The Cultural Heritage of Coastal Suffolk

PETER WILLSHER

Cover photograph by Alison Rawson

Cover and page design by Katherine Gibney

The author dedicates *The Cultural Heritage of Coastal Suffolk* to his
family, especially the new arrival, Daniel (born 2011)

British Library Cataloguing in Publication Data.
A catalogue record for this book is available from the British Library.

ISBN 978-0-9540991-2-1

Published by

Courtyard Publications
Kenninghall
Norfolk
NR16 2AW
United Kingdom

Printed in Great Britain by
4edge Limited
7a Eldon Way
Hockley
Essex
SS5 4AD

CONTENTS

PROLOGUE

IN WRITING ABOUT what could be described as somewhat of a celebration of the cultural heritage of coastal Suffolk, I am fully conscious of the fact that perhaps no area of any English county has the right to stand alone with its literary, artistic, theatrical and musical associations. However, I do feel confident in venturing the opinion that the Suffolk coastal area is certainly unique in its association with the major arts over a period in excess of two hundred years.

Various counties have their own unique geographical features and, although the coast of Suffolk lacks, say, the spectacularly rugged cliffs, pounded by crashing waves from an azure sea as is the case in far-off Cornwall, there are attractive compensatory factors pervading in coastal Suffolk. These are represented by not only the serene and almost mystic quality of its marshes, but also the miles of often-deserted sandy and pebble beaches before anyone can even begin to think of promoting the area's phenomenal cultural heritage. As far as I am aware, this is the first attempt to record a holistic account of a remarkable number of connections that must surely be unique in the annals of our traditional English culture. Amongst those featured are national as well as international icons in the world of twentieth-century art, literature and music who have been attracted to living, visiting and working in this cherished section of the Suffolk coast

'The Suffolk Coast and Heaths Area of Outstanding Natural Beauty (AONB) is one of Britain's finest landscapes. Located on the coast of East Anglia, it covers 150 square miles and includes wildlife-rich wetlands, ancient heaths, windswept shingle beaches and historic towns and villages.' This is a direct quotation from the website of The Suffolk Coast and Heaths Unit, an organisation that manages this largely undeveloped area which is indented with no less than three estuaries and the confluence of two wide rivers. However, my study deals hardly at all with the magnificent landscapes, seascapes or indeed the wildlife, even though many of the painters, writers and musicians mentioned within these pages have certainly drawn inspiration from these features in one form or another. I have described this work as a 'celebration' because, to my mind, the accumulative creative output per square mile is probably well in excess of that of any serious competition from other areas of similar size in the whole of England, with the possible exception of the capital city. Specifically, I should perhaps explain that I have written about the towns of Southwold and Aldeburgh as well as the villages of Walberswick and Snape. With this in mind, perhaps I should now confess that from time to time I have permitted myself to stray just a little farther afield when it was considered justified. Because of coastal Suffolk's rather benign topographical features, the invasive North Sea has been an ever-present threat that has on occasion succeeded in swallowing at least one community, with several others still in peril. In these circumstances, and knowing that without continued support and interest the longstanding cultural activity could also fade way, there is certainly a considerable need for an influentially protective arm for more than merely the physical factor.

Whilst walking around each of the named towns and villages, a visitor, new to the area, would become aware of a certain degree of gentility but this is, by no means, overwhelming in nature. Life in each of the towns tends to be unhurried and the atmosphere is certainly friendly. It is also the case with the area's numerous village communities. Happily, the legacy of Benjamin Britten's Snape Maltings complex is situated away from the village of Snape and it is fair to say that this small local community is spared all the hustle and bustle associated with an evening performance at the concert after a warm summer's day. I now regard the Snape Maltings International Concert Hall as standing like a colossus where it overlooks the nearby marshes. Walberswick, on the other hand, has a massive parking problem in the months of high summer so the local residents are not spared from peak activity. If a majority of the local population of these villages and towns carry an awareness of the existence of their cultural heritage they do not show it. Nevertheless, I would wager that the inhabitants might be persuaded to discuss the benefits or perhaps even the disadvantages of the various artistic and literary associations over the years. Some of these are ever present, such as the case in Aldeburgh where the impressive presence of the Britten-Pears library stands alongside The Red House, the former home of Benjamin Britten and Peter Pears, as well as The Red Studio, once the working place as well as residence of the artist, Mary Potter.

Several authors and biographers have already visited the life and works of more than a few of my chosen subjects but I wished to create the opportunity to learn more about this specific area within a single volume covering the various cultural aspects I have chosen to feature. From time to time I shall relate a few anecdotes that helped me to understand more about the personalities of the people involved, as well as their work.

At this early stage, I find it worthwhile to explain why there have been some much-overworked words in this book. One particular noun is 'inspiration', coupled with the verb 'inspire', to which I must add 'influence'. Musicians have been influenced by other musicians, as well as inspired by poets and other writers, just as most painters have always been inspired, as well as influenced, by other artists. Added ingredients have been landscape, seascape, huge East Anglian skies and even certain areas of coastal Suffolk itself. It will be shown that certain writers have been inspired and influenced by places and elements of local history as well as by other authors. There is also the mentor-pupil relationship to consider, such as that between composer Frank Bridge and Benjamin Britten. John Constable was an admirer of the work of Claude Lorrain, the seventeenth century landscapist and it was none other than JMW Turner who found himself spellbound when viewing a work by this Frenchman, the painter who has been regarded as Turner's mentor. The latter is just one of the multitude of affinities that interconnect throughout the history of art. Painting is perhaps the easiest example to illustrate how admiration for the work of one, indeed many in some cases, can inspire another, although the same applies also in literature and music. It's not plagiarism that rears its ugly head here, but those close but very much more respectable cousins, inspiration and influence. It can be the technique or approach of one that influences the style adopted by another, in music, painting, art and writing. Actors and directors are also to be included when considering such matters. Some might even regard these practices as flattery but, whatever the case, the world of the arts generally has reaped considerable benefits for us all to enjoy for the rest of our days. Long may it continue, because there is no way that anyone would ever seek to put a stop to such conduct. That would be to deny cultural progress.

Bearing in mind what is already known about Walberswick and its residents, past and present, it is interesting that one of them, artist Richard Scott, should refer to the fact that between World War I and

World War II, the village attracted not only artists but also the sort of literary and theatrical intelligentsia which gave rise to the description 'NW3-by-the-sea'. Augmented by the odd media personality (I have avoided the word celebrity), this trend has continued to the present day. Modern broadcasters seem to be obsessed with links in terms of one item leading to another, especially on radio discussion programmes. The links I discovered were friendships and interrelationships between writers, painters and even musicians or perhaps more accurately those that appreciate the musical form. Ex-Prime Minister, Margaret Thatcher famously said in her rather dismissive way, 'There is no such thing as society.' Well, she should have taken more notice of the nineteenth century when there was certainly plenty of society on the coast stretching from Southwold to Dunwich and beyond. On the basis that this particular form of social community certainly did exist, it follows that society generally is something that cannot be eliminated from humanity, even by politicians, as long as there are sociable people ready to enjoy all that life has to offer. As one outstanding example, I cite the late Benjamin Britten, surely a great modern Elizabethan: he worked very closely with a number of his numerous artistic and literary friends and it seems to have been his ability to form such cultural friendships that served to make such an important contribution to his distinctive music. The collaborative work undertaken by these talented exponents of their particular form of creative art served to illustrate the composer's musical compositions. We should also bear in mind the host of internationally known musicians who have performed at the Aldeburgh Festival each year. During Britten's lifetime, many members of artistic society were entertained as guests at his successive Aldeburgh homes and they soon came to regard the Suffolk coast in general, and Aldeburgh in particular, as an inspirational part of England. For his part, Britten made no secret of his overwhelming desire to compose music for the people of Aldeburgh and for the Aldeburgh Festival. He once wrote

> 'I belong at home...in Aldeburgh. I have tried to bring music to it in the shape of our local festival; and all the music I write comes from it.'

In his speech, in California in 1964, when accepting the Robert O Aspen Award in the Humanities, Britten was at pains to express his gratitude to the United States of America because of his providential discovery of the poetic works of George Crabbe in July-August 1941 whilst based in Los Angeles. He said that he suddenly realised where he belonged and what he lacked. He confessed that he had become without roots and when he got back to England six months later he was ready to put them down, once and for all, in his beloved coastal Suffolk. He added that the older he got he found that working away from home got more and more difficult and he realised that he belonged there – specifically in Aldeburgh. Despite his need for regular travel, 'with a congenial partner' in order to give concerts, his music had its roots in where he lived and worked.

Coming across this story in the course of my research, and reflecting on what I subsequently learned about the inspiration for much of his music, I cannot agree more with those who describe Britten as one of the most literary composers. This is not just because a number of his close friends and collaborators were writers, and in this respect I am thinking of people such as W H Auden, E M Forster and Christopher Isherwood as well as Stephen Spender and William Plomer. There were others, but even then this Suffolk composer was a man who had always been known to read very widely. To have eliminated the North Sea together with its changing moods and then deprive Benjamin Britten of literature, we would surely be left speculating what else might have been left to inspire him. On the other hand, I'm quite sure he would have found something.

However, this book is not just about Benjamin Britten, although at times you may be forgiven for believing that this is indeed the case. My research has led me in many directions and in Britten's case I have to agree with exactly what Donald Mitchell has written. He maintains that there is very little in Britten's life that has not proved of interest and of some significance for his evolution as a composer. You will learn later that Mitchell is Britten's authorised biographer.

The Aldeburgh Festival has had its detractors over the years, and by this I refer to those who voiced the opinion that it was little more than a get-together for passionate admirers of Benjamin Britten and Peter Pears. Others have felt that it was no bad thing for the festival to have its own personality and that those looking for something else had plenty of alternatives. As far as I am concerned, it is not at all difficult to support the latter point of view but, in any event, as the years have passed since the deaths of the two stalwarts, changes have taken place and, like any other important musical event, it will continue to develop as long as the artistic direction continues to be of high quality. In my view, the Aldeburgh Festival is in very safe hands and matters are unlikely to change to any material extent as far as its international reputation and importance are concerned.

The Earl of Harewood KBE (1923-2011), one time Artistic Director of the Edinburgh Festival and for a great number of years an acknowledged expert on opera, wrote a personal introduction to the programme for the First Aldeburgh Festival that ran from 5-12 June 1948. He acknowledged that since the Second World War ended in 1945, 'the Festival in this country has become something of a national habit'. This seemed to indicate that festivals as such were then rather commonplace and therefore perhaps rather passé. However, later in his piece he described various items on the programme as 'belonging' to Aldeburgh and Suffolk in the sense of what Mozart did for Salzburg. Harewood also finished with a comment to the effect that 'One hopes that visitors to Aldeburgh may feel that the hosts have at least not hired the entertainment for their guests, but have provided it for themselves'. Now over sixty years into its impressive history I cannot conceive a greater illustration of what Benjamin Britten and Peter Pears, two of the original founders, set out to achieve. This is not to forget that many performers at the Festival over the years have been not only famous nationally but also of worldwide fame. The fact that they were drawn to Aldeburgh, and later to the Snape Maltings Concert Hall, provides irrefutable evidence that the localised element plays a predominant part in creating the unique atmosphere and continues to do so on a regular annual basis. It was with this thought in mind that I became most intrigued by seeing, in the third volume of the *Selected Letters of Benjamin Britten*, an image of the handwritten minutes of the first meeting of the Festival's Executive Committee. This was held at a private house within the town on Monday, 27 October 1947 when it was determined that funds be raised locally to guarantee the sum of at least £1,000 in the event of a financial loss. Of this sum the founders, Benjamin Britten, Peter Pears and Eric Crozier each contributed the sum of £25. In the event, in the weeks leading up to the festival, the total sum by way of guarantees reached £1,400. Over the years, there have been many administrative and financial difficulties, not to mention occasional artistic tensions and disagreements, but here we are in the second decade of the twenty-first century and this unique festival continues to retain its special place in a crowded international music calendar. As far as I am aware, the festival committee no longer relies on the support of local guarantors.

Perhaps it might be useful for me to try to clarify further my thoughts on what I wrote earlier. This was my reference to the inspiration that Britten drew as a result of observing a raging North Sea, perhaps together with a darkened and angry sky, from the window of his study, at home in Crag House. Just how long did it take before he was inspired to compose the score of *Peter Grimes*, once his imaginative mind had converted the natural drama taking place outside and married it with George Crabbe's now immortal poetic character? An added but essential ingredient was, of course, the creative work of Montagu Slater, poet, novelist, playwright and librettist. Yehudi Menuhin's words on this theme were:

> 'The screech of seagulls, the clatter of pebbles, the constantly shifting moods of the sea – all are powerfully evoked by Britten's score'.

My mention of Yehudi Menuhin reminds me of the musical association he formed with Benjamin Britten, an occasional alliance that resulted in the virtuoso's visits to the Aldeburgh area and the occasional performance, including *Mozart's Violin Sonata in A major, K 402* for a Festival concert at Framlingham church on 22 June 1958. Their rehearsals together were held at The Red House.

Adverting to the inspirational themes, in observing the sky, especially on a summer's day, would have had a different effect on John Constable (1776-1837) before he embarked upon another landscape. His particular bailiwick was the area surrounding the River Stour, East Bergholt and Dedham Vale rather than what can be seen looking out over the pebbled beach at Aldeburgh. However, Constable is certainly known to have visited Walberswick and the many other artistic visitors to this village, however briefly, play an important part in this book. Let us consider also Maggi Hambling, a fellow artist of a far more modern era, looking intently at the unsettled North Sea *en plein air* at Aldeburgh. Her painting entitled, appropriately enough, *Crashing Wave* (2007) will be discussed elsewhere but just to ponder such an angry movement of water on a wild day has always been enough for her to return to her studio and set about creating a highly dramatic work of art. However, it must be borne in mind that the musician and artist cannot use the sea or even the sky as a permanent model because each is constantly changing, although perhaps not quite so often on a rare cloudless day during an English summer. My point is that both musician and artist have to hold a personal image of a particular natural phenomenon in mind when setting about interpreting what they have seen before starting on their creative work.

Maggi Hambling, Summer Wave Rolling

They have to rely not only on memory but also on their imagination. Not only that, I have come to the conclusion that artists tend to have an individual freedom in the way that they approach their work, in that they need to explore their subjects and not just represent them in their personal approach.

The same could apply to an actor or composer, and also the writer who might be inspired by a particular sight in nature before storing it away somewhere, in the mind or otherwise, for use when setting a particular scene in a novel or short story. All of us are affected, not only by surroundings but also by other people and our personal experiences. The creative artist uses these moments in time in order to share them on some occasion in the future, perhaps with a particular audience in mind. In most cases the writer, painter, musician and dramatist work alone but they toil at their work for the benefit of others, even if this notion is not uppermost in their thoughts at that particular time.

An early decision, after receiving some professional advice, was to divide the four arts - namely music, literature, painting and the theatre - into separate sections. However, scores of personalities are involved, as well as their range of associations and connections. For example, notable painters and writers have, to a significant extent, worked with, as well as socialised with, equally famous musicians. It is inevitable that I have had to introduce a limited number of overlaps here and there. I have endeavoured to keep these to a minimum in order that the narrative can flow in a manner that enhances, rather than diminishes, the effect of what I regard as an intriguing story that needed to be told holistically.

PART ONE

MUSIC AND MUSICIANS

If Music and sweet Poetry agree
As they must needs (the Sister and the Brother)
Then must the love be great, 'twixt thee and me,
Because thou lov'st the one, and I the other

Poems: in Divers Humours, An Ode

Richard Barnfield (1574-1627)
Barnfield was said to have had a close relationship
with William Shakespeare

If music be the food of love, play on

Twelfth Night

William Shakespeare (1564-1616)

Chapter One

The Lowestoft Lad

IT IS QUITE impossible to write under this heading without getting straight to the point. Edward Benjamin Britten (1913-1976), latterly and only a matter of a few months before his death, created Baron Britten of Aldeburgh, OM CH, was born auspiciously on St Cecilia's Day, Saturday, 22 November 1913. Dame Edith Sitwell (1887-1964), in a letter to him dated 23 August 1963, wrote 'How right it is that St Cecilia's Day should be your birthday', it being well known that St Cecilia was the patron saint of musicians. All honours were conferred upon him in recognition of his thoroughly deserved reputation as a twentieth-century musical colossus in coastal Suffolk, let alone the United Kingdom and the rest of the world. He was born in Lowestoft, the most easterly point of England, but it is his enormously close association with both Snape and Aldeburgh that really marks him out for this particular epithet. To say that he was a born musician is not to exaggerate the truth because music certainly dominated his life from a very early age.

The Britten family's home from 1908-1936 was at 21 Kirkley Cliff Road, Lowestoft. The youthful Benjamin started his education at South Lodge Preparatory School, Lowestoft where he became Head Boy. Below, you will find a schoolboy photograph of him there and a reference to early sporting activity at the end of the narrative to this book. His initials, 'E.B.B', have been photographed as carved on a brick at the former school that was subsequently destroyed by fire.

Britten's birthplace in Lowestoft

At the age of thirteen, Benjamin Britten attended a performance, by the Queen's Hall Orchestra, at

Norwich in October 1927. Included in the programme that evening was an orchestral piece by a modern composer. It was entitled *Enter Spring*, part of an overall composition entitled *The Sea*. It appears that Britten had heard the entire orchestral work previously at the Norwich Triennial Festival; this was in 1924. There is no doubt that this work had made a deep impression on the youthful Britten. It had been conducted by the composer himself, Frank Bridge (1879-1941). Bridge subsequently agreed to become teacher to the promising young musician, who had been introduced to him by Audrey Alston. This composer was to become Britten's role model and mentor and the then middle-aged Bridge succeeded in opening a number of doors for someone he perceived to be a young man

Schoolboy Britten at South Lodge Preparatory School, Lowestoft

with a powerful ambition to progress in music. Bridge and his wife virtually adopted the boy, taking charge of his artistic development. Britten publicly acknowledged the debt he owed to the older man in 1937 and his works often demonstrated the influence Bridge had imposed upon him. Britten's *Variations on a Theme of Frank Bridge*, for string orchestra, was based upon the second of Bridge's *Idylls for string quartet* (1906). He also went to work on some compositions of Frank Bridge in future years, sometimes in live performances as well as recordings. In the light of what I will be revealing later about the inspiration that Britten derived from his long association with the North Sea, his attendance at that concert in Norwich was surely providential in many ways.

According to his biographer, Britten himself was never quite certain how good a composer he had become. It seems that he was perpetually asking himself whether he had achieved the technical goals set by his hero, Frank Bridge. That composer's portrait was invariably hanging alongside Britten's desk in his studio. He also treasured an etching of Mahler, a portrait of Mozart and an early photographic study of Chopin. To Britten, this was an ever-present, soundless array of mentors, which should serve to tell us quite a lot about Britten the human being as well as Britten the composer

Incidentally, the American composer, pianist and conductor, Aaron Copland (1900-1990), who wrote *Fanfare for the Common Man*, a work that has become a patriotic standard in his native country, came across Britten's *Variations on a Theme of Frank Bridge* and admired, in his own words, 'its technical adroitness and instrumental wizardry'. They had met in London in 1938 when Britten was aged twenty-four. Copland later received an invitation to visit Snape where Britten was then living. During that visit, Copland entertained his host by playing and singing all the parts of his work, a school opera, *The Second Hurricane*. Britten responded by playing to the American his recently completed first version of *Piano Concerto No. 1*. Copland, conscious that Britten had expressed enthusiastic pleasure at listening to his own performance found himself having reservations as to the substance of the musical materials in Britten's composition. Thankfully, his frankly expressed opinion served only to consolidate their growing friendship. Britten later revised the concerto but, sadly, this work has been somewhat neglected.

To get back to Britten's education, he went on from the Lowestoft preparatory school to become a boarder at Gresham's School, Cromer Road, Holt, Norfolk where he was *'taught'* music, an expression that I have parenthesized in order to speak minor volumes about how little he might have gained from these lessons. However, given the circumstances relating to what we know about Britten's early talent, it is not surprising that what musical tuition was available at Gresham's could hardly have satisfied a boy with such immense potential. According to his biographer, it was at this time that it became noticeable that this particular student possessed preternaturally long fingers. This physical attribute must have assisted his early piano playing, in that his first compositions had been made as early as 1919, when he was only five or six years old. He joined Gresham's on 20 September 1928 and left in August 1930. His piano teacher at the school was Mr Harold Samuel. Young Benjamin was not happy there, but his precociousness led him to compose music even in his periods of ill health that were spent in the school's sanatorium. I find it fascinating how Benjamin Britten managed to write so many musical compositions at school, even when he was suffering almost continuously from homesickness as well as from a far from robust constitution. Perhaps his art served as some form of escape from everything he hated about being away from home. He missed his mother desperately. Apart from the maternal interest in her son, it seems clear to me that Mrs Britten's own musical talents as a singer and pianist must have provided the young Benjamin with so much encouragement, even inspiration, in pursuit of his own ambitions in music. His mother was absolutely determined that he should succeed, even talking in all seriousness, to an 'approved' friend of Ben's, of the four B's, namely Bach, Beethoven, Brahms and, yes, Britten. She was just as ambitious as Benjamin that her son should succeed. This represents a clear indication of the influence she had over him in terms of his music. I shall be writing further on the subject of the very close 'Freud' family connection with coastal Suffolk but the following quotation from Sigmund Freud's *A Childhood Recollection* quoted in *Sigmund Freud: His Life in Pictures and Words* seems particularly apt when applied to the very close and loving relationship between Mrs Britten and her son, Benjamin:

> '..if a man has been his mother's undisputed darling he retains throughout life the triumphant feeling, the confidence in success which not seldom brings actual success along with it'.

In contrast, Benjamin's father was a dentist by profession, a very useful one at that, but not at all musical. Because of this, he was very concerned about his son's fixation on becoming a successful musician. He just did not understand how anyone, let alone his son, could possibly make a living out of what he might have thought of as economically unproductive activity. He was not really a hard man but he was concerned that having four children to educate clearly represented a considerable strain on the family's finances and it seems only natural that he should be anxious that, should Benjamin not make the grade, his lack of qualifications in any other field could prove to be a financial problem to him in the years to come. He was clearly a practicable man who thought only of the family's future. With the benefit of hindsight, we all know that he need not have worried, but Britten senior was not to know that at the time. Despite his father's reservations, Benjamin grew up in an atmosphere that ensured that music was, quite literally, the centre of everything in the household and, almost certainly, by

Mrs Britten's command. In later years, music was to feature just as importantly in the home shared by Benjamin Britten and Peter Pears in Aldeburgh. This brings me to impart a remarkable fact that Dr Donald Reeve, a childhood friend of Benjamin, felt compelled to reveal. This was that the singing voice of his friend's mother bore an astonishing similarity to that of Britten's life partner, Peter Pears, who sang tenor. Beth, Benjamin's sister, had also noticed what amounted to a striking resemblance. Reeve considers this factor to have made an enormous contribution to the success of the Britten – Pears musical, as well as personal, partnership. This lasted for thirty-seven years; in other words, until the former died. Donald Reeve was the 'approved' friend that I mentioned previously. This indicated that he had been officially approved by Mrs Britten, who held very decided views on whom Benjamin should count amongst his friends and acquaintances. She was certainly not someone to be ignored in this respect. Britten had one elder brother, Robert (1907-1987) and two elder sisters, Beth (1909-1989) and Barbara (1902-1982).

The schoolboy Britten maintained the equivalent of a National Service 'demob chart' during his time at Gresham's, literally ticking off each day in his diary until the end of each term he stayed there. As we have seen, Britten's mother was a capable amateur musician and she held the position of honorary secretary to the Lowestoft Music Society. She hosted musical soirées at Kirkley Cliff Road where she and her gifted son would often be centre-stage. There seems to be no doubt that these experiences prompted the future composer's enthusiasm for the activities of the future Aldeburgh Music Club. Benjamin Britten commented, in the diary that he kept at school, on the very low net profit of £4.00 resulting from two concerts staged by the Society at Lowestoft. This caused him to despair of what he clearly thought was an unacceptably low level of music appreciation in the town in those days. His mother was involved with these productions, so this lack of financial success with the Society's musical offerings must have affected him in one way or another. It may well have been on his mind at the time that he was so deeply involved in the establishment of the Aldeburgh Music Festival in 1948 when he acted as one of the guarantors.

Because of the rapid advancement in his musical competence, Britten was not at all impressed by the teaching at Gresham's, although it seems quite clear that there was a remarkable amount of musical activity at the school. This was under the supervision of the music teacher, Mr Greatorex, known as 'Gog'. There was certainly an enviable commitment to the arts, which must have had some positive influence on the young Britten in his artistic development. This leaves me wondering if he would ever have admitted anything like this, given his obvious unhappiness there. In 1930, his final year at the school, Benjamin Britten was awarded an open scholarship to the Royal College of Music, Prince Consort Road in Kensington, London where he was taught piano by the Australian-born composer, conductor and pianist, Arthur Benjamin (1893-1960). Britten was in good company when his name was inscribed on the school's Honours Board in 'Big School' for 1929-1930. Notable alumnae included poets W H Auden, (1907-1973) and Louis MacNeice (1907-1963) as well as painter Robert Medley (1905-1994) and the composer Lennox Berkeley (1903-1989). Another notable pupil was the future poet, Stephen Spender (1909-1995) who attended Old School House, the preparatory school for Gresham's. Spender's elder brother, Michael, was already a pupil at the senior school. Because the powers-that-be at Gresham's decided that the younger Spender was not sufficiently educationally advanced at the time he was turned down for promotion to the senior school. He ended up at Repton, after attending other minor schools for short periods. More will be written of Stephen Spender later but if he had been viewed more favourably when being considered for admission to Gresham's senior school he might well have become acquainted with both W H Auden and Benjamin Britten much earlier in his life. So, despite being only a junior within the Gresham's educational establishment, the school was only too willing to include Stephen on 'Big School's' Honours Board, thereby laying claim to its part in Stephen Spender's future success in the literary field. Hmm!

Stephen Spender later went on to be a fine translator of poetry. This has been recognised by *The Times* newspaper, when in 2004, it established an annual Stephen Spender Prize for the translation of any poem from any language, classical or modern, into English.

As it happened, Spender and his wife Natasha eventually became good friends of Dame Edith Sitwell who knew them all. From what I have read from her correspondence with Stephen Spender, Sitwell rated him highly not only for his poetry, which received international recognition, but also for what he had to say about the work of other poets, including hers as well as that of Robert Graves and Auden. Dame Edith will feature in a later chapter in connection with an appearance at the Aldeburgh Festival.

It may not be generally known that Stephen Spender had a great passion for music, an interest he shared with Isaiah Berlin (1909-1997), a Russian-British philosopher and historian of ideas, regarded as one of the leading thinkers of the twentieth century, and as the dominant liberal scholar of his generation. They met at Oxford University in 1929 and they were to become life-long friends. It was at Berlin's house in 1981 that the hosts and their guests found themselves discussing the 'future of the human race'. The philosopher, who, like Spender, had witnessed so much of life in the twentieth century, confessed that he 'didn't mind very much about everything coming to an end'. Spender rejoined with 'I do care – meaning that what I care about is the civilization the world produced'. The pianist, Alfred Brendel (born 1931), a fellow guest and a regular performer at Aldeburgh Festivals, said, to Spender's relief, that he too 'cared'. Brendel had given a recital at the Festival the night before the première of Britten's *Death in Venice*. The virtuoso has been known to say that he found the 'away-from-it-all atmosphere' of Aldeburgh very refreshing and believed that he has given some of his finest performances there. That represents a considerable accolade by any measure and on that particular occasion he was said by a critic to be at his best.

When Benjamin Britten was still fairly young he insisted to anyone who deigned to enquire that he wanted to be a composer, to which the response was usually, 'Yes, but what else?' As it turned out, he was to become not 'just a composer' but also an active and accomplished pianist and conductor. What is more, we must certainly not overlook his responsibility for founding his own opera company as well as the now internationally known festival of the arts at Aldeburgh. There will be more on these achievements later, but it will also be learned that that this seaside town had at least one significant connection with the music scene before there was any thought of the Aldeburgh Festival. Imogen Holst had attended an English Folk Dance (and Song) Society Summer School held at Aldeburgh in 1921, some thirty years or so before her future and very close association with Benjamin Britten and his Aldeburgh Festival.

There is a well-documented history of Benjamin Britten working closely with a significant number of people and I will start with none other than W H Auden, the Anglo-American poet, born in England, later an American citizen, regarded by many as one of the greatest writers of the twentieth century. In my view, he certainly qualifies for inclusion

Britten's studio at Crag House

in this volume not just because of his collaboration with Britten in connection with a number of notable works but also having regard to his regular visits to Aldeburgh, including the festival where he gave a lecture in the 1950s. He was often a guest in Britten's home, Crag House, which overlooks the town's popular beach.

Auden had recognised that Britten had an extraordinary musical sensitivity to the English language at the time they worked together on Auden's Coal Face, a film made by the GPO film unit as early as 1935. However, in his diary entry of 1 December 1936 Britten wrote 'Wystan arrives at tea-time ... It will be nice having him, if I can conquer this appalling inferiority complex that I always have ... with vital brains like his'. Nevertheless, their working partnership became one of mutual

A view of Crag House, Aldeburgh, from the beach

admiration. On the visit just mentioned, Auden had indicated his intention to go to Spain to fight in the Spanish Civil War. He did indeed go to that country, but not to fight. This somewhat dramatic change of heart was not necessarily because Britten had opposed such a notion in the belief that no possible gain by the Spanish Government as a result of any heroic efforts on Auden's part would have compensated the world for being deprived of the poet's writing. Unlike his friend Benjamin Britten, the poet certainly did not appear to hold any brief for pacifism and he wrote saying just this to Stephen Spender in 1941. Auden went on to add 'as if one could do all the things in one's personal life that create wars and then pretend that to refuse to fight is a sacrifice and not a luxury.' Was this a swipe against both Britten and Christopher Isherwood (1904-1986)? The latter discovered that he was a pacifist in 1939 and remained so for the rest of his life, but as far as I am aware Britten never tried to conceal his own pacifism, as will be seen later.

Chapter Two

Literary influences: W H Auden, Thomas Mann and Henry James

MY RESEARCH INTO Benjamin Britten has taken me on quite a journey and one obvious port of call had to be an extended examination of his relationship with W H Auden. I have written elsewhere about problems with the particular liaison between musician and poet, albeit the latter with strong views on personal musical appreciation. However, from a distance, their working together seemed to be dominated by what appear to have been a series of misunderstandings. The two had collaborated again in 1936 on *Our Hunting Fathers*, which the Britten-Pears Foundation describes as follows:

> 'Written as a commission from the Norfolk and Norwich Festival and described by the composer as 'my real opus 1'. Britten's first mature song-cycle is also his first work to deal with a recurring theme in his output: man's inhumanity to man. *A tour-de-force* of vocal bravura (for either soprano or tenor soloist) and of orchestral virtuosity, *Our Hunting Fathers* is becoming increasingly recognised as one of Britten's most original and brilliantly daring early works.'

So where did W H Auden come into this obviously important work? As it happened, he was the source for the text although not the actual libretto; this form of collaboration was not to take place until well over a decade later.

However, it seems that between 1935 and 1942 Britten regarded Auden as his 'writer-in-residence' and, in turn, Auden considered Britten to be his 'musician-in-residence'. There were certainly a number of other examples of their teamwork, including *On This Island*, the composer's first published group of songs with piano. This set five poems by Auden from the collection *Look, Stranger!* Notwithstanding their working relationship, it also seems clear that Auden was in love with his 'Bengy' as well as appearing also to be jealous of Peter Pears in his relationship with Britten. Britten and Pears had first become friends in May 1937, a close personal relationship that was consummated later in the USA. We also know of the Britten-Auden link through Group Theatre, but more will be written on this subject later.

Incidentally, the BBC recognised Britten's reputation as a musician in March 1936 when the Corporation featured a broadcast on the National Programme of his composition of a suite for violin and pianoforte performed by Britten and Antonio Brosa (1894-1979), a Catalan violinist. During the following month they performed this work in Barcelona. The two became friends and in March 1940 Brosa launched his career as a solo violinist by performing the première of Britten's *Violin Concerto, op.16* at Carnegie Hall with the New York Philharmonic Orchestra, conducted by John Barbirolli (1899-1970). At this performance, Brosa had chosen, as his instrument, a Vesuvius Stradivarius made in the year 1727. If proof was really needed of his international status, Benjamin Britten had certainly arrived. He happened to be in New York at that time and I feel sure that he would have attended this important milestone in his career. This composition was his first completed work after his arrival in America in 1939.

What has fascinated me was perhaps, at the time, an unintentional admonitory letter written by Auden to Britten from New York in 1942 when the poet was sending the composer some of his completed work. When Britten as well as Pears was in New York they had, for a time, shared a home with Auden, the only instance they were to do so. However, it seems that the composer was hard to please because, in a letter to his sister Beth in May 1941, Britten described Auden's residence as 'quite nice & convenient but a trifle too bohemian for my liking'. The building was an old brownstone house in Brooklyn Heights; 7 Middagh Street for those who may be intent on paying homage to these stalwarts of British literature and music. Wystan Auden was by then an established collaborator with the musician as well as a close colleague. As we now know, they worked together in the GPO Film Unit, established in 1933 as a sub-division of the General Post Office, as well as in broadcasting on BBC radio programmes. This close association and Auden's reputation for what has been described as a 'self-appointed, albeit affectionate, prosecutor even with friends', led him to write to Britten upon a subject in which he felt personally qualified due to his own admitted torments. He obviously believed that what he wrote would benefit his friend, hence the wording he chose to use before imparting his advice:

> '...I think I know something about the dangers that beset you as a man and as an artist because they are my own.

Goodness and [Beauty] are the results of a perfect balance between Order and Chaos, Bohemianism and Bourgeois Convention.

Bohemian chaos alone ends in a made jumble of beautiful scraps; Bourgeois convention alone ends in large unfeeling corpses. Every artist except the supreme masters has a bias one way or the other. The best pair of opposites I can think of in music are Wagner and Strauss. (Technical skill always comes from the bourgeois side of one's nature.)

For middle-class Englishmen like you and me, the danger is of course the second. Your attraction to thin-as-a-board juveniles, ie to the sexless and innocent, is a symptom of this. And I am certain too that it is your denial and evasion of the demands of disorder that is responsible for your attacks of ill-health, ie sickness is your substitute for the Bohemian.'

There followed some advice that seems intended to persuade Britten to be less secretive for his own good, but this need not detain us unduly here, but I was very interested to learn from a book written by Christopher Isherwood in 1976 (*Christopher & His Kind*) that it was a first visit to Berlin in 1929, at Auden's bidding, that caused him to meet the anthropologist, John Layard. Layard had once been a patient and pupil of American psychologist, Homer Lane and a writing by Lane-Layard proclaimed that it was a sin to disobey the inner law of a person's own nature. Isherwood used this as justification for a change in his own life. There is no doubt in my mind that the Lane-Layard words had influenced Auden when he later urged his dear friend, Benjamin Britten, to be more outgoing with his sexuality. That was certainly the case as far as Christopher Isherwood was concerned. His time in Berlin in the 1930s caused him to be quite open about his own homosexuality and this eventually led to a very long term and loving relationship with Don Bachardy who will be mentioned later. Isherwood had met Bachardy on a beach in California when the writer was nearing fifty years of age and the future painter of some note was merely a teenager.

It is no secret that Britten was in awe of Auden's intellect and the subject matter of the letter must have given him cause for serious consideration. As far as Peter Pears was concerned. He felt that later meetings between Britten and Auden were uneasy as the relationship had changed, and not for the better (see below). In commenting on the letter, Dr Donald Mitchell (born 1925), Benjamin Britten's authorised biographer and lecturer on *Britten and Auden in the Thirties*, shares the views I express at a later point when writing specifically in this context about the Suffolk composer's *Death in Venice*, an opera based upon the novella by Thomas Mann.

Peter Pears had previously expressed the view that as both Britten and Auden appeared to enjoy living in a state of chaos, when sharing the house in 1940-1941, this may have inspired at least some of the thoughts behind Auden's tirade against Britten. Who could possibly provide the answer after all these years?

Further on the subject of the Britten-Auden relationship, it seems that it was not just the fact that Britten regarded the poet as his intellectual superior; it was more the fact that the composer perceived Auden as having an outstanding command of the English language, a subject on which the musician felt decidedly inferior in comparison and who could blame him? In addition, he was, of course, Auden's junior by some six years and this appeared to be at the forefront of his mind when reviewing their relationship along with his own sensitivity about feeling somewhat inarticulate in comparison with the poet. It also occurs to me that having shared a common *Alma Mater* the difference in age groups tends to appear much more significant to a young, impressionable boy and perhaps this feeling was never really eliminated from his mind when dealing with the senior figure that was Auden as an adult.

Britten had, of course, always expressed himself in a musical way as this was undoubtedly his calling, not to mention his training. Perhaps, in his own mind, he had dwelt far too sadly upon Auden's donnish exuberance, verbal dexterity and mental adroitness. Having set a fair amount of Auden's words to music, he was an obvious admirer of his writing and I am wondering if this served to underline his inferiority and at the same time almost to discount any thought of his own very rare talent in the world of music. It seems rather sad that he was not to know that his admirers, including some of superior academic status, had expressed the view that such feelings on the composer's part were thoroughly unjustified. Add to all this evidence the fact that Britten regarded Auden as far too overbearing, authoritarian and dogmatic in his expressed views and attitudes, even in criticising his music, and there was certainly a recipe for a broken relationship. Dr Mitchell has written that words seeped and leaked from Auden as much as notes tumbled out of Britten. In these circumstances, we must be grateful for the legacy of the work they did together, before they went their independent ways and, as is the case with many facets in life, some things just do not last forever. One notable bequest from their collaboration was undoubtedly Britten's *Paul Bunyan*, a choral operetta for which Auden wrote the book and words during their joint stay in New York in 1940. This was not too well received when it was given its first performance on 5 May 1941 at Columbia University but Britten revised the work as late in his life as 1976 and the operetta still gets an occasional airing. Somewhat to the surprise of the critics and the public, the exiled company of the Royal Opera House had a great success with their production of *Paul Bunyan*, just before Christmas, 1997. In the view of Dr Mitchell, *Paul Bunyan* represents both a summation as well as a consummation of Britten's earlier collaborations with Auden in film, theatre and radio.

I have become aware that Peter Pears had expressed the view that Britten remained full of admiration for Auden as well as full of gratitude for their earlier years together. This was, no doubt, referring to their very close collaboration on a number of notable projects from the mid-thirties to 1942; works that included *Our Hunting Fathers*, described as a cycle of songs on animals. Such feelings must have been uppermost in Britten's mind when he was convalescing from a major operation many years later. On hearing of a memorial service for his old friend on 27 October 1973, just over three years before his own death, Britten further learned that *Hymn to St Cecilia* had been performed as part of that day's proceedings at Christ Church, Oxford. This was a choral piece, composed by Britten and based upon the setting of a poem by none other than Auden himself. Dr Donald Mitchell, in his writings on Britten and Auden, commented that it was perhaps only then that Auden's death had suddenly become real to Britten and the years of unease were, at least momentarily, erased. It appears that gratitude and affection then surged from the composer and accompanying these emotions perhaps a very sharp sense that the loss was in the exact words of Peter Pears 'major/And final, final'. Donald Mitchell recalled in an article, written twenty-five years after

Britten's death, that he would 'never forget the torrent of tears that engulfed [Ben] when I brought him the news of Auden's death. It was the only time I ever saw Ben weep'. It now seems clear that although Britten could easily justify the ending of his relationship with Auden in his own mind, bearing in mind the anguish it had caused him, there was a genuine remorse at Auden's passing and perhaps, more importantly, just the odd feeling of personal regret on the passing of so many wasted years.

In effect, *Hymn to St Cecilia* was, more or less, the last major setting by Britten of words by Auden, a work that is said to be of notable inspiration and flawless in technique. On the other hand, there was also Britten's *Spring Symphony* (1949), a work that included part of Auden's poem *A Summer Night* that contained the first line, 'Out on the lawn I lie in bed'. This is a composition that many are on record as having also admired and it has been, no doubt, a source of inspiration to others.

As a final note on the relationship, the Britten-Pears Foundation website records that:

> 'In reality Britten last saw W H Auden in 1953, when the poet gave a lecture at the Aldeburgh Festival. Britten then kept his distance from the former friend who, it will be remembered, had provided the words for *Paul Bunyan*, many other notable vocal pieces and the classic *Night Mail*. Auden was sad, but not surprised at his estrangement from Britten. Since following the poet to the United States, and sailing back home more than a decade before, Britten had done his best to put clear water between himself and Auden's often domineering influence'.

It is perhaps best that I now let matters rest there, but only with the thought that such a highly individual relationship between two such artistically gifted individuals could not, perhaps, have been expected to follow a much more conventional path.

In October, 1971, before getting down to serious work on *Death in Venice*, Britten and Pears travelled to Venice in order to absorb the atmosphere; Peter Pears is on record as having described this romantic city as a 'heavenly place...the last refuge of non-motorised humanity'. After their return, Britten was inspired to work hard on the opera, partly in Aldeburgh and partly in Wolfsgarten, where Britten was a frequent visitor. This is a former hunting seat in the German state of Hessen, and at that time the home of his friends, the Prince and Princess of Hesse. He wrote to Pears from there, telling him that although he missed him dreadfully, he was inspired by the thought that he was working for his partner in the intended role of Aschenbach, the main character in Mann's novella. Britten was In Germany with Myfanwy Piper, who was working with him on the libretto. He also referred to the aircraft noise from Frankfurt airport and said how nice it would be for the nuisance to be doing something sensible for once, as the means whereby Pears could have been flown to his side. In October 1974, Peter Pears wrote often to Britten when he was singing the role of Aschenbach at the New York Metropolitan Opera, remarking on one occasion that the house was 'sold out, of course'.

Britten and Pears were often annoyed by the intrusive sound of low flying aircraft in Aldeburgh and in 1970 acquired a country home in Horam, Suffolk. This was known as Chapel House and they bought the property to serve as a welcome refuge from the uncomfortable noise at Aldeburgh. During the last years of his life, Britten spent a lot of time there, where he composed a number of his later works initiated by the made-for-TV opera, *Owen Wingrave* that was completed in 1970 and performed on BBC TV in November that year.

The first night of Benjamin Britten's opera, *Death in Venice*, which has been described as 'Britten's most heartrending and personal opera', was at Snape Maltings on 16 June 1973. It was also performed at the Royal Opera House, Covent Garden in October that year. It must be remembered that this work was composed under very dire conditions, Britten having put off major surgery in order to finish it. He had been too ill to attend rehearsals and he turned for urgent assistance to the conductor Steuart Bedford (born 1939) who was one of the Artistic Directors of the Aldeburgh Festival for many years. Bedford also became known for his collaborative association with Britten's works, particularly his operas, and the English Opera Group. All of this has taken him to venues around the world. He has an extensive operatic repertoire and has worked with many of the world's greatest opera companies including English National Opera, the Royal Opera Covent Garden, San Diego Opera, New York City Opera, Royal Danish Opera and the Teatro Colon. Britten's last opera was obviously trusted to extremely competent hands.

Steuart Bedford toiled exhaustively on the score, along with the composer, and was obliged to make many final decisions due to Britten's indisposition. Because of his illness, Britten was not in attendance at the first night at Snape. However, he was seated prominently in a box at the Royal Opera House a few months later in October. After the final curtain, the ailing composer was picked out by spotlight and, with the cast moving to the front of the stage, he was accorded an all-round standing ovation. Britten's illness also rendered him unable to attend the debut performance of *Death in Venice* at the Metropolitan Opera in New York (premiere, 18 October 1974), an event that was subject to a live broadcast.

Despite his unfortunate and ill-timed heart disease, Britten was delighted to be present at the Covent Garden performance in order to witness Peter Pears in the role of Gustav von Aschenbach. He viewed this opera as a public tribute to his life-long companion and greatest interpreter of his work. It seems clear that he knew at the time that *Death in Venice* was to be his last major composition. He had been composing music since the age of five and although it has to be considered that he died prematurely at the age of only sixty-three he had played a long musical innings and an attacking one at that … a cricketing metaphor that he might well have appreciated. He was an enduring lover of sport and apart from cricket, a game he played regularly, he was also commendably active with Peter Pears in regular tennis and swimming, as well as sailing in the North Sea.

As far as the Thomas Mann connection is concerned, it is perhaps now the time to mention another literary influence. I do, of course, refer to Britten's opera entitled *The Turn of the Screw*, which was taken from the well-known ghost story by Henry James (1843-1916). This opera was commissioned by the 1954 Venice Biennale, which was quite a significant international tribute to the English composer. Bearing in mind Dr Mitchell's status as a former Professor of Music at the University of Sussex and, perhaps more importantly, a close friend of Britten of long standing, perhaps I have gone too far with my own thoughts in making my personal observations at different stages in this book. Perhaps it is best that I leave it to others to pass judgment but the fact remains that the theme of *The Turn of the Screw* deals with the corruption of childhood innocence and its disturbing ambiguities. This certainly struck a chord with Britten and he later described the work as the 'nearest to me of any I have chosen (although what that indicates of my own character I shouldn't like to say!)'. The music that he composed for this work has been described as atmospheric in that he captured the mood of James's dark story beautifully. Another interesting comment was that the music was somewhat cinematic, thus causing speculation that Britten was influenced by the cinema when composing the score. On the other hand there has been speculation that this work has perhaps influenced subsequent generations of film composers but that might be a step too far, although having listened to the music on *YouTube* whilst writing a section of this book I am inclined to think that there might be something in this. In any event, Britten's choice of librettist, Myfanwy Piper, was to my mind, nothing short of inspired.

Henry James's ghost tale was published in 1898 and has been a favourite with post-Freudian critics who have set out to uncover rich pickings in particular aspects of the story relating to certain relationships, especially with the children, as well as the 'real' or imagined ghosts and which character sees what. These are issues that James leaves tantalisingly unclear. As a result of what I have already written and what Myfanwy Piper once confessed to Britten, of which more later, the composer and his librettist appeared to set out to make the sexual implications of all this much more explicit than the author of the book decided to do. Such ill-disguised innuendo is revealed in the dialogue of an opera that is as much about child abuse as it is about ghosts. Few critics are prepared to confront these features but they are undoubtedly there ... although I am not going as far as to give you precise extracts because I do not consider this to be the place to deal with what are disturbing issues of a truly sensitive nature in an age of all-too-common, and decidedly unwelcome, paedophilia.

This now leads me to introduce, somewhat tentatively, an unlikely name that became closely connected with the composer, the town of Aldeburgh, Crag House, the home of Britten and Pears, as well as the opera to which I have just referred, namely *The Turn of the Screw*.

Britten enjoyed a very close relationship with the actor David Hemmings (1941-2003) when the latter was but a youth. Hemmings had then possessed a fine singing voice (boy treble) and appeared as Miles in *The Turn of the Screw* at the age of twelve, having been selected from many others at audition. Hemmings' debut as a performer was described as remarkable in an English Opera Group production with the composer conducting. The performance of the young Hemmings in the original recording of the work has been described as 'reconciling childish innocence with wicked knowledge', which is, to me, an astounding accolade for the acting ability of an artist not yet in his teens. The work went on to be performed in Paris in 1956, when it is alleged that David's voice finally broke. Hemmings had already performed in several works by Britten and, despite rumours to the contrary and considerable jealousy demonstrated by Peter Pears, the boy treble has always strenuously denied any question of a sexual relationship with the composer who was said to be infatuated with him. Hemmings has said that this was probably true, although it has been stated that Britten regarded Hemmings as something of a muse and, to my mind, there is nothing at all wrong with that. In any event, my view is that Britten, being an honourable man, could not have possibly allowed his personal feelings to take precedence over his duties to the singer's parents, reflected by the high level of trust that they had placed in him. Of course, David Hemmings did go on to make quite a career for himself as a film actor, notably *Blow Up* where he played alongside Vanessa Redgrave and Sarah Miles. This movie was said to be indicative of the Zeitgeist at the end of the 1960s. It also needs to be said that not many ever doubted Hemmings' heterosexuality. He married four times and one of his wives was the American actress, Gayle Hunnicutt (born 1943). He also directed a number of films, including *The Survivor*, starring Robert Powell and Jenny Agutter.

David Hemmings went on to say that he may well have been cast in the part of Miles in *The Turn of the Screw* more for passion and personal favour rather than for his talent as a singer. He was not destined to learn the absolute truth but, as far as he was concerned, there had never been any question of the composer demonstrating any homosexual responsiveness towards him in any physical way whilst sleeping in the composer's bed, notwithstanding Peter Pears having been known to have described the Britten-Hemmings relationship as 'nearly catastrophic'. This seems to suggest that perhaps Britten was at best, or perhaps I should say worst, sailing rather too close to the wind for comfort. In these circumstances, perhaps Pears might have been more accurate in describing the relationship as 'potentially' catastrophic' if he was confident that nothing untoward took place between a homosexual adult and, on the face of it, an innocent youth. After all, we do have Hemmings' own words of denial and what evidence is there to suggest that he was telling his readers anything other than the truth?

During the period that Britten worked on *The Turn of the Screw* it was thought that the composer, who liked to have tangible, visual stimuli, such as stage designs, in close proximity during the period of composition, might well have regarded David Hemming's presence in his own home as quite desirable. The youth would have been learning the role and Britten needed to be quite certain that David would be able to sing the part. Hemmings describes in his biographical work entitled *Blow-Up and Other Exaggerations* just how much he felt that coastal Suffolk in and around Aldeburgh was so evocative of Britten's opera *Peter Grimes*, a work with which Hemmings was already familiar when he first arrived in Aldeburgh. It was in the town as well as in his own home that Britten assumed the role of David's guardian, with the full and very open consent of the boy's parents.

Imogen Holst was present at the David Hemmings audition at the Scala Theatre in London and Hemmings met her again at Aldeburgh where she often sat in a corner when Benjamin Britten was working at the piano on the score of *The Turn of the Screw*. At first the youth was puzzled about what she was doing there with a sheet of blank musical manuscript in front of her, but he soon discovered that 'Imo' was recording all of Britten's musical meanderings, almost like taking dictation, and Hemmings was of the opinion that this was an extraordinary achievement. It seemed to him that all those at Crag House, including the other singers, were working on the tricky passages of the music and it became clear that Britten was writing specifically for the various voices. It was not lost on the impressionable young singer that all of this was taking place in happy surroundings, overlooking the North Sea, with all concerned becoming drawn into the creation of Britten's latest opera, happily ensconced in the composer's most favoured section of the English landscape. For this particular writer such a scene appears to signify virtually everything you need to know about an undoubtedly major source of inspiration for certain creative work emanating from that part of coastal Suffolk. Sadly, my research revealed that David Hemmings' voice broke in the middle of one of the performances of *The Turn of the Screw* and this more or less ended his connection with the Suffolk composer. Hemmings did, of course, have the compensation of going on to make his name elsewhere and in other branches of the entertainment business. It seems that Britten gained something of an unfortunate reputation for dropping people once they had left his close circle of friends and associates, but this can perhaps be explained by a phenomenal work rate that put such pressure on his available time for keeping up with various individuals, once they had ceased to be of prime importance to him.

Incidentally, *The Turn of the Screw* was also the first full-length opera by any composer to be broadcast on independent television in Britain. Act I was broadcast on 25 October 1959, followed by Act II three evenings later. Fittingly, both broadcasts were introduced by the Earl of Harewood. This groundbreaking production featured the original designs by John Piper, but realised specifically for television by Michael Yates who had as a life-long friend, W H Auden, who, as it happened, was an English master at a school where Yates was educated.

Because of the rich store of artists, musicians, actors and, of course, writers associated with this section of the Suffolk coast, it might now be appropriate to mention the popular crime writer, P D James (born 1920) if only for the fact that she has also written on the subject of Britten's opera, *The Turn of the Screw*. James has expressed a personal view that, for her, it is the most terrifying ghost story of all as, when she came to it in adolescence, she found it more disturbing than *The Strange Case of Dr Jekyll and Mr Hyde* (Robert Louis Stevenson, 1850-1894) and *The Picture of Dorian Gray* by Oscar Wilde (1854-1900). She also regards the work as having not only the moral ambiguity of physical beauty but also the seductive power to subvert moral judgment. James cites that the tale is about responsibility, or indeed the lack of it. I can only marvel at James the writer's interpretation of a story that has puzzled many over the years. I certainly find it impossible to arrive at any firm judgment on what the American writer, Henry James author of the novella, *The Turn of the Screw*, intended to convey in this particular work. However, I will now go as far as to say that I now believe that he probably had it firmly in his mind to create, quite deliberately, all the literary controversy the story has aroused since its publication and adaptation in various forms. P D James describes the book's enduring power to not only puzzle but also to discomfort the reader. Add to these remarks the very personally individual approaches of both Benjamin Britten and Myfanwy Piper and we have a subject of never-ending discussion by all who have encountered the work.

Compared with *The Turn of the Screw*, Baroness James describes another of Henry James' works, *Owen Wingrave*, also an opera by Benjamin Britten with libretto by Myfanwy Piper, as 'nothing more than a tale to frighten children'. Henry James's plot dealt with a young military student who rejects his ancestors' oppressive history of soldiering for a life of peace. Britten read this novel when composing his *War Requiem,* a work commissioned for the consecration of the city of Coventry's new cathedral in 1962, the original being destroyed by the Luftwaffe on the night of 14 November 1940. Incidentally, Britten, not unsurprisingly, considered his opera *Owen Wingrave* to be a companion piece for *The Turn of the Screw*.

The operatic première of *The Turn of the Screw* took place at the Teatro Fenice in Venice in September 1954 during the Venice Biennale for which it was commissioned. The Venice Biennale is a major contemporary art exhibition that takes place once every two years (in odd years) in Venice, Italy. The Venice Film Festival is part of it, as is the Venice Biennale of Architecture, which is held in even years. A dance section, the 'International Festival of Contemporary Dance', was established in 1999.

As a footnote to the writing of *The Turn of the Screw*, Britten found himself working at a furious rate being forced to make use of his left hand when an inflammation of his right hand made it virtually unusable.

Chapter Three

Britten and the Pipers

IN WRITING ABOUT people connected with Aldeburgh and its Festival, familiar names will keep cropping up from time to time, particularly those who, as well as working with him, also became close friends of both Benjamin Britten and Peter Pears. An example is the celebrated painter, designer and printmaker, John Piper (1903-1992), husband of Myfanwy Piper who has already been mentioned. Piper, out of necessity because he had to make a good living in order to provide for his family and educate his children, wore more than a few hats during his career and he was also known to have collaborated with none other than Richard Ingrams on certain projects. These included the book, *Piper's Places* and *John Piper in England & Wales*. Ingrams is, of course, a co-founder and second editor of the British satirical magazine *Private Eye*, and now editor of *The Oldie* magazine. These ventures represent a considerable departure from his work with John Piper.

After the two became friends, Ingrams was a frequent visitor to Fawley Bottom Farmhouse, the Pipers' home near Henley-on-Thames. However, and this is the main point as far as this book is concerned, John Piper was also to become a major collaborator with Benjamin Britten on a considerable number of his operas and you will very soon be hearing much more of him, certainly as an artist whose auction record for a painting in oils has been as high as £325,250. This was set at Sotheby's on 15 July 2008 for *Forms on Dark Blue*, a canvas measuring three feet by four feet that was painted as far back as 1936.

John Piper and his wife Myfanwy were certainly a very talented married couple and it is good to know that one or the other has been so closely associated, not only with coastal Suffolk, but also Norfolk and elsewhere in East Anglia. John Piper first met Myfanwy Piper (née Evans), then an art writer, in 1934 at the seaside cottage of Ivor Hitchens (1893-1979) near Sizewell in Suffolk. Hitchens was also an artist and his work can be seen at the Tate. When the Pipers married they did more than become parents to four children because they also enjoyed what has been described as a 'creative partnership'. At their family home, a farmhouse in south Buckinghamshire, they were famously hospitable to their many friends and, with their productive garden, led what has become known as 'the simple life'. Most friends were either their editors or professional collaborators, with Benjamin Britten, Kenneth Clark and John Betjeman amongst them. Others were their patrons who included music critic and novelist, Edward Sackville-West (1901-1965) as well as the late Queen Mother, who had been known to assist with the washing-up at their home. The Queen Mother also became patron of the Aldeburgh Festival, being entertained on occasion at The Red House. Edward Sackville-West is known for being an early and sympathetic writer about Britten's music after the composer returned from America. In 1943, Britten recognised this support by dedicating his composition, *Serenade*, to him.

By way of historical fact, I have discovered that in the autumn of 1936 John Piper and a man named Robert Wellington launched a commercial business called Contemporary Lithographs, the purpose being to put contemporary art on the walls of schools by persuading various artists to make lithographic prints that could be sold cost-effectively. The scheme was administered by Wellington. Included amongst the ten artists originally commissioned was Graham Sutherland. The collective work of all ten painters attracted favourable reviews, including one entitled *Pictures in School* in the *Architectural Review*. Such good publicity made an important contribution to the venture's commercial, as well as artistic, success. Encouraged by this, Piper and Wellington, in the following year, went ahead with a second series of prints and amongst the range of representational artists commissioned was Mary Potter, who became such a good friend of Benjamin Britten and Peter Pears in Aldeburgh. You will learn much more of her later. In any event, Contemporary Lithographs Limited continued to prosper and, in researching this book, I came across a lithograph from their collection. This was on sale at a price of £2,000. The online print shop confirmed that it was entitled *Charade* by Barnett Freedman (1901-1958) from the first series of Contemporary Lithographs published in 1937 and printed at the Curwen Press in a limited edition of four hundred. This set me speculating about whether or not the other three hundred and ninety-nine have survived but I suppose we shall never know. One thing is certain however; if some have done so these will have gained in value, subject, of course, to condition and the popularity of the artist.

John Piper was probably one of the most versatile of Great Britain's twentieth-century artists, it being said that no other has done more to celebrate the 'British Landscape' and its architecture. In addition, and in order to demonstrate his remarkable versatility, he worked on no fewer than eight operas and one ballet with Benjamin Britten, arguably the country's most exceptionally successful composer of that era as far as the professional critics were concerned. Piper remarked, on one occasion, that 'I've never known anyone who left me so much alone on the job or was a better supporter when it was finished'. He was also heard to say that Britten's music had sounded right to him from the first moment that he heard a few phrases being played. The Pipers' biographer, Frances Spalding certainly concluded from this that the two men took mutual pleasure from each other's work and who would dispute this, bearing in mind the much available evidence? Apparently, Britten recognised in John Piper a sensitivity to texture and nuance that matched his own. The rest is now history.

Incidentally, Benjamin Britten and John Piper first met in 1932 at a concert in London's Queen's Hall, but it was only when they met up in Group Theatre later in the 1930s that a friendship began. I shall return to this subject before too long because this particular organisation was also to bring into being other artistic collaborations. Britten and Piper were additionally involved with the mounting of Group Theatre's lectures, exhibitions and debates for members and associate-members. It was with Group Theatre that Piper made his début as a stage designer, producing sets for Stephen Spender's play, *Trial of a Judge*, where Benjamin Britten had a hand in the incidental music.

W H Auden described John Piper's set for Britten's opera, *Gloriana*, as 'superb' and music critic, Eric Blom (1888-1959) writing in the Observer declared that 'none may ever witness anything so gorgeous at Covent Garden'. It has been said that the critics floundered obtusely about Britten's music for *Gloriana* but were unanimous in their praise for John Piper's décor and costumes. Benjamin Britten wrote in glowing terms to Piper and I quote as follows:

'There is such a great noble sweep in it all and the impact of the colour is tremendous. Especially I liked the criss-cross of green in the garden scene, and the screen at the end is a stroke of genius.'

John Piper had worked laboriously on the scenery and costumes for the huge production of Britten's *Gloriana*, an opera written for Her Majesty the Queen's Coronation in 1953. Piper went on to receive widespread acclaim for his wonderful designs. In this same year the Arts Council mounted an exhibition of his work by way of another celebration of the Coronation. This was in the form of a retrospective shown at the Arts Council Gallery in Cambridge and the Cecil Higgins Museum in Bedford. Others so honoured by this national event were the artists Thomas Gainsborough and Graham Sutherland. John Piper was indeed in distinguished company.

Piper's friend and collaborator, John Betjeman, was said to have written 'about time too' in 1972 when John Piper, having refused a CBE (1949) as well as a knighthood (1963) was made a Companion of Honour. This was regarded as public recognition of the immense esteem in which he was held. This certainly increased the demand for his art. In his seventieth year John Piper held seventeen exhibitions, some of which were solo as opposed to being exhibited with works by others.

It is sad to relate that, at one time, Piper fell out with John Betjeman but their relationship was eventually restored and Piper was pleased to be asked to illustrate Betjeman's book, *Church Poems* in 1980. I particularly enjoyed reading Betjeman's lengthy verses in his poem entitled *Churchyards*. Looking, for the first time, at one of John Piper's drawings, of a grave, reminded me of Margaret Mellis's painting of tulips, long past their sell-by date, hanging over the edge of a vase. It struck me that both artists found not only beauty but perhaps also a little pathos in what they saw before deciding on their subjects for that particular day.

Sadly, I have been unable to trace any connection between John Betjeman and John and Myfanwy Piper's close association with Aldeburgh, Snape Maltings or indeed, Benjamin Britten. I regard this as something of a disappointment but there is probably someone out there who knows differently. I am aware that there were *Shell County Guides* for Norfolk as well as Suffolk, of which more will be written later, but any Betjeman connections with the arts featured in this book are unlikely. By way of Suffolk connections it is perhaps worth mentioning Betjeman's poem, *Felixstowe,* or *The Last of Her Order* and, of course, his famous poetic visit to the town of Diss (famous in this particular Norfolk town, anyway). On that occasion, he was in the company of Mary Wilson, who has had books of her own poetry published. Betjeman's poem was entitled *A Mind's Journey to Diss* and featured the line 'Yes it will be bliss ... to go with you by train to Diss'. Her response was to write the poem, *Reply to the Laureate,* and the two poems were published in her second book, entitled *Mary Wilson: New Poems.* In the town's museum there is a photograph allegedly commemorating this occasion; the two poets are pictured standing together by the side of the town's famous Mere. However, I have since learned from the manager of the local

The Town museum's imaginative portrayal of the poets' visit to the Mere in Diss

museum that this photograph was his own personal mock-up. He made the use of two look-alikes and the result could, in my view, fool practically anyone. It certainly attracts the eye when on display, in large scale, in the museum's show window. I see no harm in such inoffensive subterfuge to mark a poem that is well liked in the area. Mary Wilson, Baroness Wilson of Rievaulx (born 1917) is, of course, best known as the wife of former British Labour Prime Minister, Harold Wilson. She was born in Diss and was the daughter of a Congregational Minister who preached in a chapel in the town. Betjeman's poem commemorating their visit to the town contains the lines:

> The train slows down into a crawl
> And stops in silence ... Where is this?
> Dear Mary Wilson, this is Diss.

John and Myfanwy Piper attended Benjamin Britten's funeral in Aldeburgh parish church on 7 December 1976 and the couple spent the night with fellow artist, Mary Potter. Later John Piper designed a memorial window for Benjamin Britten in Aldeburgh church. The subject matter was Britten's *Three Canticles*. This was suggested by Myfanwy Piper and the finished work has been widely regarded as extremely fitting.

A Service of Thanksgiving for the Life and Work of Benjamin Britten was held at Westminster Abbey on 10 March 1977. In 1979 the newly-built, Benjamin Britten High School was completed on the northern outskirts of Lowestoft and in 2008 the school was designated by the Department of Education and Skills as a specialist school in mathematics and computing with applied learning. In catering for some eight hundred students, it seems to me that an opportunity has been missed in that the school's prospectus has almost nothing to say on the subject of music. The curriculum mentions that year 9 students of music will be able to work on certain elements of the subject but what has been listed does not appear to be designed to uphold the values of the composer after whom this educational establishment has been named. Am I being too cynical in thinking that perhaps a politician conjured up the name to honour a distinguished local composer? However, as far as music is concerned that appears to be the extent of the association with the great man.

John Piper's Benjamin Britten Memorial window

After John Piper's acclaimed personal success with *Gloriana*, but with the exception of Britten's *The Turn of the Screw*, this much overworked artist, feeling absolutely drained of energy, refused to undertake any more costume designs for Britten in order that he would be more able to concentrate only on the sets.

But to get back to John Piper's life in art, a visit by him as a young boy to the Tate Gallery while his mother went shopping in the Army and Navy Stores in Victoria Street commenced his lifelong love for the work of J M W Turner, the well-known and in these modern times, famous artist who also became associated with the Suffolk coast. John's father recognised this keen interest and gave his son a packet of 'Turner' postcards for being brave at the dentist. Later on, when his interest in painting further developed, John Piper made watercolour copies of paintings by some of the artists he admired, Turner certainly being one of them.

Bearing in mind the John Piper association with Aldeburgh, Snape and Walberswick I find myself wondering if he was aware of Turner's paintings and drawings made on a journey along the Suffolk coast from the River Orwell to the River Waveney in the late 1820s or even the early 1830s. I rather suspect that he did, as he would almost undoubtedly have viewed examples of the work of Turner that depicted this particular area of coastal England. On the other hand, Geoffrey Munn, author and a regularly appearing jewellery expert on BBC TV's *Antique Roadshow*, has been given credit for the comparatively recent unearthing of, or perhaps I should say identification of, a number of Turner sketches of Southwold which date from this period. According to this author's research, this famous painter arrived in Southwold in 1824 on the way from Aldeburgh, en route to Lowestoft. Munn tells the readers of his book, *Southwold ... an Earthly Paradise*, of his excitement at the privilege of handling several of the delicate drawings of views of Southwold and Walberswick, all preserved in Turner's original leather-bound sketchbooks held at Tate Britain. More will be written in a separate chapter on the subject of Turner's connections with the Suffolk coast.

I was interested to discover that John Piper's wife, Myfanwy Piper was taught how to paint 'Turner' skies by her art teacher at North London Collegiate: Miss Monkhouse demonstrated to the young Myfanwy that by wetting coarse watercolour paper and dropping in colour from the top she could produce the dramatic Turner effect. That strikes me as a good tip but does it always work for, say, a painter of modest talent? I doubt it.

John Piper went on his own East Anglian tour in May 1939 where his theme, not for the first time, was *Beauty in Decay*, as seen through the painter's eye. Piper was impressed by the clear light in East Anglia and was an admirer of John Sell Cotman (1782-1842), an English Romantic painter, not at all unknown in the region. Piper was undoubtedly influenced by this topographical artist's great understanding of the relation of the church to the landscape. In discovering this, I am reminded of John Piper's painting of the Walberswick church tower. Over a forty-year period he completed a large number of watercolour and mixed media paintings of churches in Suffolk and in the fenland area just south of The Wash. His painting, *Three Suffolk Towers*, which includes Walberswick church, is in Tate Britain almost

The interior of St Edmund's Church, Southwold by John Piper – a watercolour – courtesy of Prudential PLC: © The John Piper Estate

a century after the young Piper first visited the galleries whilst his mother was shopping. That should provide an ideal inspiration to many a young artist, particularly as Piper was accorded the accolade of a retrospective exhibition there in 1983. The study of *Three Suffolk Towers* was painted *en plein air* in the intervals between rehearsals for the 1958 Aldeburgh Festival. The former Poet Laureate, John Betjeman, occasionally travelled with Piper although it is not clear whether such journeys included those in East Anglia. It is well known that the poet's formidable interest in churches was pursued on a nationwide basis. An image of one particular watercolour painting by John Piper that has impressed me by its intense colouring and abstract qualities is his 1965 work featuring the interior of St Edmund's church, Southwold. The original was owned by the Prudential Assurance Company, but has since been sold.

St Andrew's Church, Walberswick, originally Catholic but now a ruin, much painted by local and visiting artists, was the village's second church. The tower to the present church of St Andrew's, standing next to these ruins, is ninety feet tall and was built after

1426, with the church being finally completed in 1492. Some say the present-day St Andrew's is the village's third church. The very first parish church had been constructed, complete with thatched roof, more than a mile way. Its bells and stained glass windows, as well as the images, were transferred to the new church. A chapel of ease was formerly on the site of the 'new' tower to the present church and this is probably why St Andrew's has been described as the village's 'third' church. The tower was built to enhance the original structure of the chapel but this was demolished to make way for the new church. Many artists have been inspired by the history of St Andrew's, including J M W Turner and, of course John Piper (part of the abovementioned *Three Suffolk Towers*).

The work of such notable artists such as Cotman and Turner, as well as others, had shown Piper the important place that medieval ruins occupy in the romantic imagination. On reading Ian Collins' book, *Making Waves*, I was intrigued to be able to compare two paintings of the ruins of Covehithe Church, one by Cotman and the other by Piper. It is difficult to imagine that John Piper, at one time, had more than a brief flirtation with abstract painting, including inspiration drawn from the arrival of American Abstract Impressionism in the late 1950s. Collins' book contains an image of an abstract painting entitled *Southwold II* by John Piper. This was done in watercolour and gouache and comprises various vertical column-like images in blue, black, grey and other contrasting but subdued colours.

The ruins of the old St Andrew's Church, Walberswick with the tower of the new church in the background

In 1937, John Piper wrote an essay on John Constable for the *Architectural Review* because, at this time, there was a revival of interest in a wide range of earlier English art. This led him to immerse himself in John Constable's life, letters and work although such an interest had also sprung into Piper's life in the 1920s, after a period of personal neglect of the great man. What has been described as a re-awakening was John Piper's conclusion that Constable was 'one of the greatest artists that England had produced'. It was from Constable that John Piper learned so much about skies and most people would agree that these are in plentiful supply in Suffolk, a county with an abundant resource of the type of terrain that allows the sky to dominate the view of any landscape, or seascape for that matter. On the other hand, and in contrast to his admiration for Constable, I have seen John Piper described to the effect that no other artist since Turner had done more to celebrate the British landscape and its architecture. Art experts have written about his immediate style of painting in which he manages to convey his love of the countryside and nature in a lively and vibrant way. He had an ability to bring his subjects to life through his use of colour and his loose brushwork.

In 1933 John Piper described the sea as 'a powerful emotive force' in English art but during his journeys to the coast of Britain in the late 1920s and early 1930s he did not appear to find his way to coastal Suffolk. It was to be the 1950s before he turned up at Aldeburgh, a town that I have seen described as the aristocrat amongst holiday towns. In contrast, Southwold is termed as merely an aristocrat. It appears to me that this is a very fine distinction but as the book in question was published as far back as just before the outbreak of World War II maybe that might explain it. However, it also confirms that it was not the town's reputation for good music that earned such an accolade. After all is said and done, the Aldeburgh Festival of Music, as it was then called, was not brought into being until the year 1948. John Piper was supportive of the Festival in the early years, having been also a co-founder of the English Opera Group, but he was also more than a little removed from it. Benjamin Britten started this festival notwithstanding that a cynic had stated that fifty percent of the annual event's catchment area was covered by the North Sea. I remain convinced that such a commercial fact of life did not even enter the composer's creative mind.

In terms of John Piper's attitude towards being in a position to design reasonably for the stage he felt it best not to have to think about it all the year round and by doing this he was affirming his determination to pursue his preferred vocation as a painter and writer, believing that travelling greatly assisted his natural creativity. This was an important factor in his success and perhaps we could draw the conclusion that there is also something to be said for being brave at the dentist in your youth if you are at all interested in a successful and rewarding future career as an artist.

John Piper developed an interest in the music of Rachmaninov in the early 1950s and he somewhat hesitatingly mentioned the name of this composer to Benjamin Britten. 'Ah, there's a great composer' was the immediate response and thereafter John Piper, relieved that he had not made a fool of himself by admitting a liking for a composer that might not have received Britten's approval, bought all the Rachmaninov records he could find. Somewhat ironically, he had confessed, whilst being interviewed on BBC Radio Four's *Desert Island Discs* in 1983 that he never listened to music when working as he found it too distracting. This suggests to me that he was a serious lover of music and not at all interested in 'musical wallpaper'.

Despite the pressing need to paint in his studio at home, and thus be able to better support his family, John Piper had sometimes felt that perhaps he should have done more to help with Britten's Aldeburgh Festival. He later recognised this annual event as being destined to be 'a permanent and important English Institution'. However, in the years to come he and Myfanwy did become regular attendees at the festival's performances and exhibitions, often staying with Benjamin Britten and Peter Pears at Crag House and later at The Red House after the couple moved there from their home overlooking the beach. Otherwise, they were accommodated and ate meals at their favourite Wentworth Hotel.

This might be a good point at which to provide some more background to the various exhibitions that are mounted at each Aldeburgh Festival. I have no precise information on how these are organised in present times but I am aware that, in his day, Peter Pears in particular went to immense pains in setting them up. He was always determined to cover every necessary aspect by managing the exhibits once they had been gathered together (he was often very hands-on in this respect), supervising, directing, hanging and staging. His attention to detail was legendary as he wanted everything to look good so that anyone going to the trouble of acquiring a catalogue in anticipation of visiting the exhibition would not be disappointed at viewing what was on offer. As far as both he and Benjamin Britten were concerned, a successful exhibition was directly comparable to a triumphant performance and each knew a thing or two about that subject. I feel quite certain that local residents as well as visitors would never seek to take the Festival's exhibitions for granted, but I can see no harm in reminding everyone of the care that is taken in making all the necessary arrangements once the various themes have been agreed upon.

To get back to John Piper's design work for Britten's operas, in making clear his requirements for *Billy Budd*, the composer let it be known that he thoroughly enjoyed working with his chosen artist. This was not merely because he was always happy with the designs. There were other reasons and this mutually profitable association became further recognised when publishers and record companies began approaching John Piper for cover designs for the composer's sheet music as well as his recordings.

The personal friendship between Benjamin Britten and John Piper became well established and Britten became Suzannah Piper's godfather. She was the Pipers' third child and second daughter after Clarissa. Edward, their son, also an artist, was born in 1938 but died in 1990. More will be written about Edward a little later.

Benjamin Britten and Peter Pears accumulated a substantial art collection over the years. This embraced a number of John Piper's own paintings, including a watercolour of Aldeburgh church. Britten certainly shared John Piper's interest in churches and together they went on 'church-crawling' expeditions in the county of Suffolk. It was during such time together that Benjamin Britten would talk about the difficulties and complexities of his life and John Piper learned much more about the man and not just about his music. He recognised Britten's need for creating a coterie of close friends and associates and for his part, Piper even went as far as to cement their relationship by venturing to bathe with Britten in the usually chilly waters of the North Sea at Aldeburgh. This was on no less than three occasions within the first twenty-four hours of one of his regular stays at Crag House in August 1950. This action seems to have been above the normal call of duty, if friendship with Britten could ever be described as a duty.

John Piper had, on occasion, been forced to neglect the Aldeburgh Festival because of the need to create income from his other vocational interests. In 1978, he managed to combine the two after being invited by the General Manager of the Festival, William (Bill) Servaes (1921-1999), an ex-Royal Navy officer, to exhibit some of his works at Snape Maltings during that year's event. Seeing a welcome commercial opportunity, Piper supplied an entire exhibition of new work. It was seen by no less than some two thousand people and he earned £4,000 worth of 'The Festival of Britten' sales, which would be worth more than £14,000 in today's purchasing value. As for the current aggregate market value of such items, I would have thought that this figure would be substantially in excess of this sum. For nearly ten years, Bill Servaes was general manager of the Aldeburgh Festival. When Benjamin Britten and Peter Pears interviewed him for the job, he confessed he was more used to running ships than music festivals but, as it turned out, he was particularly well suited to this latest venture in his career. The years from 1971, when Servaes took up the position, to 1976, when Britten died, were among the most fruitful in the somewhat chequered financial history of the Festival.

As mentioned previously, Edward Piper, the Pipers' eldest son became a professional painter and it was very pleasing to his parents that after some twenty years it became clear that he was certainly not regarded as merely John Piper's son but as a significant artist in his own right. Coastal Suffolk residents and Aldeburgh Festival visitors had the opportunity to view his work when he held a solo exhibition at the Festival when his father was in his eighty-fourth year. This was 1987 and, in this same year, Edward showed work with some by his father at the Beaux Arts Gallery in Bath. It was a terrible family tragedy when he died from cancer, two years before the death of his father who had, in turn, suffered mental debility and other illnesses during the last four years of his life. During this distressing period, Piper senior was nursed by his wife, Myfanwy. Edward had studied under Howard Hodgkin at the Bath Academy of Art in Corsham, Wiltshire and later at the Slade School in London. He produced photographs for the *Shell County Guides* and undertook graphic design commissions to make a living. However, his real passion was figurative art and the painting of female nudes in particular. Later he painted landscapes in Corsica, France, Italy and Spain. A number of his lithographs and screen prints are to be found in the Tate Gallery collection. Edward

Piper's son, Luke, is also an artist and the younger son, Henry, is a sculptor. It seems that the Pipers' genes march onwards and upwards.

As John Piper has tended to dominate this particular chapter, I feel that it is time that I started to write something more of Myfanwy Piper. As Mary Myfanwy Evans she was born into a Welsh family in London. She attended North London Collegiate School where her art teacher, as we already know, was Miss Monkhouse. She went on to read English Language and Literature at St Hugh's College, Oxford. She married her husband, John, and they lived in rural surroundings at Fawley Bottom, Buckinghamshire for much of their married lives. She also went on to collaborate with Benjamin Britten on several of his operas. I came across one endearing and quite irrelevant anecdote: in 1950, Myfanwy Piper acquired an Aga and from then on swore that she would never be without one. In that respect she appeared to be just as devoted to this particular brand of cooker as my own wife, but I digress.

Incidentally, the name '*Myfanwy*' occurs in John Betjeman's poems. It was writer Julian Barnes meeting Myfanwy Piper for the first time at dinner at Mr and Mrs John Mortimer's home, who first realised that the wife of John Piper, who was at that moment enjoying his company, was none other than the actual Myfanwy, immortalised in verse by the former Poet Laureate. Having read the line about a bicycling Myfanwy with 'Soap-scented fingers I long to caress', Barnes had been inclined to believe that such a person did not really exist, unless only in the imagination of the poet. For my own part I love the poem entitled *Myfanwy*, a young person that had clearly captivated the poet. Barnes clearly found it extraordinary to be chatting with a person around whom myths had gathered and who, even in advanced years, still had 'vitality and youthful intelligence in her eyes'. Once, in answer to a question, Myfanwy Piper explained that her name means 'my darling'. So was Betjeman in love; perhaps even unrequited love? John Piper had met Myfanwy when he was almost thirty and she was twenty-three. She was Piper's second wife, the artist having previously been married to painter, Eileen Holding. It was said that the pair were sexually incompatible. Piper and Holding separated in 1934.

As far as Myfanwy Piper's collaboration with Benjamin Britten was concerned, it might be a good idea to make a start with *Owen Wingrave*, an opera with music by Benjamin Britten (*Opus 85*) with the libretto by Myfanwy Piper. Britten was inspired to create this opera by his coming across a short story by American author, Henry James, of whom I have already written in Chapter Two. BBC Television had commissioned an opera from Britten in 1966 and two years later he and Myfanwy Piper started working on the libretto; it was completed by August 1970. In the event, Britten did have reservations about the viability of an opera on the small screen but the successful broadcast of his opera, *Peter Grimes*, in 1969 convinced him of the possibilities for this latest work to be featured on television. Britten had been aware of the story since his work on the previously mentioned opera, *The Turn of the Screw*, also based on a Henry James story of the same name. The première of *Owen Wingrave* was performed and recorded at Snape Maltings in November 1970 and first televised on BBC2 on 16 May 1971. Britten originally intended the work for both television and the stage, although after the stage première on 10 May 1973 at the Royal Opera House, Covent Garden, it has rarely been seen in either medium.

The next Benjamin Britten – Myfanwy Piper collaboration was the opera, *Death in Venice*. It is interesting to note that the composer had previously written to Thomas Mann's son to see whether what he intended to create would be favourably received by him and the author's widow. It was only then that he learned that Luchino Visconti's film of the same name, and also based upon the novella, was currently in production in Venice. Britten was determined not to be influenced by the film and we now know that his music for the opera brought to the principal character, Gustav von Aschenbach, aspects of Britten's own personal predicament relating to perhaps a similar young boy, imaginary or otherwise. Added to this were his own self-confessed and personal vulnerabilities, especially so, bearing in mind his position as an established and honoured composer in his sixtieth year. In his particular film adaptation, Visconti identified Aschenbach with the composer Mahler, as evidenced also by the film's haunting theme music, but Britten had no plans in this respect as far as his own work was concerned. He preferred to go along with Aschenbach as an author in accordance with Mann's original plot. Britten's libretto for *Death in Venice* was written by Myfanwy Piper and, strangely enough, she was able to bring to her libretto some memories of an experience of a similar nature from her own childhood, also whilst on a beach holiday. As a result, she shared a particular understanding of

Aschenbach's relentless pursuit of the young boy, Tadzio, by means of contrived encounters and developing indiscretions. It seems that writing this opera rather took it out of Britten, the composer. Peter Pears had told their friend, artist Sir Sidney Nolan, on whom more will be written later, 'Ben is writing an evil opera and it's killing him'.

In researching these facts, it brought to my mind the so-called maxim that in order to be convincing a writer should have a thorough knowledge of the subject upon which he or she is writing. In the case of *Death in Venice*, it appears that both Benjamin Britten and Myfanwy Piper could identify themselves with the plot in one form or another, each from their own personal feelings and experiences. The same could also be said for Thomas Mann, who had once become obsessed with a Polish boy; this was during a holiday of his in Venice in the year 1911. Who can fail to be other than captivated by the particular circumstances surrounding both Visconti's film and Britten's operatic work? This is not to mention the fact that, as far as I am aware, no single individual involved with either of these creative works had ever before sought to identify publicly, explore or even share with each other, their very personal feelings, let alone experiences.

As far as the origin of *Death in Venice* is concerned, it seems that the work was very much in Britten's mind by 1965 at the latest, although the composer had acquired a copy of Mann's text in either the 1950s or 1960s. It was not until September 1970 that Britten opened discussions with Myfanwy Piper and, after further conversations involving her husband John, a start was made on the libretto in January or February 1971. It was not until June 1973 that the opera had its first performance at Snape Maltings concert hall. I repeat these facts if only to illustrate that the gestation period for an important work can indeed be prolonged. It must have been particularly satisfying for Britten to have managed to complete his opera, despite the serious heart condition, as well as to go on to see it being performed at Covent Garden, four months after the première at Snape. However, it was by no means altogether a close run thing as he lived on until December 1976, albeit in steadily failing health. Nevertheless, given the length of time since it was first mooted I can't help thinking that the world would be a poorer place without this notable operatic work, especially when it is borne in mind that it was composed at a time of great physical as well as psychological stress for Britten. I have traced numerous performances of this opera in the UK and internationally over the years, to which must be added the recordings and broadcasts, all of which stand testament to an outstanding work.

After her husband's death in 1992, Myfanwy Piper was unable to escape the artistic path she had enjoyed with him, even if she had wanted to, which I am inclined to doubt. Amongst other engagements in June, 1993 she travelled to Woodbridge, Suffolk to stay with Norman Scarfe (born 1923). He is an historian and the author of *Suffolk in the Middle Ages: Studies in Places and Place-Names*, the *Sutton Hoo Ship-Burial*, *Saints, Mummies and Crosses*, *Domesday Book* and *Chronicles of Bury Abbey*. He is responsible for numerous other books of an East Anglian nature as well as others that relate to the Second World War. He also worked on the *Shell Guides to English Counties* in respect of certain of those in East Anglia. This probably explains the connection with the Pipers. During the course of this visit to Suffolk, Myfanwy Piper took part in a public discussion at Aldeburgh on the subject of Britten's opera *Owen Wingrave*, which event preceded a concert recital of the opera, dedicated to the memory of her husband.

All in all, John and Myfanwy Piper can be looked upon as having established and maintained a mutually profitable association with Benjamin Britten and certain counties in East Anglia with coastal Suffolk being much to the fore having regard to their work on Britten's operas and their great affection for the Aldeburgh Festival. I have found it very pleasing to be able to place these matters firmly on the record in a book that celebrates this intensely cultural area of a county that has earned enormous popularity for even more reasons. These include having its many physical attractions, as well as an inspirational atmosphere, which have attracted so many creative artists of one sort or another over many years.

Chapter Four

Imogen Holst and her long association with Benjamin Britten, Peter Pears, the town of Aldeburgh and its Festival.

BENJAMIN BRITTEN, ALTHOUGH an exceptionally gifted musician and composer, was by no means a financial genius or indeed a superbly efficient administrator. It follows therefore that in order for the Aldeburgh Festival to grow to its current status and importance in the national as well as international calendar it has experienced vicissitudes in the form of various fiscal crises and organisational difficulties. So the co-founders, being Britten, Pears and Eric Crozier (1914-1994) came to rely on other, very special people before they could even think about realising their most optimistic ambitions after the original purpose of the festival had become far less important to them. Over the years, there have been significant contributions from what amounts to a remarkably modest number of talented and extremely dedicated individuals. Some of these people were not necessarily merely administrators and managers. Quite the opposite; more than the odd one have been and indeed continue to be very gifted musically, so much so that there have been contributions of such quality that these individuals have stood out from the others.

One such person was Imogen Holst (1907-1984), daughter of the English composer, Gustav Holst (1874-1934), his only child. He was most celebrated and renowned for his orchestral suite known as *The Planets*. His daughter, a composer, conductor, arranger of folksongs as well as a writer, wrote a biography of her father in 1938. She was also a fine administrator and was a tireless worker for the Aldeburgh Festival. In some respects she could also be considered as a rather ideal choice, given that it was Britten's wish that the music performed there should be works that did not fit into the usual repertoire. Some names cropped up frequently in his day, including Purcell, Mozart, Schubert, Bach and Frank Bridge, Britten's most revered teacher. It can be said that his choice of composers other than himself, provided a programme written in his own image. His successors' programme builders continued in this spirit, which seemed to be only fitting, given the festival's history. However, now that we are in the twenty-first century there is an undoubted change of emphasis. I will deal with this aspect to a certain extent later.

Imogen Holst became Britten's first amanuensis, his musical as well as literary assistant. She had attended, albeit briefly, the inaugural Aldeburgh Festival in 1948 as a visitor, not a participant. This celebration of music and the arts has, of course, now become a regular annual event and it was the combined reputations of the formidable founding trio of Britten, Pears and librettist, Crozier that succeeded in bringing together a multitude of international stars, as well as an array of emerging talent. The artists included world-renowned figures such as lyric baritone and conductor, Dietrich Fischer-Dieskau (1925-2012), violinist and conductor, Yehudi Menuhin (1916-1999), pianist, Sviatoslav Richter (1915-1977) and cellist and conductor, Mstislav Rostropovich (1927-2007), as well as young stars in the making such as soprano, Elisabeth Söderström (1927-2009), concert pianist and conductor, Murray Perahia (born 1947) and guitarist and lutenist, Julian Bream (born 1933). There have, of course, been numerous others, and of the contemporary performers I must certainly mention pianist, Alfred Brendel (born 1931), conductors John Elliot Gardiner (born 1943), Vladimir Jurowski (born 1972) and Pierre Boulez (born 1925), all distinguished and acclaimed musicians. Altogether, just these comparatively few names provide you with a graphic and very practical illustration of the international importance of this magnificent festival. You will learn of many other prominent figures associated with this part of the Suffolk coast as we move the story along but I cannot resist providing a note from a critic regarding the finale of the 2010 Festival on 26 June as follows:

> 'Pierre Boulez brought Ensemble Intercontemporain to Aldeburgh. This is a major coup, which London venues can't easily arrange. But Aldeburgh can bring Boulez and his amazing orchestra to a hall seating barely 500, in a small country town, because Pierre-Laurent Aimard is Festival Director. They go back together since Aimard was a boy.

Aimard, a French pianist (born 1957), became the Artistic Director of the Aldeburgh Festival for an initial contract of three years in 2009 and they are indeed very fortunate to have him. The *Financial Times* music critic has described him as a 'ferociously intelligent musician' and his artistic and musical skills are also recognised in America where he is Artist-in-Residence at New York's Mostly Mozart Festival. There was also a 2010 performance of his on piano with the Chamber Orchestra of Europe playing works by J S Bach and Elliott Carter at the Tanglewood Festival, Lennox Massachusetts, and summer home of the Boston Symphony Orchestra. Previously, and at the invitation of Pierre Boulez, he had become a founding member of the Ensemble InterContemporain, a French chamber orchestra, based in Paris.

For the sake of accuracy, I must point out that the details in the extract quoted above are not strictly correct. The concert certainly took place at Snape Maltings Concert Hall, not in Aldeburgh, and this magnificent hall seats at least 830, although I must confess that I find it hard to believe that the evening's performance was played to considerably less than fifty percent of full capacity on that evening. I cannot believe that a serious critic would mistake Snape for Aldeburgh. Do you think that he was really there on the night in question? After all, it is not unknown for these things to happen and critics do tend to get caught out from time to time.

As for Pierre Boulez, who has been described as the *éminence grise* of new music, he was never a great fan of Benjamin Britten when he was alive, as the Suffolk composer was never thought by Boulez of as 'cutting edge modern'. Indeed, Boulez is even quoted as saying 'The most elegant way of solving the opera problem would be to blow up the opera houses'. An additional comment referred to the fact that, in his opinion 'All art of the past must be destroyed'. I feel sure that Britten would have said 'Perish such a thought'.

There is, therefore, a certain irony to Boulez appearing at the Aldeburgh Festival at the age of 85, due to the recent policy of moving gradually towards focusing on contemporary living composers, and it is thought that it is Aimard who has been providing the pulling power. On the other hand, it is worth mentioning that Benjamin Britten's works are performed more widely now than at any time since his death, whereas it is yet to be established whether or not the music of Pierre Boulez will survive anywhere near as long or as strongly. Only the passage of time will provide the answer to that particular conundrum.

The Britten-Pears Young Artist Programme is run from Snape at the School for Advanced Musical Studies, which was initiated as far back as 1972. The Britten-Pears Foundation website informs us that the establishment of a school to nurture advanced musical talent in the young was a project dear to the hearts of both Britten and Pears from as early as 1953 when the former first mentioned his ambition to Imogen Holst. However, five years earlier Britten had already demonstrated that he was very interested in nurturing young musical talent. This is best illustrated by the case of Benjamin Zander (born 1939), nowadays the Music Director of the Boston Philharmonic Orchestra as well as its conductor, a position he has held since 1979. Born in Buckinghamshire, Zander was initially trained in cello and composition by his father, a Holocaust survivor, but at the age of nine, Britten took an interest in the young Zander's compositions and invited the family to spend several summers with him in Aldeburgh. Britten became a mentor, as did Imogen Holst, giving the youth lessons in music theory and composition respectively. This led to a long association between the three of them, even though Zander left school at fifteen to study in Spain and Germany before eventually ending up in New England and taking American citizenship.

Incidentally, the 2010 Aldeburgh Festival did not for one moment forget that this was the centenary year of one of its founders, Peter Pears. I have written elsewhere about aspects of this tenor's career and his life with Benjamin Britten, but this seems as good a time as any to quote what I have read about him being 'a very different sort of tenor, and one of only a few whom even Placido Domingo' (born 1941), now in any event singing baritone, 'will probably never surpass in terms of versatility and influence'.

From the above list of distinguished musicians associated with the Aldeburgh Festival, it is certainly worth mentioning that Yehudi Menuhin performed for allied soldiers during World War II and went with Benjamin Britten to perform for inmates of various concentration camps, including the infamous Bergen-Belsen concentration camp after its liberation in April, 1945. Britten acted as the virtuoso violinist's accompanist and in August of that year, following his return to England, the Suffolk composer embarked upon the task of setting the Jacobean poet, John Donne's (1572-1631) *Holy Sonnets* to music and these became known in Britten's works as *The Holy Sonnets of John Donne*. This composition, described as a 'feverish and virtuosic song-cycle', was completed within a week, as it happens in the wake of the highly successful première of *Peter Grimes*, and was first performed in London in November of that year. This was in a programme commemorating the two hundred and fiftieth anniversary of the death of Henry Purcell, one of Britten's favourite composers. The work was also performed at an Aldeburgh Festival by the composer and distinguished violinist. According to the Britten-Pears Foundation notes, the cycle certainly seems to capture some of the bleak intensity of the emotive experience shared by the soloist and accompanist. Although born to Jewish parents, Menuhin's family was not involved with the Holocaust as they were living in America during those horrific times in Nazi Germany. However, the violinist caused a critical stir amongst the Jewish community in 1947 by returning to Germany to perform with the Berlin Philharmonic Orchestra under the baton of conductor Wilhelm Furtwängler (1886-1954) in what he described as an act of reconciliation. He was the first Jewish musician to do so and justified his action by stating that he wanted to rehabilitate Germany's music and spirit. I have not been able to establish that this ever did any harm to his wonderfully successful and distinguished career as a virtuoso performer who was capable of producing the warmest and most golden sounds of his era. After all, why shouldn't musical artistry be seen to overcome any thought of emotional barriers?

I was very interested to come across a quotation attributed to Yehudi Menuhin where he referred to Britten's extraordinary affinity with the sea, especially where some of his best music was concerned - 'If wind and water could write music, it would sound like Ben's'. If ever there was any one thing said about Benjamin Britten that could be considered relevantly memorable, it must be that single utterance from a man who not only knew the composer very well but was aware of Britten's somewhat pessimistic view of humanity as expressed in certain elemental aspects of his music, especially in the tragic episodes of *Peter Grimes* and his deep personal feelings of despair when visiting the concentration camp. Menuhin had also made it known that he regarded Britten as having a 'unique and extraordinary balance'. He further stated that as far as Britten was concerned 'He reminded one of one's ideal of a bishop ... witty, warm, reliable, wise and totally incapable of petty reaction'. On the other hand the distinguished virtuoso also had something to say about Peter Pears to the effect that he thought the tenor 'capable of cold fury in the face of any act he deemed as moral turpitude'. Such anger was thought to be thankfully rare, but when it did arrive, usually on professional matters, it tended to come as a formidable shock to others. To some, Peter Pears was regarded as both saint and demon but isn't this the case with other extraordinarily artistic people? I am inclined to believe this to be so.

To return to the subject of Imogen Holst, she returned to Aldeburgh in the two years following her visit in 1948, after her employers had released her for a whole week at a time. She had been at Dartington Hall in Devon, where she had held a teaching post for some years. Holst immediately became intoxicated by the unhurried atmosphere, beautiful surroundings and, of course, the musical environment in Aldeburgh. She later wrote that it was during her third visit to the Festival that she finally had time for anything other than enjoying the musical events. She then relaxed by sitting on the beach as well as visiting exhibitions. After that, she became very much involved with the proceedings. It seems that during her earlier visits to the Festival, Holst must have met Britten personally as in 1950 she had written to Britten from India saying:

> 'I wish I could send you some of the sunshine as a Christmas present! But on second thoughts, the sea at Aldeburgh is even better than the warmth and the jasmine and the banana trees and the fireflies.'

I am not entirely convinced that the second sentence refers to actually bathing in the sea on a daily basis with Britten but there seems to be little doubt that they had certainly taken to each other in one way or another. However, there seems to be little history involving the two of them with Peter Pears in tow, although it must not be forgotten that it was Pears who first reported to Britten of his admiration for the work of Imogen Holst at Dartington, following one of his visits there. Perhaps I should explain this below.

In writing this book, I am conscious that my emphasis has been far more on Benjamin Britten than Peter Pears but somehow this seems inevitable given that one was a creative musician with the other concentrating on his role as performer, although his contribution to the ultimate success of the Aldeburgh Festival has been immense. As I have already written, it was Pears who was the first of the two to express his admiration for Imogen Holst when he came across her at Dartington Hall. Pears had also been teaching there and had attended one of her classes in which she had been studying a Bach chorale with her students. Pears wrote regular letters to Britten back at Aldeburgh whilst at Dartington Hall and he later reported to his partner on the opinion he had formed of Ms Holst. 'She is quite brilliant – revealing – exciting' and at the end of his stay Pears gave an account of this when back safely in Crabbe Street, their home in Aldeburgh. He used the words:

> 'I am quite sure that somehow we have got to use 'Imo' in the biggest way – as editor, as trainer, as teacher etc – she is most impressive.'

Britten would have taken this opinion of Pears on Imogen Holst very seriously indeed and he did indeed act upon it as we have already seen.

From 1958, Peter Pears went to Dartington Hall on several occasions where he taught at the Annual Summer Schools of Music. With him there, engaged in similar capacities, were the well-known broadcaster, classical music critic, music administrator, and writer John Amis (born 1922), William Glock (1908-2000), whose career followed more or less the same lines, Julian Bream who has been mentioned elsewhere and Raymond Leppard (born 1927), who is both conductor and harpsichordist.

Peter Pears and Julian Bream often performed as a duo after 1954 and Benjamin Britten wrote his *Songs from the Chinese* for them in 1957, the work being scored for tenor and guitar, from Chinese poetry. That particular musical accomplishment by Suffolk's outstanding composer strikes me as providing something of a challenge. The Bream-Pears partnership lasted some twenty years in all. Bream had performed at the Aldeburgh Festival in 1952 and, at a party at Crabbe Street afterwards, Pears invited Bream to try over a lute song with him. They also played other works to the assembled guests, which must have made for a memorable musical evening in Aldeburgh after the earlier performance at the Festival. Bream also played lute for Elizabethan songs with Peter Pears from time to time at their recitals together, as well as guitar for their modern repertory. Interestingly, although Julian Bream got on well with Benjamin Britten on an individual basis, when Britten and Pears were together he felt that their manner was more distant and consequently somewhat cliquey. Perhaps this could have been due only to the fact that the pair were in their very personal environment in Aldeburgh, either at home or at a musical venue before the advent of The Maltings Concert Hall in the late 1960s.

Benjamin Britten and Peter Pears have, of course, left, in the Aldeburgh Festival of Music and the Arts, the priceless legacy of one of the planet's best-known and extremely popular celebrations of classical music that, even after more than six decades, retains its unique character. This is due, in no small part, to the Festival's headquarters being matchlessly located within the surrounds of the Alde Estuary and its extensive nature reserves, which are protected from any possible undesirable development. Contrast the audience leaving

Snape Maltings Concert Hall: a venue located in superb tranquillity

the spectacular Snape Maltings concert hall on a bright and warm summer's evening, having enjoyed blissful music, with, say, the promenaders exiting the Royal Albert Hall amid the malodorous and dusty, hustle and bustle of London's traffic. In my view, there can be no contest and I feel many would agree with me.

To return once again to the subject of Imogen Holst, she had first visited Dartington Hall in 1938. It is a 1,200-acre estate in South Devon and was founded as a school in that same year. Sir Clement Freud, who will be mentioned elsewhere, happened to be partly educated there and wrote that 'the air was suffused with the smell of wild garlic and the natives spoke a language we could not understand'. His and his siblings' native language up to that point in their lives had, of course, been German. It was not long before the school's potential was recognised in terms of an important arts centre where 'music and other arts could be a living experience for the locality'. The Elmhirsts, who founded the school, invited Imogen Holst to make the Hall her home while she worked elsewhere in Devon and Cornwall and she took up this offer as it served to give her a permanent base. She got heavily involved there in one way or another but especially with the musical courses for young musicians. She stayed there until 1951 as Director of Music, by which time she had caught the 'Britten bug', having, as we now know, already attended her first Aldeburgh Festival.

Britten and fellow eminent composer Sir Michael Tippett (1905-1998) were certainly no strangers to Dartington Hall, being looked upon as major creative musicians. There was mutual admiration between Britten and Tippett and the latter wrote two song cycles for Peter Pears and Benjamin Britten, *Boyhood's End* (1943) and *The Heart's Assurance* (1951). As for Imogen Holst, she came to be regarded as one of the world's great music teachers and to have such experience at his disposal in Aldeburgh was a wonderful bonus for Britten, Pears and their Festival.

Imogen Holst visited Benjamin Britten in Aldeburgh in September 1952. This was at his personal invitation to discuss with her the preliminary plans for the 1953 Festival. It was during this time that he persuaded her to move to the town for the whole year. She ended up staying there for the rest of her life. In the event, she had first visited the town in 1921 in order to attend an English Folk Dance (and Song) Society Summer School held at Aldeburgh where she heard Cecil Sharp (1859-1924) play the piano. Sharp was the founding father of the folklore revival in England in the early twentieth century, and many of England's traditional dances and songs owe their continuing existence to his efforts in recording and publishing them.

In the 1930s, and especially in 1936, Imogen Holst's star in the folk music firmament of the country had risen on a steady basis. In January of that year, she arranged the music for the National Festival of English Folk Dance and Song at the Royal Albert Hall in London. This was a major event, and during the same year she was heavily involved with judging at a competition at another festival, at which the fellow adjudicator was none other than Ralph Vaughan Williams

(1872-1958). This distinguished composer's interest was demonstrated by his personal collection of English folk music and song. Imogen Holst also had a vast number of musical achievements to her credit, but I trust that I have succeeded in providing adequate evidence of the musical credentials that Benjamin Britten was later to find so valuable. Incidentally, I understand that Vaughan Williams had been introduced to the delights of Southwold in 1910 by a local resident, a fellow composer, George Butterworth (1885-1916). Butterworth is perhaps best known for his tone poem, *The Banks of Green Willow*, and his settings of A E Housman's poems, of which the cycle *The Shropshire Lad* is probably the most widely recognised. This Southwold composer had met Vaughan Williams at Trinity College, Oxford and they became firm friends, both being interested in English folk songs. Butterworth was also an expert folk dancer, being particularly fond of Morris dancing.

The composer's new recruit lost no time in responding positively to Britten's entreaty and Imogen Holst's first 'home' in Aldeburgh, from that same month of September, 1952, was a small bed-sitting room in a house in Brown Acres, which had once been the Vicarage. This was situated behind the parish church and only a short walk up the hill from Benjamin Britten's house on the seafront in Crabbe Street. Britten was not paying her very much for the work she was doing for him and she described her living conditions as spartan. Her employer seemed unaware of her personal circumstances. A former pupil of Holst described her room as containing nothing more than a bed, chair, table and the *Bach Gesellschaft*, this composer's complete works. Following the security afforded to her by the job at Dartington Hall, Holst found her hand-to-mouth existence occasioned by her financial precariousness more than a little worrying. She did not stay at Brown Acres for too long and, after what she described as a period of 'camping out' with friends, in September 1953 she moved into a flat in Crag Path, not too far from Crag House. The composer and Peter Pears lived at their home there for ten years, the property having been purchased in the summer of 1947. However, to get back to Imogen Holst, it was not too long before Britten came to fully recognise the true worth of what Holst had been doing for him, as well as for the Festival. I can only assume that she went on to become better paid, as well as progressing to become a very close friend and a valuable associate of Benjamin Britten. There seems to be little doubt that she thoroughly enjoyed their professional collaboration.

The confidence that the two musicians had in each other grew and Holst once told Britten, not long after he had finished the opera, *Gloriana*, in 1953, that he had given English music what had been needed, which was the equivalent of romanticism. She made it known that, in her opinion, English music had stopped with Henry Purcell (1659-1695). Benjamin Britten, who had been known for a certain lack of self-confidence, had, somewhat surprisingly agreed with her. In that same year Imogen Holst found herself walking, bathed in brilliant spring sunshine, with her employer beside the sea in Aldeburgh. This was just prior to his leaving for a holiday in Ireland where he felt could relax. He did, however, confide in her that he was experiencing some mixed feelings. He said, 'I wish I wasn't going away as there is no place like Aldeburgh.' Britten's fondness for the sea, not to mention bathing in it, started from activities whilst at the family beach hut in Lowestoft. Little did he know at that much earlier time, that in July 1951, his extraordinary musical career would be recognised by the town of his birth. The authorities there granted him the Honorary Freedom of the Borough. The ceremony took place at Lowestoft's Sparrow's Nest Theatre. Thirty-four years previously, and at the age of only three, he had appeared there in a dramatic performance of Charles Kingsley's (1819-1875) *The Water Babies*. He recalled this occasion when delivering his acceptance speech. Incidentally, the Borough of Aldeburgh conferred the Honorary Freedom of their own town on Britten in October 1962.

His birthplace at 21 Kirkley Cliff Road, Lowestoft, from where his father operated his dental practice, afforded him wonderful views of the North Sea immediately in front of him and the town's harbour a few hundred yards to the left. The building is now operated as a guesthouse and the owners utilise the Britten connection in their promotional brochure, even to the extent of nominating the composer's bedroom as a special feature of their establishment. The building enjoys an elevated position, set back a little from the seafront, and it is easy to see how the origins of Britten's fondness for sea bathing derived from regular visits to the family's nearby beach hut.

Unlike other creative people within these pages, Benjamin Britten was not exactly drawn to the Suffolk coast; it just so happened that he had been born there. Having made this obvious point, there can be no dispute that he drew enormous inspiration from the sea views at Crag House, Crabbe Street, Aldeburgh and the results became expressed in his music. He was to build upon this throughout his life but I have no doubt that his formative years were also very important to him. All this has caused me to speculate on whether Britten ever thought about the view from Crag House when relaxing occasionally on the waterfront in Venice during his working visits there.

Britten's love affair with Venice was conducted over a period of some years and it is pleasing to record that during his final trip there in November, 1975 when, already very frail, he was able to make use of a wheelchair to make visiting his favourite palaces, other buildings, galleries and gardens that much easier. On that occasion, he was accompanied by William Servaes, General Manager of the Aldeburgh Festival since 1971. Servaes and his wife Pat were also accompanied by Rita Thomson who, since 1974, had been Britten's full-time nurse. He had first met her in 1973 at the London Heart Hospital after he became ill. According to Britten's biographer, Thomson's subsequent professional skill and personal devotion enabled the composer to continue to work up until the very last few weeks of his life. As for Venice, that is a place that never failed to stir the composer and must have been one of his motives in becoming interested in Thomas Mann's novella, of which much has been written elsewhere.

In the absence of Benjamin Britten and Peter Pears on holiday in the Far East in March 1956, Imogen Holst took the opportunity to stamp her authority on every particular facet of that year's Festival, her first as Director. She was involved with all programming along with a variety of other aspects, including the choice of the preacher for the Festival service: This was a personal friend, the Bishop of Chichester. She also demonstrated her versatility by conducting Handel's oratorio, *Samson*, in the opening choral and orchestral concert. That year the Purcell Singers held a concert at Blythburgh church: this was the first time that the Festival had made use of the imposing surroundings for such an event. Another notable occasion was in June 1965 when none other than Sviatoslav Richter, widely considered one of the greatest pianists of the twentieth century, performed Mozart's *Piano Concerto in B flat* there: Benjamin Britten conducted the orchestra. This was just one of multiple appearances by Richter at the Aldeburgh Festival and many of his recitals were recorded. He disliked the recording process in a studio atmosphere and much preferred this taking place at a live performance. In June, during the previous year, Rostropovich was there playing Britten's *Symphony for Cello and Orchestra*, a work that was dedicated to the distinguished cellist for whom Britten wrote four other major works. This was the first English performance, the première having been given by Britten's Russian friend in Moscow during March 1964. I just can't stop myself marvelling at the wonderful array of virtuoso talent that Britten succeeded in attracting to coastal Suffolk during what must be regarded as the golden years of his musical life. The establishment of the Aldeburgh Festival and its emergence as a major fixture in the international music calendar is rightly regarded as an enormous achievement, bearing in mind the humble beginnings at the original Jubilee Hall and elsewhere in the general locality.

Another Russian connection for both Britten and Pears was one of the most celebrated composers of the twentieth century, Dmitri Shostakovich (1906-1975). He was recognised as a good friend and his *Symphony 14* was conducted by Benjamin Britten as a Western première at the Aldeburgh Festival in 1970. This particular symphony, a song cycle based on a number of poems on the theme of death, was dedicated to Britten. However, Donald Mitchell, the English composer's biographer, felt that the music also brought an assurance that there is implicit in the very act of creativity a victory of life over death. This strikes me very much as a positive expression that would have been appreciated by Britten. The Britten-Pears Foundation library at The Red House hosted an exhibition of materials from a Russian Shostakovich archive to mark his centenary in July 2006. This occasioned an exchange of views and experiences with his widow. She had been his third wife, then aged about 73 years; some Russian archivists also became involved. The visitors took the opportunity to see some of the local sights at Southwold and Blythburgh as well as those at Aldeburgh and Snape. If what they saw, and may have heard, during the course of this visit gave them the impression that the whole of England looked and sounded the same this must have done wonders for this country's topographical reputation in Russia, let alone our musical attributes.

The Russian connection extends even further. I have written much about the work of Britten and the performances of his music in and around Aldeburgh, as well as at the Snape Maltings International Concert Hall. Each year a number of significant composers have been, and continue to be, featured and because it gives me the opportunity to mention, a little later, one of my favourite poets I am going to introduce the name of Igor Stravinsky (1882-1971) whose name is certainly associated with the Festival, even if he never appeared there. This is not too surprising, as, although he lived in his native Russia, Switzerland, France and America, he had never resided here in the UK. He is far too prominent as a composer for his work to be ignored and in scanning the festival's programmes I have discovered ample evidence of his compositions being featured in performances.

For example, Steven Osborne (born 1971), a Scottish pianist, was there in 2009 when he took part in Stravinsky's *Concerto for Piano and Wind Instruments*, a composition written in 1920. Osborne portrays it as 'witty, touching, exuberant, and marvellously structured'. He described the acoustic at the Snape venue as 'sumptuously resonant'. Music from the 1910 ballet *The Firebird* was on the programme for 2010 following other works in 2004, 2008 and 2009 which makes Stravinsky a regular 'visitor' in all but person. But my reason for mentioning him is a poetic one in that this famous composer was a fan of none other than Dylan Thomas (1914-1953) whom he had met in person. Stravinsky dearly wished to compose an opera on a libretto with the text to be written by the greatest ever Welsh poet. The initial approach to Thomas in this respect came via the Opera Workshop of Boston University with a fee proposal of $1500 in advance and a similar amount on completion. In the event, the university appeared to have some problems with raising the money but Stravinsky indicated that he wanted to make a start anyway. On this basis, the proposal was met with some enthusiasm, only for the composer's plans to come to nothing because of Dylan's sudden and very tragic death in New York en route for California where the composer was then living. A recent biography has indicated that his life might well have been saved if his medical condition had not been mistakenly attributed to his heavy drinking. Not to be entirely deprived of being associated with such a great Welsh poet he chose the poem that Thomas had written in memory of his father, *Find Meat on the Bones*, and Stravinsky's *In Memoriam Dylan Thomas* was sung by Peter Pears at the 1957 Festival, thus establishing the Aldeburgh connection. As for my favourite poem by Dylan Thomas, it has to be the lyrical work, *Do Not Go Gentle into that Good Night*, written in 1951 and considered to be amongst his finest compositions. As was the case with Stravinsky, Dylan Thomas never appeared at the Aldeburgh Festival but it pleases me that the distinguished composer's name, allied with that of Dylan Thomas, was linked to Aldeburgh by that performance of Peter Pears in 1957.

The Festival continued to grow but the Jubilee Hall in Aldeburgh could hold only a little over three hundred people. However, the demand by audiences was satisfied by the staging of other events at the Parish Church and other venues in the county, several quite close to Aldeburgh. Nevertheless, for many years the organisers had been looking for a much more appropriate 'headquarters' venue for such a growingly prestigious annual fixture. It was in 1965 that it was discovered that an exciting building, the recently disused Maltings at Snape, just five miles inland from the town of Aldeburgh, was available for leasing. Given Benjamin Britten's previous history of living at Snape Mill in the village he was immediately inspired and one wonders why he hadn't thought of it before. I shall be writing much more fully about this magnificent building in a later chapter.

It seems clear that over the years Imogen Holst, despite being only six years his senior, developed an almost maternal interest in Britten and clearly enjoyed doing things for him on the domestic side as well as working as his musical assistant (from 1952-1964). It was also quite apparent that she became his confidante. There were times however, when the composer found her somewhat irritating but this seems to be around the time that Holst became ill and was forced to spend some time in hospital, after surgery. Afterwards she convalesced at Dartington Hall. It was at that time that Britten had been admonished by Imogen's mother, who felt that the composer worked her daughter far too hard. Britten's patience with Imogen Holst had worn thin as she had tended to spread her wings with other work; work that was not associated with Aldeburgh. The late Rosamund Strode, Imogen Holst's meticulous successor, had described her 'disciple-at-his-feet' attitude in that Holst had a tendency to carry dutifulness to extremes. It became known that all was not universally well between the composer and his amanuensis. In my experience, this is understandable between two very talented people and it is only to be expected that some tension tended to creep up into their relationship from time to time. There always seemed to be some measure of pressure associated with their work together but the fact that Holst referred to her so-called gynaecological operation in such a way that it had unfortunately become something of a joke within the Britten entourage. How she tended to describe her surgical treatment served to 'curl Ben up'. Nevertheless, Britten retained a deep admiration and affection for her, notwithstanding his occasional experiences of exasperation with 'Imo', the name by which she became widely known amongst her friends and colleagues. It should never be forgotten that he was also an ardent admirer of her style and on regular occasions she was assigned her own personal concert at the Festival. Britten was known to have said, 'Who would not cross England to see Imo conduct?' She was particularly expert at conducting brass bands. I'm not certain if this was ever done at the Aldeburgh Festival but she did share the rostrum with the Commanding Officer when the band of the Royal Military School of Music, Kneller Hall, Twickenham played at Framlingham in 1975. On that occasion, she had a dress specially made for the occasion, taking great care to ensure that the colours she chose matched those of the Bandsmen's tunics. The Band's response in terms of their performance was said to be terrific and they subsequently 'played like demons' under her baton.

To revert to a previous reference of mine on the subject of Imogen Holst, it was interesting for me to learn from her writings that she had regarded her father's musical career in terms of his having been something of a 'John the Baptist' figure, making the mistakes that needed to be made, at the same time clearing the path for a greater English composer to follow. It is necessary to understand that her musicianship and literary skills were such that she was able to write an accomplished biography of Gustav Holst and followed it up with a book entitled *The Music of Gustav Holst*, which was, as was the case with her earlier biographical work, well received. For her, the saviour was undoubtedly Benjamin Britten and it was to him, her employer, that she dedicated her new book. There were inevitable comparisons by Imogen Holst of the works of her father with those of Benjamin Britten and this extended even to the way they chose to practise their musical craft. Her father died in 1934 and his daughter continued to miss him terribly, almost throughout the rest of her life. In some ways, it seems clear that Britten may well have been regarded by her as something of a surrogate and it was with joy that she was able to watch her employer work on a day-to-day basis. This must have been when such comparisons came into her mind. Britten became aware of this and even encouraged it by going out of his way to discuss her father's scores with Imogen.

This might be a good opportunity to mention what I heard on a BBC R4 programme, *Tales from the Stave* (15 December 2009) on the subject of Gustav Holst's *The Planets*, an incredibly well known, seven-movement orchestral suite. I learned that Imogen donated her father's original score of several volumes of that immense work to the Bodleian Library in Oxford in gratitude for the manner in which they had looked after all of her father's original works during the Second World War. It was subsequently found that many pencilled notes made by subsequent conductors had been erased from the original score. Imogen Holst was later to have said to have regretted this action on her part, as a result of which she probably had her wrists slapped, metaphorically of course, by a critical archivist or librarian. This professional would have made known an insistence that such appendages were part of the history of any musical score, let alone one of such importance. Gustav Holst had composed *The Planets* from 1914-1917, a most difficult time by any standards. It was first performed, in concert to an invited audience, in 1919 and this composition must have had its pages turned by several distinguished conductors before it was printed and published two years later. This first private performance of *The Planets* was conducted by the composer's friend, Adrian Boult, and there seems little doubt that some of this future knight of the realm's personal annotations would have been amongst those regrettably rubbed out or otherwise expunged by Imogen Holst.

On a personal note, it seems that Imogen Holst's attitude to Britten's sexuality appeared to vary between being almost totally naïve in the early days to ambivalence over time. As to her own sexual inclinations, she had worked hard on suppressing these from as far back as her teenage years and the result was, not unsurprisingly, an enormous appetite for a remorseless working schedule.

It is now appropriate to mention Rosamund Strode (1927-2010), a fine light soprano who had appeared previously in an artistic role at the Aldeburgh Festival. She became music assistant to Benjamin Britten as well as part-time to the festival generally on Imogen Holst's 'retirement' from this work, thus taking over the role as amanuensis to the composer in 1964. Britten described this development in a letter to William Plomer as a new 'cog' in the music machine under his control. Fittingly enough, she had previously studied under Imogen Holst at Dartington Hall. Ms Strode went on to become the founding Keeper of Manuscripts and Archivist at the newly formed Britten-Pears Library at The Red House, eventually retiring in 1992. She also chaired the Holst Foundation. She was an undoubted authority on both Benjamin Britten and Imogen Holst and they became close colleagues.

Incidentally, and only in passing, Dartington Hall was the newly-opened co-educational school where Ernst Freud, son of Sigmund Freud, sent his three children when the family arrived in this country as refugees from Nazi Germany in 1933. These three grandchildren of the founder of psychoanalysis, Sigmund Freud (1856-1939) were scholars, not fee payers, due to their distinguished ancestry. At the time they arrived at Dartington Hall, then a preparatory school, Stephen Gabriel was aged eleven and a half, future portrait painter, Lucian Michael just ten and a bit, with Clement Raphael, Jill Freud's future husband, almost nine years old. Clement wrote more than a little about his time there in his autobiographical book, *Freud Ego*. Dartington Hall had apparently found it commercially advantageous to be seen to be educating children of eminent people. Other examples were the distinguished philosopher, Bertrand Russell (1872-1970) and Nobel Laureate for Literature, as well as author of *Brave New World*, Aldous Huxley (1894-1963). Sigmund Freud did not flee his native Austria until June 1938 when he travelled by Orient Express to London and settled in Hampstead. During the following year it would appear that, due to prolonged pain derived from oral cancer, his death was assisted at his own request by an act of euthanasia by his personal physician and friend. More will be learned about the Freud family later, because their close connections with coastal Suffolk are particularly strong.

Nowadays, the organisation behind the Aldeburgh Festival of Music and the Arts is responsible for more than just what goes on in the summer, as there are other events and occasional performances during the course of each year. There are also the activities associated with a succession of schools for young musicians throughout the year at Snape. In addition to the world-famous concert hall, the Snape

Maltings complex is also home to the new Hoffmann Building and the Britten–Pears Building, both of which contain a mixture of rehearsal and performance space, including the Britten Studio and the Peter Pears Recital Room. Visiting artists generally stay in Aldeburgh, just five miles away on the coast. We now know that this small fishing town has inspired many generations of musicians, writers and visual artists. The Pumphouse, Jubilee Hall, Cinema, Parish Church and even the beach in Aldeburgh are all frequently used for concerts and events, as are other nearby venues, including the churches at Orford and Blythburgh.

In 2013 it will be the centenary year of the birth of Benjamin Britten and Norwich City Council, disappointed at not being nominated for the UK's City of Culture for that particular year, are nevertheless pressing on with their intention to stage 'The Festival of Britten' by working with the Britten Sinfonia, regarded as one of Europe's most celebrated and innovative chamber orchestras. The venue will be the city's Theatre Royal and during that particular year a host of other cultural events are being planned. Although the Council's proposals appear to include a somewhat belated bid to climb on the Britten bandwagon, their geographical location not qualifying for consideration as part of the cultural heritage of coastal Suffolk, it is nevertheless gratifying that the regional significance of Britten's internationally famous work will be recognised in such a demonstrative manner.

Chapter Five

The Britten-Pears personal and professional relationships, the opera, Gloriana, and a disastrous flood

IT IS INTERESTING to note that Peter Pears' biographer has asked the rhetorical question 'Would Peter Pears have become a great singer without Benjamin Britten?' He felt that the answer is probably 'no'. After his partner's death Pears was known to have remarked 'He really made me'. Benjamin Britten has reciprocated on the subject of Peter Pears by saying 'He liked to take the line that he would never have got anywhere without me'. These underlying points are undoubtedly interesting but they are, of course, entirely academic in that we shall never know the answer to the question that has been posed by Christopher Headington. The same would apply to the question 'Would Benjamin Britten have been the same composer without Peter Pears?' The answer is again 'probably not' and we are left in ignorance of whether or not Britten would have been a lesser or greater overall musician without his partner. Perhaps it is best summed up by saying that their respective gifts and talents flowered together but I remain convinced that this will not, by any means, be the end of this particular debate.

I wrote earlier of my greater concentration on the life and work of Benjamin Britten compared with that of Peter Pears, but perhaps this is a convenient point at which to mention a creative element to the long-term collaboration between the two. This was in respect of *A Midsummer Night's Dream*, an opera with music by the former and the libretto by both. This work was first performed at the Aldeburgh Festival in June 1960. From time to time, we all find ourselves reading on the subject of what can only be described as some rather gruesome operatic settings of some of Shakespeare's works. Nevertheless, it is true to say that the Bard has inspired four or five of the best operas ever written, works that include Giuseppe Verdi's (1813-1901) *Othello* and then *Falstaff*. Alongside such distinguished company has been the Britten-Pears rather free adaption of *A Midsummer Night's Dream*. Pressure on time, due to the opening of the enlargement of Aldeburgh's Jubilee Hall being required to take place well within a period of twelve months, led Britten and Pears to complete the entire work involved with *A Midsummer Night's Dream* as a rather hurried collaborative venture. This, by any standards, was a remarkable achievement given their usual workload. Despite being unwell, the composer conducted this operatic work on the opening night with some of his favourite singers playing the lead parts. These were Jennifer Vyvyan (1925-1974), soprano as Tytania, Owen Brannigan (1908-1973), bass as Bottom, with Peter Pears in the minor, comic 'drag' role of Flute. The Aldeburgh pair thoroughly deserved their critical success.

Imogen Holst had always formed, as well as voiced, opinions of her own and these have been well researched by her biographer. It is clear that Holst had her doubts concerning Peter Pears, reservations that not only related to his musicianship but also to his attitude to his life-long relationship with Benjamin Britten, particularly around the time of the latter's death. There is also evidence in her writings of what she conceived to be Pears' indifference to what Britten was working on at any one time if there was not to be a singing part for him. I do not intend to dwell upon this subject, but I have certainly come across several of her criticisms of his singing performances. However, I feel sure that Benjamin Britten would have always defended his partner, such was the clearly-stated loving relationship he had with the tenor. Whilst on the subject of their respective 'live' performances, there were a considerable number together over the years but Donald Mitchell, has referred almost reverentially to such recitals being 'composer-oriented' rather than 'performer-oriented' which, to my mind, is perfectly understandable given what these two remarkably talented people meant to each other. They gave their first recital together at Balliol College, Oxford in 1937. Britten and Pears, each being a pacifist, later left to live in America, just a few months before the outbreak of the Second World War became inevitable. There, in 1940, Britten composed *Seven Sonnets of Michelangelo*, the first of many song cycles for Pears. Upon their return to England in 1942, they performed this song cycle at Wigmore Hall on 23 September, and then recorded their performance of the work for EMI. This was their first recording together. Whatever may be thought about Pears as a tenor when performing away from Britten's compositions, from what I have read about him it was his 'Englishness', a style of interpretation, expressiveness and nuance that is perceived differently from that of the well-known Italian tenors. There seems to be no doubt that these qualities served to make his formidable reputation more secure.

Having said that, Britten himself had become depressed after a bad performance by Peter Pears in *Gloriana*, a work with which the singer appeared to be thoroughly despondent at being so closely involved. Pears had made no little secret of being unhappy at being cast, at Britten's insistence, as Lord Essex who was looked upon as a young ardent lover, having had a relationship with Elizabeth I. In the end, Britten got his own way and this was usually the custom on such matters when he was clearly in charge. It had been thought that Lytton Strachey's (1880-1932) book, *Elizabeth and Essex*, would be a good starting point when this opera was being planned and William Plomer's (1903-1973) libretto was certainly based upon this work. To make matters worse, the young Queen Elizabeth II was said to be not all together happy with this opera as a result of watching her famous predecessor represented in amorous alliances. This was quite apart from the twentieth century Queen's unease at the earlier Queen's character being portrayed as sympathetic but flawed, motivated largely by vanity and desire. Even Britten conceded that he had made many mistakes with *Gloriana*, which was specially commissioned as part of the celebrations for Her Majesty Queen Elizabeth II's coronation. This almost certainly had a depressive effect on the composer after it became clear that the work was not destined to receive immediate critical acclaim. For his part, Britten felt 'kicked around, so bewildered by the venom' of the press criticism. He was, however, sustained by what he described as so many lovely friends 'of sense and courage'. He later recorded in his diary that, by the end of the run, the public attended performances in large numbers. This was undoubtedly a great comfort to him. *Gloriana* was first performed at the Royal Opera House, Covent Garden, six days after the Coronation in 1953.

In his memoirs Lord Harewood, who died on 11 July 2011 aged 88, described *Gloriana* as 'one of the greatest disasters of operatic history' but, in fairness he felt that this apparently widespread view arose owing to the exact nature of the audience for the gala occasion. Inevitably, those who had attended on such an historic occasion had comprised the 'great and the good', government ministers, the diplomatic core, foreign dignitaries and this list goes on. It could not possibly have been seen to be a gathering of 'artistic Britain', members of which theoretical group might well have been better disposed to appreciate what Harewood described as 'the passionate, tender drama inside the public pageantry that Ben had contrived'. It seems that the critics had been unduly influenced by the muted audience reaction as, thankfully, not totally everyone was as scathing. It was also felt that, given the anxieties of the period, Benjamin Britten might well have been more in touch with his time than the pomp and circumstance of a Royal gala might lead the country to suppose. It was, after all, the time of the Cold War and not long after a change of Government with the Labour Party being defeated in 1951, a Labour Party that had brought about much social change. In further defence of *Gloriana*, a 1966 revival at Sadler's Wells, in commemoration of Britten's fiftieth birthday, stimulated renewed interest, not at all unfavourable. This was taken as indicating that the Coronation year performance might perhaps have been seriously underestimated but the damage had, of course, been done, certainly as far as the composer was concerned. *Gloriana* went on to receive more frequent performances and recordings, certainly during more recent years. The Britten-Pears Foundation now suggests that the unjust critical furore surrounding the première has now passed into history and the work can be seen as a worthy successor to *Billy Budd* with which it shares a number of important features.

As a footnote to what I have written about *Gloriana*, it seems that the Earl of Harewood was subjected to rather mixed emotions all those years ago. The fact was that in March 1952, whilst he and his wife were on a skiing holiday with Britten and Pears, it was the peer who first suggested that Britten might compose a Coronation Opera that would be dedicated to his first cousin, Her Majesty, Queen Elizabeth II. On 18 May 1953, the Harewoods gave a dinner party at their London House in Orme Square, Bayswater at which the Queen and the Duke of Edinburgh were present. It was on that particular occasion that Peter Pears and Joan Cross, who were to play the leading roles as the Earl of Essex and Queen Elizabeth I respectively, sang parts of the opera accompanied by Benjamin Britten on piano. The Royal couple was polite but Joan Cross said something later to the effect that it was not 'an easy evening. I don't think they enjoyed the occasion any more than we did '. With the benefit of hindsight, this seems to me to have been somewhat of a prophetic remark.

It was probably the last time that Benjamin Britten was to receive such poor 'notices' as we all now know that during the succeeding twenty years or so of his life he went on to be responsible for some well-received and enormously impressive musical compositions that served to underline a memorable career that thoroughly deserved the internationally acclaimed reputation that he enjoys to this day. His work continues to be performed all over the world. Not only that, his beloved Aldeburgh Festival goes from strength to strength. How sad that he was taken from us before such international recognition of the annual event had achieved its current elevated status.

This may not be a bad point at which to return to more personal matters affecting the composer. I have already written about Britten and his sexuality, especially in the context of the advice given by W H Auden which rather put paid to the latter's friendship with the composer. In direct contrast, and in terms of his own sexuality, Peter Pears did not consider himself to be either proud or ashamed of the way he was. His life with Benjamin Britten must surely have served as an enormous inspiration to his work over a long and distinguished musical career. In my view, the reputation earned by British music would never have reached such heights without the results of their extraordinarily close personal relationship, allied with their professional collaboration over such a lengthy period.

This Britten-Pears relationship, not only personal but also professional, must have been almost, if not totally, unique during their reign at or near the top in recent British classical music history. Quite near to the end of his life, Britten wrote to Pears that he regarded his lifetime partner as 'the greatest artist ever' and added;

'What have I done to deserve such an artist and man to write for?'

In reply, Pears who, at the time, was making his personal début at the Metropolitan Opera, New York, singing the role of Aschenbach in Britten's opera, wrote in reply:

'... it is you that has given me everything, right from the beginning'

He went on to say:

'I am here (now) as your mouthpiece and I live in your music – And I can never be thankful enough to you and to Fate and for all the heavenly joy ...' (sic)

If ever proof were needed that these two stalwarts of British music had enjoyed such a creative and emotional partnership over a long period of time, this exchange of letters would do it for most people.

Having said that, it was towards the end of his life that Pears gave the impression to Donald Mitchell that he was concerned that, after Britten's death, his 'unique role in Britten's life and creativity might be undervalued', a concern that the editor of the Britten diaries found it difficult to take seriously.

Britten and Pears in happy times

Perhaps the year 1953 was, to coin a phrase used during a speech of HM The Queen on 24 November 1992, something of an *annus horribilis* for Benjamin Britten. On 31 January, a severe storm blew up on the East Coast and this led to disastrous flooding as well as the loss of over three hundred lives in the area. The lower floors at Crag House, 4 Crabbe Street, became flooded but thankfully Benjamin Britten's manuscripts and scores were rescued from the ground floor sitting room by Elizabeth Sweeting. She was general manager of the Aldeburgh Festival from 1948 to 1955. The entire ground floor of the house had become flooded and much residual mud needed clearing before some form of normal life could be resumed in that musical household. 'It might have been much worse' was the eventual verdict, according to Peter Pears. The house certainly needed re-wiring and the inconvenience caused was considerable. The occupants' extensive record collection was damaged and many labels had floated clear. Britten wrote that sound production was badly affected, as were the plans for the Aldeburgh Festival that year. Much had been stored in the cellar which, inevitably, was also very badly flooded but I cannot help thinking that, with the extensive loss of life in the region, the problems suffered by Britten, Pears and their associates should be seen as rather minor and the observation of Pears should be seen in that context. However, just one thought has occurred to me. This was Benjamin Britten's beloved North Sea that had inflicted such devastation on Coastal Suffolk. I have been speculating on how this might have affected his general attitude to the North Sea, even though the opera *Peter Grimes* must have remained fresh in his mind at that time. It's an intriguing thought.

Chapter Six

A well-connected Peer of the Realm, an opera and further sightings of the novelist, E M Forster

A REGULAR VISITOR from the world of the arts to Crag House was Lord Harewood and, as we already know, he was a first cousin of Her Majesty the Queen. He was a man who confessed to having had a passion for opera since his childhood. His varied career in the arts had been on the managerial side, rather than in a creative or performing mode, and his extensive involvement had been with Covent Garden and the Edinburgh Festival as well as the English National Opera. A man of considerable influence is a description that would appear to fit the bill on the subject of the arts generally as far he was concerned and with E M Forster, an honorary fellow of King's College, where Harewood read English, he found that they had, in common, amongst other things, a great liking for, and an interest in, the life and work of Benjamin Britten.

Harewood was thrilled to be asked to be President of the then newly founded Aldeburgh Festival in 1948. At that time, he was still an undergraduate, although, it has to be said that he had made a late start at the age of twenty-four, due to the outbreak of war. To receive such generous recognition from someone whom he admired meant a lot to the young man and when E M Forster urged him to accept he was delighted to do so. Harewood celebrated by hiring a bus to take a large party from Cambridge to Aldeburgh where they attended a performance of Britten's *Albert Herring* at the Jubilee Hall. The composer had always described this building as the opera's 'real home' as well as its main venue in those early days of the music festival. The Jubilee Hall is not more than a just a few doors away from Britten's former house in Crabbe Street. As a setting to stage an opera or a concert this venue became very much a favourite with audiences, even if only for the fact that the intervals presented an opportunity to spill out on to the beach, close to the building that houses the town's lifeboat. The record company, Decca, released recordings of some Aldeburgh concerts in a *Festival Series* and this certainly helped to put the annual event firmly on the musical map. A further visit by Forster followed not long after when he lunched with Britten, his sister Barbara and Peter Pears before moving on to a concert in the Parish Church. This was the second performance of Britten's cantata, *Saint Nicolas*, which was first performed at the opening concert of the Festival, the work having been written in the same year, 1948.

The full programme for the inaugural festival that ran from 5-12 June 1948 included not only the performance of *Albert Herring* with Joan Cross and Peter Pears in the principle roles but also much other British music. There were works by Purcell and Lennox Berkeley as well as Britten's own *Saint Nicolas*. Other attractions were exhibitions featuring works by East Anglian painters such as John Constable and Thomas Gainsborough, as well as modern paintings of Suffolk by various local artists. Models of the stage settings for *Peter Grimes* were also on show. There were lectures on the great literary figures of the district given by what were described by the Countess of Cranbrook, chairman of the Festival's Executive Committee, as 'notable novelists, poets and critics of today'. Tickets were said to be strictly limited, as was the local accommodation, but the town's hotels and bed and breakfast establishments all did extraordinarily well during that special week in the summer of 1948.

Lord Harewood continued to attend the Festival in succeeding years where he again met Forster and each of them stayed at Britten's home on a regular basis. In later years, Harewood backed a stage adaptation of Forster's first book, *Howard's End*. He was amused when he heard that an elderly lady, who had attended a performance of the play at a matinee, had remarked to a neighbour 'it's just what I should have expected from Lord Harewood: nothing but music and sex'. He felt that he could never have written a braver epitaph than that.

It must be mentioned, however, that Lord Harewood would not have hesitated to criticise Britten's work when he saw fit to do so, even though he remained a great admirer of the composer's musical works. He was of the belief that Britten had brought a feeling of renaissance to English music as a whole. I mentioned the English Opera Group once or twice earlier and it is a sign of the close relationship that Harewood had with Britten that the composer became accustomed to asking Lord Harewood to introduce various operatic recitals or programmes. These featured a number of different singers, each invariably accompanied by Britten at the piano. These events became a feature not only of the Aldeburgh Festival, but also of the life of the English Opera Group, even on short tours with the latter. These had the added purpose of keeping the Group's name in front of the public. These concerts were also needed to raise much-needed funds.

There is no doubt that the Britten-Harewood relationship became a close one, both personally and from the point of view of their close professional collaboration, but the break-up of the Earl's marriage to his first wife, Marion, hit the composer hard and this resulted in Britten putting an end to their association in 1964. The couple had married in September 1949 and Britten's, *A Wedding Anthem*, received its first performance at their wedding in London's fashionable Mayfair area.

Britten's deeply personal reaction to the divorce caused deep distress to Lord Harewood. Such an emotional reaction was by no means mitigated when the Queen's first cousin heard that the composer later regretted the break, in that it had brought about a parting from the man whom Britten had assumed was his most single-minded and devoted supporter. Regrettably, the breach was never healed, as it seemed clear that the composer could not bring himself to accept Patricia, Harewood's second wife, whom he married in 1967, not long after the divorce from Marion had become absolute. Britten had been very close to the peer's first wife. Harewood was surprised to learn that, quite soon after the separation, Marion had invited Britten to stay at Harewood House, his family seat in Yorkshire, along with a fellow guest who was none other than a fellow composer, Mstislav Rostropovich. Harewood's former wife's maiden name was Marion Stein (born 1926), who had previously enjoyed a career as a distinguished concert pianist. She made the national news headlines in 1973 when she married the Liberal politician and former party leader, Jeremy Thorpe (born 1929) whose career ended in disgrace six years later, after he was charged, tried and subsequently acquitted, with others, in connection with attempted murder and conspiracy to murder. I well remember the extensive publicity given to these proceedings, which would almost certainly have caused Benjamin Britten many mixed feelings.

Tentative moves by Harewood to keep in touch with the composer were not altogether discouraged by Britten and there were to be further visits by the Earl and his new Countess to the Aldeburgh Festival where they attended performances in the town and also at the new concert hall at Snape Maltings. On one such occasion, they did manage to have a few words with Britten who by then was already very ill, but a further meeting at a later date made it clear to the Harewoods that it was too late to renew the friendship and, somewhat sadly, that proved to be the final scene. On this particular matter, time did not appear to have been a successful healer.

It will be recalled that Lennox Berkeley was another person who had a personal, as well as a professional, relationship with Benjamin Britten. I have already mentioned that this composer had attended Benjamin Britten's school, Gresham's, some ten years or so previous to his younger friend's own time there and in later years these two composers were to collaborate on various works, including twenty three musical settings of poems by that other Gresham's alumnus, W H Auden. Sixteen of these were completed by Britten with the remaining seven the responsibility of Berkeley. When the latter first became aware of Britten's work, as it happens in Spain, probably around 1936, he was astonished by the younger man's musical maturity. It was in Barcelona, where they had met at the ISCM Festival in 1936, that they cooperated with each other on a four-movement orchestral suite, *Mont Juic,* based upon popular tunes they had heard in that city. They later went on holiday together in Cornwall and it is said that whilst there they had discussed composition as well as pacifism. It is generally felt that Britten's talent was superior to that of Lennox Berkeley, but this is not a subject upon which I am able to offer any informed judgment.

In addition to the foregoing evidence of a professional relationship between the two composers, they also had a very close personal association resulting in some form of love affair. I understand that there has been a recently published book on this subject. Berkeley eventually married and Britten became godfather to his eldest son, Michael (born 1948), now an established composer in his own right. In Britten's lifetime, twenty-four performances of work by Lennox Berkeley took place at the Aldeburgh Festival. According to a biographical record of this composer, a première of his opera, *A Dinner Engagement*, was an instant success at the 1954 Aldeburgh Festival, following which it had a mixed reception at Sadler's Wells.

This leaves me wondering if Britten had made known his approval of his friend's work, thus helping to ensure the critical acclaim at the festival, but this is pure speculation.

I now come to a well-known name that now needs to be more formally introduced because of a relationship with Britten that certainly achieved longevity. For my part, it also serves to demonstrate just how much Benjamin Britten enjoyed composing music in the company of friends whom he trusted to make valuable contributions to his work. This latest name is the novelist, E M Forster, whom we have already learned became a frequent visitor to Crag House. Imogen Holst wrote of Britten and Forster enjoying each other's company during the latter's stays at Aldeburgh although it is known that there was the occasional note of discord between them. In those days, the late 1940s and early 1950s, the author was more or less living at King's College, Cambridge, so his journeying to Aldeburgh could not have been too arduous and probably accounted for the frequency of his visits there. I am now able to tell you that E M Forster (1879-1970) had worked on the libretto with Eric Crozier (1914-1994) for Britten's opera, *Billy Budd*, a work that was first performed in December 1951. It also received a first television airing on NBC-TV in America in October 1952.

Billy Budd was first performed in this country on 1 December 1951 at the Royal Opera House, Covent Garden. We already know that the artist, John Piper, was responsible for the stage design. *Billy Budd* was based upon a novella, *Billy Budd, Sailor* by American author, Herman Melville (1819-1891). A start had been made around 1886 but the book was left unfinished at the author's death and not published until 1924. It has been central to Melville scholarship since it was discovered in manuscript form among Melville's papers in that same year. Melville was perhaps better known as the author of *Moby Dick*, a metaphysical whaling novel written in 1851.

E M Forster had discussed the Melville novel in his 1927 Clark Lectures, which were sponsored by Trinity College at Cambridge University. These lectures were subsequently published as a book entitled *Aspects of the Novel*, a useful book that contained Forster's analysis of the literary form but which also reveals his reluctance to omit what is described as his habitual irreverence, wit and wisdom.

Perhaps it was these rather attractive features that endeared this author to Benjamin Britten and his friends, even if they felt unable to refrain from criticising Forster behind his back from time to time for what they perceived as less engaging personal characteristics. I am sure that some people would describe such attitudes as typically English. In all, Forster had five of his own novels published in his lifetime: another, *Maurice* appeared shortly after his death in 1970. This latter novel was notable for the plot featuring a homosexual love affair and, given that the author's sexuality had not been previously known outside what must have been a very small circle, it caused some controversy. The book had been written nearly sixty years earlier, over a half century before Lord Wolfenden's famous Report was followed by homosexual acts being made legal in the United Kingdom in 1967. Seven years previously, Forster added what he described as a 'Terminal note' to his novel. After I had read this, I felt that I had somehow learned more about the novelist's craft than I had gleaned from his already mentioned book *Aspects of the Novel*, written in 1927 and categorised as Literary Criticism. It is just that in those comparatively few words it is possible to understand how such a master contrived to achieve such success in writing literary fiction.

In June 2010 it was reported in the press that a secret cache of E M Forster's papers had been discovered, locked away at his former lodgings at Cambridge University. Part of the contents of this discovery, which included a diary, made it clear that the explanation for Forster having ceased to write novels after *Passage to India* was published in 1927, was his admission that his creative drive had been curbed after consummation of his sexuality. This was followed within a few years by a long-term affair with a married policeman. This does not seem to be too surprising, as Forster had made his name by writing about heterosexual, English middle-class themes, examples of which are *Howard's End* (1910) and *A Room with a View* (1908). One gay author, commenting on the new revelation about E M Forster, said that 'It is certainly true for quite a few writers and certainly for Forster that suppression (of sexuality) was a strong creative force'. Forster added a poignant note of his own in his diary when aged eighty-five. He expressed annoyance with society for wasting his time by making homosexuality criminal. He would have preferred to have avoided all the subterfuges and the self-consciousness. There must be countless others who would agree with this sentiment.

A seventh novel, *Arctic Summer*, was never finished and has been described as an incomplete fragment, written in 1912-13 and published posthumously as late as 2003. At one time during his life, referring to his writing, Forster is reputed to have said 'I can't be considered a great novelist because my characters can be slotted into only three categories: "The person I think I am, people who irritate me, and people I'd like to be"'. I feel that it would be necessary for me to undertake a back-to-back reading of perhaps four or five of his novels in order to determine whether or not I am prepared to accept that this statement is other than an additional example of a tendency towards a waspish sense of humour. Perhaps I should also mention that at the time Forster was quoted on this subject he added 'Tolstoy was truly great because he did not operate with any such constraints'.

I have read somewhere that this highly respected and now academically recognised novelist had met Britten before the Second World War. They went on to build up a solid friendship. On the other hand, it has been reported elsewhere that the composer first met Forster in 1942. It is certainly known that, in 1945, the author was present at the Sadler's Wells performance of *Peter Grimes*. Whichever is correct I do know that in 1948, at the inaugural Aldeburgh Festival, Forster gave a lecture on the subject of Crabbe's poem, *The Borough*, linked with both Britten's opera and the town of Aldeburgh and wondered aloud what he might have done had he been invited to write the libretto for Britten's latest work. Britten obviously took the hint and, in 1949, Forster was once more invited to Aldeburgh where he worked on the libretto for *Billy Budd* with Eric Crozier. The latter was called upon to collaborate, as Forster had never before written for the theatre. We now know that since 1947 Morgan Forster had often stayed at Crag House and despite referring to Aldeburgh, on at least one occasion, as 'a bleak little place' he must have liked the town for one reason or another and not just because Britten had given him some interesting work to do. My own impression is that Forster enjoyed the social as well as the cultural activity, ever present as long as Britten, Pears and their various friends were in attendance.

Benjamin Britten later expressed the view that writing his opera, *Billy Budd*, which was commissioned by the Arts Council for the 1951

Festival of Britain, was 'my own happiest collaboration' and wrote of Forster:

> 'I think the writing of the libretto gave him great pleasure. Certainly the summer of 1950, when he stayed for a long time at Aldeburgh, when the sun seemed to shine continuously and we would go out for relaxation in a boat with a fisherman friend (curiously resembling the Billy we were writing about).'

In this respect, it appears that it was during Forster's stay at Crag House in August 1948 that Melville's novella, *Billy Budd*, was first chosen as an appealing subject for an opera. It was almost two years later, when Forster was convalescing at Crag House after a prostate operation, that a weekend house party there was entertained by Britten playing through Act I of *Billy Budd*. The guests included not only Forster but also the Earl and Countess of Harewood and music publisher, Ralph Hawkes (1898-1950) whose family company, Boosey & Hawkes, remains well known for publishing the work of many major twentieth-century composers. These included Benjamin Britten (signed up in January 1936), Aaron Copland, Gustav Mahler, Sergei Prokofiev and Sergei Rachmaninoff. It was not until over three years later that, as previously mentioned, *Billy Budd* was to receive its first public performance at the Royal Opera House, Covent Garden. Britten dedicated the opera 'To George and Marion, December 1951' and subsequently presented them with his manuscript full score. This is now held by the Britten-Pears Library at The Red House in Aldeburgh, presumably because the pair decided that this was where such a valuable work truly belonged. I have visited the library for the purposes of research and remember being impressed by the sight of young people, in all probability students of music, poring over original scores by Benjamin Britten, no doubt complete with annotations by this very Suffolk composer.

I would now like to repeat something of a somewhat anecdotal nature about E M Forster and George Crabbe. The well-known East Anglian author, Ronald Blythe, in *Aldeburgh Anthology*, a thoroughly interesting book that he edited and had published in 1972, included what had been a little known essay by E M Forster on the subject of the formidable George Crabbe. Forster wrote 'To talk about Crabbe is to talk about England'. Forster was writing about a man who left his native country only once and that was only to venture across the border into Scotland, an experience that he happily survived. Not for the first time, Forster was rather scathing about Aldeburgh, which seems rather strange bearing in mind his frequent visits to the town which must have provided him with more than a little interest bearing in mind that he was mixing freely in the Britten and Pears social circle. Anyway, he had already portrayed Aldeburgh as a bleak little place: but he also added 'not beautiful. It huddles round a flint-towered church and sprawls down to the North Sea – and what a wallop the sea makes as it pounds the shingle!' Moreover, he describes the nearby expanses of mud and 'saltish' commons with marsh-birds 'crying as melancholy'. To my mind, he recovers somewhat by stating that George Crabbe got all of this, especially the melancholy, into his verse. This was because the Suffolk poet remembered the experience from his childhood of rolling barrels of butter on the nearby Slaughden Quay, under orders from his father who was also called George. This activity, which involved the young Crabbe having to store the barrels in his father's warehouse, was hated by the youth. His mother had died and this had made his father angry with life. It certainly appears as though this had to be taken out on his son, perhaps in the absence of anyone else being near to hand at the time.

Writing a little earlier about *Billy Budd* has left me speculating if the title character could possibly, but certainly not probably, pass as an oblique but entirely unintentional reference to Billy Burrell (1925-1999), a local fisherman in Aldeburgh. Billy Budd was, of course, a character in the Melville novel but we must bear in mind Forster's 1948 talk, which included the hint about wanting to write a libretto. Add to this the existence of an available namesake and perhaps we have what inspired Britten to create an operatic version. For many years, Billy Burrell was coxswain of the Aldeburgh lifeboat and a firm friend of Benjamin Britten since 1947. Billy had been in the habit of providing the Britten household with freshly-caught fish and shellfish, especially lobsters. Billy had once run a bathing station on the beach outside Crag House. As both Britten and Peter Pears were frequent bathers, it is not surprising that a friendship developed. Billy eventually married Barbara, a local woman, in the early nineteen-fifties and the composer was known to take the couple on the odd outing at times when they confessed to be feeling bored with their lot in Aldeburgh ... 'just for a change of scenery'. They lived just across the road from Crag House and Britten has written about them as being happy together, which showed that he cared for their wellbeing. I found it rather touching to read a letter from Benjamin Britten to E M Forster in October 1953 in which he announced the couple's marriage. So Billy Burrell, local fisherman and expert seaman, was certainly known to at least two notably creative people in those days and I feel sure that more names could be added to the list. Benjamin Britten was present when the Burrells' child was christened in 1957. Six years earlier, Billy had been included with other friends of Britten and Pears in a sixteen-day boating holiday on a thirteen-ton diesel-engine launch called 'Midas' which belonged to a regional businessman. They sailed across the North Sea and amongst other passengers was the director of opera, stage and television, Basil Coleman along with Billy Burrell's brother, John and a local engineer, Vic Tripp. Somehow a local schoolboy, Robin Long, had also been included in what must have been a somewhat of a motley crew. Incidentally, it was Basil Coleman who produced Britten's opera, *The Turn of the Screw*. Coleman had known Britten and Pears for some twenty-five years and had always regarded them as a 'wonderful couple', regarding it as a privilege to be with them. He had even remarked that the two behaved like any other conventional married couple but this was long before the days of civil partnerships which afford same-sex couples rights and responsibilities comparable to civil marriage.

Having regard to the Melville literary connection, Billy Burrell was quite obviously not the inspiration for the opera *Billy Budd* but, as it has already been seen, the composer did remark on a resemblance. At first, this had led me to speculate on whether this was just an afterthought, rather than the fisherman being a possible source of the inspiration, but we must remember that Melville's Budd was a sailor in the British Navy who was hanged for murdering a fellow crew member. So now we all know that the only common factor between the two Billies was the name, although both can be described as seamen. As far as the working relationship between Forster and Crozier was concerned, it was Crozier who researched the naval history and was responsible for the dialogue, leaving the author of *Passage to India* to the production of 'big slabs of narrative' that were written in prose. Britten commented that this factor strongly influenced the opera's musical character, which leaves me wondering whether Forster would have been aware of such an outcome at the time he was putting in all the effort. This was, after all, a new genre for him and, as far as I am aware, it was the only libretto that he had ever been asked to write.

I consider it to be worth mentioning that much has been made of the homoeroticism that runs through *Billy Budd*, the cast being exclusively male, but this is not the only reason for such a conclusion. It has been said that the composer's heavy orchestration does suggest a sense of sexual tension. Quite naturally, this brings me back to Forster's writing of the libretto being reflected in the opera's musical character. Or is this too simplistic? Britten must have enjoyed working with the largest orchestra he had ever used. This enabled him to apply the sound of mass wind instruments to the sea-pictures, with brass and lower wind instrumentation contributing to darker and more ominous textures for the evil Claggart, the master-at-arms. A trilling trumpet and gulping wind section announced the stammering Billy Budd character, a press-ganged recruit to the Royal Navy.

As mentioned previously, there are no female characters in the opera, a fact that Crozier felt offered insuperable problems from the operatic voice point of view and the atmosphere is depicted as being rather stark and tragic. In the words of Eric Crozier, 'the central problem concerns the eternal conflict between good and evil, and the inadequacy of human justice in exceptional circumstances'. Britten felt that he could compose music that would allay Crozier's fears and could even make a virtue of the lack of female voices but the librettist was far from convinced on grounds that an all-male cast would have a very limited appeal for an opera repertory. In the end the quality of the writing in Melville's novel was considered to have won the day.

Crozier and Forster worked meticulously on producing a series of drafts of the script and as soon as complete copies were available, Britten's musical ideas began to take definite shape, but only after making known his criticisms of the text with suggestions for improvements. Crozier admitted that what he and Forster had created was a dramatisation of the novel and not a libretto, so work then started on producing what was really needed for an opera. The distinction is not an easy one to describe, so I will not even attempt to do so. However, Crozier has described a libretto as a springboard for the music, something that could not be accomplished by a mere script for a play written for the theatre and performed by actors. Perhaps this brief explanation of what an expert has written on the subject will suffice.

Benjamin Britten's personal views on E M Forster have left me somewhat confused at times but there seems no doubt that there was a genuine friendship between them. In December, 1947, after a two-day visit to Cambridge where the composer came across certain celebrities, he mentioned in passing that he noticed E M Forster coming and going 'like an old bat' and this found me wondering if John Piper ever came across the author of *Passage to India* at Crag House during any of his stays there, bearing in mind the artist's design responsibilities for the opera. One way or another, maybe because of his demeanour or perhaps it was the way he chose to dress, Forster somehow brought forth more than a little critical comment from intelligent people whom I feel quite sure he would have regarded as his friends. When attending a dress rehearsal at Covent Garden for *Billy Budd* (see below), Stephen Spender observed that the author was there with his cloth cap and satchel, looking 'like a piano tuner', whereas William Plomer thought that Forster more closely resembled 'the man who had come to wind the clocks'. Being almost universally known amongst his friends as 'Morgan' he must have been held in affection as well as respect but I do find these recorded 'digs' a little below the belt. On the other hand, I suppose that this is just human nature: but does this really provide an excuse for what most people might perceive as a lack of respect? On the other hand, we have to remember that we are dealing with a comparatively small group of talented and creative people who never seemed shy in criticising each other's work ... although not necessarily always to their face. Stephen Spender, in particular, had something to say about E M Forster as well as himself when he wrote in October 1944, after a lunch with Cyril Connolly (1903-1974) and E M Forster:

> 'Morgan Forster always gives me the impression that, in his extremely diffident way, he is making moral judgments on everyone. The very reticence of his personality shows up everyone else like a patch of colour, which placed beside other colours, makes them tawdry and vulgar. The effect of his presence was that I talked a great deal about myself. All the time I was thinking, while he looked at me with his head a little to one side, "how abominably vulgar I am"'.

It seems that Connolly, at the same lunch, took a more materialistic line on Forster's censoriousness: 'When I served the steak I wondered whether Morgan would notice that I had taken the largest piece?' Spender's biographer noted that 'while Stephen talked too much Cyril munched – without any uncomfortable remorse'. This was judged to be Connolly's way. The only comment that I am able to make on these exchanges is that I have always understood that steak was probably difficult to come by in those war-time days but there is little doubt that certain of the more fashionable grand hotels and restaurants of London's West End had their sources for such culinary luxuries, as long as there was a profit to be made. The cynical might reflect that the wartime clientele who could afford to patronise these establishments clung to their privileges like limpets and seemed quite happy that the majority of the population could possibly suffer degrees of hunger as long as they were able to continue to be amply foddered.

Stephen Spender often seemed to come across characters in life that he compared with Morgan Forster. On his way back from Australia via India on a tour as a free-ranging cultural ambassador for the Congress for Cultural Freedom in 1954, it was at Madras that he was met by a delegation which he went on to describe in these rather comic terms:

> 'The men looked terribly scruffy, with dirty clothes, dishevelled grey hair, and stomachs protruding under their costume. There was a writer who looked like an Indian dressed up as E M Forster dressed up as an Indian in the days when Forster wore a walrus moustache'.

In passing, it is perhaps worth mentioning that Stephen Spender, like his friend Morgan Forster, was invited to give the Clark Lectures at Cambridge University in 1966, returning from America to do so. He had been lecturing there and was always in demand by American audiences, as seems to be the case with the former Prime Minister, Tony Blair, but for altogether different reasons. Spender had stayed at Trinity College on the nights after the lectures, as the guest of its Master, R A Butler (1902-1982), the former Conservative politician. It seems that Spender found the accommodation far more luxurious than the monetary value of the stipend. E M Forster was amused to discover that Spender received precisely as much as Forster had received in 1927, described as 'a measly £150, a couple of glasses of vintage claret and some high table conversation'. Spender's lectures, like his fiend's before him, were published in a book, *Love-Hate Relations: Study of Anglo-American Sensibilities* (Hamish Hamilton 1974). These lectures were instrumental in getting American Literature established as a respectable academic subject at the university and were a natural outgrowth of Spender's long fascination with Henry James and poet, playwright and literary critic, T S Eliot (1888-1965) who was considered more Anglo-American than James, even though the latter spent the last forty years of his life in England.

Chapter Seven

Joyce Grenfell, a regular at Aldeburgh and an admirer of Imogen Holst

IT MUST NOT be forgotten that the Aldeburgh Festival also provided a venue for other arts. Imogen Holst wrote to Benjamin Britten, in January 1953, discussing a sculpture exhibition featuring Austrian-born, Georg Ehrlich (1897-1966) which, apart from his pieces, would also include works by such eminent sculptors as Henri Gaudier-Brzeska (1891-1915), Jacob Epstein (1880-1959, Reg Butler (1913-1981), Lynn Chadwick (1914-2003) and Elisabeth Frink (1930-1993). Subsequently, the Arts Council organised successive sculpture exhibitions at Aldeburgh, all of which played their part in making the town's annual Festival a hugely important event on an international basis. Incidentally, Ehrlich is known for his strikingly impressive busts of both Benjamin Britten and Peter Pears, both of whom were his friends. These works can be viewed at The Red House in Aldeburgh.

During the period of Holst's magnificent efforts at the Aldeburgh Music Festival, the annual event attracted many distinguished visitors and a regular was none other than the late, lamented actress, comedienne and songwriter Joyce Grenfell (1910-1979). She wrote the following to a friend in 1966, after attending a lecture delivered by Imogen Holst entitled '*What is Musical History*', illustrated by the Purcell Singers:

> 'It was utterly fascinating and absolutely first class. She (Imogen Holst) came on trippingly, head down. Not a trace of powder or lipstick on that fifteenth-century head painted on wood. A pale beige dress blending in with face and hair. Almost invisible really. And then she began. It was a miracle of erudition, simplicity, interest, passion and wit. Haven't enjoyed anything more during the whole Festival and it's been a very good Festival'.

I, of course, never met Ms Holst but I have read enough and have seen a sufficient number of photographs, sketches and even a portrait painted by Mary Potter, to appreciate that Ms Grenfell got Imogen Holst just right. It is difficult to find anything more gratifyingly complimentary or so entertaining as that piece of appreciation of what Gustav Holst's daughter had to offer the world of music. In terms of the description of her appearance on that occasion Imogen Holst was by then approaching the age of seventy, but as far as I am concerned photographs taken much earlier in her life depict a young woman of rare beauty.

At more or less the same time Joyce Grenfell also wrote direct to Imogen Holst in the following terms, the quotation being given verbatim:

> 'The whole thing gave enormous delight to me – from timing, humour & wit & above all from perfect communication with us, the audience. You are a born communicator…I found I could very nearly make myself believe that I'd never heard 2 parts before & felt I was in a spare, light monastery somewhere a long time ago suddenly making a discovery.'

'Imo' also had her own individual way with words. In 1980, at the age of over seventy and enjoying a much more relaxed way of life, Imogen Holst wrote;

> 'If one lives in Aldeburgh there are advantages of walking at Andante piacevole* speed, for it leaves time to look at the changing colours of a sunset or at the pattern of bare branches of a tree or the contrapuntal circling of the gulls as they fly above Crag Path.'

> * 'Andante piacevole' is probably best described as 'agreeable and moderate'.

I like to think that the most important of her past employers would have approved of that elegant example of literary skill.

Joyce Grenfell and her husband Reggie visited the Aldeburgh Festival every year from 1962 until her death. She described their attendance as 'such an enjoyable part of our lives' and offered the accolade 'certainly one of my Pleasant Places'. Steven Isserlis (born 1958), a distinguished cellist, who has admitted that he grew up with a resistance to the music of Benjamin Britten, has written that he believes that Snape is the only place he knows that changed his attitude to a particular style of music. Earlier in his career, he had hated Britten's *Cello Symphony* and his stance was changed only when in the late 1980s EMI asked him to record the work for them. It was whilst walking across the marshes at Snape before a concert that it came to him that Britten's music came from the haunting silence that he had then experienced for himself. He has expressed in words that, from that memorable occasion, everything changed and he remains a passionate fan of the *Cello Symphony* and, just as importantly, of much the composer's other music ... with the rider, 'but not yet all'. I have recounted this story because Isserlis has also spoken of the sight of Joyce Grenfell striding into a concert at the Aldeburgh Festival, seemingly oblivious to the excitement she was stirring up among her fellow audience members.

Ms Grenfell particularly enjoyed her first visit to the then new concert hall at Snape in 1967, writing to a friend it is

'All so light and rural looking, without being the least "folksy." Very spacious and gay looking'.

She went on to write that

'I'd say it's a great success as a building – lots of parking space, a big lawn with a huge "Henry Moore" on it looks well, and the theatre skilfully built within the walls of the original Maltings'.

It must not be forgotten that Joyce Grenfell was also an occasional performer at the Aldeburgh Festival. When she was first invited to participate by Benjamin Britten himself, she regarded it as the accolade of her professional life, particularly so, as, in her opinion, the composer and co-founder always maintained a standard of excellence. On that original occasion, Miss Grenfell gave one of her standard one-woman programmes but her contribution must have created a good impression as she was invited back to perform at the Aldeburgh Festival's twentieth anniversary. For this performance, she had co-written a song in praise of Britten and Pears, with a recitative aria, full of puns of Ben's name – *bene, beneficial, benefactor, benefit, beneficent* and even *Big Ben*. She later wrote that both of them had been pleased by the tribute, Britten having confessed that he had been much moved by her performance of the piece. This had been at The Red House, as Grenfell had been reluctant to sing the piece 'cold' during the evening performance. It was at their home that the composer rewarded her with an affectionate hug and asked her to sing it again. This reception made her feel a lot less apprehensive about performing the piece in public and she was thrilled that there was also a call for an encore at the performance during the festival programme that evening. This concert took place at the Jubilee Hall but in June 1972, she appeared at The Maltings where she took part in a programme of music and verse, together with harpsichordist, George Malcolm (1917-1997). They were accompanied by actor and singer, Max Adrian (1903-1973). Britten dedicated his setting of the *Mass, Missa Brevis in D* to George Malcolm, along with the boys of the choir. This was on Malcolm's retirement as organist and choirmaster at Westminster Cathedral in 1959. Britten's work received its première there on July 22 1969.

Ms Grenfell was also a big fan of both the town of Aldeburgh, as well as the North Sea. She has written of her 'childhood pleasure of a first sight of the sea, and at Aldeburgh the first sight of the sea comes into view over the rooftops, as you turn the corner by the parish church and descend the sudden and unexpected hill that goes down to beach level'. As for the North Sea, so beloved by others within these pages, she concedes that it is more beige-grey than green-blue but, for her, 'it is the most romantic and somehow a more friendly sea than any other around our coasts'. To my own mind, this opinion can be regarded as a somewhat debatable point, given the North Sea's many moods and the somewhat lower average water temperature than that regarded as being even mildly acceptable by most human beings. This may not, of course, be the case during the warmer summer months. Nevertheless, there must be many of an artistic, as well as an idealistic, leaning who would nevertheless have agreed with the late Ms Grenfell.

I was intrigued by what Joyce Grenfell felt able to write after first meeting the artist, Mary Potter in the year 1938. This was at the London home of Philip and Mary Nichols, who were friends of the Potters. Ms Grenfell acknowledged her 'as a very distinguished painter, well known and highly regarded'. She described her as dressing 'in her own dateless fashion, in the colours of her own individual palette that she uses in her paintings – chalky terracottas, pale turquoise, faded blues, whites, creams grey and stone colours, sharp yellows, pale sage greens, soft browns and reds'. I found it fascinating to have an artist's clothes described in such a way, but I suppose only another artistic woman would ever make an attempt at something like this. It was in early 1939, at a party at the Potters' London home in Chiswick, that Joyce Grenfell met the man who started her on a career that became such a passport and door opener for her future life in the theatre. His name was Herbert (Bertie) Farjeon (1887-1945) who wrote two successful revues that were performed at London's Little Theatre in the Adelphi. He was also well connected in that he was theatre critic of the *Tatler* magazine. It was at that party that Joyce Grenfell responded to a request by Stephen Potter; he requested that she might perhaps perform a piece that derived from a Women's Institute lecture that she had recently attended. Grenfell had been struck by the delivery of a talk by the visiting speaker on the subject of *Useful and Acceptable Gifts and how to make something from nothing*. Grenfell had listened intently and later described the presenter's 'performance' in terms of 'vowels aslant', sharply finished consonants and careful diction as a 'collector's item and I collected it'.

Stephen Potter had heard Grenfell's rendition at the Nichols' house, where and when they had first met, and he wanted the Potters' guests to witness a repeat performance. Somewhat surprised by such a request, bearing in mind that her stage career had not yet been launched, Joyce nevertheless set about entertaining her hosts and fellow guests, click-finishing her consonants and sliding her vowels, as had the original lecturer. At the same time she offered her audience not only what she remembered, including the actions and mannerisms, but also choosing to make up what she hadn't recalled. It seems that Bertie Farjeon treated this piece as some form of audition and he asked Joyce Grenfell if she knew who had written it? She then recounted the full story and confessed her own 'embroidery'. He asked her to write it down as he wanted to use the piece as a sketch in his latest revue entitled, *The Little Revue*, a production that had a company that included no less than Hermione Baddeley (1906 – 1986) and Bernard Miles (1907 – 1991). Miles went on to become a popular broadcaster and later founded the Mermaid Theatre in London. But there is even more to this charming story of the 'birth' of Joyce Grenfell as a popular entertainer. She went on to perform the WI piece at Bertie Farjeon's *Little Review*, and thus made her début on the London stage. Despite not being too comfortable in rehearsals, where there was, of course, no audience, her 'First Night' was an unqualified success; Grenfell left the stage acclaimed by prolonged applause. A star had been well and truly born and the rest is indeed history. This is a cliché that will be repeated in relation to other matters in this book so you will have to bear with me on this personal weakness.

Perhaps, this popular performer's ultimate 'success' was when Joyce Grenfell appeared on the Ed Sullivan Show (the second of three appearances in all) at the CBS studio in New York. A fellow guest was none other than the twenty-one year old Elvis Presley (1935-1977). The 'King', on introduction to the British performer, greeted her with 'Nice to know you honey'. She described him as a roly-poly boy, but a good singer 'of his sort of hill-billy songs' which strikes me as rather quaintly bizarre, not to say somewhat understated, given this Rock 'n Roll singer's phenomenal career and his status as a cultural icon. She wasn't sure how to respond when Presley put his arm round her neck and 'breathed down my ear-hole'.

Chapter Eight

The story of Snape's 'Moore' and other statuary

JOYCE GRENFELL'S REFERENCE to the Moore statue at Snape reminds me that I also saw it there at the time of my being in the audience at a recital given by the renowned, if not to say legendary pianist, John Ogdon, in the late 1980s. During the course of a more recent visit to Snape, Moore's work was no longer there, so I set out to find the story behind its removal. It transpires that the statue *Reclining Figure* (one of several under this name) by Henry Moore was removed from its location at Snape in autumn 2003 as it was in need of cleaning. It was returned to Perry Green (the home of the Henry Moore Foundation in Much Hadham, Hertfordshire) for restoration. The plan then was for it to remain there for the 2004 season and be sited at the entrance to the gallery at Perry Green, as part of the exhibition entitled *Imaginary Landscapes*. As I had previously learned of a rumour that the statue was subsequently stolen, I sought confirmation of this but all Aldeburgh Music could tell me was that there was indeed a statue stolen from the Foundation with the same title and date (1969-1970). I subsequently received confirmation that this was indeed the work that was removed from Perry Green in December 2005. This is a sad story and, by now, this fine piece of irreplaceable statuary has probably been melted down and sold for comparatively modest pecuniary gain by an organised gang. For some considerable time, Aldeburgh Music have been very much hoping that 'when the time was right' it would be possible for the Moore Foundation to make available, on loan, another statue by Henry Moore, so that it could be enjoyed in the future, should the Trustees' generosity stretch this far. I was very pleased to find a discreet way to pass on this information to my contact at the Foundation as I felt an additional, albeit modest voice might make a contribution.

In December 2011, I was delighted to be informed by Aldeburgh Music that their wishes had been granted in that during the preceding month a statue by Henry Moore arrived at Snape, again on loan from the Foundation. This magnificent work is entitled '*Large Interior Form*' and, with the kind permission of those at Snape, I reproduce on the following page an image from their website. It is preceded by a photograph of the original 'Moore' at Snape.

The 'new' Moore at Snape, Large Interior Form installed during November 2011, between the entrance to the Concert Hall and the River Alde, with the marshes in the background

Sun rising over Henry Moore's *Reclining Figure*, at Snape before its removal in 2003

In the meantime, I have been told that Aldeburgh Music will be staging an exhibition about Henry Moore and Barbara Hepworth's relationship with Benjamin Britten in June 2012. I regard this event as something of a celebration of the meeting of these two branches of the arts in coastal Suffolk.

In the meantime I have been amused by various references on the Internet to previous sightings of the 'Moore' statue at Snape Maltings, often accompanied by pictures which are easily identified as depicting one section of Barbara Hepworth's set of *The Family of Man* (bronze, 1970) in three figures. These are described by the sculptor as Figure 1 – *Ancestor I*, Figure 2 – *Ancestor II*,

Barbara Hepworth's *The Family of Man* at Snape

Figure 4 – *Parent I*. This statuary is on loan to Aldeburgh Music at Snape by the owners, the Fitzwilliam Museum at The University of Cambridge. I am hoping that this information may clear up one or two misunderstandings that have arisen. Nine other figures by Hepworth in this *The Family of Man* series are also on exhibition at the Yorkshire Sculpture Park, Wakefield.

Reacting to the lure of Snape, is Alison Wilding (born 1948), another sculptor of considerable note. An example of her work has been twice nominated for the annual Turner Prize. She became a Royal Academician in 1999 and has worked at Snape. Her site-specific work, *Migrant* (2003) is located in the stream leading from the river towards the Maltings Concert Hall. Arts Council England, through Dance East, celebrated the National Lottery's 10th birthday celebrations in 2004 by commissioning dancers from the Richard Alston Dance Company of The Place, London to perform in front of *The Migrant*. Alison Wilding has written about this particular work as follows:

'Snape is shaped by water, and Snape Maltings is now a concert hall which bears the traces of serious flood defences. In high summer you can lie on the grass and watch the brown sails of boats gliding past, just visible through purplish reed beds. *Migrant* is about travelling, not destination. It's nature is changeable, secretive – a glimpse of bird and boat.'

As an enormous fan of the wildlife of the magnificently serene marshes of coastal Suffolk, as well as north Norfolk, I can't add anything to what Alison Wilding has written because those few lines seem to say it all, for most people anyway.

Alison Wilding's Migrant, close by the Maltings Concert Hall, Snape

You will come across quite a few references to what I consider the almost magical marshes of Suffolk and other parts of the region in this book but I am well aware that these are very readily appreciated by others, not necessarily just sculptors or even musicians. Simon Barnes, award-winning sports and wildlife journalist with *The Times*, often gets very lyrical on the subject. Writing recently about Darsham Marsh, he described how the art of knowing, and therefore unsubsidised birdsong, is just a part of the true appreciation of nature. This led him to describe how the spell that works for the marsh and every other part of the wild world is so effortlessly available to all of us. Perhaps we tend to forget this at times when there are so many pressures in modern, everyday life.

In 1991, a major retrospective of Wilding's work, *Alison Wilding: Immersion – Sculpture from Ten Years*, was held at Tate Liverpool. Images of her work can be viewed on the Tate website. Other major exhibitions devoted to her work have been at the Serpentine Gallery, London and the Museum of Modern Art in New York.

On a final note for this remarkable sculptor, I was delighted to learn that Alison Wilding was awarded the Royal Academy of Arts Charles Wollaston Award at the RA's 2011 Summer Exhibition. At £25,000, this is one of the largest and most prestigious art prizes in Britain. The exhibit is entitled *Take a deep Breath* and was featured in a special programme on BBC2.

It is not possible to write about coastal Suffolk and its statuary without featuring Maggi Hambling's magnificent work known as *The Scallop*, now the subject of a book by its creator. As far as the artist herself is concerned, she is now linked, hopefully in perpetuity, to Aldeburgh. There, standing on the beach, a short distance north of the town centre, stands a sculpture that is not only a magnificent example of her highly individual art but, to my own mind, a wonderfully appropriate commemoration of a lifetime of the composer's work that is so closely associated with this town of culture. Dedicated to Benjamin Britten and aptly entitled *The Scallop*, this highly individual monument marks an area where Britten used to walk along the beach in the afternoons. Now an undoubted tourist attraction, this impressive sculpture, unveiled in November 2003, was created from stainless steel and stands four metres high. The piece is made up of two interlocking scallop shells, each broken, the upright shell being pierced with the words: 'I hear those voices that will not be drowned'. This text is taken from the libretto of Britten's opera *Peter Grimes*. The sculpture is intended to be enjoyed both visually and in a tactile manner; people are encouraged, especially by its creator, to sit on it and watch the sea. The day I visited, young children were playing a game of hide-and-seek around it and I felt that this famous musician as well as the sculptor would have approved of this activity in what could well be described as his spiritual presence. Let me just add Maggi Hambling's own words:

> 'An important part of my concept is that at the centre of the sculpture, where the sound of the waves and the winds are focused, a visitor may sit and contemplate the mysterious power of the sea'.

This, again, says it all as far as I am concerned because I am now a great admirer of both the work and its subject.

The Scallop took about seven months to produce at a local foundry run by Sam and Dennis Pegg (J T Pegg & Sons Limited, established

1912), now a father and son team running a steel fabrication and stockholding business. They had never made anything remotely like this particular sculpture before, and were said to be bursting with pride over it. Sam told an interviewer it was '[s]imple really - we had the model, and we just had to scale it up by thirty-seven times, nothing to it. We've had a tonne weight hanging off that top bit, and it didn't budge - it'll stand up to anything'. What a wonderful story and I find those people who declare the sculpture to be controversial and unwelcome in the town to be missing the point. Some had even stopped so low as to deface it and, sadly to say, on more than one occasion. Someone has written that perhaps Hambling's sculpture draws attention to itself a little bit too self-consciously, being just a little too, well, you know, 'Thorpeness'. I am happy to restrain myself from commenting too critically at such pretentiousness; just consider my eyebrows being raised to a significant extent. It is my personal view that the sculpture is a glorious work of art and does an enormous justice to the memory of Benjamin Britten, surely the town's most famous son, albeit adopted. He was responsible for putting the town of Aldeburgh on the international map of culture.

When interviewed by Libby Purves on her BBC Radio 4's *Midweek* programme, Hambling was happy to contradict a comment from her interviewer that the sculpture had been commissioned. She declared that the concept was entirely hers and the project came to fruition in that she had been perturbed that the leading citizens of Aldeburgh had not sought fit to commemorate the achievements of the world-famous composer who had made the town his home, let alone establish an international festival of music there. Hambling was rather vague on where the money came from but Simon Loftus, who ran Adnams, the well-known Southwold brewery, at that time, was mentioned. It turns out that the company was never involved with the funding. Loftus did, however, play a vital role in raising money from various sources and had assisted with setting up an indirect charitable status for the project.

Hambling had first set about producing the maquette, a sculptor's small preliminary model, usually in wax or clay but in this case consisting of various scallop shells 'sort of gummed together'. She somehow got halfway through the funding of the project and then took a leap of faith and set about completing the sculpture in earnest. It's a remarkable story, now recounted in her the book, *The Aldeburgh Scallop* published by Full Circle Editions who specialise in publishing from East Anglia's 'fertile cultural landscape'. The book tells us that It was Hambling experience of a storm at Thorpeness on the last day of November 2002 that later caused her to paint the sea from memory, with, as she puts it 'the sea in charge of me'. This proved to be the first of her *North Sea Paintings*. In 2003, an Aldeburgh Festival Exhibition of her work bearing this title raised money for *The Scallop*.

Maggi Hambling's iconic sculpture, The Scallop, at Aldeburgh

Other contributions soon followed, due to the efforts of friends of hers such as George Melly. The rest seemed to come from various Foundations and Trusts as well as Eastern Arts.

Hambling described to Purves how she wanted the sculpture to look as if it had forced itself up through the shingle or perhaps dropped from the sky or had even been found washed up on the shore by the force of the waves of her beloved North Sea. *The Scallop*, being made of stainless steel, has never succumbed to rust. The fact that it does appear to look rusty in places is merely the effect that the artist has successfully achieved. The brown-coloured stains that are now in evidence were created by a deliberate galvanizing process in a very hot oven. Maggi Hambling had been aware of the controversy from the first day of the sculpture being located at the chosen site. This served only to gladden her heart in that she regarded local opposition as people who were merely responding to her art, no matter whether their attitude was negative rather than positive. She described *The Scallop* as being deliberately 'site-specific and user-friendly'. As for her connections with the county, she maintained that she was a 'Suffolk person through and through just like Britten and the Peggs'. According to Hambling, her art began in Suffolk at the age of fourteen.

We shall learn later that this was at the school run by Sir Cedric Morris (he succeeded to a baronetcy in 1947), and Arthur Lett-Haines where, as you will discover later, some of the alumni can be described quite accurately as noticeably distinguished.

More will be written on the subject of various forms of 'sculpture' by highly individual artists, but the foregoing can be said to relate only to coastal Suffolk and, of course, its rich cultural heritage.

Chapter Nine

Britten, Pears and literary friends during the 'American interlude' and the 'birth' of the opera, 'Peter Grimes'

THIS SEEMS TO be an appropriate juncture to relate some details about Benjamin Britten reading E M Forster's article on George Crabbe (described elsewhere as an essay) whilst he was in California, in July-August, 1941. Britten and Peter Pears had been in America together from later on in 1939 to 1942, their having first arrived in Canada in May 1939. In August 1939, the pair travelled to New York from Canada, ostensibly to 'look up' W H Auden and Aaron Copland. By then the Britten and Pears relationship had developed to the extent that Peter Pears told a friend, Basil Coleman, in Toronto in June 1939, that the two had realised that they were in love with each other. A physical relationship was to follow and according to his biographer, with evidence from letters, that it was consummated during a stay in Grand Rapids when some form of commitment was made between them. The tenor later referred to this as a 'pledge' and, as I will no doubt say yet again on other matters, the rest is history.

During their stay of approximately three years in America, Britten earned something of a living conducting as well as touring as a soloist during the course of which he performed his own *Piano Concerto*. There were also recitals, accompanying Peter Pears as well as composing and arranging various works. As far as Britten's conducting was concerned, he was appointed as conductor of the appropriately named, The Suffolk Friends of Music Orchestra, Suffolk County, Long Island in time for their 1941 season. When they first arrived in the USA, Britten and Pears took up residence for a period of time with Dr and Mrs William Mayer within the ambit of their household in Amityville, Long Island. The Mayers had first met the couple in New York City. At their new American 'home', Britten and Pears made use of Stanton Cottage, which was situated within the Mayer's extensive grounds in Amityville. According to an entry in the Mayer's Visitors' Book, Britten and Pears had intended to stay only for a weekend. If so, this must have been one of the longest weekends in history as the pair left their Long Island residence as late as 16 March 1942. The fact that a piano had been thoughtfully installed made this an ideal home for the pair. In her youth, Elizabeth Mayer had studied at the Royal

Conservatory of Music, Stuttgart, when her ambition was to become a professional pianist. Because she was so enthusiastic in her support and encouragement of artists, her Long Island home acted as a magnet for many of the outstandingly creative people living in the USA in the late 1930s and 1940s. Dr and Mrs Mayer had created something of a cultural salon at their residence and the cultural activities there must have acted as some sort of buffer against the depressingly regular news headlines featuring the tribulations of war-torn Europe.

Whatever the exact date of the reading of Forster's article in *The Listener*, it appears that, very soon after, Peter Pears purchased a volume of Crabbe's Poetical Works in a Los Angeles bookshop. This led to the birth of Britten's opera, *Peter Grimes*. This chance reading by Britten not only helped to emphasise the importance of Suffolk in his life but also led him to his initial foray into the world of opera composition. The first work was indeed *Peter Grimes*, being a character taken direct from Crabbe's incredibly lengthy story-poem, The Borough. A whole section of this work is entitled Peter Grimes and sub-titled '*The Father of Peter a Fisherman - Peter's early Conduct - His Grief for the old Man*'. In itself, this part of the poem comprises over 3,200 words. We now know that Benjamin Britten's opera of the same name received its first performance at Sadler's Wells on 7 June 1945, shortly after the German surrender at the end of World War II. The libretto was adapted by Montagu Slater, with the assistance of Britten, Pears, Ronald Duncan and Eric Crozier, direct from the text of Crabbe's poem. Britten had known Slater in the 1930s when they were both working with W H Auden on the GPO film documentaries, notably *Night Mail*. I heard an Auden reading of his poetry on what might well have been the soundtrack recently, and he sounded remarkably like John Betjeman when the former poet laureate was reading his own work. The composer had seen the theatrical possibilities of the sections of Crabbe's poem that told of a sadistic fisherman accused of murdering his apprentices. Britten was also encouraged to pursue this imaginative operatic project by the offer of a commission of $1000 from the Koussevitzky Foundation. This is a Music Foundation established in 1942 by Sergei Aleksandrovich Koussevitzky (1874-1951), a Russian-born Jewish conductor, composer and double-bassist, known for his long tenure as music director of the Boston Symphony Orchestra from 1924 to 1949 and as a champion of contemporary music. $1000 in 1944 would be worth approximately $12,000 today if set against the US Consumer Price Index but much more if calculated by taking into account the significant growth in the nation's Gross Domestic Product. Comparison with the purchasing power of sterling is much more difficult, due to exchange rate fluctuations, but it was by no means an inconsiderable sum of money for a young composer with no experience of operatic composition.

It is now widely recognised that *Peter Grimes* is not only Britten's most celebrated opera and it was immediately acknowledged as being 'of major importance'. It became the first by an English composer to enter and remain in the international repertory. However, to return to the quote from Yehudi Menuhin, the opera contains the most brilliantly evocative music that Britten ever wrote. No one listening to the work can fail to recognise the overpowering presence of the sea as the opera's dominant force. I have been to confirm that *Peter Grimes* did not have an airing at the first Aldeburgh Festival in 1948 but I can record that E M Forster was determined to be a member of the audience of at least one performance during that inaugural week. I now feel quite sure that this would have been that of *Albert Herring*, three performances of which took place between 5-13 June. He described the cramped atmosphere of Jubilee Hall and the welcome intervals when the audience 'partly in evening dress and partly dressed anyhow, and exempt from the smartness of Glyndebourne' spilled out on to the Aldeburgh beach. He recollected that in the first interval a man in a pub said:

> 'I took a ticket for this show because it's local and I felt I had to. I'd have sold it to anyone for sixpence earlier on. I wouldn't part with it now for ten pounds'.

Forster, at that time in the late forties and not too long after the end of the Second World War, felt that this new music Festival showed considerable promise and he hoped that it had a future. His hopes have certainly been realised many, many times over. Within three years of its première, *Peter Grimes* was translated into seven languages and had been produced in sixteen opera houses in Europe and North America. It became the stimulus for the writing of opera in the English language. Britten's first full-scale opera is now generally considered one of the great masterpieces of the twentieth-century repertoire.

At the time Britten and Pears were resident in the United States they did, of course, come into contact with a number of American musicians and music lovers. This is, of course, where they met Serge Koussevitzky who became a champion of the young Britten's work. The Koussevitzky Music Foundation was set up to support the encouragement of new music and it was through this that Benjamin Britten was awarded the $1,000 commission to write an opera. Britten realised his debt of gratitude to the conductor and *Peter Grimes* is dedicated to the memory of Koussevitsky's wife, Natalie. It was at Koussevitsky's direct request that Britten's manuscript of the full score of *Peter Grimes* should remain in America and it can seen at the Library of Congress in Washington DC. The first American production of this opera was largely a student production and it took place in August 1946 at, appropriately, Serge Koussevitzky's Berkshire Music Festival at Tanglewood. The conductor was one of Koussevitzky's pupils, the soon to be extremely famous composer, author, music lecturer and pianist, Leonard Bernstein (1918-1990). Sadly, I cannot trace that Bernstein ever visited Suffolk, let alone Aldeburgh or Snape. We shall have to be content with the *Peter Grimes* connection, albeit rather indirect.

The poet, W H Auden was, of course, an enormously prominent literary name associated with Britten and the town of Aldeburgh. It was in 1939 that Auden emigrated to the United States of America with writer Christopher Isherwood. The latter eventually settled in California, whereas Auden returned to this country in the mid-fifties and became Professor of Poetry at Oxford (1956-61). Both became American citizens and had been lovers. The pair had already visited New York together on their return from China, where they had travelled to in 1938. In his own early years, as well as theirs, Isherwood was said to have acted as literary mentor to both E M Forster and W H Auden but I found no direct evidence of this in Isherwood's own biographic writings. Indeed, the opposite seems true in that in 1932, Forster sought Isherwood's opinion on the typescript of *Maurice*, a novel that you will recall was published some sixty years after it was written. Isherwood told Forster that Maurice was both 'inferior and superior' to the other novels; 'inferior as an artwork, superior because of its purer passion, its franker declaration of its author's faith'. When Forster asked Isherwood, 'Does it date?' the latter replied 'why *shouldn't* it date?' This response cheered Forster greatly as well as also serving to provide Isherwood with a great deal of pleasure. Morgan Forster became full of pride at this spontaneous reaction so it appears that there might be some mileage in the literary mentor theory after all. As for Isherwood acting as mentor to W H Auden, there is considerable evidence that they collaborated on plays, both those written jointly as well as those originated by Auden and intended for production by Group Theatre, with Rupert Doone producing as well acting in a leading role (he will be mentioned again a little later).

I note from the edited diaries of Kenneth Tynan that, dining on one occasion with Isherwood at his residence, when Gore Vidal (1925-2012), American author, playwright and screenwriter, was also present, Tynan asked his host to name the twentieth-century figures whose letters and/or journals he would be most excited to read. Isherwood replied that it would be E M Forster (many of whose letters he had received), but later adding that anything unpublished by Jean Cocteau (1889-1963) poet, novelist and dramatist, would come a close second, claiming that somehow his literary generation had avoided the French. Vidal's preferences are not recorded but perhaps he wasn't asked. This disappointed me because any reported response would have been interesting, bearing in mind his reputation for wittily acerbic literary and political essays that have been published in various collections, although I am not sure that everyone has appreciated his sense of humour. I know him best for his novel *Myra Breckinridge* (1968) which I recall reading in the late 1960s. This was a spoof story about a transsexual hero/heroine … take your pick … in Hollywood. Quite predictably, this novel was made into a film although selecting Raquel Welch, a Hollywood sex symbol, to play the title role was perhaps a little unexpected, thus causing it to be classified as qualifying for inclusion in the category of being one the worst movies ever made. I am of the opinion that this is a typical Hollywood story where 'the money' dictates the cast, meaning box office 'pull'. No doubt, Vidal was happy to go along with it on the basis that if the movie failed, the outcome could always be used by him as a heavily-embroidered dinner party story.

Isherwood and Benjamin Britten undoubtedly came across each other in New York, almost certainly through their mutual friend W H Auden. In a note in his diary of 16 January 1942, Isherwood stated that he met up with Britten and Peter Pears after he attended the first performance by Paul Wittgenstein (1887-1961) with the Philadelphia Orchestra of Britten's *Diversions for piano (left hand) and orchestra*. Wittgenstein was an Austrian-born concert pianist, who became known for his ability to play with just his left hand, after he lost his right arm during the First World War. Isherwood recorded Britten's expressed wish to return to England in order to register as a conscientious objector for the duration of the 1939-45 war. This was not stated as the sole reason, in that the composer had become increasingly homesick for Suffolk as well as his many friends. Both Britten and Pears completed their registration under this heading in April 1942, after their return to the UK on board *MS Axel Johnson*. They had embarked in New York on 16 March and the voyage took nearly five weeks. This was due to the need for various calls along the eastern seaboard, although the actual crossing from Halifax, Nova Scotia took only twelve days. Britten took the time at sea as an opportunity to compose both *Hymn to Cecilia* and *A Ceremony of Carols*, only to have the manuscripts temporarily confiscated by the English Customs. The pair were later exempted from military service, with the composer being required to write radio incidental music as well as to give concerts for CEMA (Council for the Encouragement of Music and the Arts – later to become known as The Arts Council).

It would be incorrect to conclude that Britten had been totally miserable in America. The composer not only worked very well there but also became inspired enough for an editor of his diaries to record that the composer enjoyed 'an irrepressible creative exuberance and fertility'. His productivity in the USA has been seen as Britten getting into his stride as a composer and this interlude in his life must have had an overall beneficial effect on his future career in music.

To get back to the political aspects, Britten had already been known as a pacifist and had argued the cause for peace during the clamour for preparations for war, although some people would have perhaps regarded this as support for appeasement at that time. This had partly taken shape in the form of a very short documentary film, the *Peace of Britain*, made by Paul Rotha (1907-1984) for Strand Films and commissioned by the T.U.C. & League of Nations Union. Rotha was a well-known British documentary film-maker, film historian and critic. At the time this film work was in hand, Britten was still only twenty-two years of age but already showing considerable musical maturity. Included amongst Britten's anti-militarist works were *Ballad of Heroes*, written in early 1939. In this composition, he developed certain techniques and foreshadowed those used in his *War Requiem* in 1961. *Ballad of Heroes* was written in honour of the men of the British Battalion of the International Brigade who had fallen in Spain during that country's civil war (1936-1939). We must remember that Auden once expressed a wish to fight in Spain and had returned, I suppose as what must be described as a non-hero in 1937, not having fought in that war-torn country. However, he did write articles for the *New Statesman* and later a poem, *Spain 1937*, a work it has been said he later felt it necessary to describe as 'trash'.

Christopher Isherwood left the USA temporarily and visited Paris in 1948, where he met up with Auden and was introduced to Gore Vidal. He also journeyed to England and in June attended, with a photographer friend, William Caskey, the first ever Aldeburgh Festival, where they saw Britten's opera, *Albert Herring*, on 7 June. During the course of Isherwood's visit to England with Caskey, Caskey photographed the artist Graham Sutherland (1903-1980) at his home. Sutherland was famously known for his 1954 portrait of Sir Winston Churchill (1874-1965), a work so intensely disliked by the former Prime Minister's wife that it was destroyed on her orders. It is said that studies for the portrait have somehow survived.

Britten enjoyed a lengthy career in operatic composition and it proved interesting to me to learn that his final work under this heading, *Death in Venice*, was based on the Thomas Mann novella of the same name. I was further fascinated to find that W H Auden married Thomas Mann's daughter, Erika, in 1935 for the sole purpose of providing her with a passport out of Nazi Germany. This was quite obviously a marriage of convenience, to coin the well-known phrase. Auden had visited Berlin many times in the mid-thirties and whilst there he spent time with Christopher Isherwood, who was earning money teaching English. Isherwood later went on to write one of his best known works, *Goodbye to Berlin* (1939), based on his experiences in the decadence of post-slump, pre-Hitler Berlin. In September 1935, the author described this work as nothing more than a short, loosely-connected sequence of diaries and sketches. He had originally planned a huge episodic novel of pre-Hitler Berlin to be entitled *The Lost*. Because I became engrossed in reading some of Christopher Isherwood's work, I felt very fortunate to come across an omnibus edition of his writings of these times. In a second-hand bookshop I spotted a title that the publishers called *The Berlin of Sally Bowles*. This book included *Mr Norris Changes Trains*, a highly amusing account of the life and times of the highly devious Arthur Morris, a fictional character whose political and other activities left me marvelling at the author's imagination in creating not just the title character but also his so-called fictional associates that included a young English teacher of English in Berlin. Isherwood has always denied any autobiographic leaning in these particular writings, even though in *Sally Bowles* he writes in the first person, the 'I' concerned being none other than 'Christopher Isherwood'. The author maintained that this character is nothing more than a ventriloquist's dummy. I have never come across this device before, but I don't suppose for one moment that it is at all unique. In a recent reading of *Christopher & His Kind*, I became accustomed to the author writing about himself in the third person.

It is no secret that the plot of the highly successful film, *Cabaret*, appears to bear striking similarities to that section of Isherwood's life. The movie starred Liza Minnelli as Sally Bowles and Michael York played the part of a writer (Brian Roberts) who teaches English to earn a living, enabling him to complete his German studies. Now that I have read and fully appreciated the omnibus mentioned above, I do not find the author's denial on the autobiographical aspect to be entirely convincing, particularly as far as the movie is concerned. On the other hand, I do not believe that Isherwood ever intended anyone to accept it literally. There are certainly similarities between Minnelli's exuberant portrayal and the Sally Bowles character in the book.

Chapter Ten

More of Britten's operas, their inspiration, the English National Opera and Group Theatre

INEVITABLY, WHILST WRITING about the cultural impact on coastal Suffolk in just two of the locations, Aldeburgh and Snape, the dominant factor just has to be the music. Not only that, the foremost and most influential personality is unavoidably Benjamin Britten, a man who was born to love music and spent his entire life in its cause. Along the way, he accumulated numerous friends and acquaintances and we have learned that a significant number of these entered into mutually rewarding collaborations with the great man. This was to be by exercising their particular talents in one form or another, but all in the cause of mutual creativity. There would be fellow musicians, poets and writers that became librettists, as well as artists who worked diligently as designers. The operatic works that flowed from Britten over the years owed much to the inspiration provided by others, mainly from the composer developing a genuine interest in their work. Even then, some became friends without getting directly involved, but the society that built up around Britten in Aldeburgh was undoubtedly dominated by the arts in its various forms. The names that will crop up will, in the main, be rather well known but not always in the context that I shall seek to introduce them.

This might be a useful point to provide you with a little background on the formation of the English National Opera (ENO), Britain's only full-time repertory opera company. Its origins date back to 1898 when Lilian Bayliss presented a series of opera recitals at London's Old Vic Theatre in Waterloo Road. In 1928, she added a small group of dancers to the company which then became known as the Vic-Wells Ballet. The company eventually moved to Covent Garden to become The Royal Ballet. The world-famous Sadler's Wells Theatre opened in 1931 and the Vic-Wells Opera Company came into its own. After World War II, the opera company became known as the Sadler's Wells Opera Company and the Old Vic Theatre reopened in 1945 with a production of Benjamin Britten's opera *Peter Grimes*. This was indeed the world première of the work. In 1968, the Sadler's Wells Opera Company moved its base to the London Coliseum and, six years later, it became known as the English National Opera. It is known for all its opera productions being performed in the English language and has a well-deserved reputation for charging lowish prices at the box office; in other words, highly competitive with the other principal opera company in London, the Royal Opera, Covent Garden. The ENO also performs internationally and collaborates closely with other companies, including the Metropolitan Opera in New York. In contrast, the Welsh National Opera and the Scottish National Opera are mainly touring companies within their own countries, as well as elsewhere in the UK.

You have already seen more than a few references to the Aldeburgh Festival, but it might be useful if I supply just a little background on its formation. In this context, it seemed worthwhile for me to explain the origins of the English National Opera so as to distinguish it from the English Opera Group, a small touring company formed in 1946-47 by Benjamin Britten with a small and quite limited number of musicians. The composer used this repertory company as a platform to promote his own chamber operas, although not exclusively, often in performances under his own baton, both in the United Kingdom and in Europe. By then, Britten's reputation had grown to the extent that he was recognised as the leading British composer of his generation and those touring Europe with the English Opera Group were proud that, in the words of Eric Crozier, England was at last making some contribution to the traditions of international opera. The success of *Peter Grimes* contributed much to this status but it was the touring of *Albert Herring* and *The Rape of Lucretia* across Belgium, Luxembourg and France to Switzerland that was also to play such a significant part. However, the huge costs involved with touring made this venture heavily uneconomic and it was decided that the English Opera Group, which had previously relied on funds from supporters, should be based at a home venue. This decision gave rise to the establishment of the Aldeburgh Festival of Music and the Arts, as it was known at its founding in 1948. It was Peter Pears who first suggested 'Why not make our own Festival? A modest Festival with a few concerts given by friends. Why not an Aldeburgh Festival?' In late August 1947, Britten had, of course, moved to his new home in Aldeburgh from the nearby, Old Mill, at Snape, near where the Maltings would eventually be the permanent home of the Festival. Britten and Pears' new residence was Crag House on Crabbe Street, a property that overlooks the beach, near the town's lifeboat station

Not too many years had passed before The English Opera Group together with the Aldeburgh Festival were described as 'two of the most influential art institutions in Europe'. Nevertheless, it cannot be said that Britten's opera group did not remain without its share of financial problems, even though the formation of the festival at Aldeburgh had taken place. Christopher Isherwood recorded in his diary for 8 May 1948 that a party of friends at the Tudor Court Hotel in London included Benjy (Britten) 'looking mortally weary and beset with financial troubles for his opera company'.

It was also in 1948 that the English Opera Group printed a new leaflet with a cover designed by John Piper. By then, Britten's three operas, *Peter Grimes*, *The Rape of Lucretia* and *Albert Herring* had placed England in the front rank of opera-producing countries. Overall, it can be safely said that, given Benjamin Britten's achievements, his standing as a composer was not equalled, let alone surpassed, by any other British composer in the second half of the twentieth century.

Incidentally, Britten's opera, *The Rape of Lucretia* received its première at Glyndebourne in 1946, where the famous contralto, Kathleen Ferrier (1912-1953) starred in the role of Lucretia. Eric Crozier's first opera libretto for Benjamin Britten was *Albert Herring* in 1947. This opera was premièred on 20 June in that year, also at Glyndebourne, and conducted by the composer. It was written as a companion piece to the much starker, *The Rape of Lucretia*. Crozier also directed Britten's first opera, *Peter Grimes*, at Sadler's Wells in June 1945. Their association extended over many successful years. In describing *Peter Grimes* as Britten's first opera, I am mindful of the 'choral operetta', *Paul Bunyan*, which was premièred at Columbia University in America in 1941. Perhaps I am just being pedantic in exploiting the descriptive elements of the work in 'operetta' and 'opera', but *Peter Grimes* was the first of his operas to attain both critical and popular success and I feel perfectly justified in the view I have taken, particularly as it was the first opera to be performed at Sadler's Wells. In any event, Britten had regarded *Bunyan* as something of a disappointment, so the success of *Peter Grimes* must have been particularly gratifying. The composer had been working on *Peter Grimes* before the war had ended, so in describing this work as 'topical', it seems clear that the violence and pain contained within the opera were, in his mind, bound up with what happened had during the war years. Not only that, this production proved to be more than a turning point for the better in the history of English music … and to think that all this came from coastal Suffolk! This first opera was the starting point for many others, all carefully chosen for their subject matter, more than a few having their origins in literature, others from poetry, the theatre as well as the Bible. Britten was to fully justify his position of being at the forefront of English composers of not only his own generation but of also that which succeeded his death at the early age of sixty-three in 1976. This followed a number of years of ill health. We must remember that Britten's schooldays were often accompanied by periods of debilitating sickness. He clearly lacked a strong constitution.

I was very touched to read that in the summer of 1976, David Hockney and Christopher Isherwood, accompanied by the latter's long term friend and partner, Don Bachardy, decided to make a diversion on a car journey to Scotland in order to call in at Aldeburgh to see Britten. Isherwood knew that the composer was ill, but not at all sure how ill he was at that time. Later, Isherwood wrote of Britten that 'Any emotion was bad for him. He was so moved at seeing us again that he could hardly trust himself to speak. The others left us, and Ben and I sat in a room together, not speaking, just holding hands.' Bachardy (born 1934) is an American portrait artist whom Isherwood met in 1953. The difference in their ages was thirty years, but this did not prevent them being relatively happy together until Isherwood's death in 1986. Isherwood's nickname for Bachardy was 'Kitty' and he was known as 'Old Dobbin', the stubborn workhorse. Both Isherwood and Bachardy knew David Hockney and the artist painted the two together in 1968. This work demonstrated not only Hockney's passion for colour but also his liking for still life, in that the couple are seated in a sparsely furnished room in comfortable chairs on one side of a low table facing the painter. On the table are two piles of hardback books, without dustcovers, one pile before each of them with a bowl of fruit in between. I found this a pleasing work and would have liked to reproduce an image here but the extent of the copyright fees proved to be prohibitive as far as I am concerned. However, the painting can be viewed on Mr Hockney's website, which is managed from America.

To get back to the composer's work, *Lucretia* was the first project resulting from a decision by Peter Pears, Eric Crozier and Joan Cross (1900-1993), a leading soprano, to resign from Sadler's Wells in March 1946 following differences over a change in policy. With Benjamin Britten, this trio was determined to set up their own company 'dedicated to the creation of new works, with the least possible expense and capable ... of being toured'. This led to the establishment of the previously mentioned English Opera Group. Although the first run of thirteen performances of *Lucretia* was relatively successful, the provincial tour proved to be a disaster. John Christie (1882-1962), opera manager and owner of Glyndebourne, bore the financial responsibility but he made it clear that after honouring his agreement to stage *Albert Herring* he had no wish to continue collaborations between his opera house and Britten.

It is interesting to contrast the above with what was written in Glyndebourne's brochure for the 2010 season. I offer this verbatim quotation:

> 'Glyndebourne's proud association with the operas of Benjamin Britten stretches from its world première productions of *The Rape of Lucretia* and Albert Herring in 1946 and 1947 through to Jonathan Kent's 2007 Festival staging of *The Turn of the Screw*, taking in memorable reappraisals of *Peter Grimes'*, *A Midsummer Night's Dream*, *Owen Wingrave* and *Death in Venice* along the way. However, Glyndebourne has never, until now, staged *Billy Budd*, the 1951 all-male opera, with a libretto co-written by E. M. Forster. Based on Herman Melville's allegorical tale about the battle between pure good and blind evil, the opera takes place amidships on a British man-o'-war'.

It seems that now all is forgiven and how very pleasing it is to be able to record this particular example of time acting as an essential part of the healing process.

It seems almost invidious to single out any one of Britten's operas, but I have learned that in the case of the popular, *Albert Herring* the work is in some ways reminiscent of the comic operas of Gilbert and Sullivan and in some ways of a work by Richard Strauss, *Ariadne auf Naxos*, which was first performed in Stuttgart in 1912 and directed by Max Reinhardt (1873-1943) whose name will appear again in a later chapter. Parts of the *Albert Herring* libretto are genuinely funny, and there are myriad musical quotations within the score, despite the light subject matter. I have seen a reference to the work's comic perspective being likened to the way small-town Suffolk society deals with an oddball. I regard this as somewhat disingenuous but I suppose it is fair to concede that a genuine point is being made. Like *Peter Grimes* and other works by Britten, this opera explores society's reaction to an odd individual, although, in this case at least, it is from a generally humorous and light-hearted perspective. Some of Britten's contemporaries saw, in the title character, a satirical self-portrait of the composer. In the words of the fictional character created by Michael Dobbs, Francis Urquhart in BBC TV's *House of Cards* (1990 serial) 'You may say so but I could not possibly comment.' I cannot offer any clarification on the significance but Britten dedicated *Albert Herring* to none other than his friend and regular houseguest, the author, E M Forster. Forster was awarded the Order of Merit by Her Majesty the Queen in 1969, the year before his death at the age of 91.

Peter Grimes is also deserving of special mention, bearing in mind that it was the composer's first attempt at the genre. It has already been seen that the libretto had been adapted by Montagu Slater (1902-1956) and others from the *Peter Grimes* section of George Crabbe's poem *The Borough*. Interestingly, Christopher Isherwood had previously declined the offer to write the libretto, no doubt the request being made by Britten when he was still in the USA. This does not surprise me as, although I am aware that in the 1930s, Isherwood had been commissioned to write a screenplay for a film, the thought of writing a libretto for an opera might well have overwhelmed him. As for Isherwood's venture into the world of the movies, he viewed this with mixed feelings although he did describe it as 'a new and absolutely necessary phase of his education as a writer'.

The 'borough' of the opera is a fictional village which shares some similarities with Crabbe's, and later Britten's, own home town of Aldeburgh, on England's east coast, albeit with its fictional counterpart set in around the year 1830. We already know that the work was first performed at Sadler's Wells in London in June 1945. This performance was conducted by Reginald Goodall (1901-1990) and was the first of Britten's operas to be a critical and popular success.

It is still widely performed, both in the UK and internationally, and is now considered part of the standard repertoire. In addition, Britten's *Four Sea Interludes* were published separately and are frequently performed as an orchestral suite. Indeed, this work was included in the BBC Promenade Concert Season at the Royal Albert Hall in 2010.

Mentioning an Albert Hall concert and the *Four Sea Interludes* reminds me of an anecdote I came across which featured the distinguished conductor Sir Thomas Beecham (1879-1961) who was very well known also for his caustic wit. This story was, however, not an example of this in that it features Beecham at a somewhat of a rare disadvantage. It seems that Thomas Beecham once programmed the *Four Sea Interludes* by Benjamin Britten at an Albert Hall concert. Near to him, a young man was following the music from the published score. Feeling somewhat proud and rather gratified, Beecham felt that a few words of amity were indicated and opened a conversation with, 'I see you're interested in Benjamin Britten.' 'Of course I am,' came the response. That sounded encouraging to Sir Thomas. 'Why "of course"?' Beecham asked the stranger. 'Because I *am* Benjamin Britten,' was the immediate reply. Nonplussed, Beecham came out with 'Oh, are you indeed?' and there this encounter ended, leaving Beecham unconvinced, not to say rather bemused. Later Beecham recounted the tale to a friend, who disturbed him greatly by remarking, 'Maybe he was Benjamin Britten'. From what I have learned about each of these master musicians, I feel sure that it was indeed the great man.

Another story about Sir Thomas Beecham is an example of how critical he could be about what he considered musicians to be performing below his exacting standards, in so doing offering some spontaneous wit, but perhaps not always in the best of taste. On the occasion I have in mind, he was guest conducting a provincial orchestra and it was a female cellist who experienced a typical Beecham barb. When pained by the lady's efforts at rehearsal, he stopped the music and proclaimed, 'Madam, you have something there between your legs capable of giving pleasure to millions, yet all you can do is sit there and scratch it'. Perhaps another story might help to redress the balance about this remarkable individual. At a reception, somewhere in the north-west of England, he noticed a woman who looked vaguely familiar but he was not successful in trying to place her. He engaged her in polite conversation by asking about her health, together with that of her husband, as he felt sure that she was married. The woman confirmed that they were both well and Sir Thomas rejoined with, 'What is he doing nowadays?' She smiled, typically mischievously and assured the conductor that, 'Oh, he's still King'. She was, indeed, Queen Elizabeth, the late Queen Mother, and when this particular encounter took place King George VI was certainly very much alive and on the British throne.

Putting such anecdotes aside, now is perhaps a good as time as any to tell you about a previously mentioned organisation known as The Group Theatre. This had been founded in 1932 by the dancer, choreographer, theatre director and teacher, Rupert Doone (1903-1966) who wished to adapt the principles of classical ballet to the training of actors. He insisted on a choreographic use of space: no movement or gesture could be made and no position held that was deemed inexpressive. The Group Theatre was determined to avoid the established repertoire of plays, and instead concentrated on folk and medieval sources as well as on experimental re-workings of classical drama. John Piper and his wife, Myfanwy had become involved with the Group Theatre on being introduced by a friend, Robert Medley (1905-1994), a fellow artist. Other participants and contributors included writers, artists, actors and musicians. W H Auden just happened to be one of the writers although I have seen it written that this enterprise existed largely as a vehicle for Auden's work. We know that amongst other writers were Christopher Isherwood, Northern Irish poet, Louis MacNeice and Stephen Spender, who has featured many times in previous chapters and will do so again. Auden, MacNeice and Spender had been contemporaries at Oxford. These erudite and well-read individuals became responsible for the production of avant-garde and all-too-often, left wing poetic dramas on which the fame of the Group Theatre depended. As far as I can ascertain, the Auden-Isherwood collaborations started here. Kenneth Tynan commented in his dairies (April 1977), having just finished reading Isherwood's *Christopher and his Kind (1929-1939)*, that English Literature between the wars was something of a 'buggers' banquet', naming, by way of illustration, Isherwood, Auden, Spender, Forster as well as writer and critic, Lytton Strachey (1880-1932). He could also have added William Plomer, as he was often found within this group. In *Christopher and his Kind* (1976), Isherwood recorded an account of what he considered the most remarkable ten years of his life – his time in America and a candid account of what we would now describe as his 'gay' experiences in Berlin.

W H Auden, being two years the senior of Stephen Spender, was already something of a legend at Oxford when Spender arrived there in 1927. Each had expressed a wish to become a poet as early as fifteen years of age and as far as Stephen Spender was concerned Auden had a tremendous impact on him, although the younger poet's biographer expresses the view that Auden's direct influence on Spender's poetry is hard to find. He went on to say that Auden's touch left an indelible mark on Spender, if not on his work then certainly on his idea of what it was to be a poet. It was Christopher Isherwood, who was known to have described England as 'the land of poets', went on to act as Spender's mentor, an involvement he appeared to treat with more than a little complacency. Spender became one of the 'Gang' which also consisted of Auden, Isherwood and novelist and short story writer, Edward Upward (1903-2009) whom Isherwood had met at Repton and who became his life-long friend. Spender went to Berlin in the early 1930s because of what he described as the 'hypnotic fascination of Christopher's life there'.

As far as the 'Gang' was concerned, Cecil Day-Lewis (1904-1972) was regarded as a colleague rather than a member and it is interesting to record that when in 1972 the position of Poet Laureate became vacant on the death of Day-Lewis, Spender's name was put up as a successor. He wasn't interested but he did lobby for Auden, in a discreet manner, apparently overlooking the fact that Auden was an American citizen. Since 1970, the appointment is made by Her Majesty the Queen following advice from the Prime Minister. On this occasion, the post eventually went to John Betjeman, whom both Stephen Spender and Philip Larkin (1922-1985), widely regarded as one of the greatest English poets of the latter half of the twentieth century, were certainly known to have approved.

In 1935, Auden had brought in to Group Theatre a young composer who at first sight seemed to be the epitome of convention. At rehearsal in the semi-darkness of a London theatre, someone noticed a 'slim young man, unobtrusively dressed in a sports jacket and grey flannel bags'. He had what Robert Medley described, in his memoirs, as 'irregular features and crinkly hair and was wearing a pair of slightly owlish spectacles which emphasised his watchful reticence.' By the end of that year, Benjamin Britten, and yes, it just had to be him, became the composer for Group Theatre and I have read that he regarded himself as the house musician. It seems that this is where the composer laid the foundations for his future as a musical dramatist.

As far as Britten's opera, *War Requiem*, is concerned, this 1961–62 work requires a large production in that almost two hundred musicians and singers are required. It has been described as 'a monumental piece ... one of the great masterpieces of twentieth century music'. Elsewhere it was portrayed as 'a challenging work, both to perform and to listen to, but also a rewarding experience for being both sombre and sublime'. Britten, who was, of course, a lifelong pacifist, decided to combine the Latin Requiem Mass with nine war poems by Wilfred Owen, who was killed on the Western Front in World War I, just one week before the 1918 armistice. The work was composed with soloists from three different wartime countries in mind. These were Britten's partner, tenor Peter Pears, German baritone Dietrich Fischer-Dieskau and Soviet soprano Galina Vishnevskaya (born 1926), wife of Mstislav Rostropovich. Unfortunately, the Moscow Cold War authorities refused the Russian soprano a visa for the première. However, she was able to travel to London during the following year to perform in a recording of the work with the other soloists and the London Symphony conducted by the composer. Within five months of its release, the album sold a record 200,000 copies. Incidentally, in 1963 Benjamin Britten wrote his *Cello Symphony* (some might call it a concerto) for the soprano's husband and later dedicated three solo *Cello Suites* to him: Rostropovich gave a first performance of each of these works. It was pleasing to read a BBC review of a recording of two of these compositions by Pieter Wispelwey (born 1965, in Haarlem, Netherlands) written in August 2010, which contained the words '... making this disc the sort of recording which sends expectant prickles up one's neck even before the play button has been pressed'. Happily, it did not disappoint elsewhere and the Dutchman, now one of the world's leading cellists, earned an excellent review for the *Symphony and Suite No.1*.

I have already written a great deal about Benjamin Britten and his work and the origins of the Aldeburgh Festival where performances, in the early years, took place in various buildings in and around the seaside town, but principally in the Jubilee Hall. Inevitably, the Festival's popularity grew and it became clear that Britten and Pears had long dreamed of having a larger and more permanent concert hall for the annual celebration of music. Festival concerts lost money when they were held in the Jubilee Hall in those days and a scheme for a larger hall, purpose-built for 500-600 people was announced by Lord Harewood in the 1954 Festival programme. However, it would be more than a decade before matters took a more positive turn.

Benjamin Britten and Peter Pears were once residents of the village of Snape, having lived in a former windmill there. When it was learned that the disused Maltings, prominently situated alongside the River Alde within a short distance of the village, were to be placed on the market for sale, these dedicated musicians, amidst no little excitement, recognised their potential. After all, Snape was the matter of just a few miles from Aldeburgh. Their dream was to be realised probably much more quickly than they could have reasonably hoped.

The Snape Maltings Concert Hall was opened by Her Majesty the Queen on 2 June 1967 and Aldeburgh Festival concerts began being held there during that year. In her speech, the Queen said '...you have built up a festival and you have encouraged the arts to flower in the soil of this pleasant part Suffolk'. Perhaps she had not been made fully aware that, on the soil of coastal Suffolk, the arts in their various forms had been blooming for very many years but Her Majesty could perhaps be forgiven for this omission. Perhaps the research, as well as accurate speech writing, was not up to scratch on that occasion.

Quite justifiably and it has to be said, quite extraordinarily, given its history, the outstandingly attractive Snape Maltings building has been described as one the finest concert halls in Europe. The conversion at the Maltings was made in 1966 and 1967. The overseeing structural engineer was Derek Sugden of Arup Associates, a firm that had worked on the world-famous Sydney Opera House, but as far as the much-admired Maltings Concert Hall is concerned, it is the high quality of the acoustics that is considered his special triumph. It may not be generally known that Benjamin Britten played a considerable part in agreeing all manner of detail for this large construction undertaking, even to the extent of being specific about the colour of the external guttering. As to the funding of this very ambitious project, the finance came from the proceeds of a public appeal, grants from the Arts Council and Gulbenkian Trust, donations from the Decca Record Company as well as from Benjamin Britten himself. A matter of only two years afterwards, on the first night of the 1969 Festival, what is best described as a major disaster took place. The concert hall tragically burned down, its roof finishing up as a heap of charred timbers and blackened iron on the ruined floor of the auditorium. One can only speculate on what Britten and Pears really thought about this enormous tragedy, but it must surely be a tribute to their resourceful tenacity that only one year later it had been rebuilt and the Queen was graciously happy to accept the invitation to perform the reopening ceremony. Her gracious presence at the original opening must have influenced the insurers in making some quick decisions for a change. Her Majesty had telephoned Benjamin Britten personally in order to express her sympathy for the calamity occasioned by the fire not long after it happened. When she attended the re-opening the Queen quipped that, as great as the occasion was, she hoped that the building would remain intact so that she did not have to perform this particular duty for a third time. In 1965 she had appointed Britten a member of the Order of Merit, an honour in her personal gift. In the Coronation Honours List of 1 June 1953, the composer had been made a Companion of Honour. It was 1978 before Sir Peter Pears received his own knighthood.

As a follow-up to the restoration of the concert hall at Snape and its reopening in 1970, I must mention here that William Plomer wrote a poem that commemorated the fire that caused so much damage to the building and its subsequent triumphant return as a venue for artistic events. It is entitled *A Note from a Cello*. It is certainly worth recording here:

'A blameless calm night, the people have gone.
Dark thickets of reeds feel a breath of disquiet:
Moorhens awake; fear saves the vole
About to be hooked by the soft-flying owl:
In the marshes of Snape a sluice and a pool

Make suddenly shapes of flame-coloured light.
Crackle of fire! An undeclared war,
Motiveless, strikes at those who contrived
That resonant shell, at ears that have heard
Rejoicings derived, in nights darker by far,
From greater fires, wells deeper, deep dreams,
Granite, violets, blood, the pureness of dew.

The shell is restored. The orchestra settles.
A baton is raised. Renew what is old!
Make known what is new! From a cello the bow
Draw its hauntingest tone, confiding, profound:
And immured in the bone the marrow responds
To the endless, exploring inventions of sound.'

To my mind this is a truly inspirational piece of work from someone who fully appreciated everything that coastal Suffolk, more specifically around Aldeburgh and Snape, had to offer, not only artistically but also in terms of long-lasting friendships with the social circle of Benjamin Britten and his friends. Like everyone associated with Britten and Pears, together with their work, William Plomer must have been devastated at the loss of the Maltings Concert Hall, only to be consumed with admiration of the determination and energy that saw its rebuilding, followed by its reopening, in such a short space of time.

It says much about Britten's love for the arts that he asked Aldeburgh resident, Mary Potter (1900-1981), an artist and close friend, to design a silk screen print to commemorate the calamity that befell the new and much treasured concert hall. She worked in collaboration with William Plomer who wrote the above poem. Potter's work portrays an owl flying over the marshes with a background depicting the fire at the concert hall, but in its early stages. The text of the poem is integrated within this notable piece of creative art. William Plomer, the poet and librettist for several works by Benjamin Britten, including *Gloriana and the Prodigal Son,* carried out a regular correspondence with Britten as well as being a frequent guest at Crag House. The two had hoped to work together on a children's opera, as well as something based on some characters created by Edward Lear, but these projects never came to fruition.

Since 1979 the complex of buildings that surround the main concert hall have been the home of the internationally-famous Britten-Pears School for Advanced Musical Studies, a major part of their tremendous musical legacy to coastal Suffolk.

Briefly reverting to the surroundings of the former Maltings at Snape, the attraction for the thousands of visitors, usually intent upon only the musical offerings, there are also the river and the other facilities that have accrued by way of visitor-related businesses over the years. In addition, there are the wonderfully glorious marshes. It is alongside these that the magnificent concert hall has stood since HM The Queen opened premises for the second time in 1970. What add to the glory of the river Alde and these splendid marshes, some sixty acres in all, are the thin-looking meres set against the enormous, constantly changing sky. This area is home to abundant wildlife in the form of literally thousands of birds, including redshank, shelduck, the odd heron and cormorant and no doubt a multitude of reed warblers and

River Alde flowing through the marshes at Snape Maltings. Courtesy of Alison Rawson

water rail, as well as other species. By no means are all of these are easy to see, given the vast expanse that awaits even the most casual birdwatcher. The author, P D James has written that she has also seen a white owl hunting low over Snape Marshes, now a nature reserve, but I am allowing my wildlife interests to divert me from the chosen subject. However, it is comforting to be aware that such an industrious writer of crime novels, of whom more later, can find the time to enjoy what Snape has to offer in all its natural facets.

It might be just as interesting to be aware that a succession of views of the river and marshes at Snape can be viewed on the Aldeburgh Music website. Two webcams show east-facing vistas taken automatically each hour from dawn to dusk throughout the seasons from Snape Maltings Concert Hall. It is incredibly relaxing and restful to view these images, which serve to illustrate the ever-changing conditions of light as well as tone and texture that artists have sought to capture, each in their own individual way, over many decades. It is not only here that you find such artists; they can be seen in other similar locations but not too far away. It is particularly pleasing to be able to appreciate how effectively the River Alde mirrors the sky throughout the day and the intervals between the images serve to provide the viewer with excellent contrasts on, say, showery days when the sun occasionally breaks through the clouds revealing patches of blue sky and puffy white clouds formulated on the surface of the water.

As a generously extensive footnote to the Benjamin Britten era at Aldeburgh, I wish to record that the composer was a prolific writer of letters, especially to friends. These were all hand-written apart from those that were typed when he was suffering from bursitis in his right arm. Spelling was never his strong point and even his typing was often quite hopeless but his temporary disability provided a justifiable explanation for this. He favoured the personal touch in his correspondence and he would never have contemplated dictation to the secretary-cum-chauffeur he had acquired in 1951 for what he then described as professional purposes. There have been attractions for me in writing so much about Benjamin Britten and one of these were his admirable qualities, not just as a composer, but also as a human being. He always seemed to be surrounded by people and he invariably seemed to know when it was time to relax, especially with his swimming, sailing and the occasional game of cricket as well as tennis. He was never slow in offering to give the odd session of tennis coaching to his younger friends where he felt that this would be appreciated. Whether he was immersed in his work, or just busying himself with domestic arrangements, Britten just never seemed to be alone in his chosen home. Each of his residences in

Aldeburgh, Crag House and The Red House, were usually filled with friends, guests, festival workers, visiting musicians and many others, including royalty, but it was on the stony, pebbly beach and empty marshes where he could be often found and where, perhaps, he was at his happiest and most inspired. As for the locals, seasonal visitors and others, it has to be said that the Aldeburgh Festival audiences found particular enjoyment in 'rubbing shoulders' around the town with most of the well-known people often to be seen in the audience when attending performances. Both Britten and Pears were regularly to be seen wandering around their chosen bailiwick and the local inhabitants became not only accustomed to these distinguished residents but also seen to thoroughly enjoy their informal presence when they were pursuing their domestic and leisure activities. On the other hand, the famous people who made their appearances at the Festival, whether as performers or as members of the audience, were often a source of wonder and no doubt more than a little pride. Aldeburgh's principal claim to fame is inextricably linked to Benjamin Britten and his music. The local hotels and guesthouses, not to forget the more informal bed and breakfast establishments, played host to the mighty and the owners, quite understandably, indulged in a little one-upmanship when discussing who was staying where during the Festival weeks. It was not always the case as, in the early days, there was a distinct lack of enthusiasm at the thought of the annual invasion, but this soon wore off. The considerable economic benefits became all too apparent to the town's population. A local fisherman was known to have said to a father and son who were in awe of being able to see Britten working at his orchestrations in his studio at Crag House when they were walking on the beach, 'It was Mr Britten that made this place'.

Writing about the rather famous visitors to Aldeburgh, due exclusively to the Britten influence, brings to mind the mezzo-soprano, Dame Janet Baker CH (born 1933) who has written about 'Approaching his (Britten's) kingdom, which begins for me where one leaves the A12 and makes that right turn "to Aldeburgh", feels exactly like going home'. She has regarded her time at the Festival as being quite marvellous years and she has expressed considerable praise for Britten's understanding of performers, a quality that she has found particularly valuable. That is perhaps the reason why she is known for being so closely associated with his works. She has performed at the Festival, during Britten's lifetime, in *Albert Herring*, *The Rape of Lucretia* and *Owen Wingrave*. As far as the latter is concerned, she recalls her character of Kate being discussed with the composer at length when sitting amidst the tombstones in Blythburgh churchyard. It seems that Britten rather objected when, on occasion, a performance of hers at Glyndebourne precluded her appearing at Aldeburgh, but she felt that it was not really bad thing, not being always at 'the Master's call'. The last rehearsal that she did for Britten was for *Phaedra* during the summer of 1976. This was a dramatic cantata written by the composer especially for her. On the day of the first night Britten, although in very poor health by that time, appeared at the final run-through and expressed astonishment that Baker felt able to do the first performance from memory. This caused her more than a little panic but she stuck to her guns and the night's performance on 16 June 1976, 'beautified by the perfect acoustics at The Maltings' went very well. This accomplished singer wrote that 'everyone was stunned by the power and passion of Ben's writing at a time when he was so frail physically'.

On the subject of Britten's writing of music, I have read somewhere that the composer was terribly accurate in the way that he wrote things down. One singer remembered going up to him and asking how he should interpret one of his songs. Benjamin Britten's reply was, 'I do not wish to be interpreted. You sing what I have written and that will suit me well'. It is perceived to be true that every single nuance was written in his score, both vocal and instrumental. If the music was played exactly as it is written, that was how it should sound: it was as simple as that to his mind and he was certainly someone who knew what he was talking about on such a subject. Perhaps in that brief exchange the singer was rewarded with what amounted to a Master Class as far as Britten's music was concerned.

Writing about the influence that Britten's music had on others brings me to another distinguished musician who speaks of Britten in glowing terms. This is Judah Adashi (born 1975), a fine example of a youngish man, born just a year before Britten's death. He is on the composition and music theory faculty at the Peabody Institute of the Johns Hopkins University in Baltimore. He is also a composer in his own right and I have chosen him as an example because he is on record as to why he singled out Benjamin Britten. He has said that so many of the things that he values in music go on in Benjamin Britten's work, in that the composer was able to communicate with a personal intensity and integrity. Adashi's view is that there was nothing typical about what Britten was doing: he had these personal relationships with Peter Pears, Julian Bream, and Rostropovich, artists for whom he wrote regularly and, in his opinion, these associations come through in Britten's music. Adashi felt that there must have been an intimacy to it that was deeply felt and very genuine – 'There was altogether something very personal about it'. This just serves to illustrate what I have written elsewhere about Benjamin Britten, his being so gloriously happy to be surrounded by and working with his exceptionally talented and creative friends. Adashi has also referred to how he assists his own students with their compositions. For example, if one wishes to write a piece for solo guitar he is always able to find a work by Britten that will be of real assistance. The fact that Britten worked in many idioms has enabled Adashi to guide his students to other pieces for, say, the harp or for strings. I can now appreciate the nature of the debt that Adashi feels he owes to Britten's music, music written by an Englishman in genres that were not easily accessible in an American environment. All this seems ironic, bearing in mind that Britten felt unable to stay in America for more than a limited number of years before being drawn back to Suffolk. Yet, now we learn how his work has inspired a Baltimore-based musical academic. Interestingly enough, Adashi confesses a Britten similarity in that about eighty percent of his own composition work has some kind of a literary connection, even if it acts only as an inspiration or a springboard for what is to follow. Adashi is a fine example of an American, Yale educated, award-winning twentieth-century musician inspired by a twentieth century English composer from coastal Suffolk. This is yet another legacy that can be claimed for the area's cultural heritage.

Britten's association with the particular part of Suffolk not so far away from his place of birth certainly left its mark and, as far back as early 1935 and at the age of twenty-one, his diaries record a great deal of his work with the Bungay String Orchestra, with which he conducted rehearsals of various pieces with varied results. Aged only nine, Britten was already composing music. By the age of nineteen, he had over eight hundred compositions to his credit, a fact that I find quite astonishing. In later years, having kept all of these, he would often revisit his childhood works seeking inspiration. He enjoyed writing for local audiences. His energies shone through in everything he did ... both at work and at play. There certainly seemed to be lots of bathing whenever and wherever he was near the coast and it is fitting that Maggi Hambling's *Scallop*, on the brow of the beach towards Thorpeness at his beloved Aldeburgh, commemorates his love of the North Sea. Jeremy Cullum, Britten's secretary from 1951-1969 recalls that his employer worked at Crag House in a room that faced the sea. I have tended to refer to this room as his studio. The close proximity of the beach and its waves, in all weathers, was often distracting to Britten when dictating a business letter. He would see something going on out there and sometimes a quarter of an hour would be lost as they both watched what was happening. Cullum told how the two of them would often watch storms going past and described the effect as 'very sort of Peter Grimes-ish'.

Whilst writing about Aldeburgh as well as George Crabbe's character from *The Borough, Peter Grimes*, it is worth mentioning that the poet was officially recognised by the town of his birth in that the street that runs parallel with the seafront is named after him. We already know that Crag House, 4 Crabbe Street was home to Benjamin Britten and Peter Pears for ten years from 1947. Previously, Britten had lived at The Old Mill, an already converted windmill, within the village of Snape, also for a period of ten years. This property had been bought with £2,000 provided to Britten through a legacy from his mother. In those days Britten also shared a London flat in Finchley Road with his sister, Beth, but by February 1938, Britten and Pears had found a flat at 43, Nevern Square and they moved in together shortly after. Although this apartment had 'two very nice rooms', by the end of the year the two had moved on to 67, Hallam Street, London W1, a property situated near BBC's Broadcasting House. Nevertheless, Britten had continued to enjoy Suffolk and he wrote his opera *Peter Grimes* whilst living at The Old Mill, often to be found looking out on a large and attractive building that was to become the future home of the Aldeburgh Festival, some twenty years later. Who knows what thoughts might have been stored in his subconscious during his stay there?

There seems to be no doubt that it was the view of the beach, and its backdrop of the North Sea, which had always retained for the composer an enduring fascination. This finally decided Benjamin Britten and Peter Pears to make their home in Aldeburgh. By living at Crag House, their almost daily swims in the North Sea were greatly facilitated in that they were able to gain access with the minimum of inconvenience by merely opening their garden door and proceeding across the narrow expanse of Crag Path to the beach and, to my mind, the far from welcoming waters of the North Sea. I am inclined to the view this is so even in summer, but this couple seemed to relish their confrontation with the chilly waves on an all-the-year-round basis. This reminds me of the hardy souls who brave the winter weather to go swimming in the Serpentine, at London's Hyde Park on Christmas Day each year, as well as other like-minded enthusiasts from beaches in the UK and Europe on New Year's Day. Although the architectural arrangement of Crag House appeared to suit Britten at the time, it seems not everyone was as impressed. The writer of one book of the tourist guide genre stated that 'Aldeburgh has an odd back-to-front appearance in that the backs of many buildings face the sea' as if this was a major disadvantage. Perhaps it was in more than one sense, as I shall now explain.

In their early days at Crag House Britten and Pears had certainly considered their new home to be an ideal location. The composer later told an interviewer: 'I've always felt I wanted to live by the sea. I've tried living away from the sea but something has gone slightly wrong, I always felt. I have needed that particular kind of atmosphere that the house on the edge of the sea provides'. We now know that Britten composed many of his musical works there at his 'studio' desk, overlooking the sea. These include the operas *The Little Sweep*, *Billy Budd*, *Gloriana* and *The Turn of the Screw*. I have written about the devastation caused by the major floods on the east coast in 1953, resulting in the loss of a significant number of lives. We also know that the worst that happened to the Britten household was that the ground floor and basement were flooded and the clearing-up operation took some considerable time. As he was then under great pressure to complete the opera *Gloriana*, this intervention by nature was massively inconvenient to say the least. However, if the flood couldn't drive Britten away from his cherished home, eventually the effects of the constant public gaze certainly did. The windows at Crag House were easily visible from the sea front and passers-by would increasingly stop to watch the composer in his study. I have written elsewhere of the mutually opportune house-swap with artist, Mary Potter, that followed before too much time had passed.

Now that I have more or less come to the end of my references to Benjamin Britten, I cannot resist adding just one personal note. It seems that the composer was a committed melodist when writing his music but he was fearful of sounding too much like Giacomo Puccini (1858-1924), whose music he apparently loathed. There I must differ very strongly with him and I feel certain that this must be the case with literally millions of others who have been held in rapture by Puccini's melodies and dramatic arias from *La Bohème*, *Tosca*, *Turandot* and *Madame Butterfly*. On the other hand, I am conscious of the fact that perhaps Britten felt that Puccini was far too inclined to, shall we say, 'play to the gallery' when composing his operas. Everything I have read about Britten, whether in music or in his personal life, seems to indicate that he was very much his own man and I cannot imagine him being involved with composing any piece of music just because he felt that it might prove to be popular. Whatever reasons he had for his attitude towards the Italian composer, he has my strong support on another matter - he was not reticent in demonstrating his impatience on the subject of atonality. Music that it is not written in any key or mode also happens to be an affront to my admittedly untrained ear, but Britten earned billions of brownie points from me when he infamously walked out of the first performance of Harrison Birtwistle's (born 1934) *Punch and Judy* (his very first opera), at Aldeburgh of all places. This was in 1968 and the action that Britten took on that occasion seems to me to be very much akin to the host abandoning his own party long before the event had ended. In later years, certainly after Britten's death, Birtwistle's work was again performed at the Festival, notably *The Io Passion* in 2004 and *The Corridor* in 2008, each of these being premières.

It will be of the many painters who have been attracted to coastal Suffolk that I will be writing later. In the meantime I would like to tell you about some of the writers who have come from far and near as well as a number that, like Britten, were simply born locally.

PART TWO
WRITERS AND LITERARY ASSOCIATIONS

'You know who the critics are? The men who have failed in literature and art.'

Lothair (1870)

Benjamin Disraeli, Earl of Beaconsfield (1804-1881)
Politician as well as a literary and social figure

'Fool' said my Muse, to me, 'look in thy heart, and write.'

Song II: Have I Caught. Certain Sonnets, To the Tune of a Neapolitan Villanelle

Sir Philip Sidney (1554-1586)

If a man write a better book, preach a better sermon, or make a better mouse-trap than his neighbour, tho' he build his house in the woods, the world will make a beaten path to his door.

Mrs Sarah S B Yule (1856-1916) credits the quotation to Ralph Waldo Emerson (1803-1882) in her *Borrowings* (1889), stating in *The Docket*, Feb. 1912, that she copied this in her handbook from a lecture delivered by Emerson. The 'mouse-trap' quotation was the occasion of a long controversy, owing to Elbert Hubbard's claim to its authorship.

Chapter One

Henry James, Edward FitzGerald and other writers

IT IS WORTH recording here, now that we know so much about Henry James and his work that so inspired Benjamin Britten to write his opera based upon the American author's book, that James was persuaded to visit Southwold in 1897. He was then staying in England, but as far away as Bournemouth. Whilst there, he had been reading about Suffolk's famous nineteenth century poet and writer, Edward FitzGerald, of whom I shall be writing more a little later on. It seems that not long after his arrival in Suffolk James had been exploring the general locality on a bicycle and had come across the place name Saxmundham. Later that day he met a Suffolk boatman from that same town who just happened to have, as a brother, FitzGerald's very own and much-loved boatman. The Suffolk literary hero was a very keen sailor on East Coast waters. To take the coincidences one stage further, James returned to where he was staying to find, waiting for him, a letter from an American cousin. This invited him to visit the family in Dunwich, now just a small coastal village but before the now famous, terrible storm in 1328 that destroyed 400 houses, an important town and seaport.

However, the decline at Dunwich had started in 1286, following an equally violent storm. All in all, Henry James was resident in England for some forty years or so, living in both London as well as Sussex. His visit to Suffolk brought about, initially, a magazine article entitled *Old Suffolk*. This eventually became a chapter in his series of beautifully illustrated travel sketches, published as *English Hours: Portraits of a Country and its People*. This work was re-released as recently as March 2011; a new paperback edition entitled *English Hours: Portrait of a Country*, this time with a new foreword by Colm Tóibín (born 1955), a multi-award-winning Irish novelist, short story writer and critic. His fifth novel, The *Master* (2004), is described as a fictional account of portions in the life of Henry James so he was undoubtedly a fan of the American's life and work.

Henry James had a niece, Ellen Emmet (1875-1941), just one of a generation of talented women painters in the family. She visited London en route to study in Paris with her sister, Rosina. The aim was to meet the American author who had been keeping an encouraging eye on them and their more than promising artistic talents. This was in late 1896 and in 1900 she painted a portrait of her uncle when he was at Rye in Sussex, writing his famous novel, *The Ambassadors*, now considered to be a classic. Her artistic career prospered and in 1933, when using her married name Ellen Emmet Rand, she was commissioned to paint the official White House portrait of Franklin D Roosevelt (1182-1945), President of the United States during World War II. Some years before, she had abandoned a portrait of Teddy Roosevelt, complaining that 'he couldn't keep still'. Theodore Roosevelt, 'FDR's' fifth cousin, was the 26th President of the United States, from 1901-1909.

Contained within *English Hours* is an essay on *Old Suffolk* which states that the author was with a friend, Edward Warren (1856-1937), a British architect and archaeologist, with whom he had been bicycling within the county in 1897, when he is reported to have been bemused by Dunwich. A quotation reads 'a month of the place is a real education to the patient, the inner vision'. According to Norman Scarfe (born 1923), an expert on the history of Suffolk, it moved James to much incoherence. On the other hand, like many reflective visitors to Dunwich the distinguished author saw that 'there is a presence in what is missing – there is history in there being so little'. At first glance, this seemed to me to be an obvious statement that refers to a large community laid waste by the ravages of an angry sea but, on reflection, I agree with Scarfe who feels that James 'was well content with the sensation, with the presence of absence, with the incentive to brood'. Scarfe goes on to scoff at the so-called legend of the bells of no less than seventy churches of the sunken Dunwich being heard ringing out from beneath the waves. This seems justified as, quite apart from the questionable practicality of the local legend, my researchs tell me that even at its height the number of churches in Dunwich never reached double figures.

Henry James was undoubtedly inspired by the highly invasive North Sea being responsible for the history of coastal erosion in Suffolk. His thoughts were concentrated upon man's perpetual struggle with the omnipotent sea. This led him to write:

> 'The coast, up and down, for miles, has been, for more centuries that I presume to count, gnawed away by the sea ... which moves for ever, like a ruminating beast, an insatiable, indefatigable lip'.

South of Dunwich, and a little inland, is Leiston Common, once the home of a remarkable, eccentric figure and old-fashioned Communist, A L (Leslie) Morton (1903-1987). He lived in a building that was a converted twelfth-century chapel. This Marxist historian, an accomplished critic, served with T S Eliot on *The Criterion* (a literary magazine published from 1922 to 1939) and wrote a scholarly study of Blake's prophetic books called *The Everlasting Gospel*. Amongst his other works are the classic *The People's History of England* (1938) and *The English Utopia* (1952). He also wrote a Communist Party pamphlet in 1949 entitled *The Story of the English Revolution*. I must have missed that in more ways than one. Morton studied at the University of Cambridge from 1921 to 1924. There he encountered socialist ideas, possibly from the communist group that formed around Maurice Dobb (1900-1976), a Marxist economist, and a lecturer (from 1924-1959) and Reader (from 1959-1976) at that university. He was also a Fellow of Trinity College from 1948-1976. Later, Morton went on to teach at Summerhill, a progressive, co-educational, residential school, founded in Suffolk in 1921 by A S Neill (1883-1973). He was a Scottish progressive educator and author. The school, not to mention its methods, continues to remain more than a little controversial and it was the subject of an excellent drama, entitled *Summerhill*, that was specially made for BBC Children's Television at the school in the summer of 2007 and directed by Jon East, Head of BBC Children's Drama.

Edward Thomas (1878-1917), the Anglo-Welsh writer of prose and poetry, stayed in one of the coastguards' cottages on Dunwich Heath in 1908, while writing his biography of Richard Jefferies (1814-1877), a prolific nature writer. The National Trust team room displays a letter written during that visit. Thomas was commonly considered a war poet, although few of his poems deal directly with his war experiences. Already an accomplished writer, Thomas turned to poetry only in 1914 and a year later he enlisted in the army but, like so many of his fellow soldiers, he was killed in action during the Battle of Arras in 1917, soon after he arrived in France. During his life he gained a fine reputation as an accomplished writer with many poems and essays to his name. He wrote just one novel, *The Happy-Go-Lucky Morgans* (1913), the story of the London suburb of Balham and of a family that lived there. He dedicated the book to his parents. What might be of some interest is that in his 1980 autobiography, *Ways of Escape,* novelist Graham Greene (1904-1991) makes reference to Thomas's poem *The Other* (about a man who seems to be following his own double from hotel to hotel) in describing his own experience of being bedevilled by an imposter.

Chapter Two

Aldeburgh's famous 'Poet of the Poor', a 'Marmalade Cat' and some other literary figures of considerable fame

APART FROM BENJAMIN Britten, we already know that another famously positive and certainly distinctive connection with the town of Aldeburgh is the name of George Crabbe (1754-1832). He is said to be probably Suffolk's most distinguished literary figure, having lived in the county for the first third of his life, an initial seventeen years or so in Aldeburgh. I feel that I am far from qualified to make such a judgment on this poet's qualifications for such an exalted position in the county's literary hierarchy but perhaps it would be useful to examine the available and enormously convincing evidence.

George Crabbe was born in Aldeburgh, the eldest of six children and son of a tax collector. The simple beach-man's dwelling where Crabbe was born at Slaughden Quay was swept away by the sea in 1779. Later in life, he became an ordained clergyman, being appointed curate to the rector of Aldeburgh, having previously trained as a doctor, a career that proved to be unsuccessful. Crabbe had first discovered that he had a love for poetry in childhood but circumstances dictated that he needed to make a living in other ways. After Crabbe left Aldeburgh in 1782, he lived for a while at Rendham, where he was to write *The Borough*. His house there, 'Ladywhincups', still stands in Grove Farm Lane, off the B1119, and a blue plaque commemorates Crabbe's residency. Eventually he became vicar of Trowbridge, Wiltshire and died there in 1832. Earlier he had been the so-called 'poetical' chaplain to the Duke of Rutland at Belvoir Castle Leicestershire. Indeed it was poetry that seemed to dominate his thoughts and Crabbe's two best known works are undoubtedly *The Borough* and *The Village*. If there was ever any doubt concerning the way he was regarded in his lifetime, the fact that he was, in effect, a protégé of Edmund Burke (1729-1797), the distinguished Anglo-Irish statesman, should assist in settling the matter. Burke assisted Crabbe in having his poem *The Library* published in 1781. George Crabbe was also befriended by William Wordsworth (1770-1850), a former Poet Laureate, as well as by historical novelist, playwright and poet, Sir Walter Scott amongst other major literary figures of the time. Lord Byron (1788-1824) certainly admired Crabbe's poetry and called him: 'Nature's sternest painter, yet the best'. He was also the favourite poet of Jane Austen (1775-1817). In all, ten of George Crabbe's works were published but it is probably fair to say that the connection with Benjamin Britten is best responsible for his name being so widely recognised today.

It was, in effect, just a character study of Crabbe's, sub-titled *Peter Grimes*, merely one section of his poem, *The Borough*, that was to provide Benjamin Britten's inspiration to write the opera entitled *Peter Grimes*. This is somewhat ironic as George Crabbe was said to generally dislike music. What is important is the fact that the whole of the original poem by Crabbe is regarded as a major work in its own right. *The Borough* is comprised of no less than almost 70,000 words and was first published in 1810, which makes Crabbe one of the earliest of the creative people mentioned in this book.

The Borough is made up of a collection of poems arranged as a series of twenty-four letters that illustrate various aspects of a small fishing village. Crabbe seemed to specialise in writing not just about the pastoral concerns that feature in his work, but also biographically about the lives of individual inhabitants of a mean and primitive place, just like Aldeburgh in Crabbe's time. *The Village* is very much shorter in length than *The Borough* and, in general, Crabbe's writings are regarded nowadays as a somewhat unsentimental commentary on provincial life and society.

The 1954 Aldeburgh Festival celebrated the bicentennial of Crabbe's birth, the poet being born on 16 June 1754. A lunch was held at the East Suffolk Hotel at which E M Forster and William Plomer were the guest speakers. What followed this indoor event was a tour of sights and houses associated with the inspirational poet, ending at Glenham House where Plomer, who stepped in for publisher, Sir John (Jock) Murray (1908-1993), read from a selection of Crabbe's writings. The poet's memory was also honoured by the Festival mounting an exhibition of first editions, manuscripts and letters in Aldeburgh's Moot Hall, a well-preserved Tudor building that is the current home of the town's museum. In earlier years, Murray's long established family firm of publishers had published Crabbe's work. More latterly, they became publishers to Sir John Betjeman, John Piper and Sir Kenneth (later Lord) Clark, all of whom are mentioned within these pages.

Although George Crabbe junior was later to be regarded as 'a poet of the poor', particularly as his own family's circumstances were so straitened, this was not a social circumstance that appealed to him and as far as he was concerned the working classes were not to his liking. This strikes me as rather strange, with Crabbe having been a man of the church. He eventually left, or as Forster puts it, 'escaped' from Aldeburgh but he never left it in spirit. Forster concludes that this was the making of him as a poet. Once again, it was the Suffolk coast with its North Sea, the estuary and the flat land, as well as the people, which inspired the creative mind of an Englishman, as we have seen so often within these pages. As a lengthy footnote to what Forster had written about Aldeburgh and its famous poet this particular author not only attended the inaugural Aldeburgh Festival in 1948 but also gave a lecture in the town's Baptist Chapel on the subject of George Crabbe and *Peter Grimes*. This leaves me speculating as to whether or not Forster met up with Christopher Isherwood during that visit, having regard to the close relationship between the two men and the fact that in his early years Isherwood had acted as some sort of literary mentor to both W H Auden and E M Forster. In his writings, Forster remembers that at the performance of *Albert Herring*, in the intimate atmosphere of Aldeburgh's crowded Jubilee Hall, the temperature had soared making it uncomfortably hot. During the intervals, wrote Forster, the audience, 'partly in evening dress and partly anyhow burst out on to the nearby beach' the distinct impression being given that the occasion was 'exempt from the smartness of Glyndebourne'. Somehow, I feel that the Festival's organisers would have approved of this comparison to the famous operatic institution established in an English Country House atmosphere in 1934. If nothing else, I have never understood Aldeburgh's festival to be in any way associated with social snobbery and the 'London/English Summer Season'. I also feel quite certain that this would not have been a feature that Benjamin Britten and Peter Pears would have encouraged. That first Festival also had, as one of its events, a lecture by William Plomer on the subject of the previously mentioned writer, Edward FitzGerald. Forster had described this as 'brilliant and provocative' even though Plomer concentrated more on the author's character rather than his work. All in all, E M Forster was impressed by the Festival and felt it to be an encouraging start that would make a contribution to preventing people 'trailing up to London for their art'. Amen to that! However, it has left me speculating about whether Forster may have been disappointed that it was *Albert Herring* that was on offer at the first Festival in 1948. After all, it was Forster's article on Crabbe that had first attracted Britten and Pears to the poet, leading him to write *Peter Grimes*. It will also be recalled that Isherwood had declined Britten's request to write the libretto for *Peter Grimes*. This leads me to the conclusion that perhaps Forster might have jumped at such a chance had it come his way. He was similarly disappointed to have to wait until Britten's *Billy Budd* invitation came along before he was entrusted with a libretto by the composer, this time in collaboration with Eric Crozier. I have since learned from an archivist at the Britten-Pears library that *Peter Grimes* was, quite surprisingly, not performed at the Festival until the year 2000. This was at the Maltings (by ENO). The point was made that due to the restricted size of the Jubilee Hall stage it would have been near impossible to have *Peter Grimes* performed there in 1948. Thus, my curiosity was satisfied.

From the literary sublime to the almost ridiculous, although very large numbers of children would, no doubt, disagree, I now seek to draw your attention to a rather less obvious connection with Aldeburgh. Kathleen Hale (1898-2000) was a British artist, illustrator, and children's author. She is best remembered for her series of books about the wonderfully eccentric *Orlando (The Marmalade Cat)*. In her book *A Seaside Holiday* (1952) as part of her extensive Orlando series, the feline family enjoyed the delights, as did many others, offered at post-war Aldeburgh and the River Alde. In the book, these were thinly disguised as Owlbarrow-on-Sea, complete with lifeboat, a land-girl and the River Owl. I loved one of the child characters in the book describing Owlbarrow as being 'like a big open-air bathroom'. This long-lived author substituted sand for the Aldeburgh pebbles but I suppose that is a matter of artistic license, not to mention personal taste. Pebbles don't tend to invade the contents of picnic sandwiches ... or do they?

Kathleen Hale was brought up and educated in Manchester and her early talent as an artist was recognised at school by an enlightened headmistress. She went on to attend art courses in Manchester and at Reading University. In 1917, Kathleen moved to London to make a life for herself as an artist. She worked for some time as secretary to the distinguished painter and portraitist, Augustus John (1878-1961) whilst developing a wide circle of friends in the artistic community.

She first met this notable artist when she was aged twenty-two and John, then at the height of his fame, was some twenty years her senior. Their working relationship was, in her own words, 'friendly and mutually slightly teasing'. She termed this as an aberration that served only to add certain warmth to their friendship. This may well have been the case then, but on one occasion she allowed him to seduce her. It was about this time that Kathleen Hale also had a loving relationship with another artist, Frank Potter, some ten years her senior, who had a strong influence on her work. Together, they visited Étaples in Normandy where she produced a series of highly accomplished pencil drawings of fishermen's wives and children, very much in the manner of her 'mentor' and possible muse, Augustus John. During the 1920s, Hale managed to earn a living as an illustrator, accepting commissions for book jackets as well as selling her own drawings. She is best known for creating Orlando and his fascinating world to entertain her children at bedtime, for the simple reason that she had become weary with reading and constantly re-reading the work of children's authors such as Beatrix Potter (1866-1943) and Edward Ardizzone (1900-1979), both of whom illustrated their own books. Beatrix Potter had connections with Suffolk but this was in respect of a large house now owned by the National Trust, Melford Hall in Long Melford, the home of the Hyde-Parker family to whom she was related. *Orlando (The Marmalade Cat)* 'with eyes like twin gooseberries' was one of the classic children's book characters of the 1940s and 1950s when Kathleen was married to Douglas McLean, a doctor. Her fictional feline character, Orlando, is said to be based upon her husband because he was 'wise, reliable and kindly'. Her stories are known for their eccentric wit and extravagantly gaudy illustrations by the author. These popular stories combine adventure with friendship and family life and the illustrations in the book I decided to read, in the interests of my research, certainly cover more space on the page than the text. As the creator of Orlando, Kathleen was awarded the OBE in 1976. I write more about Kathleen Hale as an artist and her connection with the East Anglian School of Painting and Drawing run by Cedric Morris and Arthur Lett-Haines at Dedham, and then at Benton End, in a later chapter, because there have been other very famous names numbered amongst its alumni.

Edward FitzGerald has been mentioned once or twice before, so perhaps now is the time to tell you more about this remarkably famous man. First, we must look a little further afield in Suffolk. Staying on or near the coast we travel south and come to the town of Woodbridge, the home of the previously-mentioned writer, Norman Scarfe and a town that stands proudly upstream on the River Deben, which like its more southerly sister rivers, the Orwell and the Stour, flows into the North Sea. This brings us to the English writer who lived in and around Woodbridge, the said Edward FitzGerald (1809-1883). He was best known as the poet who produced the first and most celebrated, free and imaginative English translation of a selection of Persian poems that became known as *The Rubáiyát of Omar Khayyám*, this being the title he gave to his work. It has been described elsewhere that what he accomplished with this renowned masterpiece was nothing more than a paraphrase of the original composition. That may well be so, but as a work of English literature, FitzGerald's version has become known as a high point of the nineteenth century and has been greatly influential. Omar Khayyám was a Persian poet, mathematician and astronomer. FitzGerald may also have been involved with the publication of a selection of the work of a fellow Suffolk poet, none other than George Crabbe. He was certainly an admirer of Crabbe, who died when FitzGerald was aged only twenty-three.

I have been fortunate to have access to a rather elderly edition of Edward FitzGerald's translation of the *Rubáiyát* and have read with interest the Introduction by playwright, writer and illustrator, Laurence Housman (1865-1959), younger brother of the classical scholar and poet, A E Housman (1859-1936). Housman comments on the fact that FitzGerald, being very much a writer of the Victorian era, brought this particular dimension to his translation of the original work. It is described as being done 'divinely well'. FitzGerald studied Persian poetry at Oxford and there seems no doubt that the *Rubáiyát* presented him with a challenge which he was eager to accept. Laurence Housman felt that FitzGerald brought his own special flavour to the now famous, indeed revered, translation into the English language and at the same time he was, of course, not only adding his personal poetic beauty but also his own version of 'westernising' as well as modernising the text. It was indeed Housman that went as far as to say that FitzGerald was paraphrasing rather than merely translating his selection from over one thousand original poems in the Persian language. I put this down to FitzGerald being an undoubted admirer of the original text, even though there were matters where perhaps he felt inspired to agree as well as to take issue, especially when it came to discussing belief in the Almighty. All this reminds me of my own belief or, more precisely, my trust. It is difficult for me to believe absolutely but I am more than willing to trust. I would like to think that both Omar Khayyám and Edward Fitzgerald shared at least a small portion of my personal views on this perennial subject.

Ruth Rendell has written that it was FitzGerald who defended Suffolk when others slighted it, even though he was said to have described Boulge, a village near Woodbridge, as 'one of the dullest and ugliest places on earth'. This is an opinion that Rendell finds it very hard to accept in that she regards Boulge and its environs today as 'beautiful pastoral countryside, thickly wooded, serene in sunshine, bleak and wild in winter'. FitzGerald refused to live at Boulge Hall with the rest of his family and chose instead to live in a single story thatched cottage on the family estate for all of sixteen years. The writer ended his days in Woodbridge, having been born in the town in a residence named Bredfield House. Amongst his friends was George Crabbe the younger, son of the Aldeburgh poet but, sadly, he did not inherit his father's genius. In the family tradition he became a clergyman and subsequently the Vicar of Bredfield, also in Suffolk where he built a somewhat extravagant vicarage. Incidentally, the FitzGeralds were once one of the wealthiest families in England.

Apart from brief visits to London and the fact that his family moved to France for a short period, FitzGerald spent all of his life in seclusion in Suffolk. His marriage, in Chichester, to Lucy Barton, daughter of a Quaker poet, was very short-lived with separation taking place within only a matter of months. Amongst his great friends were English satirical novelist, William Makepeace Thackeray (1811-1863), Scottish satirical writer, essayist and historian, Thomas Carlyle (1795-1881) and Alfred Lord Tennyson (1809-1892), all of whom who need no further introduction. FitzGerald is buried in the churchyard of St Michael and All Angels, Boulge, near the foot of the church tower. In 1893, his grave was further marked by a group of admirers who planted a rose tree on top of his remains. This plant had been raised from seed grown in Kew Gardens, the seed having been brought from a rose growing on Khayyam's own grave in Persia. In 1972, six rose bushes were planted where he continues to lie buried today. These had been sent from Naishapur to mark the 2,500th year of the Persian Empire. Naishapur is a town in the Khorasan province of Iran. The story of the single rose tree is what I would describe as thoroughly deserved international recognition of Suffolk's own Edward FitzGerald. Incidentally, Omar Khayyám was born in 1047CE and died in 1123 CE (the Arab Period). This planting of the rose tree was organised by Edward Clodd and more will be learned of this notable resident of Aldeburgh a little later.

Mentioning Aldeburgh once again leads me to the fact that Thomas Carlyle moved from his native Scotland to Chelsea in London in 1834 and became known as the 'Sage of Chelsea'. Being friends with Edward FitzGerald resulted in a visit to the latter's home in Suffolk. On an excursion to Aldeburgh he remarked '...a beautiful little sea town, one of the best bathing places I have seen...If you have yet gone nowhere, you should think of Aldeburgh'. FitzGerald was equally praising with his 'There is no sea like the Aldeburgh sea – it talks to me'. Where have I heard that before? He is also responsible for writing of Aldeburgh thus: 'I was ruthlessly ducked into the Wave that came like a devouring monster under the awning of the Bathing Machine – a Machine whose Inside I hate to this day'. He obviously preferred his sailing to venturing out from the beach into the waves at Aldeburgh without the comforting feel of the planks of his vessel beneath his feet. In the spring of 1862, Fitzgerald was in Aldeburgh 'to have a Toss on the Sea and a Smoke with the Sailors'. This seems to confirm his preference, as far as nautical activities were concerned. 'Fitz' had declared himself at his happiest 'going in my little Boat round the coast to Aldbro' with some bottled Porter and some Bread and Cheese', presumably sailing from the River Deben which was known to be his favourite haunt. I believe that I have read somewhere that it was known as Fitzgerald's river. By way of an additional note, Fitzgerald was said to go sailing in a top hat, which he tied on with a strap tucked beneath his chin. He obviously had style but of a nature not normally observed at Cowes in our modern times.

Being a keen sailor, FitzGerald often sailed off the coast of Suffolk and we now know he included Aldeburgh in his itinerary. His best-known vessel was a 45ft schooner, launched at Wivenhoe on the Essex coast in June 1863. It was originally named 'Shamrock' but soon became known as 'Scandal'. This is said to be a name by which the sailing yacht is remembered throughout the English-speaking world as Edward FitzGerald's 'dear little ship'. Scandal became very well known, along with its tender, 'Whisper' on the rivers Deben, Alde, and Orwell. Perhaps the Stour was too shallow at low tide for such a fine craft as Scandal. *Sea words and phrases along the Suffolk Coast* was written by FitzGerald and published in 1869. I understand that this book, rather unique in character, can still be found today although the Amazon website states that it's currently unavailable from them.

Returning to FitzGerald's friendship with Thomas Carlyle I have come across a connection between them which refers to the former's love for the sea and sailing. It is by virtue of a letter written by FitzGerald to Thomas Carlyle in 1870. It seems that, before this date, Carlyle had written a book entitled *On Heroes, Hero-Worship, and The Heroic in History*. This was released again as a paperback in 2007 by the Echo Press. FitzGerald's letter referred to an earlier edition of this book and he set out to introduce a hero of his own, a fisherman partner of his named Joseph Fletcher, known to FitzGerald as 'Posh'. A book by the late James Blyth has been published in electronic form (an eBook) by the Project Gutenberg and it is entitled *Edward FitzGerald and 'Posh': 'Herring Merchants'*. This is the letter written by FitzGerald to Thomas Carlyle:

'DEAR CARLYLE, Your "Heroes" put me up to sending you one of mine— neither Prince, Poet, or Man of Letters, but Captain of a Lowestoft Lugger, and endowed with all the Qualities of Soul and Body to make him Leader of many more men than he has under him. Being unused to sitting for his portrait, he looks a little sheepish—and the Man is a Lamb with Wife, Children, and dumber Animals. But when the proper time comes—abroad—at sea or on shore—then it is quite another matter. And I know no one of sounder sense, and grander Manners, in whatever Company. But I shall not say any more; for I should only set you against him; and you will see all without my telling you and not be bored. So least said soonest mended, and I make my bow once more and remain your

"Humble Reader"

E. FG.'

In his introduction to the book, James Blyth described how he set out to track down 'Posh', the fisherman friend and partner of

'Old Fitz', for that was how the eminent literary man was known to the fishermen of Lowestoft. It seems that the author and fisherman separated after some form of quarrel but it is clear that FitzGerald thought the world of Joseph Fletcher who died some time after his landlady who passed away in 1906. James Blyth, who spoke to 'Posh' in the twilight years of his life, was responsible for publishing some of FitzGerald's letters to the fisherman, thus affording the retired man of the sea some much welcome financial benefit at the end of his days, although he did admit that he had rid himself of 'sackfuls of them' without realizing their value. I find this a touching story and a fine example of the popularity and humanity of Edward FitzGerald, a man who wrote to Thomas Carlyle in such glowing terms about his friend, 'Posh'. I find myself wondering if Henry James's coming across the brother of FitzGerald's boatman resulted in any connection of his own with 'Posh'. It is not important but not a little intriguing. The relevant dates do not render this at all impossible.

Edward FitzGerald's boatman, 'Posh'

FitzGerald's estranged wife, Lucy, was the only daughter of Bernard Barton (1784-1849), born of Quaker parentage and educated at a Quaker school in Ipswich. Barton's wife had sadly died in childbirth. He was known as the Woodbridge Poet and sometimes as the Quaker Poet. During the course of her relationship with FitzGerald, Lucy published a selection of her father's poems and letters, to which her husband prefixed a biographical introduction. As it happens, Bernard Barton was an admirer of the work of George Crabbe and although he never achieved Crabbe's status, his work was said to have found a home in many hearts. During his lifetime, he sought advice from both English essayist, Charles Lamb (1775-1834) and Lord Byron (1788-1824), the leading romantic poet. Each of these notable literary personalities was prepared to be helpful but cautioned Barton against abandoning his main source of income as a bank clerk in order to write full time. Another of his correspondents during his lifetime was the distinguished Suffolk poet, Robert Bloomfield (1766-1823), who made his reputation with his poem *The Farmer's Boy*, a work that earned international success. Bloomfield was born in the village of Honington in Suffolk and his grave is in the grounds of the parish church there. Capel Lofft, a Suffolk squire of literary tastes as well as being Bloomfield's publisher, wrote to Barton that both he and the poet had 'read with pleasure your verses on Felixstowe, but with particular delight that calm, and soothing, and soul elevating poem, *The Valley of the Fern*'. Writing this in the twenty-first century it is extremely difficult to think of the United Kingdom's largest container port being the subject of romantic poetry. Undertaking a little research I found that the valley described in the poem was probably just off the road leading from Woodbridge to Melton, a spot where, at near the end of the nineteenth century, a noticeboard warned the wayfarer that it was 'criminal to leave the footpath that crosses the Valley of the Fern'. I wonder if this sign, or possibly a successor, remains to this day. Maybe a rambler would know.

After Barton's death, Edward FitzGerald likened his father-in-law's poetry to its author watching his volume 'at last afloat', as a boy watches a paper boat committed to the sea. Being aware that such a flimsy craft was unlikely to survive for very long leaves me struggling to decide if this was intended as a compliment. Perhaps it is best to leave others to decide. The book of poems was published posthumously, having been written in a humdrum life of a bank clerk whilst struggling for years to be published.

As a footnote to the activities of Edward FitzGerald, it is said that it was during a stay in a house in Dunwich that he worked on his translation of the *The Rubáiyát of Omar Khayyám*. Over sixty years later, the writer and humourist Jerome K Jerome (1859-1927) stayed at the same house. In a room, said to have been used by FitzGerald, Jerome wrote his autobiography, *My Life and Times* (1926). Jerome's most important work was, of course, the comic novel, *Three Men in a Boat*, a book that he started writing in 1888 on return from the honeymoon which followed his marriage to 'Elsie' Maris who was also known as 'Ettie'. The couple had spent their honeymoon in a boat on the River Thames between Kingston and Oxford. For the book,

Jerome substituted the names of two of his long-time friends for that of his new wife, as well as introducing a fictional dog named Montmorency. Their humorous adventures were such that, even in the twenty-first century, devoted fans have been known to recreate the epic journey, once for the benefit of a TV audience. Thanks to Jerome's detailed and painstaking descriptions, the route and pubs appear to be easily identified.

An admirer of FitzGerald's work on the *Rubáiyát* was Algernon Swinburne (1837-1909) and this fellow poet was no stranger to either Southwold or Dunwich. He was a self-confessed lover of the deep and has been described as the 'laureate of the sea'. He had found Southwold quite boring during his short-stay address at South House, Middle Cliff, apart from a chance discovery of what he described as a 'lake of freshwater'. He described this as 'only parted from the sea by a thick and steep pebble-ridge, half encircled by an old wood of oaks and ash trees'. He went on to compare this discovery to Dante's *The Wood of Suicides*, especially if seen in the winter months. This caused Swinburne to revise his views on the locality. A quotation from this work is:

'The leaves not green, earth-hued;
The boughs not smooth, knotted and crooked-forked;
No fruit, but poisoned thorns'.

Believed to be hanging in Balliol College, Oxford is a portrait of the highly-strung Swinburne by a non-Suffolk artist, William Bell Scott (1811-1890) who was also a poet. The fact that the painter chose the sea and the seashore as a background to this work served to underline Swinburne's other reputation as the 'Seagull Poet'. During his visits to the east coast he often bathed naked in the sea, being attracted by the physical presence of the water. From what I have read, however, this must have been early morning if he chose Southwold for his skinny-dipping, as nude bathing was permitted solely at the north end of the town and only before 6am. Swinburne's affection for the East Coast is generally thought to have been inspired by his mother, Lady Jane, who was born at Barking Hall in Suffolk, the daughter of the third Earl of Ashburton. Sadly, the background to the portrait described above is said to have been the poet standing before the wild seas off the Northumberland coast and not in Suffolk.

Swinburne must have thought a lot of his portraitist as his poem *To William Bell Scott* illustrates:

'The larks are loud above our leagues of whin
Now the sun's perfume fills their glorious gold
With odour like the colour: all the wold
Is only light and song and wind wherein
These twain are blent in one with shining din.
And now your gift, a giver's kingly-souled,
Dear old fast friend whose honours grow not old,
Bids memory's note as loud and sweet begin.
Though all but we from life be now gone forth
Of that bright household in our joyous north
Where I, scarce clear of boyhood just at end,
First met your hand; yet under life's clear dome,
Now seventy strenuous years have crowned my friend,
Shines no less bright his full-sheaved harvest-home.'

The above poem was written in April 1882.

Illustrating his love for the sea, and especially his almost rampant desire to immerse his body within the waves, he writes in his poem *In the Water*, from his *A Midsummer Holiday* thus:

'As we give us again to the waters, the rapture
of limbs that the waters enfold
Is less than the rapture of spirit whereby,
though the burden it quits were sore,
Our souls and the bodies they wield at their will
are absorbed in the life they adore--
In the life that endures no burden, and bows not
the forehead, and bends not the knee--
In the life everlasting of earth and of heaven,
in the laws that atone and agree,
In the measureless music of things, in the fervour
of forces that rest or that roam,
That cross and return and reissue, as I
after you and as you after me
Strike out from the shore as the heart in us bids

and beseeches, athirst for the foam.'

Swinburne's poem, *By the North Sea*, refers to the terrible fate suffered by the town of Dunwich and the dramatic ruins that remained of its illustrious history as a major seaport. Aa we already know, the dramatic erosion of the coast in that particular area began as far back as the year 1286 and all that now remains is little more than the odd cluster of buildings. There must certainly be a 'lost city' to be found under the nearby waves in the North Sea off Dunwich village. I now give you just one verse from the above poem as I consider that this gives dramatic effect to his feelings for the lost inhabitants of Dunwich:

'Naked, shamed, cast out of consecration,
Corpse and coffin, yea the very graves,
Scoffed at, scattered, shaken from their station,
Spurned and scourged of wind and sea like slaves,
Desolate beyond man's desolation,
Shrink and sink into the waste of waves.'

Amongst Swinburne's friends was writer, Thomas Hardy (1840-1928) who was introduced to Southwold by a friend he shared with Swinburne, namely the Hon. Florence Henniker (1855-1923), a woman who wrote six novels and three collections of short stories. She was the daughter of the first Baron Houghton who had a wide circle of friends that included poets, authors, artists and actors as well as members of fashionable society. Hardy had first met Henniker in Ireland in 1893 and she apparently aroused strong emotions in him. He described her as 'one rare woman' even though she was happily married to the Hon. Arthur Henniker-Major, the younger son of Lord Henniker of Thornham Hall, in Suffolk (not to be confused with a house of the same name in north Norfolk). The Prince Regent and Lily Langtree are said to have stayed in the Suffolk version, at Thornham Magna, near Eye, in the nineteenth century.

After Hardy's first wife, Emma died in 1912, Mrs Henniker invited the author to stay at the house she had taken on Gun Hill, Southwold and he arrived on 22 April 1913 to meet up with Florence Dugdale there. She had been his secretary since the year before and was a lady thirty-nine years his junior, with whom he had enjoyed a love affair since 1907. Mrs Henniker was apparently aware of this relationship and it is perhaps for this reason that the author decided it would be best for him to sleep at the Swan Hotel, rather than at Southwold House. Hardy wrote to friends from there during his stay and Southwold must have remained happy in his memories as he married Florence Dugdale in February 1914. I regret that I have been unable to find any evidence of Southwold or indeed any part of coastal Suffolk having inspired any books by Thomas Hardy but who could know for sure, bearing in mind the emotional connections? There is, however, a suggestion that there may have been some influence that affected the portrayal of at least one of his characters, as well as part of a plot.

It is, therefore, worth mentioning, having regard to my conclusions on Hardy's apparent lack of any literary inspiration in Suffolk, that Florence Henniker was known to admire Hardy's genius as a writer. Hardy did, of course, respect her as a person, and perhaps loved her, in his own way, more than she ever knew. For many years, her friendship and loyalty were a great solace and comfort to him. His early idealisation of her is said to have been to have been transferred to the heroine, Sue Bridehead, in *Jude the Obscure*, and Mrs Henniker's perceived religious conventionality affected the book's ending. Hardy's idealisation settled into steady affection, constituting one of the two great and lasting friendships of his life - perhaps the most important of all. Between 1893 and 1922, Hardy and Florence Henniker wrote many letters to each other.

These were not written with posterity in mind, although Mrs Henniker did send them to Florence Hardy (née Dugdale), thinking that they might be useful in preparing a biography of her husband. Mrs Hardy thought the correspondence formed 'a most interesting whole', quite the best letters that her husband had ever written: she even considered publishing the letters in a limited edition. Subsequently, Florence Dugdale, a writer of books for children, published two volumes of Hardy's biography in 1928. This is a work said to have been at least part ghost-written by him as he spent some of the last years of his life dictating his life story, presumably to his wife and former secretary.

Hardy was also a frequent visitor to Aldeburgh as a member of an intellectual group whose members were invited by the previously mentioned Edward Clodd (1840-1930), at Whitsun of each year to

Strafford House, Crag Path, a residence quite close to where Benjamin Britten and, later, Mary Potter once lived. Hardy was fascinated by the town, if only because of having observed that he experienced 'the sensation of having nothing but the sea between you and the North Pole'. This leaves me wondering if he had this thought when in Southwold. It must be remembered that perhaps Benjamin Britten recognised Thomas Hardy's connections with Aldeburgh by setting eight of his poems about the fleetingness of experience, which contrast brief instances ('a boy's boredom on a long train ride, the creak of an old table, a certain light in the trees in November') against the unfeeling vastness of time. This is his musical work, *Winter Words* which was composed in 1953. This was first sung by Peter Pears at the 1954 Aldeburgh Festival.

I referred just a little earlier to a resident of Aldeburgh, Edward Clodd, a banker, writer and anthropologist, who had set out to cultivate a very wide circle of literary and scientific friends, being an author in his own right. His books included biographies of the naturalist, Charles Darwin (1809-1882) and a biologist, Thomas Huxley (1825-1895), known as 'Darwin's Bulldog' because of his advocacy of Darwin's theory of Evolution. Another biographical work was of Herbert Spencer (1820-1903), the philosopher and prominent classical liberal political theorist. Edward Clodd was also a sociological scholar of the Victorian era and was also responsible for studies to popularise evolution through books such as *The Childhood of the World and The Story of Creation: A Plain Account of Evolution*. Other visitors to Clodd's residence, apart from Thomas Hardy, accompanied by Florence Dugdale, included George Gissing (1857-1903), a writer with twenty-three novels to his name, and J M Barrie (1860-1937), who created Peter Pan, the boy who refused to grow up (first performed in 1904). There was also the distinguished science fiction author of *The Wars of the Worlds* (1898), H G Wells (1866-1946) so it was clear that our friend Clodd had substantial pulling power. It is worth mentioning that another member of this literary group was Edward FitzGerald whose work is covered elsewhere in this book. I understand that Clodd founded the *Omar Khayyam Club* and was, of course, the instigator of the floral tribute at FitzGerald's grave.

To expand the rather tenuous literary connections theme just a tad or so further, the author of many children's books, Roald Dahl (1916-

1990) based his story, *The Mildenhall Treasure* on a local ploughman named Gordon Burcher finding a hoard of Roman silver of unparalleled beauty and value. This event was described by the British Museum as 'one of the most iconic finds of the Roman period'.

Robert Louis Stevenson (1850-1894) often visited his uncle in Suffolk. This gentleman was the rector at Cockfield. Stevenson is said to have thought of the idea for *Treasure Island* on one of these visits. Some say that the character Long John Silver was possibly inspired by 'Peg Leg' Brinkley, a local road man. Whether or not this is true is, to my mind, irrelevant, on the grounds that it makes a nice story.

Wissett is a small village quite close to Halesworth and, in the year 1916, its inhabitants included artist Duncan Grant (1885-1978), writer David Garnett (1892-1981) and artist Vanessa Bell (1879-1961). What they had in common was that all were members of the Bloomsbury Group. Vanessa Bell's sister was writer, Virginia Woolf (1882-1941) who wrote, after a visit to the village, 'Wissett seems to lull asleep all ambition. Don't you think they have discovered the secret of life? I thought it wonderfully harmonious'. Although, in a letter to her sister, Woolf indicated that Vanessa's life there had attracted her interest, the experience seemed to have only a minor effect on her second novel, *Night and Day*. She began drafting this work during her stay. Sadly, that is virtually all I have found in connection with Woolf's short stay in Suffolk. I have certainly been unable to discover that any of her other work was inspired by the county, let alone its coastline, especially at Aldeburgh. In *The Common Reader* (1925) she wrote of the town '... that miserable, dull sea village'. Well, you can't please everybody can you? I am able to say with absolute certainty that Woolf's novel of high modernism, *To the Lighthouse* (1927) was totally unconnected with Southwold. I am aware, however, that she was a friend of Dame Edith Sitwell with whom she corresponded quite regularly. Dame Edith's connection with Benjamin Britten was mentioned earlier and you will learn later that she performed at the Aldeburgh Festival.

It may not be generally known but the village of Kessingland, south of Lowestoft and quite a fair way north of Southwold, was once the home of Sir Henry Rider Haggard (1856-1925), a prolific as well as popular writer of mainly adventure novels set in exotic locations, predominantly Africa. Probably his most famous work is *King Solomon's Mines*, which was published in 1885, but his 'Allan Quatermain' series of adventure books also sold well. Allan Quatermain is the protagonist of Rider Haggard's *King Solomon's Mines* and its various prequels and sequels. The Rider Haggard family lived in England from 1882-1925, following his return from Africa, and it was during this period that he resided in Kessingland.

Writing about Rider Haggard leads me to mention the artist, Maurice Greiffenhagen (1862-1931), a Royal Academician who visited Walberswick on a frequent basis, as a guest of Francis and Jessie Newberry at their home in 'Rooftree'. During the early years of the twentieth century, Greiffenhagen was illustrating Haggard's books. In those days, the author lived inland at Ditchingham House, near Bungay. Greiffenhagen was perhaps better known as a portrait painter and muralist although he was also responsible for painting some rich and colourful landscapes.

There is another writer, who is not strictly coastal Suffolk by way of residence, but he does live in the countryside, close to Bungay. This is a town that can sport more than one contemporary author. He is Louis de Bernières (born 1954) whose fourth novel and best known work, is a book that brought him to national prominence. It was *Captain Corelli's Mandolin*, published in 1994 when it won the Commonwealth Writers' Prize for Best Book. The Commonwealth Foundation established the Commonwealth Writers' Prize in 1987 in order to recognise the outstanding literary talent that exists in many parts of the Commonwealth, and also to ensure that works of merit written in English reach a wider audience outside their country of origin. Translated into at least eleven languages, this book has truly become an international bestseller and led to a popular movie. Other books have intriguing titles and I find myself speculating if these were chosen by the author. My guess is that the publisher's marketing department may have had something to do with them. Perhaps you could form your own opinion: the titles are *The War of Don Emmanuel's Nether Parts* (1990) and *The Troublesome Offspring of Cardinal Guzman* (1992). Sadly his book, *Notwithstanding: Stories from an English Village* (2010) does not appear to concern Suffolk but a village in Surrey, where he grew up.

A further, very successful author living happily in Bungay, a town that in the late seventeenth and early eighteenth century was regarded as a spa, is Elizabeth Jane Howard (born 1923). She told another interviewer that she bought her house ten minutes after first seeing it. Houses had always been important to her and her current home is looked upon as her harbour after a stormy life, including recent ill-health and an unfortunate emotional misjudgement when she was duped by a confidence trickster. She used that unfortunate experience in her novel, *Falling* (1999) which was later dramatised on ITV. There have been many other books and these include *Slipstream: A Memoir* (2002) and the *Cazalet Chronicle* that comprises four volumes, *The Light Years*, *Marking Time*, *Confusion* and *Casting Off*. This family saga has been described as a classic and was set to become a major BBC Television drama, *The Cazalets* (2001) although, for reasons best known to the BBC, not all of the episodes were shown or indeed made in accordance with the original expectations. This left any completed adaptations of the final two volumes of the original books in the series failing to reach the nation's screens. Period drama never seems to diminish in popularity and this left me wondering if any independent production company might consider undertaking a major series to take in all four of the books if the estate of television and film producer, Verity Lambert (1935-2007) could be persuaded to part with the rights. Then, lo and behold, I read that at the age of 89 Jane Howard is busy writing a fifth volume. Moreover, BBC Radio 4 is engaged in dramatising at least the first four volumes, so it must be better late than never again. Re-visiting the Cazalet family after a literary absence of about seventeen years or so, Elizabeth Jane Howard must feel that she is meeting up with old friends, but instead of them telling her what they have been up to she is telling them as her imagination creates new scenes involved with their daily lives and family comings and goings.

Elizabeth Jane Howard, CBE (awarded in the Queen's Birthday Honours List, 2002, the monarch's Golden Jubilee Year) has been married three times in all. Her first husband was Sir Peter Scott (1909-1989), the naturalist and artist son of Captain Robert Falcon Scott of the Antarctic. Secondly and certainly most famously, from a literary point of view, was the author, Kingsley Amis (1922-1995). Amongst her circle of friends have been poet and novelist, Laurie Lee (1914-1997) and author, Arthur Koestler (1905-1983), novelist and poet with whom she had an affair, as well as Olivia Manning (1908-1980). Included with others were Cyril Connolly, controversial theatre critic and writer Kenneth Tynan (1927-1980), a friend of Kingsley Amis from his post-war Oxford days, and former Poet Laureate, Cecil Day-Lewis (1904-1972). It will be seen that she has outlived them all and she has had an incredible wealth of experience to draw upon for her excellent writing. Incidentally, Tynan, as revealed in John Lahr's *The Diaries of Kenneth Tynan*, claims that Elizabeth Jane Howard was once his mistress. This snippet was recorded by Tynan after attending a dinner party in April 1976 at what he described as the palatial home in Barnet of Kingsley Amis and his wife 'Jane'. This house was called 'Lemmons' and appropriately enough was once the home of writer and literary hostess, Frances Trollope, mother of the more well-known novelist, Anthony Trollope. It appears that on the particular evening when the Tynans were guests, Kingsley Amis went on one of his usual rants against socialism, whereby he accused Tynan, a self-confessed libertarian socialist, of gathering evidence against the host, there and then, in order to connive at Amis's execution by the powers-that-be in a British police state. This had been too much for Kenneth Tynan, who immediately left the gathering with his wife, Kathleen. The diarist later came to the conclusion that Amis was what psychoanalysts would call a monosymptomatic neurotic, a person who is rational on every subject but one, in this particular case, socialism. All I can add here is that Elizabeth Jane Howard must have participated in some mightily entertaining dinner parties when she was married to Kingsley Amis but I am wondering if she would view the experiences in precisely this manner. Having now met her, I am inclined to think that she would have, although she may not have been overjoyed at the degree of resentment she must have experienced at the hands of Kingsley's sons, Martin and Philip, by his marriage to Hilly. Howard and Amis had first met at the Cheltenham Literary Festival in October 1962, when the theme was, perhaps appropriately, 'Sex in Literature'. They married in June 1965 and within only a year or two an artist, Sargy Mann, was describing his moving in to a turbulent household, having previously become a frequent visitor. As it happened, it was Mann who discovered in Philip a nascent interest in painting. He then encouraged him to enrol at the Camberwell School of Art but there was nothing even approaching a supportive response from his father. Philip has since gone on to establish something of a reputation as a collagist. In turn, Jane Howard has revealed that she was responsible for Martin Amis starting to read 'properly', having introduced him to the book *Pride and Prejudice* after he had announced to her that he wanted to be a writer. She felt that perhaps he should start some serious reading before he got too far advanced in his early ambition. So he set out on his path to becoming what an article in *The Times* described in 2008 as 'one of the fifty greatest British writers since 1945'. Other people have gone further, but he has had his fair share of criticism over the years, as did his father. It seems clear from what I have read, that in the early days of her marriage to Kingsley Amis the two boys took more to Jane's brother, Colin 'Monkey' Howard than they did to her. But I suppose this was a natural reaction from sons who regarded their stepmother as wholly responsible for the break-up of the their father's marriage to Hilly.

Not being one to ignore a connection here and there and bearing in mind the Freud family's connection with coastal Suffolk, I have been unable to resist mentioning that Kingsley Amis regarded Freudianism as having been instrumental in fewer deaths than Nazism and Marxism. However, in his view, it is 'surely one of the great pernicious doctrines of the twentieth century with its denial of free will and personal responsibility'. He did, however, recognise some redeeming features in its ability in 'solving or seeming to solve (the secrets about people's inner selves) where other forms of therapy seem merely to uncover more questions'. Having regard to how Sigmund Freud brought about what has been described as one of the great revolutions of how we think of ourselves, Tynan could well have a point ... if you come to think about it! All this would seem to be an intriguing subject for debate if any dinner party appears should appear to be in danger of running out of conversational steam.

As a footnote to the subject, it was Elizabeth Jane Howard who took the initiative in the break-up of her marriage to Kingsley Amis, the principal cause being his reluctance to give up his over-fondness for alcohol.

I did not raise any of these matters when I called upon this well-known author, by special arrangement. But when I referred to her connections with people associated with coastal Suffolk, she soon began telling me that she knew the artist, Lucian Freud, and his late brother, Clement (known as Clay), when they were all in their mid-teens, having been born within eighteen months of each other. She also knew Anna Freud (1895-1982) their aunt and the sixth and last daughter of Sigmund Freud. Anna had followed in the same field as her father and made her own contribution to the then, newly-born field of psychoanalysis.

Jane Howard also mentioned John, the son of her music teacher, Harold Craxton, a Professor of Pianoforte at the Royal College of Music. Craxton's mother, Essie Craxton was a promising violinist but raising her family and being a generous and necessarily busy host put paid to any thought of a career in music. This reminds me of how Jill Raymond, the stage name of Jill Freud, gave up her own already successful acting career to raise their family while Clement was employing his varied talents in the task of earning a living to keep them all.

John Craxton (1922-2009) became a successful artist in the 1940s Neo-Romantic Movement. He shared a flat with Lucian Freud in Abercorn Place, St John's Wood as well as a studio during the early war years. Their patron, Peter Watson (1908-1956), was a well-known arts benefactor and owner of *Horizon*, the literary magazine that was said to have been originally founded by Cyril Connolly and Stephen Spender, who was editor from 1939-1941. Watson not only paid their rent but also introduced the young painters to such figures as the previously mentioned John Piper, Graham Sutherland and Augustus John as well as the art historian Kenneth Clark. Clark occasionally called in at the St John's Wood flat dressed in tweeds and a country cap, and was soon giving Craxton and Freud the run of his Hampstead library as well as being proactive in buying their pictures. Both Cyril Connolly and Stephen Spender were also friends of Elizabeth Jane Howard. Jane Howard kept up with Natasha, Spender's widow, a former concert pianist, until her death at the age of 91 in October 2010. She had married Spender, ten years her senior, in 1941, at the height of the blitz, with one of her new husband's most significant ex-boyfriends acting as one of the witnesses. Notwithstanding Stephen Spender's admitted early homosexual experiences, the pair enjoyed an unusually happy marriage.

Despite being in very poor health Natasha continued to visit Jane Howard in Suffolk during in her later years, being driven there by

Colin, Jane Howard's brother who we are now aware is known to her as 'Monkey'. Having written that, I cannot help myself thinking how just many connections there are between this prolific author and a meaningful number of people mentioned in this book. One could be forgiven for thinking that during the twentieth century most of them ended up in coastal Suffolk for one reason or another. I will refrain from reeling off all of the names but Sitwell (an admirer of Orwell), Britten, Auden, Plomer and, of course, Piper come immediately to mind.

Looking back over the years, Jane Howard just sensed that 'Johnny' Craxton was going to be successful in that he had a very sharp eye, having found a Reynolds as well as a Blake in junk shops. Over the following decade, John Craxton spent much of his time travelling in southern Europe, first settling on Poros, where he was visited by his old friend Freud. They sketched each other and exchanged the drawings, as was their custom in the old days. Back in London, Craxton joined his old friend at the gaming club, Aspinalls in Mayfair. Over scrambled eggs and champagne, Freud told his friend that, desperate for money, he had sold the drawings Craxton had given him, adding 'You don't mind, do you?' Some time later Craxton too found himself strapped for cash, and was persuaded to sell some Freud drawings. When these were put up for sale in London, Freud was called upon to authenticate them. 'Craxton is a ****', he wrote on the back, which did no harm at all to their value. Getting back to Craxton's art, he disliked being called a Neo-Romantic and preferred to be known as an Arcadian; in other words, simply and poetically rural. He lived and painted a great deal in Greece and Crete and also took time out to illustrate many dust jackets for books written by Sir Patrick Leigh-Fermor (1915-2011), a noted travel writer, war hero and long-term correspondent with Deborah, Duchess of Devonshire (born 1920), née Mitford. John Craxton was elected a Royal Academician in 1993. His last London exhibition was at *Art First* in 2001 and some of his works were exhibited at the Peter Pears Gallery at the time of the sixty-third Aldeburgh Festival of Music and the Arts 2010. Peter Pears was a patron and collector of work by John Craxton along with other artists and during the Festival a seminar took place, based upon works in the exhibition. Earlier, in April that year, an event in memory of the late artist was held at the British Embassy in Athens. This was attended by friends and people close to him and these included 'Paddy'

Fermor, a long term resident of Greece who died in June 2011 at the age of 96. His obituary described him as one of the few genuine Renaissance figures produced by Britain in the twentieth century. Craxton's association with Greece had dated back to the mid-1940s. In the 1960s, Craxton settled in Hania, Crete, in a house facing the old harbour. He led a simple bohemian life, appreciated the local lifestyle and explored the country's cultural history, especially the Byzantine churches on the island. For many years, he also served as Britain's consular correspondent in Hania.

Continuing these connections, William Plomer was Jane Howard's editor at Jonathan Cape when she was with that publisher but she had not been aware of his association with Benjamin Britten at Snape and Aldeburgh. She had been present at the first performance of *Gloriana* at Covent Garden but had been unaware that her editor was responsible for the libretto.

Jane Howard also remembers Lennox Berkeley the composer who, as we have learned, had close relationships of both a professional and personal nature with Benjamin Britten. Berkeley was married and had two sons, one of whom, Michael (born 1948) was a former chorister at Westminster Cathedral where he frequently sang in works composed by his godfather, Benjamin Britten. Michael Berkeley became a composer after studying with composer and jazz performer, Richard Rodney Bennett (born 1936). Before that, Berkeley learned composition, piano and singing at the Royal Academy of Music.

Jane Howard told me that she never had a formal education, learning French from a series of governesses and being educated in other subjects from the age of eleven, also by a governess, Miss Cobham, a woman of 'good intellect with an encyclopedic knowledge'. Howard considers herself to be a self-taught, natural writer having written in one form or another since she was aged only eight. When she was young, she had wanted to be an actress and she wrote her first play, which she described as a domestic comedy, at a very early age. She emphasised that she is also a great reader and her home is certainly full of packed bookshelves, although she confesses that she does have a bit of a clear-out every now and again. When questioned on recent reading she mentioned the entire output of Anthony Trollope (1815-1882), George Orwell (*Burmese*

Days 1934), Leo Tolstoy's (1828-1910) *War and Peace* and, of course, William Shakespeare, saying that she reads one of his sonnets each night.

She recalls travelling with her friend, John Betjeman in Norfolk for a few days when he was looking at churches. She described him as a 'lovely man' and she misses him dearly. Having been married to Kingsley Amis for so many years she particularly recalls how much she enjoyed her husband and Betjeman having a pleasant evening of jokey humour, describing their conversation as very funny indeed.

Elizabeth Jane Howard, who now suffers very badly from arthritis and is unable to manage gardening any more, lives in a wonderful period house in idyllic surroundings that include a lovely garden, a well-kept meadow and a bridge that leads to a quite magical island on the River Waveney. With her indulgently kind permission, I enjoyed a brief walk there on a beautiful sunny morning when I was able to admire masses of spring bulbs in full colour as well as vast numbers of splendid trees and shrubs. The island itself has several creeks of its own where wildfowl seemed to be in abundance: all in all, a private nature reserve that has enjoyed very close attention from its literary owner over the last twenty years. I cannot imagine more inspirational surroundings in which to work. I was struck by one of the near closing sentences in Jane Howard's memoir, *Slipstream*. I quote 'One of the good things about living longer is that we have more time to learn how to be old'. With this reflection in mind, she goes on to refer to what she describes as 'the possibility of art' when in old age. She regards this attitude 'can be made into something worth trying to do well, a challenge, an adventure'. I have written those words with the image in my mind of Elizabeth Jane Howard, sitting at her desk, surrounded by all the paraphernalia required by a writer, including what must be thousands of her books. It was only when driving home that I got the impression that I had been granted the privilege of an audience with a woman with an undoubted stately presence but this was counter-balanced by friendly disclosures from her colourful past and the anecdotes about her literary friends. Her attitude towards me may well have been influenced by the keen interest I demonstrated in her wonderful garden and magical riverside island. I like to think it did anyway.

The beautiful environmental landscape that I have described is also enjoyed by a close neighbour, the previously mentioned distinguished artist, Sargy Mann who was responsible for introducing Jane Howard to her new home in 1990. In turn, it was a visit to Jane Howard's home that prompted Louis de Bernières to find his present home, nearby in South Norfolk.

Another close friend of Jane Howard, Booker Prizewinner, Penelope Lively (born 1933) OBE, CBE had, or maybe has, a country residence not too far away, although, from what I have read she writes nowadays in her London home. However, she did once work as an assistant in a Southwold bookshop and even wrote a novel, *The Bookshop* (1978) that was set in a fictional East Anglian town, Hardborough. This is obviously an author who views some of her experiences in life as a creative writing opportunity. Her Booker winner in 1979 was set amongst the Battersea houseboat community as a result of having once lived on a houseboat moored on that particular reach of the Thames. Lively is another prolific author - many children's books as well as two volumes of autobiography, in addition to many novels intended to please her far more mature readers. She has also written numerous short stories that have appeared in collected editions. Her connection with the area is underlined by *Corruption*, only one of a collection of no less than thirty-four short stories entitled *Pack of Cards: Stories* (1978-1986). The plot of *Corruption* is set in Aldeburgh. One can sit back and only admire this lady's impressive level of productivity over the years. This particular short story features a judge and his wife, aged in their sixties, on holiday at the seaside but with the intention of paying one of their regular visits to the Aldeburgh Festival. Quite innocently, they find themselves victims of a thoroughly embarrassing, not to say very uncomfortable, misunderstanding. I was soon wondering why the author chose Aldeburgh as the setting for this tale, other than the fact that she considered the town and its reputation represented the least likely resort for what had so discomforted the distinguished visitors. On the other hand, I have come across a lengthy feature article that she wrote for the New York Times in 1991 which suggested a more than very useful knowledge of coastal Suffolk. *Entitled Essex to Suffolk: 3 Country Inns* she describes, in loving detail, the areas around Southwold, Blythburgh, Snape and Dunwich. It is certainly clear to me that she has a very useful familiarity with this area and this was not attained solely by putting in an appearance at the *Ways with Words' Literary Festival* in Southwold in 2009. All in all, I have traced that she has written no less than twenty-eight children's' books, nineteen novels and three works of non-fiction including *A House Unlocked* which is all about Golsoncott, the country house in Somerset her grandparents bought in 1923 and which was occupied by her family virtually throughout the whole of the twentieth century.

Not too far away from the Suffolk coast, or indeed Bungay, is the town of Beccles, so I have decided to include Adrian Bell (1901-1980), farmer, journalist and author of the classic rural trilogy, *Corduroy* (1930), *Silver Ley* (1931) and *The Cherry Tree* (1932) as well as a number of other books. Taken together, the three volumes that formed the trilogy have been described 'as the classic account of a twentieth century Englishman's conversion to rural life'. His writing is richly laced with humour and shrewd observation of what happens when you actually do 'go back to the land'. He was first apprenticed at the farm at Farley Hall, Darsham, no more than four miles inland from Dunwich. As the farmer that he chose to become, Bell worked the land in one form or another in a number of locations over the next sixty years. In Corduroy he recalls: 'I was upon the fringe of Suffolk, a county rich in agricultural detail, previously missed by my untutored eye. It was not but scenery to me, nor had I any inkling of what it might become.' When he retired from farming, but thankfully not from writing, he lived at 19 Northgate, Beccles where a plaque can be seen commemorating his stay there from 1954 to 1964. He is also famous for compiling the first Times crossword and although he disputed that he had any knowledge of the subject, he went on compiling them for the next fifty years. He is buried in Barsham churchyard, just on the Suffolk side of the River Waveney and about ten to twelve miles north of the village where he served his agricultural apprenticeship.

Writing about matters relating to the countryside is another author who has specialised in this genre, but who has also expanded his repertoire into gastronomically-related matters. He is none other than Richard Mabey (born 1941) whose book *Food for Free* has been re-printed many times since first appearing in 1972. He is a prize-winning writer, conservationist, naturalist and broadcaster who in the first year of recovery after illness moved to the Waveney Valley, the borderland between Suffolk and Norfolk, living south of the river near Reydon, just a mile or two from Southwold. As far as I am aware he now lives and works near Diss but he certainly qualifies for inclusion if only because I find his books irresistibly interesting. I live quite near the Suffolk Wildlife Trust's centre at Lopham and Redgrave Fen and have spent many a blissful hour there wandering the paths and observing the wildlife. I would venture to suggest that Mr Mabey may not be a complete stranger to those parts, if only for the fact that the source of the River Waveney can be found within the fen's borders.

The large number of books written by Richard Mabey includes *The Unofficial Countryside* (1973 – a later edition was illustrated by Mary Newcomb qv), *The Flowering of Britain* (1980), *The Flowering of Kew* (1988) and *Nature Cure* (2005). The latter work describes his experiences of, as well as recovery from, a depressive illness but in the context of man's relationship with landscape and nature. The latter book was short-listed for three major literary awards. Richard Mabey contributes frequently to BBC radio. '*The Scientist and the Romantic*', a series of five essays in which he discussed his lifelong relationship with science and the natural environment, was broadcast on BBC Radio 3 in 2009. All in all, Mabey has been an exceedingly busy man and he has been described by *The Times* as 'Britain's greatest living nature writer'. He has also written for *The Guardian*, *The Independent*, *Granta* (a quarterly magazine that tackles some of the world's most important subjects) and *Resurgence*, another magazine dedicated to matters 'at the heart of earth, art and spirit'. A selection of these writings from 1973-1999 was compiled as the book, *Country Matters* (2000). He has also written a personal column in *BBC Wildlife Magazine* since 1984.

Another contemporary writer, of fiction and non-fiction, as well being a broadcaster, theatre critic and columnist for *The Times* newspaper is Libby Purves (born 1950). She lives with her husband, Paul Heiney (born 1949), also a writer and presenter, including both national as well as regional TV, in the village of Westleton, home to artists in addition to Chapel Books, a regional curiosity featured later. The well-known married couple have been keen sailors over the years and Heiney's *The Last Man Across the Atlantic* (2006) is his own account of sailing that ocean single-handed. Other books of Paul Heiney have been on a variety of subjects dear to his heart such as farming, not to mention some with rather original slants on farm livestock. Purves remains a columnist with *Yachting Monthly* and she enjoys a well-deserved reputation as a social commentator.

The couple suffered a very tragic loss with the death of their son, Nicholas Heiney (1982-2006) and the book, *The Silence at the Song's End* presents the collected journals and poetry of Nicholas who took his own life at the age of only twenty-three. These vivid writings about his adventures sailing on the Atlantic and Pacific Oceans, in true family tradition, together with his poetry, remained undiscovered until after he died. His parents were urged to publish the work by Prof. Duncan Wu of Oxford University, Nick's former tutor, who realised the depth and maturity in the prose. This is described as exemplary in its sanity and clear-sightedness. Libby Purves and Duncan Wu acted as editors of this work and I found the book quite extraordinarily good reading, given the heart-rending background.

To complete the family's literary credentials I now come to Rose Heiney (born 1984), daughter to Paul and Libby. Rose wrote, as her first novel, T*he Days of Judy B* (2008), a work that was described by Victoria Hislop, author of *The Island* and other fine works, as 'one of the funniest, most profound and most affecting books I have ever read. It has literally blown me away'. Rose was nominated as a 'Hotshot' - one to watch - by *Broadcast Magazine* in 2009 and she won Best New Comedy Writer in the 4Talent Awards in 2008. She has also worked as an actress, appearing with Julia McKenzie in an Agatha Christie 'Miss Marple' TV production, *A Pocket Full of Rye* (2008). Rose played Gladys, a parlour maid who proved to be the murder victim. Her appearance attracted critical attention; otherwise I would not have discovered this item.

Before leaving this family, I am aware that Libby Purves and no doubt other members are loyal supporters of Southwold's Summer Theatre, a subject I will be writing about in a later chapter. The Heineys have been known to make it even more of an occasion by braving the odd picnic on the beach, notwithstanding the challenges provided by an English summer, not to mention the vagaries of the North Sea. Ms Purves is a champion of theatre in the United Kingdom and whilst commenting in a national newspaper on Britain's successes in the prestigious Tony awards in New York she wrote about the wealth of talent punching above their weight in the provinces. She singled out for special mention the Eastern Angles theatre company touring around the East of England and beyond, including visits to the Edinburgh Festival. This company mounted a spectacular, site-specific production entitled *Bentwaters Road*, set in an old USAF hangar near Woodbridge in Suffolk. This well-received work served to revive memories of the Cold War. Another of their regional productions was *I Caught Crabs in Walberswick* (2008) which was about three sixteen-year-olds and a period of twenty-four hours that changed their lives forever. Incidentally, Eastern Angles was formed in 1982, a date which is remarkably close to December 1983 when Jill Freud and her company, then a small group touring popular classics in East Anglia and the regions, took their production entitled *A Jolly Berry Christmas* to St Edmund's Hall, Southwold. It will be seen that this was when the hall Committee asked Jill if she would consider presenting the summer season in the town for 1984. It will be learned in Part Four that Jill and her team have been operating there ever since.

Chapter Three

An Aldeburgh Festival lecturer and some modern and latter day writers of note

OVER THE YEARS, the lectures at Aldeburgh have formed an integral feature of the festival and the planning has been both ingenious and inspired. Dame Edith Sitwell, who remains regarded as the queen of English twentieth century poetry, certainly lectured there and stayed at the Wentworth Hotel. I am inclined to the view that this was on or about 21 June 1956. It seems that on this particular occasion she was anxious about form and not wishing to speak for too long she was said to have asked the advice of a hotel housemaid. 'Would half an hour be too long?' was her question to the bemused member of staff. In any event the maid seemed to have misheard, thinking that Sitwell had said an hour and a half and answered 'Yes' whereupon Dame Edith cut her talk down to no more than twenty minutes. As a result, Kenneth Clark, the chairman for the evening, somewhat desperately, given the circumstances, found it necessary to fill in time so that the audience wouldn't feel too deprived as a result of Dame Edith's accidental brevity. This was at the 1956 Festival, one year before Britten and Pears relocated to The Red House, from where he later wrote to Edith Sitwell about the move. His words, in describing their new home, stated that the house was 'alas, away from the sea, but thankfully away from the gaping faces, and irritating publicity of that sea-front'.

The Red House, Aldeburgh

For the 1956 Festival, Britten had devised a sequence of Edith Sitwell poems in which she could take part as speaker, with some of the poems being spoken and others sung. This programme was entitled *The Heart of the Matter*. The work was revived in a shortened version by Peter Pears at London's Wigmore Hall in 1983 and some additional settings were published in 1994. Incidentally, Sitwell's 1956 visit to Aldeburgh must have been something of a burden for her because of her physical frailty at that time. She was almost seventy by then and complained, in a letter to Stephen Spender, of the pain from arthritis in both knees as well as acute rheumatism in both feet. She also suffered from frequent attacks of sciatica and, as a result, she was often able to walk only with the aid of a stick. She wrote '... I could not put my feet to the ground when I reached Liverpool Street Station, and had to be carried out of the train, wheeled along the platform in a truck, and carried into my club'. This leaves me wondering if Benjamin Britten had been made aware of what a considerable effort that journey to the Aldeburgh Festival must have been for the ailing poet. On the other hand, I prefer to regard her considerable discomfort as a wonderful personal tribute to the composer and his work.

Sitwell was a friend of both Britten and Pears and *Still Falls the Rain*, about the London blitz, remains perhaps the best known of her poems. This work was set to music by Benjamin Britten as *Canticle III: Still Falls the Rain*. Dame Edith wrote to the composer after the first performance on 28 January 1955 at the Wigmore Hall as follows:

'I am so haunted and so alone with that wonderful music and its wonderful performance that I was incapable of writing before now. I had no sleep at all on the night of the performance. And I can think of nothing else. It was certainly one of the greatest experiences in all my life as an artist...I can never begin to thank you for the glory you have given my poem...'

In turn, her poem *The Bee-Keeper* was set to music by Priaulx Rainier (1903-1986), as *The Bee Oracles* (1970), a setting for tenor, flute, oboe, violin, cello and harpsichord. It was premièred by Peter Pears in 1970. Rainier was a composer of South African birth and Peter Pears and the Purcell Singers gave the first performance of her Requiem (1956; tenor and unaccompanied chorus) at the Aldeburgh Festival of that year. All in all, I am glad I have been successful in establishing these Sitwell connections with Aldeburgh as I feel it is well worth recording and serves also to illustrate how Britten enjoyed employing the creative work of his friends in his music. Dame Edith died in 1964 and at the seventeenth Aldeburgh Festival in that year a notable success was Malcolm Williamson's piece of 'operatic entertainment' based upon her book, *English Eccentrics*. This work was originally published in 1933, although it has since been subject to some updating. Williamson's music has been described as containing some catchy parodies of the popular music of its day and is felt to be a fitting memorial to an exceptional character, although I feel sure that it was never intended as such at the time the book was written. Sitwell had been working with Williamson (1931-2003) in anticipation of the Aldeburgh performance during 1963 at a time that she had remained far from well. It must have been her indomitable spirit that kept her going.

Apropos of nothing as far as coastal Suffolk is concerned, but something I came across during the course of my research, has led me to tell you about Edith Sitwell and a Russian painter by the name of Pavel Tchelitchew (1898-1957). Strangely, she preferred to spell the name Tchelicheff. Whatever the correct spelling, it is claimed that Sitwell fell in love with this artist during the year 1927, when she was aged about forty. I have seen references in Dame Edith's letters that her relationship with Tchelitchew was said to be 'special', but also a difficult one in that she had felt hurt by his behaviour on more than one occasion. However, she seemed to have a high regard the artist's work, going as far as to compare it favourably with that of the painter of the Spanish Renaissance, El Greco (1541-1614). Sitwell had never married and the fact that Tchelitchew proved to be homosexual did not seem to deter her amorous interest in him. I came across a reference to the two of them in an essay by Myfanwy Piper entitled *The Portrait Question*. In this she sets out to explain the relationship between a painter and his (her) subject, described as:

> 'almost a marriage, built up during the time that the portrait is being painted, founded, not on what casual conversation may go between them, but upon the silent message from the bones and the skin to the painter's eye'.

I found this fascinating, particularly as, within this volume, I have referred to the various styles of portrait painters such as Lucian

Freud and Maggi Hambling as well as their particular needs from their subjects. At one stage, my research indicated that the relationship between poet and artist lasted not much more than a year but I then discovered that they kept up a correspondence, at least from 1929-1957. Myfanwy Piper wrote that Tchelitchew painted Edith Sitwell's full-length portrait in the early thirties. According to Piper this painting belonged to Edward James (1907-1984), a wealthy life-long patron of the arts, and hangs in the Tate Gallery, or it did at the time she wrote her piece. James specialised in collecting works by artists such as Salvador Dali (1904-1989) as well as Tchelitchew. This was when the output of these artists was by no means fashionable; James was shown thus to be a man who was ahead of his time. In doing this, he perhaps unintentionally amassed what has come to be accepted as one of the finest collections of surrealist art in Europe. This does not appear to have been the only portrait that Tchelitchew did of Sitwell as I have discovered another by him, but this was of head and shoulders only. This is in the possession of the University of Texas. Piper described the full-length portrait as having all the paraphernalia of the artist's surrealist affinities as follows:

'The details are emphatic and ugly; the furniture of the picture fanciful, almost false: in no respect has he underlined the natural beauty of her face - nothing is conceded. Yet it is a beautiful, affecting and convincing portrait of poet and woman'.

In 1948, a reunion with Tchelitchew, whom she had not seen since before the war, went badly and this seems rather sad for a woman who seemed to have had little such romance in her life, unless I am very much mistaken.

Edward James' connection with Dali reminds me that Dame Edith introduced James to Dylan Thomas, whom he sponsored for a while. Through Dali, James also met Sigmund Freud ... and so the Suffolk coast connections, some albeit a little on the remote side, go on and on.

Although the above two paragraphs form an admitted diversion from the theme of this book, there is a tenuous connection with Aldeburgh because W H Auden knew Pavel Tchelitchew through a mutual friend, Lincoln Kirstein (1907-1996), an American writer, impresario, art connoisseur, and cultural figure in New York City. Auden's *Vespers*, probably written in 1954, in the sequence *Horae Canonicae* opens with this verse paragraph:

'If the hill overlooking our city has always been known as Adam's Grave, only at dusk can you see the recumbent giant, his head turned to the west, his right arm resting for ever on Eve's haunch...'

This hill is not Auden's invention. It was suggested by a painting made in 1940 by Pavel Tchelitchew and entitled *Fata Morgana* (Derby Hill Theme, Summer). It really is a small world. Tchelitchew's painting corresponds closely, but not precisely, to the poem. Auden, not Tchelitchew, seems to have identified the two figures with Adam and Eve and added the detail that Adam's head is turned in the Utopian direction of the west. Auden has the male figure's right arm resting on the female figure's 'haunch'; Tchelitchew has the male figure's left arm resting on the female figure's thigh. Auden probably saw *Fata Morgana* either in Tchelitchew's studio or in the collection of Ruth Ford, where the painting is now. It seems to have been reproduced only after the poem was written.

Fata Morgana by Pavel Tchelitchew

But what of the more contemporary writers associated, in one way or another with coastal and even other parts of Suffolk? Ruth Rendell, a well-known writer of crime fiction for many years, has also written of the county as well as its literary connections. I was interested to read that it is Ruth Rendell who has regarded Aldeburgh's George Crabbe as 'the poet of the poor who wrote about the neighbourhood of the sea and the people of the coast, drawing character from life and apparently unaware that it is possible to create fiction from the imagination'. This present-day writer is clearly aware that this is precisely what authors Esther Freud, P D James and Julie Myerson do nowadays, let alone Rendell herself and her equally famous *nom de plume*, Barbara Vine.

It is not too difficult to reel off names of authors associated in one way or another with coastal Suffolk. This is not necessarily only in the area between say Southwold and Aldeburgh and perhaps a few miles inland. I have strayed even further afield, but seldom too far from the coast. The question is, were these people attracted by landscapes and seascapes or by what they perceived as the beguiling atmosphere of the general area? Perhaps it has been, and continues to be, a combination of factors: these include considerable peace and quiet that has, to a significant extent, remained virtually unchanged for decades or even, as some might say, over more than a few centuries. On the other hand, perhaps this would be going a little too far.

I have certainly come across recent novels written by authors who have made no attempt to disguise the locations for their plots. In some cases, I have recognised the use of the writer's personal experiences, family connections and local personalities, not to mention rather quaint historical facts. What has made such writing attractive to the reader is the added bonus of knowing exactly where certain of the fictional events have taken place, as far as the imagination of the author is concerned. Maybe it is not too fanciful to suggest that some devoted readers may have gone so far as to follow in the footsteps of certain characters, perhaps even the fictional murderers.

Julie Myerson (born 1960), a resident of Southwold, although not all the year round, dedicated her novel, *Something Might Happen* to a fellow author, Esther Freud. Added to Ms Myerson's dedication were the words '- who understands about the place'. That really intrigued me because I found her book totally absorbing and the subject matter quite unlike anything I had ever read before. She dealt with the intense and innermost of personal feelings of her characters with admirable dexterity. This left me wondering just how long she had taken over the choice of words when dealing with the riveting descriptions of what runs through a person's mind when the most unimaginably horrific events have taken place in the lives of loved ones. Julie Myerson does most of her intensive writing on her regular visits to Suffolk, somewhere where she feels that she can get away from the necessary chores of normal life. She confesses that when she decides to write another novel it is usually with a blank sheet of paper in front of her, although not literally. It could be the bare bones of an idea and sometimes even less. Myerson describes this feeling as being in a dark room when someone lights a candle that highlights say an object of some description. This starts her off and she describes that, when she is nearing the end of the narrative, the same room is suddenly very bright and everything has become clear. Quite predictably, she sums up her description of that particular phenonomen as a very nice feeling. I suppose every author has some sort of intensely personal method for their writing activity but this is the first time I have heard about anything quite like that. Whatever else might inspire Julie Myerson, what she has described does seem to work rather well. She has now written eight novels, the first being *Sleepwalking* in 1994 and the latest, *Then* (2011). Her advice to budding writers of fiction is to make a very real effort to set aside specific time to start writing, if there really is a desire to make it happen. She also recommends reading first novels of other authors so that people can see and appreciate for themselves what it takes for a new author to be published for the first time. All this seems to be pretty good advice. For my own part, I often hear people say, 'I have always wanted to write a book' to which my rejoinder is invariably 'Well, why don't you then?' That tends to end the conversation on that particular subject.

Esther Freud, in *The Sea House* (2003), her fifth novel, devised a plot that bears more than a casual association with local events in the village of Walberswick. She made use of characters and even family connections, all of which were cleverly disguised, in a creative work that she dedicated to her father, Lucian Freud (1922– 2011) who died after a short but grave illness, aged 88. The plot of *The Sea House* features an invitation to an artist to visit the fictional village of Steerborough in order to assist his recovery from a recent bereavement. To pass the time he set about painting every house in the village. We shall learn later the fact that John Doman Turner, a prolific and innovative amateur watercolour artist, completed a strikingly similar work in the village of Walberswick in the summer of 1931. It is not entirely coincidental because this obviously inspired Esther Freud to include this notable event in her creative fiction. Members of the Freud clan have strong connections with Walberswick, dating back to before the Second World War. Esther Freud's uncle, and accordingly brother to Lucian Freud, was the late Sir Clement Freud (1924-2009), Jill Freud's husband, a renowned raconteur and wit who enjoyed a varied career of some eccentricity. Earlier, in another novel of Esther Freud, namely *Summer at Gaglow* (first published in 1997 as just *Gaglow*), the action takes place in Germany during the First World War as well as seventy-five years later in London. One of the modern characters is a painter engaged upon a nude study of his daughter, the book's modern narrator. At first, she was merely pregnant but when the baby was born he too became part of the painting and therefore subject to very close attention by the artist.

All three of these novels draw upon locations and people that are well known to the writers and I am sure it would not be too difficult to find other examples. Interestingly, a short story by Esther Freud entitled The Visit, derived from the work-in-progress associated with *The Sea House*, was included in an anthology compiled by Peter Tolhurst. Having read both, I can now better appreciate how vital it must be for the writer to develop characters and live with their actions and emotions whilst the story unfolds and comes to its revealing climax. Short stories can often leave the reader wanting more and it was refreshing, in this particular case, to be in a position whereby I was able to become aware of the entire story. Incidentally, Peter Tolhurst founded Black Dog Books in 1996, a well-established East Anglian publisher. He is also the author of *East Anglia: a Literary Pilgrimage* published by his company in the same year. He also wrote *Wessex: a Literary Pilgrimage* with a foreword by Ronald Blythe.

Most, but not quite all, of what I have written about the coastal village of Walberswick and its many attractions concerns the numerous artists who have been inspired there. With this in mind, you can imagine how thrilled I was to come across a poet who was so stimulated by the enchanting atmosphere of the place during his lengthy stay at the Old Yacht Yard, next to the site of the old car ferry, over three seasons in 1956-57, that he wrote no less than thirty-six verses on this theme. This work was published under the title *Moons and Tides* to which was added *Walberswick* in a volume of his collected poetry that was released in 2001. The poet is Oliver Bernard (born 1925) who now lives in the village near the Norfolk-Suffolk borders where I have made my own home. To add an interesting twist to this connection, Oliver's younger brother was the late Jeffrey Bernard (1932-1997), a journalist who was famous for writing the regular and long-running Low Life column in the Spectator. Jeffrey was later immortalised on stage by Peter O'Toole in *Jeffrey Bernard is Unwell*, a play first performed in 1989 and written by Keith Waterhouse (1929-2009). Waterhouse was not only a playwright but also a novelist, newspaper columnist and the writer of many television series. The comedy's title refers to the magazine's traditional one-line apology on a blank page whenever Bernard was either too drunk or hung-over to produce the required copy before the deadline for publication. It goes without saying that the editor invariably found it difficult, in these circumstances, to rustle up a substitute article before going to press. Jeffrey Bernard's column has been described as 'a suicide note in weekly instalments'. His habitual watering place was the Coach and Horses, a stubbornly grubby pub in London's Soho. This establishment became a semi-official second office for the staff of *Private Eye* magazine.

To extend the links of Oliver Bernard to the heritage of coastal Suffolk just a little further, I am able to confirm that he became friendly with Joyce Grenfell in the 1950s. She was a friend of his mother and they were both Christian Scientists. Grenfell was responsible for sending some of Oliver's poems to Walter de la Mare, who will be mentioned in a later chapter. Oliver was pleased to learn that this great man regarded his as 'real poems' and thereafter was a source of great encouragement to him. As if he needed further confirmation of his status as a recognised poet, Bernard recalls that the first fellow to describe him as a poet was someone he met at the Anchor pub in Walberswick. This is the hostelry closest to where he was staying during his sojourn in the village, in 1957. It really is surprising where you might come across examples of poetry criticism and I suppose a pub is as good a place as any. Maybe regulars of the Coach and Horses could also have ventured some views on Oliver's poetry if he had ever considered discussing his work there when having a quiet drink with his brother. This is not too far-fetched because, during what could be described as his bohemian years in the clubs and pubs of London's Soho in the 1940s and 1950s, Oliver also mixed with the likes of Dylan Thomas, Lucian Freud and Stephen Spender, all of whom I have mentioned elsewhere. Another member of this group was the young writer and poet from

Goa, Dom Moraes who was once married to Henrietta Moraes who is mentioned elsewhere in connection with her relationship with artist, Maggi Hambling. Bernard wrote quite a lot about his early life as well as from the late twenties onwards in his autobiography, *Getting Over It* that was published in 1992. This work has been described as 'a strange and at times bewildering story written in an equally strange and bewildering style'. He is a very interesting man and, as far as I am aware, he continues to write just a little, probably remaining faithful to his highly individual style. Below, I am happy to quote, with his permission, just two verses from *Moons and Tides, Walberswick*:

'Half moon half moon the second half
The half of darkness as the first
Heavy yellow set behind
The sea wall over meadows cursed
Four years ago with floods of salt

Neaps but the wind kept up and kept
High tides high and hardly let
Ebb tides out but covered with
Hissing white and I forget
If I ever saw such fury'

Perhaps the illustration opposite depicts the disturbed condition of the sea that Oliver was describing. I captured this image on a chilly morning in January 2009.

Oliver Bernard's style is not to include the customary punctuation. The reference to meadows cursed with floods of salt is explained by the appalling East Coast Floods of 1953 that claimed so many lives. It will be recalled how the home of Benjamin Britten and Peter Pears in Aldeburgh became damaged by the swollen tidal waters of the North Sea at that time. Incidentally, in closing, Oliver Bernard is also well known for his translations, from the French language, of the poems of both Arthur Rimbaud (1854-1891) and Paul Verlaine (1844-1896). It was interesting as well as a little puzzling to read that, in Dame Edith Sitwell's opinion, Verlaine's poems, along with Charles Baudelaire's (1821-1867) were incapable of being translated, being just two of a very small number of French poets 'who simply cannot

A 'heaving' North Sea as seen from the beach at Walberswick

be translated'. It was her view that 'their poems lie entirely within the (French) language'.

The historian, writer and one-time journalist, Anthony Sampson (1926-2004) owned the smaller half of Valley Farm, Walberswick and wrote *Anatomy of Britain* in the brick-built studio adjoining the garden. Valley Farm will be featured elsewhere in this book as, in its time, more than a few distinguished artists also lived or stayed there. To get back to Sampson, he wrote a major series of books between 1962 and 1992. All of these contained within their titles the words, *Anatomy of Britain*. All of Sampson's considerable output of published work was non-fiction and included the award-winning, *Mandela: The Authorised Biography* (1999). Justin Cartwright, a contemporary writer, for whom I have great admiration, wrote of this book, 'A magisterial, detailed and invaluable account of one of this century's greatest figures. !t is hard to believe that a better biography will ever be written.' Sampson wrote other books on South Africa during the course of his notable writing career.

P D James (born 1920) is a very English writer of classic crime who has also fallen under the spell of the Suffolk coast and her most iconic character, Commander Adam Dalgleish, policeman and poet, is certainly no stranger to the area. In her book, *Unnatural Causes* (1997), Dalgleish, then merely a senior detective at Scotland Yard, becomes involved with the local police force when a planned holiday at his aunt's house is interrupted by a murder. As it happens, P D James has used East Anglia as a setting for a number of her novels and in this particular book she featured as a location the heath-lands and marshlands of the coast of Suffolk ('this most unspoilt and un-prettified of counties') around Dunwich, Blythburgh and Monksmere Head. All the residents and weekend guests at Monksmere Head (a fictional location but based upon Dunwich Heath) are either writers of some kind (romance, crime, non-fiction) or merely literary critics, not forgetting the orphaned and crippled little typist. It almost goes without saying that James's plot ensures that these greater or lesser creative people, albeit fictional, have their little quirks, their allies and their enemies.

This very successful author states that another of her books, *Devices and Desires*, (Faber and Faber 2005) had its genesis when she was exploring Suffolk with an elderly friend of long-standing. She remembers stopping for a few minutes on a deserted beach of shingle and found herself looking over what she described as a cold and dangerous North Sea. She recalled the wonderful atmosphere she then experienced, thinking that time could well have stood still in that self-same spot for the last thousand years. She emerged from her reverie and looked south and saw the stark outline of Sizewell nuclear power station, dominating the coastline. Immediately she knew that she had a new novel. It eventually took more than twelve months to research, as well as plan, this work. The actual writing took even longer but this anecdote provides an excellent example of what this book is all about: creative people drawing their inspiration from coastal Suffolk. Another of her books featuring a Suffolk location is *Death in Holy Orders* where the coastal hamlet of Covehithe is the setting. St Anselm's is set on 'this windswept desolate headland' and the Doom painting described as being within the church is very similar to the one in Wenhaston church, to which it is compared.

However, P D James has also admitted that, as is often the case with other authors, she also uses experiences in her own life as material for her novels on the basis of 'what else do we have?' However, she adds the rider that the 'novelist must be able to stand aside from a particular incident, encounter or event, view it with detachment, however painful, and fashion it into a satisfying shape'. She quoted the distinguished novelist, Graham Greene (1904-1991), by adding 'every writer has a splinter of ice in the heart'.

P D James bought a seventeenth century house as a second home in Southwold in 1995. Previously, her father had also owned a small house in the town. Her parents-in-law had similarly retired to Suffolk many years beforehand. In August 1997, she travelled from her home in London to the seaside town in order to fulfil an engagement to give a lecture to the local Archaeological and Natural History Society. That evening, she employed as her thesis 'The use of place in fiction', a subject that she felt rather remote from the Society's interests but this did not appear to present a problem to her audience. In her talk she cited, as examples, the black tower in her novel of that name as well as the nuclear installation in *Devices and Desires*. However, in the case of *The Black Tower* the remote coast is in the county of Dorset, possibly because this county has become familiar to the author as some of her oldest friends live there.

This distinguished, multi-award-winning author has written that she has been familiar with the East Coast since childhood. Her earliest memory in this respect was of her father pitching a large army bell tent at Pakefield, just south of Lowestoft, still known today as the site for a Pontin's holiday camp of long standing. This holiday centre has now been made subject to a form of gentrification by being provided with the title Pakefield Holiday Park. That tent, which her father had acquired after the First World War, was the family's regular living space for two weeks of summer holiday. This was most probably in the late 1920s and early 1930s. This reminds me of a quotation from E M Forster, recalled also by P D James in her own writing. Forster described life in England in the 1920s and 1930s as 'a long weekend between two wars'.

Baroness James of Holland Park, having been made a Conservative Life Peer in the New Year's Honours List, 1991, is yet another who grew to love the enormous Suffolk skies, bird-life in the estuaries and, of course, the ubiquitous village churches. The grandest of these, as we know, were financed and built by the wool merchants in the fifteenth century at a time of growing prosperity amongst Suffolk's cloth merchants. She has described the church at Blythburgh, the Most Holy Trinity, as 'like a great ship moored in the marshes', taking her breath away when she gazed upon it on an October day in 1997. It has also been described as a church that truly sums up Suffolk, where the county's imagination is 'writ large'. It is certainly fifteenth century and this building is distinguished by the presence of no less than twelve angels carved in the timbers of its roof. Some of these were peppered with lead shot in the eighteenth century, possibly by men shooting at jackdaws that had probably congregated in the interior, having gained access through an open door. In the event, it is most likely that this church was not financed by funds generated from the profits of wool. This medieval village did boast an important priory, and thus its church attracted enough wealthy piety on the eve of the Reformation to bankroll a spectacular rebuilding.

Reading through the author's personal writings in a book, part diary and part memoir representing a period of just twelve months in her life, I was struck by her very apt description of the North Sea seen from Southwold in September 1997. She referred to it as 'changing from grey-green to pale milky blue' set under the delicately hued skies. The North Sea from the Suffolk coast is never the deep azure blue of the waters around Cornwall; it has a colour all of its own and none the worse for it. Otherwise why would Maggi Hambling spend so many of her more recent years in painting what she sees in the waves, sometimes gentle but often just a little more on the wild side?' I offer the illustration opposite as a colourful example of her work.

P D James has been a writer for something like half a century. Using her maiden name, she had her first mystery novel, *Cover Her Face*, published in 1962 when she was in her early forties. The book had been delayed somewhat agonisingly for a year due to a crowded fiction list at Faber and Faber. It was well received and it is amusing to note that only one critic, although just a little hesitatingly, identified the author as a woman. She chose this somewhat enigmatic nomenclature as she thought it would look better on the book spine, thus demonstrating an early degree of marketing skill. It was in this literary début that she introduced the now legendary, but since promoted through a series

Crest of a Wave by Maggi Hambling

of higher ranks to Commander, Adam Dalgliesh of Scotland Yard. The fans of both the author and her principal character have multiplied many times over the years. In discussing the book, she has reminded us that although the construction of a detective novel may well be formulaic, this method should not necessarily be applied to the writing. She based the plot of her first novel in an English village but by no means identified it as being in the county of Suffolk. That notion would arrive in her later work. This first novel was accepted almost immediately by Faber and Faber who, at that time, were looking for a replacement for Gordon Clark (1900-1958), an English Judge whose pseudonym was Cyril Hare. He was one of the publisher's most successful crime writers and he had died just a year or so previous to the publication of *Cover Her Face*. It was the late Elaine Greene at MCA, the literary agent acting for P D James, who suggested to a director of Faber's that she might well have found an author to take the place of Cyril Hare. The rest, as I have written so often, is indeed history as here we are, well into the twenty-first century, and to this day Faber and Faber continue to remain loyal publishers of P D James.

P D James is also a lover of art and has written of Lucian Freud, 'He paints what he sees with total honesty if little humanity. I should like to own a Freud'. I would have thought that by now she could probably afford to acquire an example of his work, having had what must be millions of her books sold by her publishers all over the world but particularly in America, where she is very popular. In the year 2011, her name was added to The International Crime Writing Hall of Fame, alongside none other than Sir Arthur Conan Doyle and Dame Agatha Christie. This leaves me speculating, somewhat irreverently as well as mischievously, as to whether or not Baroness James would have responded positively to an invitation by Freud to have become a model for one of his portraits. Somehow, I think this would have been unlikely. We have learned that Baroness James is certainly no stranger to Southwold, her association going back over more than just a few years; she is known to be a keen supporter of 'live theatre' provided each season by Jill Freud's production company.

Ruth Rendell whom we now know as another Suffolk crime writer and her husband Don are friends of longstanding. James describes Rendell as a remarkable and prolific writer whose novels explore, with power and high imagination, the darker corners of the human psyche. She seems to agree with others that Rendell's best novels have been written under the pseudonym, Barbara Vine. One Vine novel, *No Night is too Long* is set in Aldeburgh. This author once lived in the village of Polstead which was, by coincidence, the location of the infamous 'Murder in the Red Barn'. This took place in 1827, a real-life crime of Victorian times that was made into a film in 1935 and entitled *The Red Barn Murder*. This starred Tod Slaughter (1885-1956), an actor, best known for playing over-the-top maniacs in macabre film adaptations of Victorian melodramas. Accompanying him in this movie was Eric Portman (1903-1969), best known for his portrayal of strong, sensitive men, often with a psychotic tendency. His firm, commanding voice made him ideal for his notable rôles in war movies. Although he was considered to be something of a matinée idol, he was rarely featured as a ladies' man or indeed the lover in the roles that he played.

Ruth Rendell now lives in a small village near Sudbury in Suffolk. She first moved to the county in 1970 and has gained a well-deserved reputation as a prolific crime writer, acclaimed for her fine psychological thrillers and murder mysteries. This author qualifies for her numerous mentions in a book that deals in part with the literary connections with coastal Suffolk not least because she once lived in

Aldeburgh. *Front Seat*, a novel published in 1983, is unmistakably set in Aldeburgh and I have read it also as a short story, part of a collection entitled *The Fever Tree and Other Stories*. Front Seat was an episode in a long TV Series of *Ruth Rendell Mysteries* that started in 1988. *Front Seat* was first shown in 1997 and starred the actress, Janet Suzman, another Suffolk resident who was created DBE in the 2011 Queen's Birthday Honours List. She is the niece of the staunch South African anti-apartheid activist Helen Suzman and a former wife of theatre director Trevor Nunn. I noticed that this marriage was once described as a famous theatrical alliance. Janet Suzman is a courageous woman. In 1987, before the end of apartheid in South Africa, she was running and directing at the Market Theatre in South Africa. In a brave departure from safety, she decided to put on *Othello* and being a logical woman she cast an African as Othello and a white actress as Desdemona. There are lines in the play that would surely have raised a few hackles in the audience but the remarkable outcome to this story is that Dame Janet Suzman's production created an enormous hit, playing to packed houses and critical acclaim. Her aunt must have been very proud of her.

Ruth Rendell became Baroness Rendell of Babergh in 1997, having also been created a Life Peer. In the House of Lords, she sits on the Labour benches and she is known to have been a considerable donor to Party funds. The Babergh District was created on the re-organisation of local government from five former local authorities in South Suffolk. The District takes its name from one of the old Saxon hundreds which was referred to in the Domesday survey. The District Council's offices are located in the town of Hadleigh, which derived its prosperity from the wool and cloth industries. It has a fifteenth century timber-framed Guildhall and many fine examples of timber and brick listed buildings, some with highly detailed seventeenth century plasterwork known as 'pargeting'. The town is well worth a visit and it should be remembered that Ruth Rendell lives close by. She has received many awards for her writing, including the Silver, Gold, and Cartier Diamond Daggers from the Crime Writers' Association, three Edgars from the Mystery Writers of America, The Arts Council National Book Awards, and *The Sunday Times* Literary Award. A number of her works have been adapted for film or television.

It should also be known that, in addition to what has already been mentioned, P D James has also received many other awards for crime writing in Britain as well as America, Italy and Scandinavia, including the Mystery Writers of America Grand Master Award and the National Arts Club Medal of Honor for Literature (US). She has been recognised in various other ways, too numerous to mention, but there is no doubt that she has risen to very lofty heights as a result of her prolific writing career. Suffolk can be truly proud of these two distinguished authors.

Ghost stories have also been inspired by actual local residents, a vague example being *A Warning to the Curious*, a short story by M R James (1862-1936), the son of a Suffolk clergyman. This is set in Aldeburgh where his parents had associations even though they had made their home in the village of Great Livermere, Suffolk where the writer was born. He was later Provost of King's College, Cambridge and followed this with an eighteen year spell in an identical position at Eton College. This author earned the distinction of having his writings in this genre being considered as some of the very best in English literature. His ghost stories were set in realistic contemporary settings, as opposed to the more traditional, not to say very popular eighteenth and nineteenth century fiction, associated with the supernatural or horrifying events of that period.

Montague Rhodes ('M R') James's ghost stories were published in a series of collections, an example being *Ghost Stories of an Antiquary*. I have discovered that the short story to which I referred previously was first published in 1925 in *A Warning to the Curious and Other Ghost Stories*. His first hardback collected edition appeared in 1931. Many of the tales were originally written as Christmas Eve entertainments, being read aloud to select gatherings of friends. James perfected a particular method of atmospheric story telling that has since become known as Jamesian. As far as I am concerned, after reading *A Warning to the Curious*, I felt this work was well named as the narrative conveyed exactly what the title described.

I think that this is now an appropriate time to introduce someone who could well be described as Southwold's greatest literary son, although such a statement is certain to be somewhat controversial. I do, of course refer to none other than George Orwell (1903-1950).

It now seems clear that no one could ever suggest that Eric Blair was an established writer who was attracted to coastal Suffolk and lured to Southwold specifically by the town's location, scenic beauty and an atmosphere conducive to creative writing. It was in 1932 that he decided to adopt the pen name of George Orwell. His parents had decided to live in the Suffolk seaside town in 1921 following his father's retirement from the Indian Civil Service. As for the adoption of the Orwell name, Blair took this name from the river that flows from Ipswich into the sea between the ports of Harwich and Felixstowe, in confluence with the river Stour. That in itself is a connection with coastal Suffolk but it will be seen that some literary work did indeed emanate from Southwold. Eric Blair decided to publish his book *Down and Out in Paris and London* in 1932 under an assumed name as he apparently wished to spare any possible embarrassment to his parents over its relatively seedy subject matter.

In his boyhood and youth, Orwell had won a succession of scholarships that served to considerably ease the burden of the cost of his private education. At the time of his birth, his father was nothing higher than a Sub-Deputy Opium Agent, 4th grade civil servant in the Indian Civil Service. His son, Eric, was born in Motihari, Bengal in 1903 and although he had a far from inferior education he never seemed to be in the running to gain admittance to a university. Notwithstanding what must have been his enforced disappointment at the termination of his studies after leaving public school, his almost immediate travels did influence his writing, as perhaps did the friends he made at Eton where he was a King's Scholar from 1917-1921. Amongst his contemporaries, there were the future writer and critic, Cyril Connolly who has been mentioned elsewhere in connection with other well-known writers. Another future author, Anthony Powell (1905-2000) was another pupil at this elite public school. Orwell, as young Eric Blair, rather surprisingly distinguished himself at that well known public school by being instrumental in the scoring of a 'shy' in the Eton Wall Game, which then led to a goal, a notoriously difficult achievement. Apparently, Orwell passed the ball to a boy named Longden who then completed the goal by hurling the ball against a garden door. This was a rare moment of symbolic success in a school career that one of his biographers describes as having been 'lived more or less below surface level'. Whilst at Eton, Orwell was taught French by none other than the previously mentioned Aldous Huxley. The British Pathe News website contains a short clip of the Eton

Wall Game being played at the time Orwell was there and a caption indicates that Orwell had confirmed that he was one of the players on that particular day. There was no mention, however, that this was the occasion on which the famous goal was scored.

Orwell, had previously been at school with Cyril Connolly at St Cyprian's, Eastbourne and later at Wellington College. The wife of the headmaster of St Cyprian's, who taught English as well as other subjects, encouraged all her pupils to read widely. She also urged them to try their hand at creative writing. Whilst at that particular school Orwell wrote a patriotic poem which he rather pretentiously entitled *Awake Young Men of England*. His mother was so proud of her son's effort that she decided to send this example of her son's creative work to the local paper when they were living In Henley-on-Thames. It was subsequently published in the *Henley and South Oxfordshire Standard* in 1914 (the year of the outbreak of World War I) and the wife of the headmistress at St Cyprian's, Orwell's English teacher, read the contents of the accompanying article out loud to the assembled school.

It is interesting that when Orwell, as well as Connolly, later published their somewhat critical accounts of life at St Cyprian's, W J H Christie, a younger fellow pupil wrote that he 'detected among the excellencies of their writing, some of the qualities – simplicity, honesty and avoidance of verbiage – which were encouraged by their teacher to aim at in the writing of English'. This is extracted from an article of Christie's entitled *St Cyprian's Days* in *Blackwood's Magazine* 1971 where he was a regular contributor. Christie followed Orwell and Connolly to Eton and went on to become a British colonial civil servant in India, where he played a prominent part in the post-war independence of that sub continental country, assisting in the provision of the required administrative continuity after this historical event.

It seems that his former schoolmate, Cyril Connolly, who has been described as precociously brilliant in his youth, had more than a passing admiration for Orwell's writing. In his literary reviews for the *New Statesman* in the mid-thirties, Connolly had been critical of English novelists in general, comparing them unfavourably with their American counterparts such as Ernest Hemingway (1898-1961) and his contemporary, Dashiell Hammett (1894-1961), described as one of the finest mystery writers of all time. He did however exclude George Orwell from his criticism after reviewing Orwell's novel *Burmese Days*, stating that it had 'that decent and inspiring intimation of equality'. Needless to say, Connolly's views on the literary ability of English writers were somewhat controversial but this did not appear to trouble his conscience.

So it can be established that Orwell's talent for writing developed from the early encouragement he received during his education on the south coast. He reached the vitally important milestone of having his first book published when he was based in Southwold. His novel *The Clergyman's Daughter* (1935) is partially set in the town but it appears that this was not his first book. He spent most, but certainly not all of his time in the seaside town until 1934. He then proceeded to move to London in November of that year where he decided to live in Hampstead. In those days, this leafy suburb attracted artists for much the same reasons as it had in the 1830s: pleasant views, fresher air and a sense of separation from central London. Its residents included intellectuals, writers and a group of fiercely committed modernist artists, Ben Nicholson, Barbara Hepworth and Henry Moore. Their presence turned Hampstead into the headquarters for avant-garde art in England. It also became a refuge for European artists and architects fleeing the Nazi-dominated continent. It is not difficult to understand why Orwell was attracted to such an area for his early days in the nation's capital city. He must have found the atmosphere refreshingly different from a rather sedate eastern coast resort.

Some of Orwell's early written work in Southwold included some basic poems and what has been described as a fragmentary try-out for *Burmese Days*. It was at this time that he decided he wanted to become a full time writer, revealing this ambition to his astonished, not to say somewhat horrified parents. He also lived for periods of time in Paris as well as in London over what seemed to be approximately three years or so. He never seemed to be very happy in Southwold, not being too enamoured with the social life but the existence of numerous girlfriends appeared to make life more bearable for him. In later years, he certainly became known as something of a ladies' man. One elderly Southwold resident has recalled that he came to blows with Orwell over his fiancée on Southwold Common in the 1930s.

A biographer also refers to Orwell writing to a girlfriend, Eleanor Jaques, in which he referred to one of their walks along the banks of the River Blyth and the time they spent in the wood, 'along past Blythburgh Lodge'. He recalled '... the deep beds of moss ... & your nice white body in the dark green moss'. That said, it seems clear that matters other than romancing the ladies were on his mind in that he had certainly started writing while living with his parents in 3 Queen Street, Southwold. They had moved there from their previous home in 4 Stradbroke Road, where they lived from 1921 onwards, when their son was aged eighteen. Eventually the Blairs finally settled in Montague House in the High Street. On the basis that this is where George Orwell once lived there is a plaque on the house that commemorates the property's famous past resident.

George Orwell's last home in Southwold

The building itself has been Listed Grade II as being of Special Architectural or Historic Interest and it now seems certain that Orwell completed *Burmese Days* there.

The Blair family had retired to Southwold in 1921 and on his son leaving Eton his father had expressed a wish for Orwell to join the Indian Civil Service. In the event he joined the Burma Police; this was after cramming for the entrance examination in Southwold. By 1922 he was to be found at the Police Training School in Mandalay.

It was in 1933 that *Down and Out in Paris and London* was published. This was Orwell's factual account of several years of what is regarded as the self-imposed poverty he contrived to experience after leaving Burma. This was not the first book he had written during what has been described as his 'Southwold period'. One of his biographers gives this distinction to the novel already mentioned, *Burmese Days*, published in the following year. It was in this work, often described as 'extravagantly written', that Orwell revealed a somewhat ill-disguised hatred of imperialism, in that he set about dissecting the iniquities of British Rule. It is no secret that the young Eric Blair found himself having to endure five miserable years in Burma. The book is set in that country in the 1920s and amongst Orwell's characters is a corrupt and cunning magistrate who seeks to destroy the reputation of an Indian doctor by fabricating falsehoods. E M Forster wrote A Passage to India in 1924 and this also contains the character of an Indian doctor who falls into disgrace as a result of unfounded allegations. The comparison did not appear to be lost on a reviewer in *The Saturday Review* who wrote that Orwell's work could take an honourable place beside *A Passage to India* and I find this to be a noteworthy commendation for a book that the publisher, Gollancz, originally rejected for publication. This was earlier, in 1934. Heinemann's subsequently did the same. All of this was considered surprising bearing in mind that Orwell's *Down and Out in Paris and London* had made a decided impact but both publishers were concerned about possible legal action by Burmese and Indians who might claim to recognise themselves as characters in the book. There appeared to be no such fears across the Atlantic as *Burmese Days* was subsequently published in the USA by Harper Brothers, New York, in 1932. Although not at all without precedent, this was a demonstration of rather unusual confidence in an English writer who was making his fictional debut. The Americans could well have been influenced by their own views on British colonialism and were perhaps rather sympathetic to the author's opinions, but the fact remains that Burma was regarded by its colonial masters as something of a lucrative sideline to India, strategically crucial and perhaps, more importantly, a place to get rich. It is certainly fair to say that Eric Blair was not there for that purpose, as he was merely following in his own way the livelihood followed by his father. It did not last long and George Orwell's literary career was soon to take on supreme prominence in his life. As I write, Burma seems to be taking its first tentative steps towards a form of democracy but no one seems to think that a complete transformation from years of military rule, steeped in isolation and paranoia, will happen overnight, despite the determined efforts of Aung San Suu Kyi over an extended period of time.

As it happens, whilst living in Southwold, George Orwell would often embark upon some form of down-market safari into what could be described as low-life London, such as squalor in the East End, punctuated by stays in various doss-houses. He also spent periods of time working in the hop fields of Kent where the population was swollen by annual mass emigration from working-class London when the hop-picking season was in full swing. He must have gathered copious material for more than one of his future books during the course of these forays from genteel Southwold. It is not too difficult to arrive at the conclusion that in Southwold he was most certainly living the part of Eric Blair but elsewhere it was 'George Orwell' who was making new friends and gathering valuable material for his future writing. The fact that Cyril Connolly had referred to Orwell as a writer whose work intimated 'equality' may well have arisen because of Orwell's determined efforts to be seen as a 'man of the people' despite his privileged education. He was indeed a person whose left-wing credentials were, of course, already well known. He is known to have said that until 1935 he had been only intermittingly interested in politics although he felt able to say that he was always more or less of the 'Left'. On the other hand, his views were also somewhat unconventional, certainly as far as supporters of the Labour Party were concerned, because of his expressed view that 'there is not much to choose between Communism and Fascism'.

In early 1937, George Orwell served with Britain's Independent Labour Party contingent that formed part of the militia of the POUM (Workers' Party of Marxist Unification) against Generalissimo Franco's Nationalists in the Spanish Civil War. Whilst he was away fighting, his novel, *The Road to Wigan Pier* was published by Gollancz in 'trade' and *Left Book Club* editions. In May that year, he was shot in the throat by a Fascist sniper at Huesca and taken in succession to hospitals in Monflorite, Sietamo and Lerida, before arriving at a sanatorium outside Barcelona. During the next month he escaped from Spain by train with his first wife, Eileen (née O'Shaughnessy, 1905-1945) and in early July they arrived back at their rented home in Wallington, Hertfordshire after a short stay in Greenwich with his in-laws. It was then that he began writing *Homage to Catalonia*, in which he dealt with his experiences in the Spanish Civil War. This book was published in April 1938 by Secker & Warburg, having been refused by Gollancz, just as they had done with *Burmese Days*, four years previously. On a final note regarding his time in Spain, I was intrigued to learn that in

Barcelona there is an place named after the writer, namely Placa de George Orwell. Such is literary fame, although having been wounded in that country may have had something to do with it, though this is pure speculation on my part.

It is not particularly well known that, during his period in Southwold, George Orwell acted as a private tutor to a disabled child and he followed this up by tutoring a family of three boys one of whom, Richard Peters, later became a distinguished academic. Orwell's final visit to Southwold was in 1939 and the novels which were published before this date are *A Clergyman's Daughter* (1935) where the lead character was taken from his experiences in the Kent hop fields and *Keep the Aspidistra Flying* (1936). In 1939, *Coming Up for Air* arrived on the scene. His more famous and better-known novels, the ones that established his excellent literary reputation on a very firm basis were the political satires, *Animal Farm* (1945) and, of course, *Nineteen Eighty-Four* (1949). Graham Greene read Orwell's book whilst sailing to America on the *Queen Elizabeth* in early February 1950. He was passing the time and found the volume 'very good except the sex part. That's ham'. This leaves me pondering the fact that when Orwell was living in Southwold he had a series of dalliances with local girls, including Eleanor Jaques, who he lived next door to when the family occupied a house in Stradbroke Road. In those days, and living in a town of no more than say two thousand inhabitants, it must have been difficult to have any sort of relationship without attracting attention and that is why the author and his girlfriend preferred to find themselves a quiet spot for their lovemaking. This was usually in the woods that can be found across the heath on the way to the bridge over the river Blyth that then led on, by means of a well-trodden path, to the nearby village of Walberswick. It was at the ruined church in this village that Orwell used to sit and relax with a good read. I have also seen photographs of him on the beach at Walberswick, accompanied by some of his local friends at that time.

There is no doubt that, given the enormous extent of the writing he undertook during his rather short literary career, George Orwell's public reputation far exceeds that of any other writer of his generation, and indeed of any other political writer of the twentieth century. Southwold can indeed feel entitled to lay claim to a famously unique literary son but it must be remembered that it is not only for his novels that he became so well known. Orwell became one of the most potent and symbolic figures in Western political thought, leaving behind the expression, 'Orwellian', as a byword that sums up a particular way of describing a way of life as well as literature and language. Notwithstanding this iconic status, Orwell remains something of an enigma. However, I would think that perhaps just the odd fragment of the time he spent in Southwold must surely have made some type of contribution, albeit remote from controversial political philosophy, to the way he lived what turned out to be such a pitifully short life by any modern-day standards.

It seems that this famous author did indeed pay a final visit to Southwold in 1939. This was on the occasion of the death of his father at the age of eighty-two. The latter had been suffering from intestinal cancer. In the fashion of the time, a couple of copper pennies were placed on his deceased parent's eyelids. After the funeral it didn't seem right for Orwell, having retrieved the coins, to

George Orwell (left) on Southwold Beach, with friends in 1932

merely put them in his pocket. He strolled down to the seafront and cast the loose change into the sea. This was something that one of his biographers described as a true Orwellian moment.

As a footnote to my purposely-parochial coverage of the career of George Orwell, he did undertake some broadcasting work for the BBC during the war but not without some criticism. After hearing one of the writer's talks, the Controller of Overseas Services, a certain JS Clark, wrote a memorandum which left no doubt that he regarded Orwell's voice as unsuitable, even though he found the subject matter interesting. This was in January 1943 but the author went on to get an exceptional annual report from his superiors and, in that same year, was awarded an annual salary increment of £40 to £720.

On this basis, it is fair to say that the broadcasting section of his comparatively short career can be regarded as successful. The fact that it was in this year that he also tendered his resignation from his employment with the BBC should not detract from this fact. This was on grounds of policy, as he felt that his work, being regarded as propaganda, was not achieving anything and he preferred to work in journalism, which he felt would prove to be more useful.

I must now return to other authors associated with the area. Perhaps not too many people will be aware that Wilkie Collins (1824-1889) used Aldeburgh as one of the settings for his novel *No Name*. He did not trouble to disguise the name too much by calling his fictional town 'Aldborough'. The author described the fashionable promenading along the seafront where the character, Magdalen Vanstone, determines to meet Noel Vanstone, the sickly heir of her father's estate. I have always found Wilkie Collins very difficult to read but there is no escaping the fact that he remains an important figure in British twentieth century literature.

Pat Barker (born 1943) is thought to be one of the country's most important novelists. She has won many awards for her fiction, which tends to deal with themes of memory, trauma, survival and recovery. Her work has been described as direct, blunt, and plainspoken and she is recognised for her exceptional qualities of intellectual scope and imaginative understanding. I have read her book, *The Ghost Road* (1995), the final part of a trilogy, known as the *Regeneration Trilogy*, and winner of the 1995 Booker Prize. I found reading just the one had no effect on my enjoyment of some fine writing which blended fact with fiction. The story opens with a young army officer due to be back at barracks for a medical examination. On being found fit, he was then due to return to the warfront in France for a possible fourth exposure to almost inevitable death. He had been repatriated to England just a matter of a few months previously. He had been diagnosed with 'shell-shock'. Despite doubts about his problems with asthma, his 'medical' determined him fit to go back to the front. All the characters, which include the war poet, Wilfred Owen (1893-1918) who in real life was awarded a posthumous MC for gallantry, are exceptionally well drawn and I found it a very rewarding read.

However, Pat Barker is being mentioned here because in her

book, *Regeneration* (1991), the first part of the trilogy, she portrays Aldeburgh as a grim coastal town during the First World War. The town does, of course, have as a prominent landmark a Martello tower, the largest and most northerly of a chain, designed to defend the country against Napoleon and his French forces. Barker's plot featured a psychologist, W H R Rivers, on a visit to a young officer who was recovering from the trauma of trench warfare. As in Wilkie Collins' *No Name*, the presence of a Martello tower symbolised bleakness. Rivers observed that 'ferns grew from the high walls of the moat; and the tower, where the look-out turret had crumbled away, was thronged with bindweed'. The overall impression conveyed by the author was of a dead place. For the sake of completeness, the second part of Barker's trilogy is *The Eye in the Door* (1993).

I should perhaps mention that Benjamin Britten set more than one or two of Wilfred Owen's poems to music when composing his *War Requiem* (1961-62) and also *Nocturne* (1958). In this latter work, he set another of Owen's works, *The Kind Ghosts*. Is there, I ponder, a connection with the title of Pat Barker's final book in the trilogy? This must surely be so.

Chapter Four

Coastal Suffolk's literary, acting and directing connections and the discovery of a fun bookshop

ESTHER FREUD (BORN 1963) is married to actor and director, David Morrisey (born 1964). They have a holiday home in Walberswick and they have three children. They were married in a ceremony on Southwold pier in 2006. This was about five years after the pier had been rebuilt after successive storm damage over the years. It was first constructed, with an impressive length of a length of 810 feet, in the year 1900. Morrisey has appeared in a great number of films, both in Hollywood and in the UK and has played the role of former Prime Minister, Gordon Brown on television in *The Deal* (2003). He also prides himself on being an actor who likes to direct, an example being the recent second series on BBC TV, *Five Hours*, which attracted critical approval. Such achievements are not new to Morrisey as there have been successive film and TV acting triumphs. He has also become known for what a publisher has described as a super-star detective type of character.

Another aficionado of the Walberswick-Southwold area is fellow actor, Bernard Hill, whose films include the *Lord of the Rings* film trilogy and *Titanic*, in which he played the role of the heroic Captain Smith who went down with the ship in 1912. Hill joined Morrisey in a charity abseil down the town's landmark lighthouse for the RNLI in 2009. Bernard Hill also starred in the Peter Greenaway film, *Drowning by Numbers* which was shot in Southwold, a role that started his fond association with the town.

Walberswick's charms have also drawn film director and screenwriter, Paul Greengrass, into its fold. He specialises in dramatization of real-life events and is known for his signature use of hand-held cameras. His film credits include, the screenplay for *Omagh*, which depicted the 1998 bombing of Omagh, Northern Ireland. He directed *The Murder of Stephen Lawrence* (1999), which told the story of Stephen Lawrence, a black youth whose murder was said to have been investigated inefficiently by the Metropolitan Police. The deceased mother's personal research into the case led to accusations about 'institutional racism' in this police force. Another notable film by Greengrass was

Bloody Sunday (2002) which depicted, in an almost documentary style, the 1972 Bloody Sunday shootings of Northern Irish anti-internment activists by British soldiers. This highly controversial reaction by the country's armed forces ultimately led to an official Government apology, which was given by Prime Minister, David Cameron in the House of Commons in June 2010, on publication of the results of the Saville inquiry. Greengrass's docudrama type of production shared First Prize at the 2002 Berlin Film Festival. Greengrass was hired to direct 2004's *The Bourne Supremacy*, a sequel to the 2002 film *The Bourne Identity*, There has been plenty of other impressive work in films but I think I have written enough to establish his credentials in what, at times, is a far from glamorous business.

Turning to another modern writer, I have wondered if I am being naïve in comparing *Akenfield … a Portrait of an English Village* by historian, Ronald Blythe (born 1922) first published in 1969, with the two works, *The Borough* and *The Village* by George Crabbe. The Amazon website product description of Blythe's *Akenfield*, the book that had propelled him into the limelight, reads as follows:

> 'This colourful, perceptive portrayal of English country life reverberates with the voices of the village inhabitants, from the reminiscences of survivors of the Great War evoking days gone by, to the concerns of a younger generation of farm-workers and the fascinating and personal recollections of, among others, the local schoolteacher, doctor, blacksmith, saddler, district nurse and magistrate. Providing insights into farming, education, welfare, class, religion and death, Akenfield forms a unique document of a way of life that has, in many ways, disappeared.'

The Guardian's review of the book mentioned:

> 'A hundred years from now, anyone wanting to know how things were on the land will turn more profitably to *Akenfield* than to a sheaf of anaemically professional social surveys.'

In these circumstances, Ronald Blythe certainly deserves a mention as a modern-day Crabbe and, as far as I am aware, his book and the odd follow-up have been very well received, certainly near where I live close by the Norfolk-Suffolk border. *Akenfield* was made into a film by Sir Peter Hall and the work is said to be based upon one or more small Suffolk villages that are situated near Wickham Market. This area is close by the trunk road A12, which leads travellers further along that highway in a confident manner to coastal Suffolk. When they reach, say, the village of Yoxford there remains only a modest drive to reach Southwold, Walberswick and, of course, Aldeburgh as well as nearby Snape. This will be where most journeys to discover elements of coastal Suffolk's cultural heritage will begin.

Ronald Blythe has written many short stories as well as books about the county he loves in both past and present times. Indeed, his name is synonymous with Suffolk literature and in his Introduction to his own work, *The Stories of Ronald Blythe*, he explains that the tales relate to the early years of his writing life. These incorporate what he heard and saw around him in childhood, even the ghost stories. As a boy, he had lived within walking distance of the infamous Borley Rectory as well as M R James's house in Aldeburgh. He confesses that his true interest was not in the actual stories but in the personalities of the people who saw the ghosts. This strikes me as an interesting slant on the genre. In writing in this narrative about Ronald Blythe, I have concentrated only on coastal Suffolk.

Another writer who is proud to be associated with Aldeburgh is Jon Canter (born 1953) who has written affectionately about his boyhood holidays in the town where his family had a second home in the High Ridge area. Canter was born and brought up in the Jewish community of Golders Green, North London and studied law at the University of Cambridge where he became President of Footlights, the university's theatrical club. After a spell in advertising copywriting and as a housemate of Douglas Adams (1952-2001), author of *The Hitchhiker's Guide to the Galaxy*, he became a freelance comedy writer, providing material for comedian Lenny Henry as well as writing for Dawn French, Angus Deayton, Mel Smith and Griff Rhys Jones, the latter being a resident of Suffolk and an ardent campaigner for the protection of the county's countryside. Canter was also script editor for Stephen Fry and Hugh Laurie and wrote for BBC TV as well as BBC Radio. In addition, he created the screenplay for the film *Full Monty 2*. His first novel, *Seeds of Greatness*, a comic story inspired by his upbringing, was published in 2006 and received favourable reviews, as did his second humorous novel, *A Short Gentleman* (2008).

Although this section is dealing with writers I feel that I must, at this point, mention that John Canter's wife is painter, Helen Napper (born 1958) who has had solo shows in the Thackeray Gallery at both London and Aldeburgh as well as elsewhere. She has also shown jointly with Anne Thomson in London, New York and Los Angeles. Paintings by Helen Napper are in public and private collections in the USA, Australia, Hong Kong, Germany, France, Italy and Belgium. Napper specialises in still life painting and her work has also been shown at the Aldeburgh Festival where the curator was Anne Thomson, the former owner of the Sue Rankin and Thackeray Galleries. John Canter and Helen Napper have been living in Aldeburgh since the mid-nineties and, as was the custom of Benjamin Britten and Peter Pears, Helen is said to enjoy swimming in the sea. I have not seen it recorded whether or not her husband shares this enthusiasm.

Writing about the literary connections of coastal Suffolk brings to mind a most wonderfully bizarre, but nevertheless totally intriguing, destination for all booklovers. I refer to an establishment situated quite close the Suffolk coast, right in the heart of Westleton, a village that can also lay claim to an author or two amongst its residents. Chapel Books, also known as Bob's Bookshop, is located in The Street and I can promise anyone who enjoys a good read that they cannot fail to have a rewarding experience by paying these premises a visit. You will come across a wide-ranging and eclectic selection of books, both modern and antiquarian, that can occupy even the most casual of browsers for hours on end. If you need assistance, you are invited to summon the proprietor by banging on a large empty can that formerly contained olive oil. The always-helpful proprietor has provided a stick for this purpose. In order to rest weary legs, a number of assorted chairs are dotted here and there about the premises if it is your wish for a more detailed inspection of a likely-looking tome. I can promise you that there will be many that will take your fancy. Robert Jackson himself is also likely to put in an appearance, occasionally dressed in his pyjamas, and you may well be asked whether you would like a mug of tea or coffee. This is not the sort of place you would expect a thief to set about exploiting such a casual approach to management and administration. But if someone does contemplate making off with any items of stock they might well be deterred by a warning notice to the effect that if a book should be stolen, on leaving the shop an alarm will go off in the head of the miscreant. This store is also linked to a website, the delights of which will lead you to just about any obscure book that might well have eluded your diligent search for years on end. I can vouch for this service after a very rewarding personal experience. Julie Myerson's novel, *Something Might Happen*, made use of Southwold in its text and two of the characters one day undertook an excursion to Westleton where they visited ... you guessed it ... Chapel books. You will need to read the book to find out what happened there.

Chapel Books in Westleton – media photo-collage by Tiggy Gabrielle Jackson Newcomb

The illustration shown here is a depiction of the Chapel Books premises in Westleton. It is the work of Tiggy Gabrielle Jackson Newcomb, one of four daughters of parents Bob Jackson and the artist, Tessa Newcomb, daughter of painter Mary Newcomb. I will write about each of these later but bearing in mind that Robert Jackson is also an artist it is clear that, in creating this mixed media photo-collage, Tiggy is following in her parents' footsteps. Bob describes the work as 'striking' and, as I have to agree with him, I obtained Tiggy's permission to share the image with you.

Chapter Five

Further Literary Connections

ONE WRITER WHO was born in Southwold has proved to be a little difficult to pin down due to his eccentricity in the use of names. Stephen Southwold (1887-1964) attended St. Mark's College, Chelsea from 1905 for two years and then worked as a schoolmaster. He also became a prolific author, writing just over a hundred books during his lifetime. Born Stephen Henry Critten, he used a number of pseudonyms, eventually changing his name to one of them, Stephen Southwold. He most often wrote as Neil Bell and also as Stephen Green, S. H. Lambert and Paul Martens. One book, *The Seventh Bowl* (1930) was written as Miles and then Neil Bell. The same applied to *Valiant Clay* (1931) and *The Gas War of 1940*. The story of generations of the author's boat-building family is told in *Bredon and Sons* (1933). He set two historical novels in the Bury St Edmunds area, namely *The Abbot's Heel* (1939) and *Simon Dale* (1959). His frequent change of name was apparently a reaction against his father.

Another most distinguished resident of Aldeburgh was the notable writer, Laurens van der Post (1906-1996), an admirer of the work of the painter, Mary Potter whose career I will deal with just a little later. This eminent man and his second wife, Ingaret, eventually moved permanently to the seaside town and lived in a cottage that he had used as a retreat and summer home for over thirty years. He lectured at the Aldeburgh Festival in 1957 and this married couple were certainly part of the circle of friends involved with Benjamin Britten and Peter Pears. They often played tennis with them and, on the odd occasion, also with Mary Potter, usually at The Red House. This social activity resulted in van der Post being introduced to HRH Prince Charles, with whom he had a close and influential friendship for the rest of his life. He became godfather to HRH Prince William, now Duke of Cambridge following his marriage to Kate Middleton. Laurens van der Post and Prince Charles went together on safari to Kenya in 1977. When living at his Chelsea home, in Flood Street, his next-door neighbour was Margaret Thatcher. When she became Prime Minister she often called upon his advice with matters dealing with southern Africa, notably the Rhodesia settlement of 1979-80. In 1981, he was rewarded with a knighthood. In addition to being an educator, journalist, humanitarian, philosopher, explorer, and conservationist he was also a prolific writer of fiction and non-fiction over a period of some sixty years or so. There were film-adaptations of his books, which included *Merry Christmas, Mr. Lawrence* (1983). This was based on his novel, *A Bar of Shadow* (1954). The films, *The Seed and the Sower* (1963) and *The Night of the New Moon* (1970) were about his experiences as a prisoner of war by the Japanese in World War II. Another aspect of the Britten-Pears connection, was van der Post's friendship with William Plomer, whom he had known from his time in South Africa and then Japan in the 1920s. Laurens van der Post had certainly led a very full and active life and for his ninetieth birthday party he had a five-day celebration in Colorado, USA with a This is your Life type event with friends drawn from virtually every period of his long life. A few days later, on December 16 1996, after whispering in Afrikaans 'die sterre' (the stars), he died. The funeral took place in London and included amongst the many dignitaries attending, Prince Charles and Baroness Thatcher.

Although never a resident of East Anglia, the author John Cowper Powys (1872-1963) was an occasional visitor to Suffolk, having spent childhood holidays in the county as well as staying with his brother who farmed at Sweffling, near Saxmundham. During his lifetime, he earned quite a reputation as a writer, being regarded as a great master of landscape portrayal. Such an aptitude owed much to his rendering of interpenetration and emotional experience; this was in his novels that dealt with the landscapes and seascapes of East Anglia, as well as other parts of the country. With these aspects in mind, his later work has been compared with that of D H Lawrence (1885-1930) as well as Sir Walter Scott and Thomas Hardy. Powys learned from the latter writer the technique of handling physical dimension. His novels are considered rich in a type of spatial distancing. He became a prolific writer, with over twenty novels and novellas to his credit as well as short stories and books on philosophy. It seems remarkable that he had reached his fifties before his first novel was published; this was *Wolf Solent* (1929), the first of the so-called Wessex novels, which include *A Glastonbury Romance* (1932) followed by *Weymouth Sands* (1934) and then *Maiden Castle* (1936). Powys's characters are conveyed to the reader primarily through their responses to the environment and it is said that his talent for character analysis was fed upon by the writer, Angus Wilson (1913-1991). Wilson not only lived in Suffolk but also, jointly with Malcolm Bradbury, helped to establish the now renowned creative writing course at the University of East Anglia. 'It is in his treatment of nature that Powys takes his place as one of our great romantic novelists.' This is a direct quotation from *John Cowper Powys: Novelist* (1973) by Glen Cavaliero (born 1927), a former Research fellow of St Catherine's College, Cambridge. Cavaliero is no stranger to assessing the qualities of English writers associated with East Anglia: he has also published a critical study of E M Forster (1979) in a book entitled *A Reading of E M Forster*

Amongst the many authors noted for being laborious and conscientious in their research were Agnes and Elisabeth Strickland, both born at Reydon Hall, Suffolk and educated by their father, Thomas Strickland. I mention both women as being writers on the grounds that although Agnes (1796-1874) took the credit for writing a series of non-fiction books, according to *Oxford National Dictionary of Biography*, most of the research and writing was done by Elisabeth. Amongst the various books which I will, for the sake of convenience, describe as being attributable to the sisters were *Lives of the Queens of England from the Norman Conquest, Lives of the Queens of Scotland, and English Princesses*, etc. (8 vols., 1850-1859 – also published in America where Elisabeth was also given a credit), *Lives of the Bachelor Kings of England* (1861), and *Letters of Mary, Queen of Scots*. It seems to be the case that because Elisabeth was not interested in the publicity that a writer attracts, even in those days, Agnes Strickland's name was put forward as the author. I am, however, not entirely convinced of this due to Elisabeth being specified as author in the USA. Let us settle for what seems to be a case of 'the jury is still out' on that subject. Whoever wrote these books it has been said by some that the style was mediocre, whereas others maintained that the writing should be compared only to that of their contemporaries of the time. This strikes me as a fittingly indulgent qualification of the sisters' merits as authors.

Both sisters not only lived but also died in Southwold. In his book, *A Bookman's Tale* (his account of a trip to the town on a summer's Bank Holiday entitled *Blackberrying at Southwold*), Ronald Blythe wrote 'I see these Victorian ladies putting down their pens for an hour for a gusty stroll to Walberswick, their maid banking up the fire for their return'. He described the North Sea on the particular day to which he refers as 'a steady azure until it is within sight of the horizon, when it turns to skimmed-milk blue'. I am still struggling with that description. I can understand that the sea gets paler in colour towards the horizon, but the actual sea being within sight of its horizon? Discuss; or is just me? Anyway, Agnes Strickland started her literary career with a poem, *Worcester Field*, followed by *The Seven Ages of Woman and Demetrius*. She then abandoned poetry and concentrated on historical non-fiction. One of her books was *Historical Tales of Illustrious British Children* and this was written in 1833. Two of Agnes's other sisters were also writers. These were Susanna Moodie (1803-1885) and Catharine Parr Traill (1802-1899), both of whom are famous for their works about pioneer life in early Canada where they both settled, Moodie having emigrated with her husband in 1832. Susanna also wrote children's books, but it was *Roughing it in the Bush* and *Life in the Clearings Versus the Bush* that established her Canadian literary reputation. Catharine Parr Traill also wrote what were described as children's books, including some early work, *Disobedience, or Mind What Mama Says* (1819) and *Happy Because Good*. These books tended to dwell on the benefits of obedience to one's parents. I am wondering just how popular these might have been with children in general but perhaps attitudes were different in those days. After marrying Thomas Traill, Catharine and her new husband moved abroad by crossing the Atlantic to Canada. This was much to the displeasure of her parents who must have found the family home in Southwold much less active in every way after these events. Brother Samuel had also emigrated and worked as a surveyor in the Dominion. P D James describes Agnes Strickland as a forgotten writer of sentimental biography which seems harsh, given her era, but this contemporary writer concedes that sentimental, schmaltzy or not, she was undoubtedly popular in her day and she did, of course, come from an extremely literate family.

Some, but certainly not all, of the literary connections with coastal Suffolk that I have decided to feature can be considered a little on the tenuous side. This is due to me working on the basis that if the name is strong enough, perhaps a half-hearted link is better than none at all. For example, if the name is, shall we say, in a mastery of understatement at the very least, certainly well known, to my mind it merits inclusion. For instance, let us take Blundeston, a location just a short distance to the north-west of Lowestoft and more or less the mid distance between that town and Great Yarmouth. This village is named as 'Blunderstone' and is the birthplace of the title character in the novel, *David Copperfield*, which was written in 1849-50 by Charles Dickens (1812-1870). There does appear to be some evidence that this most theatrical of writers did visit the actual village, it being understood that he might well have been attracted to the name as a result of having seen it on a signpost when visiting Great Yarmouth or perhaps Lowestoft. Whatever the truth of the matter, it does seem apparent from reading *David Copperfield* that Dickens, in one way or another, did become familiar with some of the local landmarks that can be readily found in Blundeston to this day. For example, he mentions the view of St Mary's church and the yew trees from The Rookery, the fictional childhood home and birthplace of David Copperfield. Dickens also refers to the Plough Inn, which continues to remain in business. It is also said that the character of the carter and carrier, Mr Barkis in *David Copperfield*, often departed from this particular hostelry whilst going about his business. It will be remembered that David was instructed by Barkis to give a message to Clara Peggotty, the maid servant to David's mother, to the effect that 'Barkis is willin'' (to marry Clara).

As far as the town of Great Yarmouth is concerned, this is given as the fictional home of the Peggotty family and always named in the book as merely Yarmouth. Throughout the book, the particular part of Yarmouth that David visited regularly, being the home of both Clara as well as her brother Daniel, is stated to be in the county of Suffolk by virtue of the fact that this was the county they often visited when travelling from London. Without getting too tied up with county boundaries, Great Yarmouth is certainly known as a Norfolk seaside resort and seaport. However, I am inclined to the view that as 'Dan'l', Clara Peggotty's brother's home, was an upturned boat, converted to a house, and situated on the seashore this could well have been artistic or indeed literary license on the part of Charles Dickens. On the other hand, perhaps his East Anglian geography had been found lacking.

David Copperfield is known to be semi-autobiographical and although the novelist was born in Portsmouth he clearly chose a costal location for his character and there is, of course, the town of Yarmouth on the Isle of Wight or is this just coincidence? All in all, it is nice to think that of this country's greatest literary figures, and known throughout the world, two are associated with costal Suffolk in one form or another. In the Preface to the Second Edition of *David Copperfield* (1867), Dickens wrote that of all the books that he had written, he regarded *David Copperfield* as the one he liked best. Furthermore he confessed that acting like a 'fond parent to every child of fancy ... I have in my heart of hearts a favourite child. And his name is David Copperfield'. I do not think that anything more needs to be said on that subject, other than that the two years he spent on writing this delightful story were certainly well spent.

Dickens was certainly no stranger to the county of Suffolk in that his connection with Bury St Edmunds dates back to the 1830s. His first novel, *The Pickwick Papers*, was said to have been at least part-written in room number fifteen, now known as The Dickens Suite, at the town's well-known Angel Hotel. *The Pickwick Papers* is said to be based upon the town of Sudbury, Suffolk, in those times a 'rotten borough'. Bury St Edmunds' townspeople tend to boast about the way Dickens immortalised their town by specifically mentioning the self-same Angel Hotel, a coaching inn dating back to 1432. Not only that, this distinguished author also gave readings in the nearby Athenæum, a Grade I Listed building, on Angel Square, at right angles to the Angel Hotel.

Other places in Suffolk have also laid claim to an association with Charles Dickens in one way or another. The author is said to have visited a workhouse at Barham, a village 'twixt Ipswich and Needham Market, when he was a young journalist writing about social conditions. Some say that a record book he found there contained details regarding a ten-year-old boy's apprenticeship. This was to give him the inspiration for *Oliver Twist*.

No one less than Walter de la Mare (1873-1956) who, whilst being unhappily employed by the Anglo American Oil Company in the City of London, chose to visit Southwold for the first time in 1894. This was in pursuit of a young lady resident of the town called Constance Elfrida Ingpen, or 'Effie' as he knew her. He had met this woman previously at an amateur dramatics club and she was ten years his senior. It was in Southwold that they decided to get married and it was also whilst in the town that he finally made up his mind to become a full time writer. Walter de la Mare was author of a huge collection of short stories, the majority of which were for children with many being in the genre of fairy stories. There were also four novels and numerous examples of published poetry. He was a great theorist on aspects of the imagination; he tended to divide these into two precise forms: 'childlike' and 'boy-like'. His impressive literary career earned him official recognition in the form of being created Companion of Honour and subsequently being made a member of the Order of Merit. His ashes rest in the crypt of St Paul's Cathedral in London. As far as I am concerned, he is also to be remembered for giving such welcome encouragement to Oliver Bernard who wrote those delightful verses about the endearing charms of Walberswick.

I am now about to establish a connection between Walter de la Mare and Benjamin Britten. In his boyhood, the composer had made musical settings of a selection of Walter de la Mare's poems that he eventually published in 1969 as *Tit for Tat*. This collection is dedicated to the poet's son, Richard de la Mare, who was the first chairman of Faber Music, Britten's music publisher. T S Eliot (1888– 1965), the American-born, English poet was a director of Faber and Faber at that time and warmly welcomed the idea of Faber's publishing Britten's music. Sadly, I have not been able to establish any direct association between Eliot and the Aldeburgh Festival. However, Benjamin Britten did become a director of Faber Music after initially welcoming the concept of Faber entering the music publishing business in March 1964. I am inclined to regard this as an independent non-executive appointment, although I feel quite certain that his advice to fellow board members would have been invaluable.

PART THREE
ARTISTS, PAINTERS AND ARCHITECTS

'As my poor father used to say
In 1863
Once people start on all this Art
Goodbye moralitee!
And what my father used to say Is food enough for me.'

Lines for a worthy person (1930)

Sir Alan Herbert (1890-1971)
English humourist, novelist and playwright

'Art must be parochial in the beginning to become cosmopolitan
in the end,'

Hail and Farewell (1925)

George Moore (1852-1953)
Novelist, short-story writer, poet, art critic, memoirist and
dramatist

Chapter One

Mary Potter, a convenient 'house swap' and a further painter or two

THE COAST OF Suffolk is, of course, noted for the enormity of its skies. These are emphasised by low horizons, which, combined with the reflections of the sea, generate light of exceptionally high quality. This is the extremely desirable feature that has attracted artists for over a period of two hundred years and probably even longer. I have already written about the Pipers and their association with Benjamin Britten but I would now like to illustrate the cross-fertilisation of artistic talent by describing how John and Myfanwy Piper got to know a married couple, Stephen and Mary Potter as a result of the Benjamin Britten and Peter Pears connection.

In 1954, the Pipers invited the Potters to stay at Fawley Bottom, their home in Oxfordshire, but the invitation had to be declined due to a devastating change in personal circumstances as far as Mary Potter was concerned. She was obliged to explain to the Pipers in a letter, which must have caused her much distress to write, that only the week before Stephen had announced to her that he wished to marry someone else and would be seeking a divorce. This subsequently happened but, as an artist, Mary Potter's association with Aldeburgh was to last for something only a little short of thirty years.

Mary Potter soon settled down on her own in Aldeburgh and concentrated on her chosen vocation to paint. She worked every day in her new, north-facing studio. It was clear that this was what she lived for and she was to spend the rest of her life in coastal Suffolk. She carried on doing productive painting until she reached the age of eighty-one.

I have decided to write at some at length about Mary Potter because women artists on the Suffolk coast were few and far between compared with their male counterparts. I do feel more than justified because she was undoubtedly recognised as an impressive talent, especially when three examples of her work were exhibited at the Graves Art Gallery, Sheffield's exhibition entitled *'Famous British Women Artists'*. It was also the employment of her own special interpretation of light that attracted Mary Potter's many supporters, including some of the national UK galleries such as the Tate and the Arts Council, as well as the art collection owned by the Government. In addition to these, there were also a number of provincial and overseas galleries. She was awarded a number of 'one man shows' and exhibited at any number of other galleries over the years.

At an earlier stage in her career, she was something of a portraitist although this activity was given up in the late 1960s. Amongst Mary Potter's portraits are those of people associated with the Aldeburgh Festival, principally its founders, Benjamin Britten and Peter Pears as well as Imogen Holst. At the time of writing, Mary Potter's portrait of Holst can still be seen hanging alone on the wall inside the entrance area of Snape Maltings Concert Hall. Imogen Holst is said to have confessed that when Mary Potter was working on her portrait, she was thinking of Bach, 'going over the *St John Passion* in my head'. Potter's penultimate subject for a portrait was Jacquetta Hawkes, the third wife of author and playwright, J B (Jack) Priestley (1894-1984). He became extremely well known for his BBC wartime broadcasts on Sunday nights in 1940-41. His audience was said to peak at around sixteen million, and I am just about able to remember listening to some of these popular talks with my parents. The Hawkes portrait was intended to be Mary Potter's swansong in the field but in 1968, Joyce Grenfell, of course no stranger to the Aldeburgh Festival, asked if she could sit for her. As this work involved no travelling, Mary agreed after Joyce made it clear that she was prepared to attend for sittings at The Red Studio, which was a later addition to the previously mentioned The Red House. It took three attempts at the portrait until Mary Potter was satisfied and the finished work was kept by Joyce Grenfell and included in the 1981 Serpentine Gallery retrospective of Mary Potter's work. Miss Grenfell had kept up with Mary as well as Stephen after the divorce in 1955. Earlier, as a writer at the BBC, both during and after the Second World War, Joyce Grenfell had collaborated with Stephen Potter in writing the '*How*' series of thirty satirical programmes from *How to Talk to Children* to *How to Listen*.

To get back to the after-effect of the Potters' marital problems, Mary Potter had explained to Myfanwy Piper how Britten and Pears had helped her through all the misery that she had experienced at such an emotional time. It was then that a 'house exchange' plan was hatched because the pair had already been considering a move away from the seafront. With their increasing celebrity, Britten and Pears found Crag House offered them little privacy so, as The Red House, the Potters' marital home in Aldeburgh, was far too large and expensive to manage for Mary Potter alone during the period following the divorce, an exchange of homes was deemed to be an ideal solution for all parties concerned. As it happened, it was Mary Potter's son Julian, eventually to become her biographer, who suggested the arrangement. Living in The Red House, being situated on the outskirts of Aldeburgh, resulted in Britten and Pears becoming far more divorced from the public gaze. An added advantage was the presence of a tennis court. Benjamin Britten and Peter Pears had been regular tennis players and had been obliged, in the main, to make regular use of the public courts in Aldeburgh. However, they had also become accustomed to playing, on occasion, on the grass court at The Red House during the course of their friendship with the married couple and when all had been well between the Potters. To now have their own tennis court was a very welcome feature in the active lives of the composer and singer and this must have added an attractive bonus as far as the house swap was concerned. They were also able to continue to make use of Crag House as a base for their habitual sea bathing, despite The Red House sporting an outdoor swimming pool. It seems that certain regular habits die hard. Other activities of theirs included sailing, motoring (they owned a vintage Rolls Royce in the early 1950s) and brass rubbing, working on the 'old memorial brass figures that fill so many of Suffolk's gothic churches'.

Crag House and subsequently The Red House were always full of both old and young friends as Britten and Pears loved to feel 'free and well' after hectic months of hard work. Perhaps, above all, their new home provided an essentially private, creative and social space for visiting performers and a wide variety of other musical, literary and artistic figures, who continued to arrive at Aldeburgh to work with Britten and Pears in their musical activities. Others were there to work with them on collaborative projects and were soon to draw inspiration from the uniquely creative atmosphere that Britten and Pears instilled into their new home.

The Red House, in Golf Lane, Aldeburgh remains preserved much as when Britten and Pears lived there. It continues to be open to visitors on a regular basis. Adjacent nowadays can be found the Britten-Pears Library, converted in 1963 from an old school for milkmaids. It was in this same year that Mary Potter moved into the newly-constructed Red Studio, which can be found just a short distance away from the library building. It is now a private residence.

In 1963, Mary Potter moved away from Crag House into living accommodation contained within the newly-constructed studio/ bungalow in the grounds of The Red House. She must have found this a little strange after enjoying the spaciousness and ample grounds of The Red House during the course of her married life. Crag House was placed on the market and sold. Benjamin Britten had previously bought some adjoining land at Red House in order to enlarge the garden, thus providing enough space for this new building within the grounds. This new home then became known as The Red Studio. Myfanwy Piper stayed a night there with Mary Potter in August 1964. The purpose was for Myfanwy Piper to obtain material for her catalogue essay on Mary Potter. On completion of this piece of writing, at a later date, it was said to neatly pinpoint Potter's pursuit of 'a kind of suspended extension of the moment' and the sense, in her work of 'the inescapable and extraordinary repetition of life'. However, this intended work of Myfanwy Piper had to be temporarily set aside due to her charwoman being ill and there was much domestic work that required her attention, in the way of washing and ironing, in preparation for a visit to Dame Edith and her brother, Sir Robert Sitwell at Renishaw, their stately home and family seat in Derbyshire. Sir Osbert Sitwell (1892-1969) was fifth Baronet Renishaw and he was also a writer of some note. His work included not only poetry but also novels and short stories. In later life, he became known as a 'Grand Old Man of English Letters'.

It became noticeable that Mary Potter's painting seemed to have been given a new lease of life after she had settled at The Red Studio. Her completed works were seen to steadily increase in number on the walls of her new home. Her oil and watercolour paintings had also become a significant part of each of the private collections of Benjamin Britten and Peter Pears. In Myfanwy Piper's view, these acted as 'pools of perceptive calm in their sometimes rather fraught lives'. It is thought that what she was referring to in this respect was all of the necessary travelling for their performances and other appearances, both at home and internationally. Their creative work also continued to play a significant part in their lives, to which could be added the effort involved in organising the Festival, especially in the early days. Imogen Holst stated that for Pears, the acquisition of paintings acted as a relaxation and lifesaver. Incidentally, although Benjamin Britten had arranged for The Red Studio to be built in the enlarged grounds of The Red House, he and Peter Pears had never sought any rent from Mary Potter, preferring to accept, in lieu, one of her paintings each year. Another painting was added to their collection of art after her death when her will instructed Pears to collect a painting of his choice from her studio. There seems to be no question that Mary Potter is the best-represented artist in the Britten-Pears art collection. As far as Peter Pears' own collection was concerned, during his lifetime he regularly bought paintings by artists associated with coastal Suffolk. Amongst his collection could be found works by John Constable, Walter Sickert, John Piper, John Craxton and Sidney Nolan, OM as well as Mary Potter. He also supported work by young, less well-known painters. However, it must have pleased him to be in a position to purchase the work of a number of his friends so that these could be well represented on the walls of The Red House.

Throughout her time at Aldeburgh, Mary Potter continued to remain dedicated to her painting. We have seen that her work, which often depended on a subtle interplay of closely related colours, had already achieved national recognition. Admirers of her art included poet, novelist and essayist, Stephen Spender, Laurens van der Post, and the art historian Kenneth Clark (1903-1983), later known as Lord Clark, arguably one of the most distinguished art historians of his generation. He achieved an international popular presence as the writer, producer, and presenter of the acclaimed BBC Television series, *Civilisation*. After Britten's death, Mary became close to Clark, having stayed with him at his home, Saltwood, Kent. It appears that marriage was discussed. In his autobiography Clark wrote: 'Her husband, the noted humourist, left her. Of all the women in the world whom I would not have left, Mary Potter is the first. She accepted the law of nature and went on painting better than ever'.

It is odd to think that Mary Potter might well have become stepmother to Alan Clark (1928-1999), the late Conservative MP and government minister. His reputation as a womaniser, as well as his somewhat notorious published diaries, were to make Saltwood appear somewhat tarnished due to its name appearing so often in the columns of the national press. Clark's well-publicised diaries revealed far too much detail of his various affairs and dalliances but this just seemed to add to his scandalous reputation, especially when he was sometimes seen to have over-imbibed whilst on parliamentary duties. Something of a snob, he once famously described Lord Heseltine, a former Conservative cabinet minister, as the sort of man who bought his own furniture.

Alan Clark's father also seemed to have an eye for the ladies, particularly at least two connected with Aldeburgh. I have read that he also had an affair with the previously mentioned Myfanwy Piper who wrote three libretti for Benjamin Britten. The composer once complained that 'she is so good, but is so occupied with being a wife and mother'. So perhaps there were also other distractions. The composer required total dedication, but her excellent reputation was earned as a result of her notably deep research bringing an insightful flair to her tasks. This earned her remarkable plaudits for some memorable passages in Britten's operas. Myfanwy Piper's relationship with Kenneth Clark could well have been part of an intriguing love triangle. Clark had become her editor, commissioning her to write for the *Penguin Modern Painters* series to which John Betjeman was contributing a monograph on John Piper. According to Frances Spalding in her book on the Pipers, there was evidence that Myfanwy became the poet's lover and we are also aware of his poem bearing that name in its title. I will write more on this subject later and you will also be made aware of the further links in the lives of Mary Potter, Myfanwy Piper and her husband with John Betjeman. It was Sir Walter Scott (1771-1832), novelist and poet who wrote:

> 'O what a tangled web we weave,
> When first we practise to deceive!'

Notwithstanding the marital difficulties and the obvious popularity of Mary Potter, I feel that it would be unfair if I ignored this opportunity to introduce Mary's former husband, Stephen Potter (1900-1969), a name that became quite well known in the 1940s and 1950s. He was the author of *The Theory and Practice of Gamesmanship or the Art of Winning Games without Actually Cheating* (1947). This is indeed a lengthy mouthful of a title but it is customarily shortened to the term *'Gamesmanship'*, of which Stephen Potter is generally recognised as its inventor. However, what follows seems to prove otherwise. The practice of gamesmanship tends to be deemed dubious without technically being illegal and the idea of writing the book first came to Potter in the changing room after a doubles match of lawn tennis as far back as the year 1931. On that particular occasion, his partner was philosopher and psychologist, C E M ('Professor') Joad (1891-1953) who went on to become one of the members of BBC Radio's *The Brains Trust* in 1941-42. This programme was broadcast throughout the war as well as well after hostilities ceased. In the 1950s it was transferred to BBC television. During the particular game of tennis that I have mentioned, it seems that Joad had sought to put off one of their opponent's overwhelming superior serving game by seeking his confirmation as to whether Joad's return of a serve was categorically 'in or out'. As it was quite clear to Potter that the ball was definitely 'out', having hit the netting behind the server on the volley, he judged Joad's gambit as perhaps the birth of 'gamesmanship'. This questionable tactic severely affected the opponent's ongoing service game, and this enabled Potter and his partner to win a match that otherwise was virtually certain to be lost. Why is it that a perfectly ordinary game of tennis between what appears to have been members of a tennis club should be treated seriously enough to warrant the application of such an almost childish but unquestionably dubious ploy from a distinguished academic? I am not sure that I wish to know the answer but it could hardly be called competitive instinct if at least one of the players felt compelled to resort to trickery. Whatever might be thought about that incident, it did lead to the art of gamesmanship as we know it today. I suppose a deliberate coughing noise from an opponent when a golfer is concentrating on the striking of the ball from a tee or is lining up for a put tends to come under this heading.

Moving on, it was as a result of paying several visits to Suffolk, and subsequently staying with friends in Aldeburgh, that led Stephen and Mary Potter to settle in the town in the year 1951. After seeing the town at its best on a summer's day, they bought a house just a few minutes' drive from the sea as well as being adjacent to the local golf course. As we now know, their new home was known as The Red House. They soon became involved with Aldeburgh's social life if only because they were more or less regarded as incoming celebrities, bearing in mind Stephen's success with the *Gamesmanship* book and Mary's growing reputation as an artist. It was inevitable that they would soon meet Benjamin Britten during the course of the social whirl and the composer lost no time in introducing the couple to his small dinner gathering at a local hotel during the week of their arrival in Aldeburgh. It was during that evening that the Potters socialised with Peter Pears and E M Forster. This eventually led to their becoming closely involved in the circle of those connected with the freshly-started Aldeburgh Festival. They soon became a popular part of this rather exclusive social set. When Britten and Pears' home, Crag House became flooded in the East Coast storm disaster of 1953, the regular meetings of the Aldeburgh Music Club were transferred temporarily to The Red House. The Red House soon became the club's permanent home as the drawing room was judged by Benjamin Britten to be a far better venue for the club's activities. This was the time that the Potters joined as members which, given the circumstances, was probably something of an obligation. At a later date, Mary Potter moved on from being hostess to chairman of the club. Elsewhere I shall write about how 'Westons', a Freud family home in Walberswick, became a sort of headquarters to Jill Freud's Southwold Summer Theatre Company and it strikes me as a very informal, not to say an attractive way, to set about creating artistic entertainment in coastal Suffolk.

I have mentioned, one or more times earlier, an artist, Sidney Nolan (1917-1992), an Australian who responded creatively to Benjamin Britten's music. Theirs was perhaps an unlikely friendship: or was it? Each of them gave something to the other. In Nolan's case, he unlocked the exposed landscape of his native country, described as an ancient indigenous civilization, an atavistic inner world that both chimed with and informed the composer's vision. Although the two men talked about collaborating with each other on various projects, such as a ballet, a sea symphony, maybe even Coleridge's *The Ancient Mariner*, nothing of that nature was ever fulfilled. On the other hand, Sidney Nolan's painting of *Peter Grimes Apprentice* is thought to be a vivid evocation of Aldeburgh, where the swirling grey sea constantly threatens to overwhelm the town. This work is said to retain an extraordinary, luminous presence as the boy's drowned body becomes literally part of the undersea world of fishes and seaweed, which are painted in Nolan's trademark colouring. This picture was painted for the thirtieth Aldeburgh Festival and included in an exhibition subtitled *An artist's response to the music of Benjamin Britten*. An image of the painting can be found on the Tate's website. The final, almost valedictory, connection, as far as the two friends were concerned, was for the 1991 Aldeburgh Festival's Japanese production of *Sumidagawa* (the Noh-play on which Britten's *Curlew River* is based). It was for this performance that the Australian artist agreed to design the obligatory pine tree. Britten had seen the play during the course of a visit to Japan in 1956, and eight years later he composed *Curlew River*, a dramatic work based on the story. This piece is described as *A Parable for Church Performance*, the first of three Church Parables, in effect something of a Chamber Opera, setting it in mediaeval East Anglia. It was William Plomer who wrote the libretto.

Having mentioned Mary Potter as a female artist closely associated with Aldeburgh, it is worth noting that the village of Iken, not a million miles from Snape, had as a resident for some years Amy Katherine Browning (1881-1978), a lifelong professional painter thoroughly dedicated to her art. She studied at the Royal College of Art and exhibited at the Paris Salon where purchases of her work were made by the French Government. One of her landscape paintings is of Benhall Green, Suffolk; by contrast, this is held in the British Government's art collection. There are also four more of her paintings in this official collection, including one entitled *Aldeburgh Fair*. All are oil on canvas and were purchased from the artist in 1957. In her youth, she was closely associated with the women's suffrage movement and although her work was accepted for the Royal Academy's Summer Exhibitions over a period in excess of seventy years she was never elected to full membership, a matter that made her deeply unhappy. One of her notable portraits was that of Sir Winston Churchill, after a similar painting by Sir Oswald Birley (1880-1952). She was also an exhibitor with W F Crittall's Sole Bay Group in the early 1930s, in both Southwold and Aldeburgh. More will be written on this subject later.

Browning was married to T C Dugdale (1880-1952) who was a Royal Academician, known principally for portraiture. Amongst this artist's subjects were members of the aristocracy. Two portraits by him are hung at the National Portrait Gallery. One was of Ernest Bevin (1881-1951), a prominent member of the wartime coalition and Labour

Cabinet, who was successively Minister of Labour and the Foreign Secretary. The other was of Dame Wendy Hiller (1912-2003), a notable stage and film actress with a career that extended some sixty years. One of her earlier roles was that of Eliza Doolittle in the original 1938 film of George Bernard Shaw's *Pygmalion*, with Leslie Howard as Professor Higgins.

All in all, the above represents just one or two examples of the extraordinary interconnection of artistic talent that has occurred from time to time in coastal Suffolk, all during the 'reign' of Benjamin Britten and Peter Pears.

Chapter Two

Walberswick, an enduring haven for painters for more than two centuries. Southwold has also enjoyed its supporters

NOT BEING AN amateur, let alone a gifted amateur painter, I can, nevertheless appreciate how artists have been inspired by scenes, particularly landscapes, period buildings, flowing rivers and streams, weeping willows and picturesque bridges. The word 'picturesque' is defined as 'strikingly graphic' and therefore directly relating to visual art. For example, there is a wealth of evidence in support of Walberswick because of its exceptional eastern light, added to which is its immediate environment by way of dominant seashore which backs on to delightfully tranquil marshes. These attractive features have served to contribute to the village's reputation as an inspirational haven for both notable and amateur artists who have been drawn from near and far during the course of recent centuries. Many of these made some sort of home there or have been content to enjoy lengthy, as well as much shorter, stays in the village. The owners of several local bed and breakfast establishments have not hesitated to claim that certain notable artists of the past have either lived or resided within the premises.

I find it rather surprising that the village of Walberswick has not been quite as well known as an artists' colony as, say, other coastal locations in the country, particularly in Cornwall, such as Newlyn or perhaps St Ives. The foundations for the latter colony date from 1928 when Cornish painter, Alfred Wallis (1855-1942) met in the village with his artist friends Ben Nicholson (1894-1982) and Christopher Wood (1901-1930). This is comparatively recent compared with Newlyn; this town's connection with art dates back to 1882 when the painter, Walter Langley (1852-1922) arrived from Birmingham and became the founder of the school of *en plein air* artists. Although Walberswick's development as a haven for artists dates as far back as the mid-1880s, it will be shown that artists of significant reputation for their sketching and painting were regular visitors looking back as far as the much earlier years of the nineteenth century. That may well have been the case also in Cornwall but, in this particular story, we are concentrating on just this particular stretch of the Suffolk coastline.

Over the years, many artists have sought to capture the mood and spirit of Walberswick by observing the glittering eastern light as this phenomenon allied itself with crashing waves, when the wind was seen to rise above light to moderate in strength. If further contrast was needed, there was always the serenity of the nearby marshes that make their own, highly individual contribution to the atmosphere.

Activities connected with the Southwold-Walberswick ferry have certainly attracted the attention of artists over the decades and we shall soon see that there is the lasting evidence of what is contained within the *Walberswick Scroll*. This admirable and fascinating work by John Doman Turner features every building in the village at the time of its execution in 1931. Known simply as the *Walberswick Scroll*, the real thing is a 123ft long (37.5m) roll of cartridge paper depicting each house down the full length of the village, one side on the way down and the other on the return journey. This monumental work has been restored after what had been years of neglect. It can be viewed, by special arrangement, thanks to the efforts of a local resident. The roll has been backed with linen and stored within the mahogany case of a former pub football game. It can be viewed by turning a large brass handle that operates a spindle mechanism. Although Doman Turner's painting skills were thought to be somewhat erratic, this was compensated for by other qualities associated with his undoubted love for the village and his talent for concentrated observation. It is also worth mentioning here that the fictional character, Max, the artist who painted the 'scroll' in Esther Freud's previously mentioned book was described as deaf. This was the real-life case of Doman Turner, and it was seeing the *Walberswick Scroll* for the first time that inspired her to write *The Sea House* and perhaps include certain other characters that have featured in the history of the village.

My personal viewing of the *Walberswick Scroll* afforded me a delightfully romantic image of a largely unspoilt community on the Suffolk coast. I am certainly not alone in this respect. Long may Walberswick reign as an example of a Mecca for artists, not only as a very desirable place for them to live but also as a location ideally suited to inspire creative activity in all its various forms. Walberswick's little Georgian centre has been described as 'impossibly picturesque' and continues to feel as if it is charmingly trapped in the 1950s. It gets more than a little crowded in the summer months, but tranquillity can be found in the nearby nature reserve that follows the River Blyth estuary. Over four hundred hectares (almost 1,000 acres) form an enchanting locale that features reeds, mudflats, meadows and marsh, all protected by the official designation as that of an Area of Outstanding National Beauty (AONB). It serves as a home to otter and deer, as well as a large variety of birds. One prominent local resident assured me that there is no serious problem with the vast number of summer visitors because the peace and quiet experienced by the locals during other seasons provides more than adequate compensation for the traffic congestion and crowded beach during the peak summer months.

A section of the Walberswick Scroll that depicts Doman Turner's plan of the village

Elsewhere in this book, I have written in some detail about Esther Freud's book, *The Sea House*, a novel that features within the plot the already-mentioned memorable work of art that has become known as *The Walberswick Scroll*. We now know that the 'real' artist was John Doman Turner and although he had never been a full-time student of art, he was an original member of the Camden Town Group. These were Post-Impressionist artists of considerable note that had a short-lived alliance from 1911-13. Members, some of whom had been influenced by Vincent Van Gogh (1853-1890) and Paul Gauguin (1848-1903), included the already-mentioned Walter Sickert as well as Spencer Gore (1878-1914), August John, Harold Gilman, (1876-1919) J B Manson (1879-1945)and Lucien Pissarro (1863-1944), son of Impressionist artist, Camille Pissarro. This was particularly distinguished company for Doman Turner, who was indeed totally deaf, and his creative skills owed much to his determination to seek guidance and instruction from the established artists associated with the group, especially Sickert. This was due to the fact that Doman

Turner attended Walter Sickert's life classes. In turn, Spencer Gore accepted Doman Turner as a private pupil and, because of the latter's hearing difficulties, this took the form of what would be known today as a correspondence course. The 1920s saw Doman Turner working a great deal in and around Southwold, Blythburgh, Wangford and Walberswick. He lodged at Harbour View in the last mentioned village.

To return, once again but very briefly, to Esther Freud's *The Sea House*, one of the minor characters was a local tramp and her inspiration in that regard appears to have been drawn from the fairly recent history of the village of Walberswick. A resident, Francesca Wilson, was not an artist, even though she may well have been, at least in spirit. She worked as a writer and died in 1981, by then aged in her nineties. As a result of her travels overseas, she developed an awareness of the plight of refugees as well as other unfortunates and, in her later years, became involved with their rehabilitation. She owned two properties in the village, Creek Cottage and East Point. These were used as holiday retreats where 'visitors' included not only second-generation Spanish immigrants but also several artists and writers who benefited from her generosity in terms of inexpensive accommodation. A number of these artists succeeded in not only having their work exhibited, but also in being elected to the Royal Academy. I have singled out for special mention an abstract artist named Donnagh McKenna. He arrived at East Point in 1976 and, over the years, his work was reputably exhibited at the Tate Gallery, the Arts Council of Great Britain as well as at several London embassies.

To get back to the Esther Freud 'tramp' character in her work of fiction, this fictional being must have been as a result of inspiration drawn from Peter Buxton (1925-1979), an architect said to possess unusual sensitivity and vision. Sadly, he became a drop-out for reasons that were never made known and he ended up in Walberswick as one of Francesca Wilson's 'guests'. The very welcome accommodation allotted to him consisted of a potting shed in the garden of Creek Cottage. He had graduated from a packing case situated amidst the shingle near East Point where the previously mentioned local artist, Donnagh McKenna, had come across him. The 'tramp' was immediately regarded by the painter as a friendly neighbour. The move to the garden shed at Creek Cottage came about only as a result of Buxton also being offered the use of an old gypsy caravan on the edge of the marsh. The shed was deemed to be marginally more comfortable than the former mobile home, in that Buxton was able to gain his independence as well as grow his own vegetables. It is pleasing to report that his appearance was stereotypical, not to say theatrically, biblical, having regard to a regal bearing and a flowing beard, both attributes accompanied by a soft and melodious voice. His day-to-day clothes came to be donated, one way or another, by friendly villagers who took this character to their hearts. In any event, Donnagh McKenna drew a lot of his artistic inspiration from this intriguing individual and he must have been very sad when Buxton died prematurely at the age of 54, just two years or so before the passing of his benefactor, Francesca Wilson. Walberswick had lost a charmingly engaging character but, to a certain literary extent, he lives on bearing in mind that Esther Freud saw fit to make him one of the fictional personalities in *The Sea House*. All in all, this 'cameo' came across to me as a touching story.

Another architect who truly practised his profession in Walberswick, away from his London office in St James's, London was Frank Jennings. He was on the scene well before fellow architect, Ernst Freud arrived in the village. During the first three decades of the twentieth century, he was responsible for around ten or so Arts and Craft style houses within its boundaries. More than one of these is featured in the *Walberswick Scroll*, amongst them The Mercers Hall, a Grade II Listed building. This house originally stood in Lady Street, Lavenham but was dismantled in 1908 and, according to Richard Scott, transported on haywains to Walberswick to be erected in its present location some twelve years later, complete with interlocking plain tiles, a jettied first floor and closely-spaced half-timbering. According to English Heritage many of the windows appear to be original.

The Mercers Hall, as depicted in the Scroll

Frank Jennings married Mildred Hall, an accomplished painter and Frank's brother, George was a painter of some note. Both artists had work exhibited, some in London, including the Royal Academy, as well as the provinces. George's oil painting of 1902, *Bell Cottage, Walberswick* was shown in the village as recently as 1999.

Another member of the family with close connections with Walberswick was Humphrey Jennings (1907-1950), son of Frank and Mildred. He became something of a surrealist painter who also produced collages. He was born in a house then called the Gazebo but now called something quite different. It lies behind a house named Marshway in Leverett's Lane. This was designed by his father. At the age of 27, Humphrey, with a double first from Cambridge under his belt, joined the GPO Film Unit. This must have been around the time that W H Auden and Benjamin Britten collaborated there on Auden's previously mentioned *Coal Face* and other documentary-style films. As far as coastal Suffolk is concerned, it is certainly a small world. I have seen Humphrey Jennings described as 'a genius of British cinema' by the British Film Institute (BFI) and others so this cannot really be an exaggeration. There is no doubt that he does enjoy the reputation of having been a pivotal filmmaker in the British wartime documentary movement. He was a man who was considerably influenced by George Orwell so the local connections grown in number all the time. They were even photographed together as boys. Two of Jennings' films (*Listen to Britain* (1942) and *Fires were Started* (1943), the first a twenty minute montage driven by sounds, from waves breaking to trains clanking into action, the second written for a baby born in the last twelve months of the war) have earned highly respected admiration from a contemporary filmmaker of considerable stature, one who is cast in the same mould as Jennings. This is Terence Davies (born 1945), who specialises in autobiographical films of exceptional quality. He has recently been described by Bryan Appleyard (born 1951), a distinguished journalist, as our greatest and most underrated filmmaker so the links with Jennings carry a lot of weight. Davies' latest film is a remake of Terence Rattigan's *Deep Blue Sea* (2011), starring Rachel Weisz and Simon Russell Beale. Humphrey Jennings and Terence Davies have films featured in the BFI's top 100 British Films. Davies is another admirer of Maggi Hambling and describes her *Scallop* as pure genius. Terence Davies lives in coastal Suffolk, but on the Essex-Suffolk border.

However, to get back to Humphrey Jennings, his films have become recognised as some of the key works produced in this country, not only in his time, but also in the history of cinema. He obviously achieved a great deal in the world of making movies but there is evidence that he continued to paint until at least the outbreak of the 1939-1945 war. Evidence of work away from the film business after that seems hard to come by. He died in Greece, from injuries related to a fall from a cliff, a steep rock-face on the island of Poros while scouting for locations for a film on the subject of post-war healthcare in Europe. This was a tragic loss, at such a young age, to both art and his chosen industry.

After writing about Walter Sickert in connection with artists associated with Southwold and Walberswick, it is worth mentioning here that this painter was also a member of the New English Art Club that was founded in 1886 for the benefit of those who had expressed a wish to paint in the open air. Many of the members, who included Philip Wilson Steer and George Clausen, painted in and around the Blyth valley. Sickert had, of course, visited the area earlier but he also arrived in Walberswick in the 1890s, in the company of his friend, James Abbott McNeil Whistler. It was not a happy visit, as it seems that they found the village 'too cosy, picturesque and prosperous'. Sickert was persuaded to make a return visit in 1927, when it proved just as unfortunate. It seems that the artist, instead of delivering a painting of a vivid architectural landscape for the new art room at St Felix School, had offered instead a miniscule and altogether gloomy portrait of a woman artist of French origin to whom he had become married (his third wife) only the year before. Whatever the work's merits, the painting was returned by the school, later to be replaced by something considered more suitable. His most famous portrait came about by accident, although not literally. One day in 1871 a model booked by Whistler failed to appear and he asked his mother to stand in for a portrait. This work, originally entitled *Arrangement in Grey and Black: The Artist's Mother* (1871) became popularly known as *Whistler's Mother*. The painting was later acquired by the French government and the portrait is now housed at the Musée d'Orsay, Paris.

There are undoubtedly a considerable number artists associated with both Southwold and Walberswick, as well as coastal Suffolk generally. As a result, it has been difficult to decide who is to be excluded, let alone included, but I see no reason why I should not now write about an illustrative artist, Reginald Arthur Lay Carter (1886-1949). He became a compulsive sketcher during his schooldays and he received his first commission to create comic postcards at the age of eighteen. He was born in Southwold and lived in the High Street, with a studio just around the corner in Bank Alley. Six years later, a local firm published the first of a series of his greetings cards entitled *Sorrows of Southwold* that depicted hypothetical troubles experienced by the Southwold Railway. This local service also attracted other artists of that time but not in the original lampooning style of 'Reg' Carter. He went on to become the first artist of the inaugural *Beano*, a children's comic that was launched in 1938 and is still published by D C Thomson & Co to this day. In his time, Reg Carter illustrated humorous postcards and posters for Tuck and Valentine as well as others but ultimately the constant jokes against the town of his birth wore rather thin. He moved to Sussex after building a house in the county. He later married a local girl. Reginald Carter was also known as a coastal and landscape painter, noted for his skill in composition and draughtmanship. Some of his work has survived to this day.

Postcards that feature watercolour paintings of rural and coastal scenery have been popular since the Edwardian period and attractive views of locations in both Walberswick and Southwold have featured in the work of extremely competent artists over the years. A family of professional painters with formidable talent, ideally suited to this artistic genre, was the Stannards of Bedfordshire. Harry (also known as Henry) John Sylvester Stannard (1870-1951) and Lilian Stannard (1877-1944) were brother and sister and each produced a substantial body of work from coastal Suffolk around Southwold and Walberswick. Other artists have also travelled along this course but I will concentrate upon these two, if only for the reason that for well over thirty years I have owned a painting of an enchanting river view by Henry that must have been painted before 1896 and at quite a young age. Since that year, when he was elected to the Royal Society of British Artists, he had always added 'RBA' to his signature. He painted many pictures of the royal estate at Sandringham, Norfolk, and received many personal commissions from the Royal Family. Stannard had many imitators but few equals. He made watercolours of picturesque rustic scenes his own speciality and these have earned worldwide acclaim. A gallery that features his work is of the opinion that very few artists can match his delicate touch and soft coloured palette. He was said to possess equal skill at placing images of children and small animals in appealing and charming situations. He exhibited widely, including showing thirty-five works at the Royal Academy and no less than seventy paintings at the Royal Society of British Artists, as well as the Royal Institute, Royal Cambrian Academy, Royal Hibernian Academy, and in Birmingham, Manchester and Liverpool.

A detail from a painting by Henry Sylvester Stannard (Victorian watercolour)

In his book, Ian Collins reproduced an image of an Edwardian postcard of Southwold's *Blackshore Quay* by Henry John Sylvester Stannard. The town's well known lighthouse is shown in the background. He had a reputation for imbuing his work with atmospheric presence that normally indicates being painted *en plein air*. However, Richard Scott is of the view that the odd misplacement of topographic detail could also indicate that a particular work had been completed in the artist's studio. To my mind, this is not all that important as I find what I have seen of Stannard's work made for very pleasant viewing, although I am aware that Victorian landscape painting has experienced periods when the genre was not considered fashionable. That I judge to be a marketing matter rather than a valid opinion on the quality of the painting.

The father of the family, Henry John Stannard (1844-1920) had certainly been a popular and successful landscape and 'cottage garden' artist but it appears that the coastal scenery of Suffolk did not capture his attention, unlike that of his children. Three other members of Henry Stannard's family also became accomplished in this field, as was the case with two of his grandchildren. Richard Scott has also followed in the footsteps of his father, Eric Ronald Scott (1904-1960) as a professional painter and resident of Walberswick. His work has featured and still features in exhibitions. His son, Richard has gained a well-deserved reputation for being an expert on art and artists of Walberswick, following a career in teaching and then as a lecturer the School of Art and Design at Suffolk College, Ipswich. He has always insisted that the village and its surroundings have provided a deeply atmospheric inspiration for much the work throughout his painting life, as indeed it did for

A Pigeon Colony at Covehithe by Richard Scott

his father after his family had settled in Walberswick, nearly half-a-century ago. I reproduce below a fine example of Richard's work. This is by kind permission of Geoffrey Munn, who is fortunate enough to have it in his collection.

When I visited Richard at his Walberswick home, nestling comfortably very close to the sea and the marshes, I was not too surprised to see so many of his father's paintings hanging prominently on the walls of the living room. Eric Scott's career as a painter was much encouraged by the acceptance of two of his paintings for the 1935 Royal Academy Summer Exhibition. Whilst Richard and I were chatting, a remarkable coincidence came to the fore. For some reason I had disclosed that I had done virtually no painting since I was school in the late 1940s. I then saw the reaction on Richard's face when I mentioned my art teacher, Bob Overy, whose engaging personality and teaching had created my own interest in art. Richard asked me where I was educated and when I replied that it was at a grammar school in Somerset, he remarked 'That ties up then. The Robert Overy I knew had a special interest in Montacute House and, unless I am mistaken, that building is in Somerset'. It soon became clear that Richard and I had shared the same art teacher at school. Robert Overy had obviously moved on from Bridgwater to Cranbrook School in Kent, where Richard Scott was then a pupil. It seems that Overy had also taught the young Richard Scott how to paint flowers, just as inspirationally as he had done for me a few years earlier. Richard felt that a number of people who knew his work might be somewhat surprised at this. Whatever his sensitivity in the matter, it is indeed a small world. Richard taught at the School of Art and Design at Suffolk College from 1971, at first part-time but full-time from 1982 until he retired in 1995. It seems that Richard, who is currently engaged upon writing another book, this time on the history of the Ipswich School Art, is now thinking of taking up the painting of industrial landscapes, no doubt not too far afield from his own, very special bailiwick. He still gets involved with the staging of various art exhibitions and is a founder member of the Suffolk Group of artists, which was formed in 1990. You might be interested in knowing that Montacute House in Somerset is a magnificent, Renaissance mansion, built in the late sixteenth century. It is now owned and preserved by the National Trust. Perhaps Robert Overy had been attracted to Montacute's Long Gallery, the longest of its kind in England. It displays over sixty of the finest Tudor and Elizabethan portraits from the National Portrait Gallery collection. This also seems to be a good opportunity to recognise just how helpful I found the wealth of information on Walberswick artists, past and present, contained within the pages of Richard's extremely well researched book. The same can be said for the Ian Collins book on Southwold's painters.

Incidentally, Richard's sister, Lesley Scott (born 1941), produced a substantial body of sculptural work whilst living in Walberswick and she shared an exhibition at Halesworth Gallery in 1979 with a composer, William Alwyn CBE (1905-1985). This musician decided to take up painting while living in Blythburgh. The Scott family moved to Walberswick in 1950, after a painting holiday there. It seems that it was a friend of the family, Noël Carrington, who recommended that Eric should take a close look at the village and the area generally. It was during the summer of 1949 and Carrington felt that this particular part of coastal Suffolk should be considered by Eric and his family before they were committed to buying a property elsewhere. That was all it took for the Scott family of artists to put down its roots.

When driving to talk to Richard Scott at his Walberswick home, I chanced upon an artist painting *en plein air* in the middle of the road. This was not literally the case. The painter happened to be seated on a grassy 'island', more or less at the centre of a crossroads, almost immediately adjacent to the water

Blythburgh Water Tower

tower at Blythburgh. Noting that the man concerned was still working there on my drive home, I stopped and asked permission to take a photograph, mentioning that I had just been discussing the tradition of open air painting with a local artist. He muttered that he had no objection, still intent on completing his painting whilst the light remained good. I took my digital image and then went across to take my leave. We chatted a little and when I demonstrated in interest in what he was doing, he gave me his card. Robert Soden (born 1955), studied for three years at the Royal College of Art in London, graduating MA, having previously obtained a degree in Fine Art Painting at Birmingham Polytechnic (now Birmingham City University). He could be classed as one of coastal Suffolk's itinerant artists as he is based

in Sunderland. He specialises in landscape and architectural painting, which I suppose is another way of saying 'I paint industrial landscapes', and after we exchanged emails a week or so later he very kindly sent me images of the paintings he had made whilst in the Southwold area at the time I came

St Andrew's church and ruins, Walberswick

Sizewell beach

across him. With his permission, these are shown below and depict not only the water tower at Blythburgh but also the beach at Sizewell and the ruins of St Andrew's Church at Walberswick.

Each of these demonstrates Robert Soden's passion for the vibrant colours that bring the scenes to life. A local artist, for whom I have a deep respect, commented as follows when being given the opportunity to view the same images of these three paintings.

'I liked the freshness and vitality of his work. There's a truly personal response to his subjects which is not marred by the desire to impress. Good feel for rhythm and colour too'.

These paintings are finished in acrylic and gouache on paper. Acrylics are extremely versatile, fast-drying paints, and can be used straight from the tube, just like oils, or thinned with water or an acrylic medium. This can range from thin to thick in various degrees, according to your choice, and then used like watercolours. The term gouache is applied to painting in opaque pigments, ground in the chosen material, either water or acrylic, and then thickened with a glue-like substance, sometimes even clear honey. A typical technique is to lay in thin colours at the outset in order to establish general tones and then work over each shape to revise the colours and build up the required pattern.

As far as my own artistic achievement is concerned, my art teacher's encouragement of my work led only to a solitary 'A' in my School Certificate. However, on the basis that I have been writing about only what has interested me in my research, I would like to touch upon the subject of drawing. It seems to me that an artist can make drawings for two distinct purposes: employing media such as ink, chalk or charcoal on paper as a preliminary for a painting or as a work of art in itself. In the latter case, a pencil or crayon may also be used. By sketching the elements of a composition in outline, an artist can also include patterns of light before constructing the detail of the proposed subject and proceeding to accomplish the completed work. For example, this could be a landscape, a still life of an inanimate object or even a portrait. On the other hand, there is so much evidence available from drawings that have survived from the fifteenth century, and even more so from the sixteenth, that lead us to the conclusion that Italian artists drew more prolifically than their contemporaries elsewhere. Moreover, it was the Italians who were the first seriously committed collectors of drawings and from the sixteenth century these have been regarded as works of art in their own right and not merely as preliminary sketches. It has even been said that the drawings of some artists are more impressive than the finished works. Giulio Romano (1549-1646), a principal pupil of Raphael (1843-1620) an Italian painter of the High Renaissance, has been given as an example in this respect. It was as a result of the study of the work of Leonardo da Vinci (1452-1519) that it was appreciated that a fundamental change in artistic practice had taken place during his lifetime. It was not until the 1470s that drawing came to be a record of the artist permitting us to look over his shoulder, almost to see him thinking aloud, if the mixed metaphors can perhaps be forgiven.

The above is by no means the whole story but I am hoping that these facts will illustrate that, even for the uninitiated, drawings are there to be appreciated in their own right. On this basis, we can be aware that certain artists associated with the Southwold and Walberswick areas have certainly been responsible for producing many drawings just for their own sake. In particular, these painters include J M W Turner, John Piper, Stanley Spencer and Henry Davy, not forgetting the esteemed Arthur Rackham and Charles Rennie Mackintosh and the popular flower drawings he made whilst at Walberswick.

Returning briefly to Robert Soden, I have now learned that his interest in architecture and urban life began when he lived and worked in Rome in the early 1980s. He has spent the last twenty years or so recording the changes to Sunderland, a city that has undergone substantial redevelopment. To my mind, this places his work as a continuation of the topographical tradition of Cotman, his pupil Henry Davy, and perhaps even John Piper. Soden tends to focus on what he sees as the human element of architecture, describing where and how people live their lives. In 2005 the regional critic, William Varley wrote of his work:

'You can be sure, too, that the decaying Victorian terrace will be a mongrel mix of video stores, off-licenses and chip shops. He (Soden) loves them all'.

Robert Soden tends to use weather as well as light as a metaphor for the politics of change. He works in the open air in front of the subject and, because of this, his paintings have the veracity of the 'lived' experience. I was very happy to come across Robert at work in coastal Suffolk and, even more so, to be able to bring you the images of his work. This has given me a great deal of pleasure.

I would now like to draw your attention to one former resident of Walberswick, whose connection dates back to the latter part of the nineteenth century. He was Thomas Davidson (1842-1919), who had a large house built in what is now known as Millfield Road. This residence was first named as Seahome, but later became Mulberry House. Davidson, a deaf mute, became a much-respected artist whose specialty was figures. This is demonstrated by the fact that the majority of his work featured human bodies and an appreciation of their movement. After he became firmly established in the village, despite having also a large house and studio in Hampstead, he went on to discover that the Art Club at Ipswich was to be a useful conduit for exhibiting his paintings. His work also found favour at the Royal Academy and other outlets in London. Richard Scott has written that very little of his output seemed to bear any obvious connection with Walberswick. This seems somewhat strange, bearing in mind the attraction that the village and its surroundings have had as a subject for so many other painters over the years. Paint stains, preserved under a carpet by the current owners of his former home, provide some form of memorial to his art and it is nice also to be able to record that his son, Allan Davidson (1873-1932), followed in his father's footsteps. Trained at St John's Wood School of Art before moving on to the Royal Academy Schools, Allan received prestigious awards before receiving further tuition at a famous Paris Academy. His early career was as a painter of landscapes and coastal subjects, in which he was able to bear in mind the family connections with Walberswick. The village became his main base in the 1920s but there is evidence of work with village titles dating back much earlier. He once lived next door to his parents' home and he also rented studios in the near locality. Later in his career, he enjoyed considerable success as a portrait painter and a famous commission was a miniature painting of a young girl that was to hang in Queen Mary's doll's house. Sadly, I have been unable to trace any of his work at the National Portrait Gallery but his portraits of local residents in Walberswick were much in evidence locally and three are said to continue to remain there. He exhibited prolifically at all the major London exhibitions, including twenty works at the Royal Academy between 1905 and 1931, some of which were of local windmills. His work, *Valley Farm*, where Philip Wilson Steer once stayed, was shown at the *Walberswick Enigma Exhibition*.

The nearby town of Southwold has also played its part in attracting hoards of painters over the years. The town connects with Walberswick by means of the reliable passenger ferry in the form of a stout rowing boat that plies across the river Blyth and between the respective shores. The ferry continues to operate from the end of March through to the end of October annually. The energetic work is now undertaken by a member of the fifth generation of the same family that has been associated with this almost legendary service for over 120 years. Her name is Dani Church and she has written a book about the history of the ferry. This features, in some detail, the vital part played by members of her family over such a long period of time.

As far as painters who have worked in Southwold are concerned, Carel Weight (1908-1997) certainly deserves more than just a brief mention. He was Professor of Painting at the Royal College of Art from 1957-1973 where he taught with Ruskin Spear, and he was elected to the Royal Academy in 1965, having shown there from as far back as 1931. Carel Weight was also a Trustee from 1975-1984. He was certainly an influence on other painters associated with coastal Suffolk, including Maurice 'Mike' Kelly (born 1920), an original instigator of the Suffolk Group and William Bowyer RA (born 1926) who painted *Walberswick Beach Huts in 1962*. From what I have read, I suspect that Richard Scott has a soft spot for Kelly's work. I am inclined to share this, now that I have viewed some examples. Scott describes how his friend Kelly incorporates urban architecture featuring incidents, either observed or imagined, often with a degree of humour. This can be seen in *Hurrying Vicar, Wenhaston, After the Match* and *Prodigals Return*. From what I have read about the work of Carel Weight this appears to be the inspiration for such characteristics in his own paintings as they often incorporated human dramas. As for William Bowyer, he stayed and worked in Walberswick and graduated from the enjoyment of a caravan holiday there to living in a village house, complete with garden studio. He was also another painter who liked to work at his landscapes *en plein air*. Bowyer became a familiar sight with his baseball cap and a cigar, quite oblivious to any interested onlookers that might have gathered nearby.

Returning to Carel Weight, his first, somewhat tentative ventures into Southwold were during the early 1990s when he stayed for several long weekends in a house overlooking the sea on Centre Cliff. He was not immediately happy with what he found, in that he complained he was unable to find anything worth painting in the town. In the knowledge that I have written some thousands of words on the subject of the considerable attractions of coastal Suffolk, largely unchanged for centuries and good enough for literally hundreds of other very talented painters, I must confess to finding it difficult to comprehend his alleged attitude. Thankfully, that was not the end of the story as he was soon producing work entitled *Disturbed Children*, portrayed near some backstreet garaging in the town and *Mad Woman*, an oil on canvas of an unhappy looking female walking alongside a ramshackle fence, with the lighthouse in the background. These must have been the 'human dramas' that he had been seeking locally. I am glad that, in the end, Southwold did not let him down. This was Carel Weight being true to form with his imaginative take or interpretation on what were, in reality, probably nothing more than very ordinary looking human beings in non-descript surroundings within a small seaside town. It is not difficult to appreciate how Maurice Kelly must have drawn his own inspiration from these, or similar examples, of Weight's work. As Carel Weight had been introduced to Southwold by his life-long companion, Helen Roeder (1909-1999), whom he eventually married in 1990, it seems that, in the end, his persistence triumphed on the strength of a recommendation from a loved one. She was a painter in her own right, the pair having met at Goldsmiths' College of Art some sixty years previously when they were fellow students. The fact that such a romance ended up by being associated with Suffolk's coast leaves me feeling rather happy with the story.

So, having made a start on the artists of coastal Suffolk, and bearing in mind that in Part Four I shall be writing about the early and more up to date theatrical movements and associations of East Anglia, I thought that it might be worthwhile, albeit briefly, to look into aspects of art in the region stretching back beyond the period of two hundred years to which I referred in my prologue. I became prompted to do this on first learning about an exhibition entitled *Medieval Art in East Anglia 1300-1520*. This was staged in Norwich during the city's Triennial Festival in 1973. Jarrold & Sons Limited published the catalogue and the introductions to the various periods, covering a span of 220 years, contained some useful information on the nature of East Anglia as a wealthy and art-loving society in the fourteenth and fifteenth centuries.

We have already learned that we are dealing with what was, back in those days, a prosperous region with the wealth being based on wool – the rearing of sheep and the making of cloth. This had been encouraged by the arrival of many Flemish weavers during the reign of Edward III (1327-1377). The dreaded Black Death, towards the middle of the fourteenth century, was responsible for a fairly short-lived interruption to these medieval good times. It was, more or less, on the lines of a modern day recession, but the far more disastrous effect in those days was a sharp reduction in an ever-expanding population, especially in Norwich, which lost a third of its inhabitants. Back then, Norwich was comparable in size and importance to cities such as York and Bristol, although London was in a league of its own with a population of some 35,000 in the year 1350. In comparison, nearly

12,000 were living in Norwich but, by the late eighteenth century, the population stood at some 80,000, with people starting to make homes beyond the city walls.

In medieval times, art was expressed in panel painting, stained glass, embroidery and sculpture as well as in book illumination. The latter was a costly process usually reserved for special books such as altar bibles, psalters or other books of a religious nature. Other artistic objects were made of silver as well as gold. These valuable items found a ready market with a wealthy and art-loving society in the fourteenth and fifteenth centuries. However, it was the large number of late medieval churches throughout East Anglia, unrivalled elsewhere in this country let alone Europe, that provided a home for all manner of products derived from the readily available artistic talent of the day. We are talking here of not only stained glass in situ but also architecture in stone and wood, ecclesiastical furnishings, screens, stalls and fonts along with their covers and canopies. As far as the art of manuscript painting was concerned, East Anglia developed as a major centre with influence extending to many other parts of England, so much so that this period became known as the 'East Anglian Period'. It cannot be said that coastal Suffolk achieved any special prominence in this respect, but Peterborough, Norwich as well as, to a lesser extent, Ramsey and Ely, certainly figured as being of significant importance.

The International Gothic period c.1360-1430 was one of exceptional interest in European art but sadly this country, let alone East Anglia, played no prominent part in its development. Having said this, artists began to care far more about perspective and the way scenes were constructed. Figures started to be painted with a greater degree of modelling and light came to have a more important role to play in the paintings of the day. It was in this context that England contributed her fair share to the style of the time and the regional artists figured prominently. It seems that it was this period that saw the final flowering of the artistic decorative fashions found in the earlier part of the century. The professed 'East Anglian' style, that featured somewhat delicate foliage and animal decoration, came to be replaced by the more flamboyant, and what some would call the garish, leafy plant type of decoration of the fifteenth century. This was based upon the way the Romans decorated their Corinthian column capitals.

However, to return to the art of around the end of the nineteenth and the beginning of the twentieth centuries, one favourite subject for artists that must not be overlooked, is the arched Kissing Bridge at Walberswick. One such artist was the already mentioned painter, Henry John Sylvester Stannard. This wooden structure straddles the dyke that runs from a gap in the pier wall. It enjoys a reputation as a favourite for children, as well as their parents, who never seem to tire of the gentle pursuit of crabbing. This footbridge is still in use by the public and recognised by the authorities as a popular means of making progress towards the ever-popular beach. Due to the regular ravage of the structure caused by the winter storms, not to mention the constant plodding of human feet as well as regulations that satisfy modern health and safety requirements, the bridge requires complete replacement as and when necessary. Nevertheless, as far as I am concerned, the succeeding substitutions continue to retain their natural charm and continue to attract a generous measure of artistic as well as recreational attention. You will see later that The Kissing Bridge is depicted in the intriguingly remarkable *Walberswick Scroll*.

Peggy Somerville (1918-1975) was one notable East Anglian artist who did not actually live in Walberswick although she did become a regular visitor. Her home was in the nearby village of Westleton, but she moved just the odd mile or so to Middleton in 1964. She was a painter of what has been described as rich and colourful landscapes, seascapes and beachscapes, some certainly at Aldeburgh as well as at Walberswick. She painted in a direct and impressionistic manner that I find most attractive. Somerville had been something of an infant prodigy and she was hailed as such by the national press in that she had her first exhibition at the tender age of ten. Impressively, this achieved the distinction of being a total sell-out. The fact that this was at the prestigious Claridge Gallery in London's Brook Street, Mayfair makes this event even more remarkable. A distinguished official artist of the First World War, Sir John Avery (1856-1941), in his opening speech remarked upon her extraordinary genius in the handling of oils, watercolours and crayons. Peggy Somerville became a land girl in World War II but returned to painting soon afterwards and subsequently broadened her experience by enjoying extended stays in Provence in southern France, as well as in the Netherlands. To my mind, she is the sort of painter who typifies the many that drew inspiration from coastal Suffolk in her later years. Sadly, I have been unable to trace any record of her work after referring to Tate Online. This seems to me to be a sad omission but the prestigious Messum's gallery in Cork Street, Mayfair appears to remain a keen supporter of her art. Messum's held a *Major Retrospective Exhibition* in 1997 and subsequently there have been other shows there. Her work was shown at contemporary Walberswick artist, Richard Scott's '*Walberswick Enigma – Artists inspired by the Blyth Estuary*' exhibition in Ipswich in 1994. It was Scott's book, *Artists at Walberswick: East Anglian Interludes 1880-2000* that I have already recognised as being so valuable to me during the course of my research. His own delving into the past has been vastly more extensive than mine and his personal knowledge of his artistic bailiwick must indeed be second to none, his father having been an artist in the village before him. Richard Scott (born 1938) is indeed a much respected historian of Walberswick artists and in a personal statement to the Ipswich Art Society, he described the merits of the village, in which he has lived and worked for many years, as follows:

'My work is a record of my surroundings, made usually when deserted and still. I am particularly interested in the effect of low or unusual light upon local colour. Dawn and dusk are very special - spooky, even - and frequently devoid of the implied movement of human presence.'

Walberswick is certainly special, very special, and I would like to take this opportunity to pay a personal tribute to the important contribution that Richard Scott has made to the artistic integrity of the village, not only by his work but also by his thoroughly well researched writing. He never ceases to champion what has reigned as such a unique centre for creative art over a period of more than two centuries. Ian Collins has written of Richard as 'a faithful recorder of miniaturist local scenes enlivened by major effects of light'.

One artist from the nineteenth century who preferred to be known as an 'Eastern Counties Man', after his family moved to Ipswich, was Charles Samuel Keene (1823-1891). The distinction was important to him as, having been born in London, he did not wish to be regarded as a cockney, as was the case with the famous caricaturists and satirists, William Hogarth (1697-1764) and George Cruikshank (1792-1878), described as the 'modern Hogarth' in his lifetime. Keene was best known as an illustrator and caricaturist: he worked with the *London Illustrated News* and *Punch* magazines. *Punch*, in particular, valued Keene's illustration of the social side of the periodical's political concerns, but his work was not uncontroversial, Ruskin having regarded him as 'coarse'. He was admired in France as a result of his work illustrating Louis Napoleon's answer to opposition to his coup d'état by making use of cannon, which Keene sketched as the *New Paris Street-sweeping Machines* (December 1851). The French classed Keene with the likes of Edgar Degas and Camille Pissarro, each of whom supported Keene in his own right, whereas the English seemed typically embarrassed by his illustrations. In general, his satirical sketches were of characters drawn from lower- and middle-class life. Perhaps this is what art critic and painter, John Ruskin (1819-1900) regarded with such distaste as this particular notable appeared to be a man who considered himself a cut above the rest, enrolling at Oxford as a 'gentleman-commoner'. He was, however, a supporter of the Pre-Raphaelites and was a man of considerable influence as an art critic in the Victorian era. He was also noted as a water-colourist, prominent social thinker and philanthropist. On the other hand, Ruskin has been described as brilliant, eccentric and often disturbed.

Charles Samuel Keene was, however, not just a magazine illustrator and it has been verified that he visited Walberswick, Southwold and Dunwich in the 1860s and 1870s, very probably amongst the numerous artists who could be found 'dotted around the open ground' in successive summers. He was known to have drawn a number of cartoons of Southwold scenes for *Punch* and at least some of these were produced as postcards on a commercial basis. One, much more notable work, that resulted from these travels was *View of Walberswick, Southwold and Dunwich from the Cliffs*. This was shown at '*The Walberswick Enigma*' exhibition at Christchurch Mansion in Ipswich in 1994. Keene was highly regarded by his contemporaries and, not long after Keene's death, Whistler described him as 'The greatest British Artist since Hogarth'. Keene was responsible for spreading the word about the magic of Walberswick to other artists of his era. Perhaps he was bearing in mind the fact that the village was not too difficult to reach from London.

Whilst on the subject of Charles Keene, it is worth mentioning Edwin Edwards (1823-1879), a man born in Framlingham into a well-to-do banking family. He eventually married a woman called Ruth who turned out to develop into a formidable wife. The wedding ceremony was conducted at Hendon in 1852. Both Edwin and Ruth had a great love of art and she persuaded her husband to abandon a promising legal career to take up landscape painting which he went on to study in Paris. It was there that he met the well-connected French painter, Henri Fantin-Latour (1836-1904), who numbered Édouard Manet (1832-1883) along with other leading artists as his friends. Fantin-Latour painted a remarkable double portrait of the Edwards' as a married couple in 1875. This can be seen hanging in the National Gallery's rooms that feature Impressionism. Fantin-Latour also painted a portrait of his friend Manet in 1867. The Edwards' set up their marital home in Sunbury-on-Thames where they established an art salon which attracted, amongst others, Charles Keene, the afore-mentioned James Abbott McNeill Whistler (1834-1903) and Alphonse Legros (1837-1911) who became Professor of Fine Art at the Slade School as well as Professor of Etching at the Royal College of Art. Edwin and Ruth Edwards made a habit of paying frequent visits to the Suffolk coast, an area that Edwin had known since his childhood. Their friend, Charles Keene, was only too happy to recommend that Edwards should paint there. They lodged at Dunwich and this resulted in the production of hundreds of etchings as well as oil paintings, including one of mid-Victorian Southwold as well as an etching depicting the same town in 1867. It was Mrs Edwards who became very proficient in printing the engraved plates, earning herself a remarkable reputation for the work. According to Richard Scott, Ruth Edwards was 'tireless in tiring' her husband out and he eventually died at the early age of fifty-six. Before his death, the couple hosted another salon at Southwold. We shall learn later that Whistler was known to visit Walberswick with the already mentioned German-born English Impressionist painter. Walter Sickert (1860-1942). This was in the 1890s and he may well have attended this particular Suffolk salon where Keene was an almost permanent guest. It is certainly known that Sickert was an admirer of Keene's drawings for Punch, describing them as 'on a level with the finest in the world'. It is but mere speculation that the Edwards' might also have attracted Manet and Fantin-Latour to Southwold. Moreover, on the basis that Edwin Edwards' relations, who knew various Suffolk-linked artists, continued to live in the Framlingham area, the couple could well have met up with none other than Edward Fitzgerald, the

Woodbridge poet who has been given a detailed mention elsewhere. Connections, connections ... as we have already seen, these seem to never cease. The more I delved, the more these became ever more numerous.

An influential figure in Walberswick's artistic history between the two wars was undoubtedly Walter Francis Crittall (1887-1956) and yes, he was a member of the family that once owned the famous Crittall window company before its shares became listed on the London Stock Exchange. At one time, he was a resident of Old Farm, Walberswick, a building he bought in 1928 and at least part of which dates from around the seventeenth

Old Farm, Walberswick from the Scroll

century. This house is recorded in the *Walberswick Scroll* and the distinctive green colouring of the windows is clearly shown in the following illustration.

As a lover of unspoilt old buildings, it irritates me to mention that Crittall, being none other than the son of the founder of the window company, appeared to use his home as a showcase for Crittall metal windows, a product first manufactured in 1884. On the other hand, W F Crittall should perhaps be forgiven for what really amounted to no more than an innovative marketing exercise. The protection of old buildings and the materials used in their construction that was afforded by the statutory Listing of Buildings of Architectural Merit was not introduced until the Town and Country Planning Act, 1947. He would not have been aware that stripping out original wooden windows was, in effect, an act that would eventually be considered by the authorities as the destruction of a small but significant part of Walberswick's architectural heritage. On the other hand, these metal windows would be regarded by English Heritage as part of the building's history and deserve to be retained as such.

The windows company is no longer family-owned but has become internationally famous for its products. In fact, family participation in this manufacturing enterprise ended in 1974, although it is more than possible that some members of the family continue to own shares in the business. As far as Walberswick is concerned, the Crittall connection is unquestionably for artistic reasons in that W F Crittall founded the Sole Bay Group of artists in the early 1930s. The intention was to mount beautifully and expertly presented summer art exhibitions in Southwold and Aldeburgh. It was not only the work of local artists that was on display, as Crittall and other equally enthusiastic members had succeeded in persuading a number of Royal Academicians to be guest exhibitors. These included Sir William Russell Flint, (1880-1969), Sir Stanley Spencer (1891-1959) as well as Sir George Clausen (1852-1944), who had studied at distinguished schools in both London and Paris. Clausen's painting entitled *Old Farm Garden* was also exhibited at the *Walberswick Enigma exhibition*. Crittall's praise for the delights of Walberswick seemed to have persuaded Clausen to make several visits to the village after 1934 and the two became neighbours when W F Crittal moved to Great Easton, quite close to Great Dunmow in Essex. I find myself speculating as to whether he attempted to persuade the Royal Academician to install metal windows in his home. I doubt he that he would have succeeded in this particular case but we shall perhaps never know if this was indeed the case.

It is certainly worth mentioning that Sir George Clausen, who stayed at Old Farm with W F Crittall during his visits to Walberswick, became one of the nations' foremost modern painters of landscape and of peasant life. He was influenced to a certain extent by the Impressionists, with whom he shared the view that light is the real subject of landscape art. This explains, once again, precisely why Walberswick became so popular with all of these artists, a popularity that, as we have already seen, certainly continues until the present day. After all, its reputation for light is unlikely to change merely because so many years have passed since the early nineteenth century. Clausen's pictures excel when depicting the appearance of various objects under small patches of outdoor sunlight, or in the shady shelter of a barn or stable. His *Girl at the Gate* is now at the Tate Gallery. As Professor of Painting he gave a memorable series of lectures to the students of the South Kensington Schools, published as *Six Lectures on Painting* (1904) and *Aims and Ideals in Art* (1906). Clausen was appointed an official War Artist during the First World War.

Moving once more to an artist recently mentioned, I discovered a reference on the back of a greetings card that features a reproduction of a painting by Stanley Spencer of Southwold beach dated 1937. It reads as follows:

> 'STANLEY SPENCER first visited Southwold in Suffolk in the autumn of 1924 after he had followed his future wife, the painter Hilda Carline, to the nearby village of Wangford. After their wedding in Wangford Church in 1925 they left the area. But in 1937 Spencer returned alone, having tried in vain to heal the breach in their relationship. The morning after his arrival in Suffolk he began his painting of Southwold beach. He wrote at the time of the 'dirty washing water colour sea', which was 'splashed by homely aunties' legs' and of the Southwold air which 'was full of suburban seaside abandonment'. As an escape from his own emotional distress Spencer set out to capture this carefree summer scene and the result was one of the best loved of all his paintings.'

Stanley Spencer was, as was the case with Clausen, an official War artist during World War One as well as in World War Two. He used both oils and watercolours and produced many notable drawings. Spencer also had a varied career in terms of subject matter, ranging from biblical scenes and work associated with two world wars to nudes featuring his second wife, Patricia Preece. This was a marriage that was never consummated, due to her homosexuality. These nude studies have been described as perhaps influencing the much later works of Lucian Freud, who was said to have admired Spencer's painting. As far as the critics were concerned, they could not decide whether Spencer influenced Freud or whether, on the other hand, there had been mere like-mindedness. Spencer had a reputation as being something of an eccentric, which seems a little strange as the above beach scene at Southwold depicts a totally conventional and rather idyllic setting for holidaymakers at the water's edge. I find myself wondering if this was the painting he was referring to when he wrote 'The dirty-washing colour of the sea was splashed by homely aunties' legs and the air was full of suburban seaside abandonment'. Somehow, I like to think it

Southwold Beach by Stanley Spencer (1937)

was. Spencer was also drawn to paint scenes in the countryside around Southwold, as well as scenes of gardens attached to an odd house or two or perhaps a cottage found in the nearby village of Wangford.

As a footnote to Spencer's portrayals of the naked female body, a passer-by spotted some of his nudes in the window of a London gallery as recently as the year 1950, which is hardly in the dark ages. As a result, the person pressed a prosecution for obscenity, which resulted in the pictures being destroyed. The complainant was none other than Sir Alfred Munnings (1878-1959), a notoriously ultra-reactionary president of the Royal Academy from 1944-1949, who to my mind should have known better. On reflection, I have to concede that in those days, when the Lord Chamberlain was a guardian of so-called public morals and wielded considerable power, perhaps it was not very surprising. On the other hand, and to my knowledge, major public galleries have been displaying paintings featuring female nudes for many, many years, by a large number by extremely famous international painters such as Peter Paul Rubens (1577-1640), who was Flemish and an exponent of the Baroque style.

It appears that in the previous year Munnings had fulminated against Pablo Picasso (1881-1973) and it had certainly been known for him to shout out 'Down with modern art' at students attending the East Anglian School of Painting when this establishment was located near his home in Dedham, now a museum to his memory. However, it seems that Munnings had not always been such an arch reactionary; this artist had some claim to being England's Degas (1834-1917), a French artist who was a founder of Impressionism and who was known also for depicting dancers and equestrian subjects as well as, surprisingly in this context, female nudes. I refer again to Sir Alfred Munnings and his own work and his far from humdrum reputation a little further down the line. In the spirit of reporting accurately, and not at all as a comment on any perceived deficiency in the quality of his painting, it is a matter of factual interest that Munnings had been handicapped from an early age by the loss of an eye. Whether or not this had anything to do with his outspoken views on modern art, as well as any painting that featured a naked body, is not something that I have seen discussed elsewhere. This is possibly because it is totally irrelevant. However, the fact remains that he was simply prejudiced against anything that offended him, but it is a pity that he did not keep his opinions to himself.

As a rather extended footnote to the part that Munnings played in having the Stanley Spencer nudes destroyed, I was intrigued to learn from a *Times* article of 9 September 2010 that the Royal Academy of Arts was to host the first survey of twentieth-century British sculpture in thirty years during 2011. This has been billed as an ambitious show that will demonstrate diversity by featuring works by Jacob Epstein under the same roof as Damien Hirst, which demonstrates a welcome enlightenment. It seems that for a generation of British sculptors such as Barbara Hepworth and Henry Moore (each having their work on view at Snape), the Royal Academy was regarded as a philistine institution and a recognised enemy of their art form. It appears that the cause of this cultural conflict was a series of eighteen carvings of nude figures that Sir Jacob Epstein (1880-1959), a pioneer of modern sculpture, made for the exterior of the British Medical Association's building in London's Strand in 1908. The *Evening Standard* newspaper and a body known as The National Vigilance Association led a campaign against their alleged indecency but, fortunately, this was headed off by a counter-attack from the nation's respected sculptors, critics and museum directors. After the BMA vacated the building in 1935, the premises became occupied by the then Government of Southern

Rhodesia and some of these sculptures were removed. This was on the somewhat dubious pretext that the works had constituted a danger to the public. This was done with the approval of the President of the Royal Academy, who at that time was Sir William Llewellyn (1858-1941), portraitist and landscape painter. Henry Moore was said to be appalled at what happened and was quoted as saying, 'I'll never forgive them. That's why I'll never exhibit in the Academy.' For a generation after that, no British sculptor would join the Academy. So it seems that Sir Alfred Munnings was merely following an earlier twentieth-century precedent in connection with his objections to the Spencer nudes but, in my view, this doesn't make his negative attitude any more justifiable.

Chapter Three

Philip Wilson Steer, Charles Rennie Mackintosh and other painters associated with coastal Suffolk

TO RETURN TO the heritage aspect of coastal Suffolk, it is necessary for me to refer, once again, to the past. If I am to single out any individual artist as a fine example of who might represent all those who have been attracted to Walberswick to practice their art, it must be English Impressionist Philip Wilson Steer (1860-1942). He had painted previously at St Ives in Cornwall. More famously, he brought a kind of artistic fashionableness to both Southwold and Walberswick as others had done equally at St Ives. He first visited Walberswick to work at his art in 1884 and I understand that he usually stayed at Old Farm. On the other hand, so did so many other artists on what Richard Scott describes as being 'on a random basis'. Steer was seen as a pivotal figure, even something of a star amongst radical young artists of varying merit. Steer went on to pioneer English Impressionism on the Suffolk coast in scintillating images inspired over successive summers. Unlike St Ives, it cannot be said that there has ever been a so-called 'school' of artists located within this iconic Suffolk seaside village, even though some may beg to differ. Nevertheless, it is now felt that, one way or another, Steer achieved a status almost presidential in nature, however unintended it may have been. He initially worked there for a period of five years or so, but with further visits in ensuing years. There seems to be no doubt that it was again the remarkable eastern light that attracted Steer and his contemporaries, a distinctive light that has been described as similar to the nacreous light of Venice. It follows, therefore, that although the good citizens of Walberswick did not go as far as to erect a road sign with the words 'WALBERSWICK WELCOMES ALL ARTISTS' the fact remains that for a period of some two hundred years or so that is exactly what the village has been doing. This has earned Walberswick a considerable reputation that has not being equalled elsewhere on the Suffolk coast.

Philip Wilson Steer's work at Walberswick was notable for the application of his skills with light and movement. However, I was a little surprised to learn that most of the twenty or so of paintings of scenes he started work on during his stay in the village in 1887 came to be completed in his wintry studio in Chelsea; this was during the course of the following winter. Nevertheless, it was the drawings and colour sketches he made there and then, on the beach or otherwise, that enabled him to produce finished work that appeared to declare aloud not only their naturalness but also their openness. I particularly enjoyed seeing an image of his *Two Girls on a Pierhead, Walberswick*, in oil on canvas, featured in Ian Collins' book. Steer could also be very sensual in his work and his *A Summer's Evening* caused a critic to comment, 'This is a picture you could warm your hands at, or boil eggs over, and it should be looked at – just once'. I am certainly not prepared to take that advice literally and not just because this particular oil on canvas features three slim beauties who had obviously been skinny-dipping from the beach, almost certainly at Southwold. His many admirers have found these particular qualities to be engagingly attractive and, in the words of Ian Collins, his 'use of vivid unmixed colours of Impressionism captured the sun-drenched scene perfectly'. Steer's last visit to the area was in 1894, when he painted *Children Paddling, Walberswick*. As Ian Collins has pointed out, the allocation of a title must have occasioned a lapse of memory, as it seems quite clear that it is a Southwold scene that is shown. I might add that as Philip Wilson Steer was then in his early thirties this could not have been blamed on a 'senior moment'. You will find more than the odd reference to Ian Collins in this book as, in his own writings, he has demonstrated, in the words of Ronald Blythe, a 'deep understanding' of painting which 'derives from his friendships with artists. They are his universe'. Collins' own book, *Making Waves: Artists in Southwold* was a book of the year choice in *The Times* and *Sunday Telegraph* as well as *Spectator* magazine. Collins, a former journalist, has written other books on art and has curated exhibitions at Norwich Castle, the Aldeburgh Festival and in London's Cork Street.

Local people, especially children, soon discovered that they could earn some spending money by posing in the open for visiting artists and, from the examples I have seen, it is interesting to note what these amateur models were seen to be wearing on a particular day. It is very pleasing to see their period bonnets and aprons and the young boys, often barefoot, with their hats perched at rakish angles on their heads. Both Southwold and Walberswick remain idyllic spots in which young and old alike continue to spend their leisure hours outdoors, especially when the weather is being kind. One way or another, I feel that the figures portrayed in the late nineteenth and early twentieth century paintings and sketches look far more romantic and relaxed than in any contemporary photograph. However, this is not too surprising as the artist, in perfecting the work, would have been persuaded to create precisely the impression that would be enormously difficult to capture by making use of the camera's high-speed shutter, or the modern equivalent in the digital age. I have read that one or two members of one Walberswick family that volunteered their services to act as models ended up by marrying into the artistic community. Perhaps my use of the word 'romantic' was not all that wide of the mark.

Philip Wilson Steer seemed to have converted several of his artist friends to the attractions of Walberswick, notably Francis Newbery (1855-1946), a dominant force at the Glasgow School of Art before this venerable institution moved to the innovative new premises designed by Charles Rennie Mackintosh, a highly celebrated exponent of the *art nouveau* style of decoration and architecture. This Art School building was completed at the end of the nineteenth century and remains revered as a magnificent

Eastwood and Westwood (inset) from the Scroll

example of the fashion of the period. Another painter was Arthur Rendall (1861-1936) who eventually went to live in the village in a house called 'Eastwood', with 'Westwood' in Back Lane as his studio. Both of these are recorded in Doman Turner's *Walberswick Scroll*. Newberry was also to influence Mackintosh who paid much more than the odd visit to the increasingly popular village, as we shall soon see.

Newberry, who spent much of his working life in Glasgow, proved to be an influential figure in the early years of the twentieth century and Mackintosh was not the only other visitor from Scotland. Newberry's wife, Jessie, a fellow painter as well as a designer of embroidery, accompanied her husband on his visits, as did his daughter. This artistic family visited for many years and their tenanted household there, named Rooftree, became a magnet for various visiting artists. Newbery also rented a fishing-hut studio by the harbour where he painted an oil on canvas (c1912), a work entitled *Summer's Day*, which depicted his wife reading beside an open door, with sailing boats anchored in the background.

Charles Rennie Mackintosh was undoubtedly the most celebrated long-term artist visitor to Walberswick and a great deal has been written about his talents, let alone the various documentaries that have appeared from time to time. The fact that he had found the village such an attractive location to practise his art is, to my mind, a valuable confirmation of the tremendous appeal that has survived for so many years. There were some notable architectural achievements by Mackintosh in Glasgow, one of which I have already mentioned. However, it was his habit of making summer tours around Britain that brought him to the Southwold and Walberswick area, albeit on recommendation from a friend. His most notable, as well as extended, visit to Walberswick was in 1914, when he was alleged to have fled from Glasgow. This was the time that he produced his well-known flower drawings, which arose from his long evening walks in the sand dunes. His concentration on this subject at that particular time was said to be influenced by his feelings that the war would not be a long-term affair. There were other studies that year, including a detailed drawing of work being undertaken on the reconstruction of the harbour. Mackintosh's extended stay apparently brought about local comment as well as suspicions and it is said that the artist found himself arrested as a suspected spy. This unfortunate, but now celebrated, event was due to a series of misunderstandings, amid rumours of signals to ships at sea. His unintentionally sinister reputation was not helped by the discovery in his rooms of correspondence from German and Austrian sources. Although released after intervention by friends from London, he was barred from certain counties of East Anglia. The authorities were soon persuaded to change their minds about this, but it seems that, as a result of all the fuss, he was never to return to coastal Suffolk. Whilst staying In Walberswick for a period of approximately twelve months, Mackintosh lived in rented rooms in 'Millside'. This was arranged by Francis Newbery who lived next door at Rooftree from circa 1897-1915. However, it was a few years later, when living in the South of France, that Mackintosh developed further his now highly popular landscapes and quite exquisite floral studies.

Chapter Four

John Mallard William Turner, landscapes and topography

OTHER ARTISTS OF distinction also found their various ways to Walberswick in the summer of 1884. What appears to have been the high point of the popularity of the village was reached in the two succeeding summer seasons. It was not only the notable artists that were drawn to the area, many enthusiastic amateurs also appeared on the scene. In later years, certainly well into the twentieth century, some of the young artists were to build considerable reputations in the world of art. These have been described as the 'new wave', long before this expression was used to describe rock musicians in the 1970s. So how did it really happen that so many artists became attracted to the small village of Walberswick? There have been numerous theories but, even in retrospect, it is difficult to substantiate any real evidence that might be considered as totally convincing, apart from the repeated references to the excellent light. It has occurred to me that was perhaps reason enough, but the 'word of mouth' supposition seems to be a safe bet. We already know that Suffolk's coast had already attracted Joseph Mallord William Turner (1775-1851). The reputation of such eminent painters, and where they might choose to work, must carry a lot of weight in the world of art. It is also known that this famed artist travelled by sea from Harwich to Scotland and it will be seen that during the course of the voyage, it was views of the Suffolk coast that captured his eager attention.

Turner is known as the one of the supreme interpreters of the sea in all its moods and later in this book I feature a more contemporary artist who has already established a growing reputation in this respect. Turner was certainly no stranger to coastal scenes and is known to have been responsible for a succession of engravings that depicted attractive views of the south coast of England. These were published over a period of twelve years, culminating in the year 1826. These works attracted much critical acclaim and led Turner to plan another series; this time it was to be entitled, not too imaginatively, as *The East Coast of England*. This is, of course, an area that was already familiar to him as a result of the sea voyage to Edinburgh in the late summer of 1822. It was on board that ship that he made a number of sketches, including a view of the cliff backed by the town of Southwold. It was most probably this journey that prompted him to travel northwards two years later, this time on foot, along the coast of Suffolk. Spurning conveyance by means of coach and horses, he tramped along the coastline with all the necessary accoutrements, including an ample supply of sketchbooks, watercolour paints and pencils, not forgetting his famous umbrella. Turner made use of the artist's materials as a traveller might use a digital camera nowadays. During this long hike, that must have taken some considerable time during 1824, he painted a crew bravely launching a small boat into the angry waters of the North Sea (known as the German Ocean until the early 1900s) near Dunwich, just three miles or so south of Southwold. It seems that few, if any, finished works survive from this coastal journey although some sketchbooks (now in the Turner bequest to the Nation) contain hundreds of delicate drawings, some of which have been labelled with their locations. One such sketch is of Walberswick, with a view of the village that includes the ruined church of St Andrew. Another view is of the beach, including assorted herring baskets with a glimpse of Southwold in the distant background. Even more such sketches have been identified as representing Blyth Haven, the man-made harbour between Walberswick and Southwold. As previously mentioned, we have Geoffrey Munn (born 1953) to thank for correctly identifying these East Coast treasures.

During his stay in the area I feel sure that someone would have made Turner aware of a little of the history of Southwold. At the same time he might well have been impressed by the town's architectural features, particularly those of the Georgian Period that included part of his own lifetime. He would have also been conscious of the series of greens that have, to this day, been left undeveloped. These were originally intended as firebreaks, since the disastrous fire that destroyed so much of the town in late April 1659. At that time, the timber-framed houses quickly succumbed to flames fanned by a fierce gale which rendered them beyond the control of what must have been scores of terrified residents. The town's inhabitants were driven to extreme levels of desperation at the apparent ineffectuality of their brave efforts to save their town from the inevitable destruction. This great tragedy left Southwold at the mercy of economic collapse and starvation. Some three hundred families were made homeless. This notable event seems strangely unrecorded in terms of any visual representation or indeed any first-hand account of it. Therefore it seems fair to assume that the area's artists arrived too late to capture such drama on canvas or otherwise. If it had been Aldeburgh that suffered such devastation in the time of Benjamin Britten, this composer might well have been inspired to musical composition. We shall, of course, never know, but he did have the experience of the effect of the terrible fire that all but destroyed Snape Maltings, the year after the concert hall's official opening. I have been unable to trace any music by Britten that commemorated this dreadful tragedy, but perhaps I am mistaken. However, on reflection, I find it difficult to comprehend that the composer would have felt inclined, let alone sufficiently moved, to commemorate in music what must have been considered a personal disaster of some magnitude. Perhaps after such terrible events composers feel far too inhibited, maybe by shock, and not at all inspired to create anything remotely commemorative. However, we must not forget that he did encourage both William Plomer and Mary Potter to employ their respective creative instincts in memorialising this dreadful happening in their own way.

As far as J M W Turner was concerned, during his visit in 1824, the effects of the great fire might well have still been in evidence and no doubt remained the subject of local gossip. It took nearly a whole century before the town returned to something close to normal after the fire but it is known that, by the 1750s, things were certainly looking up. There have been other fires of some consequence, as well as varying degrees of elemental destruction within the general area over the years, and some of these have certainly been recorded by artists.

It is now known that J M W Turner, from a very early age, regarded London's pre-eminent artistic institution, the Royal Academy, as a means of securing professional recognition as a painter, as well as a degree of prestige and social acceptance as an individual. He was accepted at the Academy's drawing schools at the age of fourteen and it was only a year later, in 1790, that he was successful in having one of his paintings shown for the first time at their annual Summer Exhibition. Over 250 other works were to follow during his long career. He was elected an Associate Member in 1799 and three years later he was awarded the distinction of full membership of the Royal Academy. In 1807, he became Professor of Perspective, a position he held for thirty years, and became president of the RA for one year in 1856. In his lectures to his students, Turner sought to emphasise the need for an artist to pursue an independent direction and not to regard painting a landscape as simply a record of visual facts. We have since learned to appreciate that Turner succeeded in defining his own defiantly innovative forms of pictorial imagery that so delight many of us today. In his own time, he wanted those studying painting to concentrate on what they perceived as beautiful in nature when setting about practising their art. Indeed, he wished them to follow his own very personal example. During the course of his career and travels, Turner made a study of the work of the Old Masters and made frequent copies of paintings that attracted his attention, but upon which he was keen to put his own stamp. In other words, he matched his own talents against those forerunners whom he most admired. Having said this, his trademark landscapes and seascapes that are so much admired today were produced from a background of personal criticism of the technique of artists he found problematic. These included Peter Paul Rubens (1577-1640), who he blamed for a lack of naturalism in his landscapes. On the other hand, he became enchanted by this Flemish Baroque painter's sensual portraits of young women, where it seems that Turner was not at all troubled by any lack of naturalism.

As for landscapes, this word has surely been mentioned many times over in this book and this can be due only to the vast majority of us finding so much pleasure in viewing such subjects, either in their natural state or indeed on canvas or otherwise depicted. Elysium, or the Elysian Fields in Greek mythology, is accepted universally as the place of ideal happiness and this has surely been the case over literally thousands of years. An art theorist as well as Dutch Golden Age Painter, Gérard de Lairesse (1640-1711) regarded a 'Landscape' as the most delightful object in Art, being possessed of 'very powerful qualities'. De Lairesse even went as far as to recommend that any painting of a landscape should be hung at a height to ensure that the horizon was always even with eye level. He wrote further about travelling the world without seemingly venturing outdoors, allegedly to so view the wonders of the world 'without danger or inconvenience from sun or frost'. This strikes me as rather strange, but perhaps he did not take kindly to the big outdoors ... a somewhat eccentric preference demonstrated by a man who had such an obviously high regard for landscapes. On the other hand, it was in 1707 that he also recorded:

> 'What is more acceptable than shady groves, open parks, clear waters, rocks, fountains, high mountains and deep misty valleys? All these we can see at once; and how relieving must the sight be to the most melancholy temper?'

This seems to suggest that he was not always confined to quarters. However, I trust that my point has been made after coming across such a glowing appreciation of the glory of landscape.

Even the most ardent fan will be obliged to confess that by no means all of Mother Nature's most beautiful scenery is confined to coastal Suffolk, even though it remains an inescapable fact that so very many painters have been drawn to capturing the area's abundant landscapes, not to mention the seascapes. Representations of these continue to delight us and will always do so as long as we maintain our interest in such artistic treasures.

Another, even earlier artist, than J M W Turner, and one who remains inescapably linked to the area, is William Daniell (1769-1837), a marine painter who was elected to the Royal Academy in 1822. William Daniell was the nephew of Thomas Daniell RA (1749-1840) and, together, uncle and nephew embarked upon travels to India, China and the Far East between 1785 and 1794, placing their paintings in a combined lottery in Calcutta in 1791. They then utilised the proceeds to finance their travels, during the course of which they would invariably be seen intently occupied with their sketching. However, it was William Daniell's arrival in Southwold's harbour in 1822, during the course of a *Voyage Round Great Britain* (recorded in eight volumes of aquatints), that led to his engraving of a view of the town as seen from Walberswick. In those days, Southwold was no bigger than Walberswick is today and Daniell's work is dominated by the fifteenth-century church of St Edmund and two windmills, long since disappeared. One painting by Daniell that caught my eye depicts a sailing boat riding the swell into the mouth of Southwold's harbour. It reminded me of my days of competitive racing in a sailing dinghy, returning to the mouth of the river Arun at Littlehampton 'riding on a plane' in a dinghy of the Merlin Rocket class in the 1960s.

It is interesting to note that in 1822, the year that William Daniell was elected RA, John Constable had high hopes that he might also then fill one of the vacancies but the other slot went to Richard Cook, an artist who had ceased to exhibit in 1819. It was not until he was aged fifty-two, in 1829, that the famous Suffolk landscape painter from East Bergholt became a Royal Academician. In 1823, he had again been passed over in favour of a landscape, portrait and animal painter, Ramsay Richard Reinagle (1775-1862) whom Constable not only disliked but positively despised. I consider it rather interesting to read about painters of this vintage and their likes and dislikes as well as their disappointments. John Constable met J M W Turner on several occasions in London and regarded some of his work with mixed feelings. Constable regarded the cockney artist as somewhat uncouth although, in a letter to his wife, Maria (written in June 1813), he did concede that Turner had a wonderful range of mind. He had recently dined in the Council Room at the Royal Academy, and had sat opposite his fellow artist and 'was a good deal entertained'. It should not be forgotten that Constable is known to have visited Walberswick; amongst his paintings of coastal Suffolk are *Harwich Lighthouse* and *Yarmouth Jetty*. He also worked in and around Brighton but he was never attracted to the area and is known to have corresponded with others to this effect. During his lifetime, Constable's work did not bring him any material financial success. He sold more paintings in France than in England, which seems unbelievable now that his paintings enjoy such extraordinary popularity and are valued extremely highly. With regard to the Constable-Turner relationship, this did not exclude elements of rivalry. The former often praised Turner in public but in private he had been known to describe Turner's work as 'just steam and light'. In writing to his wife in May 1814, Constable remarked that at an exhibition in Somerset House a large landscape of Turner's seemed to attract much attention but he felt that he would rather be 'the author of my landscape with the ploughmen than the picture in question'. Just to explain matters, Turner's work was *Landscape: Ploughing Scene in Suffolk* and Turner's painting was his epic, *Dido and Aeneas*. This was an oil painting on canvas and accepted by the nation as part of the Turner Bequest of 1856.

To continue with a further anecdote on the rivalry between these two Masters, I discovered that in the year 1832, on the occasion of the public exhibiting of Constable's *The Opening of Waterloo Bridge*, a painting that he had been working on for almost fifteen years, Turner was dismayed to see that his own almost monochromatic grey seascape had been hung beside it. He must have been more than a little depressed by what he regarded as a somewhat drab comparison with the lurid hues of his rival's work. It is said that he took a paintbrush and added a small red mooring buoy to his own canvas at the last minute, before leaving without saying a word to anyone. This act of one-upmanship had the effect of stealing the show as a result of that single daub of red paint. Constable was heard to exclaim, 'He has been here and fired a cannon' on unsubsidised that his own work might have appeared rather over-laboured and garish in comparison. It has been written that Turner's action on that day was taken in revenge for an alleged 'crime' that John Constable had committed at the previous year's exhibition, when he had acted as a member of the hanging committee. It was said that he reputedly replaced a work by Turner that had been given a rather advantageous position in the Great Room at the Academy with a painting of his own. Not unreasonably, J M W Turner had been intensely irritated by this act of a fellow academician. As far as I am concerned, it seems that, from John Constable's point of view in connection with J M W Turner, there was respect alongside the rivalry factor. It also occurs to me that, on the back of the anecdotes concerning these two great men of the nineteenth century, art somehow appears to become just like any other form of creative activity in that humanity and attendant personalities bring the writers, painters, sculptors, musicians and people in the theatre down to the level of the proverbial 'man on the Clapham omnibus'.

I mentioned earlier the admiration that John Piper had for the work of John Cotman in a topographical context. Although Cotman had taught drawing in Great Yarmouth and had painted throughout East Anglia, having been born in Norwich, sadly, there appears to be no evidence of his having visited Southwold or Walberswick, notwithstanding that he painted a derelict church in Covehithe. On the other hand, a pupil of Cotman's at Yarmouth was Henry Davy (1793-1865) who was born at Westhall, Suffolk and he soon made a name for himself as an artist. After Davy married the daughter of a former master mariner from Southwold, the newly married couple settled in the town in 1824. They lived there for five years before moving on to Ipswich; it was during this period that two of their sixteen children were born. Davy also revisited Southwold on many occasions in succeeding years; his parents-in-law had continued to live in the seaside town.

It is inconceivable that Davy's former art teacher and mentor, John Cotman, would not have visited his talented former pupil in Southwold, particularly as Davy's reputation had grown from strength to strength. He benefited from well over one hundred patrons, including a significant number from the English aristocracy. Henry Davy went on to produce some notable etchings of Suffolk churches and paintings of topographical scenes at Southwold, some of which featured beach settings with people handling wrecked ships. Another painting was of Southwold's Gun Hill made in 1829. An etching of Walberswick church was made by him in 1826. Sadly, Davy's life and character were not associated with financial success from his paintings, etchings, drawings and other work as an architect, even though his output had been quite prolific. Having said that, how on earth did he find time to father, let alone provide the financial resources to maintain, sixteen children? In any event, he is said to have died intestate and there was no obituary, merely a brief note in a Bungay and Beccles weekly newspaper. Henry Davy is buried with his wife in Ipswich cemetery and somehow I feel that he deserved so much better in recognition of his achievements. Perhaps Mrs Davy's considerable success in the art of raising such a large family should also be afforded a measure of credit. I feel sure that John Sell Cotman was proud of his former pupil, even though the accepted opinion is that Henry Davy's later work, always careful, lacked the flair he displayed while under Cotman's influence. However, it is now widely accepted that the record he made of his native county, spread over four decades, combined charm and delicacy with admirable accuracy.

Chapter Five

Elements of driftwood and this material's influence on an unlikely fan

MARGARET MELLIS (1914-2009) was a painter and maker of driftwood sculptures, who spent the last thirty-three years of her life living in Southwold. She was a woman with outstanding qualities and it is not overstating the case to say that her long and productive career spanned the important movements in twentieth-century British art. A person of enormous charm, vitality and forthright opinions, her slight and diminutive build belied a hardy constitution. Well into her eighties, she swam nearly every day in the chilly waters of the North Sea from the beach at Southwold.

The landscape that surrounded the town, as well as the local beaches, provided Mellis with all the materials she required to produce her later works, namely the magnificent driftwood constructions for which she became so well known, even revered.

Born in China in 1914, she was the eldest daughter of a Presbyterian missionary, who was recalled for active service in 1915 and returned with his wife and children to live at the family home in East Lothian. A precocious girl, Mellis's initial interest was music but this gave way to an increasing awareness and desire to study painting. Her ambition received the support of her parents. She attended Edinburgh College of Art between 1929 and 1933 and came under the tutelage of a notable landscape painter as well as a distinguished colourist before being awarded a scholarship in Paris. There, aged nineteen, she trained under sculptor and painter, André Lhote (1885-1962). Later she travelled elsewhere in France, as well as Spain, which helped to give her work a certain international appeal.

However, one of the two most important influences that had converged on Mellis during her stay in Paris was a visit to a large art exhibition. She had been attracted there because André Lhote was then painting under the inspiration afforded by Paul Cézanne (1839-1906), an early exponent of modern expressionism (an alternative term for symbolism). The second happening of the day was her meeting, at that particular show of Cézanne paintings, with someone who was to become her future husband. He was the author and critic of the visual arts, Adrian Stokes (1902-1972). They married in 1938 and, in the following year, with war threatening, the pair searched for a safe house in this country. They scoured the Norfolk and Suffolk coasts and almost took up the challenge, for their marital home, the Martello Tower at Slaughden. In the event, they moved as far away as St Ives in Cornwall, a spiritual home of artists since the nineteenth century. There they met and became befriended by a number of talented artists who introduced Margaret to modernism, very much a movement for change in that it was, in simple terms, a style that aimed to break with traditional forms. So it was to transpire that, during the early days of her career, she came under the spell of artistic persuasions that were to have such a powerful influence on her future career.

It was at St Ives that Ben Nicholson and Naum Gabo encouraged Mellis to make collages, albeit regarded as somewhat modest in scale during that time but it did serve to afford her a personal entry into modernism. These works were entirely intuitive and highly individual and not at all influenced by the works of her friends. She intended that this, perhaps experimental, work should be regarded as true to the materials, a creative principle that was to remain with her throughout her career. As a result, there seems no doubt that the values and methods established in St Ives, as well as her experiences there, served as a template for what was to eventually follow in later life. In the course of my research, I have developed an admiration for her attitude in terms of being extremely honest and real about her art.

However, all was certainly not destined to be too well in the personal life of Margaret Mellis and, towards the end of the war, the couple's marriage was in trouble. Stokes left her the following year. He was later to marry her sister, Ann. Margaret did remain in Cornwall for a while, no doubt wishing to remain amongst friends but, late in 1944, she returned to London, with their son, Telfer (born 1940). Through her friend, Patrick Heron, she went on to meet the poet and painter Francis Davison (1919-1984). They became a married couple in 1948, after Mellis's divorce the year before and lived at the Davison family's deserted Château des Enfants at Cap d'Antibes. It was during this period that Mellis returned to painting landscapes. These paintings refer back to an earlier period, albeit with the warmer tones of the Mediterranean.

Margaret Mellis's connection with Suffolk began in 1950 when she and Davison bought a house in Syleham after sharing a harbour-side shack at Walberswick. She continued to paint in a somewhat nostalgic mood after her time spent in France and she did not begin to exhibit her work until the late fifties when her paintings again began to follow the path towards abstraction, as did those of Francis Davison. In 1976, Davison and Mellis moved to Southwold. In 1983, Davison became ill and he died from a brain tumour the following year. Not altogether surprisingly, Margaret's work immediately after her husband's death became marked by a sombre quality. However, released from the artistic constraints that had been placed upon her, Mellis then began to explore new ideas. The driftwood constructions, made over a period of twenty years, are perhaps her most significant body of work. Her garden became her studio and the studio at the top of the house was a spectacular sight in that a visitor could be forgiven for drawing the conclusion that the outdoors had arrived indoors.

The Sainsbury Centre for Visual Arts at the University of East Anglia, Norwich mounted what was described as a 'survey exhibition' of Margaret Mellis's work in the year 2008. Portrayed emphatically and enduringly as a Modernist, this was undoubtedly a description that the artist herself would most certainly have approved. The distinctive driftwood pieces of her later Suffolk years were said to have played a role in an underplayed chapter in the history of British art. She regarded her imaginative constructions, for that is what they were, as representing objects of creativity in their own right, each one earning its own individual place amongst other objects in the world. These are not my words but my attempt at paraphrasing the writing of Professor Mel Gooding, renowned art critic, writer and exhibition organiser. As it happens, Gooding has also written appreciatively about Suffolk artist, Maggi Hambling, of whom there will be more later. Margaret Mellis is regarded by many as a strikingly original artist in all aspects of her art. I found the examples of her work that I have been privileged to see as even more attractive now that I have learned so much about her. Colour played an enormous part in the work of Margaret Mellis and it seems readily apparent that she loved colour in every form. Some colours undoubtedly had special significance, of which I will write more a little later. The abstract and modernist elements of her future work were undoubtedly born at the time of her association, still in her early thirties, with everything associated with St Ives after the Second World War. Southwold was certainly fortunate in its new resident when she and her second husband decided to move there in 1976.

As far as her own work was concerned, Mellis became very much aware of the difference between the artistic terms 'carving' and 'modelling' in creative art. The colour, blue was also to have a special significance for Margaret Mellis and ultramarine brought out the best in her. She adored the sea on the Suffolk coast, which was, no doubt, a throwback to her childhood in Berwick. It was there that she swam in and walked beside the sea when staying with her grandmother. Bearing in mind the period of her life spent in Cornwall before eventually moving to Southwold via inland Suffolk, it is clear that her close connection with the sea and its colour came to dominate her work. Blue acted as a catalyst for igniting hot tones, making the reds even fierier as was also the case with the deeper orange colours that she used. I have always enjoyed such contrasts in viewing these colours. However, not all of her work provided these distinctions as, for example, she enjoyed putting red with red, scarlet with orange as well as with magenta and vermillion. She believed in defining colours together with shapes in her own special way.

Margaret Mellis had talked about her work in terms of an overwhelming need for her to get it right, almost to the extent as if her life depended upon it. The fact that so many others have come to recognise her highly individual contribution to British art leads me to believe that her long life signified that she had manifestly succeeded in her artistic endeavours. It is an obvious statement that each individual example is undoubtedly unique by its very nature but it is now recognised that Margaret Mellis' uniqueness was distinctively personal. This was because she was absolutely meticulous in ensuring that completed works underwent a great number of careful and painstaking adjustments. On the other hand, it has been emphasised that this was not merely an artist striving for perfection. After all, art isn't anything near as straightforward as that is it? Occasionally, creativity can often be seen to have taken very little time at all, before the stage is reached when the artist becomes satisfied with what has been achieved. Margaret Mellis was known to say, 'It might come together as if it made itself'. Somehow, this makes me warm to her even more, perhaps inspiring me to collect a few diverse items during a stroll along the beach. I could then seek to combine whatever is found together in an attempt to create a modest work of art. If Margaret Mellis was inspired by others, and indeed provided inspiration for the likes of Damien Hirst, it will be interesting to see what happens. I must always remember to add no colour and certainly never change the shape of any item if I am to follow in her footsteps, maybe even quite literally. In one way or another, I might even my own, very personal tribute to the art of Margaret Mellis.

As intimated above, we all know that it is not as easy as that and there can be never be an element of mere luck about creative art. Margaret Mellis had the genius to transform beach-combed driftwood, bits of beach huts and virtually any likely discarded object into something meaningful to the extent that it would stay in the memory of her many admirers for long after they had moved on from viewing it. Margaret Mellis never saw the need to differentiate between the three dimensional 'sculpture' and painting on canvas, as she merely chose the medium or combination that best depicted her interpretation and further understanding of what she had created.

I can just imagine her seeking out, with the accuracy of the natural eye of a bird of prey, the ideal material that would generate ideas for her next study. Her methods have been compared with those of an alchemist; in other words, a Mellis transformation of sometimes diverse objects into a work that evolved only after much shuffling and rearranging. I can imagine her just letting everything breathe before the final selection. The resultant work of art by Margaret Mellis could be relied upon to not only impress her many followers but also lead people to marvel at what the study appeared to be saying, even singing, to them if they felt especially romantic on that particular day. What also interested me was a report that when she looked back on her work, even as early as the next day, she remained impressed by the magic of the entire exercise. She was often amazed by what she had done, as well surprised by what has been described as the ease and immediacy of her particular style of creative art.

I was fascinated to read a description of the way Mellis collected and stored materials. This was not only confined to her studio as storage also extended around her home; she even left her gathered material soaking in the bath or standing outside the house. This was just in case what was there had not yet weathered enough for a specific purpose. I noticed that several photographs I came across were taken of her at Covehithe, as deserted a beach as you are likely to find on the coast north of Southwold but south of Lowestoft. This found me wondering if visits there were planned specially for the reason that she was more likely to find undisturbed driftwood there. In other words, before other, less artistic beings, had scavenged amongst what had been thrown up by the tide. The ordinary beachcomber would not necessarily know just how very prized an odd object might be regarded in the eye of a very special artist. The more that I have read about Margaret Mellis, the more I have found myself marvelling at her energy, even late in life before the tragic onset of severe Alzheimer's disease. She has certainly inspired others, not least the young Damien Hirst, of whom I have written elsewhere. Actress Susannah York, who had holidayed in Suffolk as well as Norfolk as a child, performed in the role of Margaret Mellis, in the sixty minute documentary film, *Margaret Mellis: A life in Colour*. This production received its World Première in Norwich in July 2008.

During her lifetime, Margaret Mellis had some twenty-five solo exhibitions and her work has appeared in even more group exhibitions; all of these were throughout the United Kingdom, as well as in Northern Ireland. There have also been two documentary films, including that already mentioned. Her work has been featured in some detail in more than a few books. Make no mistake; her work will live on, and on, and on.

During the last thirty-two years of his life, Francis Davison, her second husband, devoted himself to the making of collages. A Cambridge graduate, Davison began as a poet but turned to drawing and painting in the late 1940s after Patrick Heron, a friend from school days, had invited him to St Ives where he was to meet Margaret for the first time. It was on the return of the married couple to England in 1950 that Davison began to concentrate fully on his artistic career, no doubt receiving encouragement from his wife. The early paintings and collages of landscapes and cottages confess their Cornish roots but, progressively, colour took over and, while a strong sense of landscape remained, any hint of mere depiction was dismissed. He never returned to painting and Davison's mature collages were made of coloured papers, butting, interlocking or overlaid, added and subtracted, built and adjusted towards their eventual, accumulative shape. By choice very much an outsider, Francis Davison is still not actively acknowledged as one of the major British abstract artists and colourists of the twentieth century and for the time being, at least, his work appears regarded as being in the shadow of that of his wife. I find that unfair and rather tragic and just hope that this fact did not trouble Margaret unduly. However, she must have been comforted by the fact that his works had been exhibited on a regular basis. The Tate lists at least one of his works, *Brilliant Black* 1982.

Having covered aspects of the work of Margaret Mellis, it now seems to be an ideal opportunity to introduce in more detail an unlikely character for a book on the cultural heritage of coastal Suffolk, coupled with the town of Southwold. I mentioned earlier what can only be described as a 'household name', due mainly for his notoriety in the world of art. Much, but certainly not all, that I have written so far on artists of the nineteenth century might well be regarded as a snub to modernism as far as Suffolk's east coast is concerned. However, it was a teenage Damien Hirst, born in 1965 in Yorkshire, who declaimed that the things he saw on a visit to the area 'blew him away' and it seems he was not referring to a strong north-easterly off the North Sea.

Hirst became an enthusiastic fan of the work of Margaret Mellis and subsequently she became mentor to the young man. Mellis had received a postcard, or perhaps it had been a letter, from him at her Southwold home. She must have been impressed by what he had written and it was not long before they were swimming, walking and working together in coastal Suffolk. Later Hirst was to recall that he lost touch with her although he didn't really know why. He thought that the estrangement might have been driven by age difference and the change in his life when he was accepted at art school. Hirst did confess that there was an affinity with her that might, in itself, have played its part in what happened between them during his time in Suffolk. I was pleased to learn that Damien Hirst was responsible for the written Introduction to the catalogue for the exhibitions of a selection from the works of Margaret Mellis at galleries in London and Penzance in 2001, so his earlier connections with her at Southwold had not been totally forgotten in the art world.

It was the discovery by Hirst of the collages by Francis Davison and the constructions by Mellis that lured the teenage Damien to

Southwold in the first place. He wanted to see some more of their work, following a visit to an exhibition of theirs at a gallery in Cork Street, Mayfair, as well as elsewhere. He abandoned any previous inspiration provided by Kurt Schwitters (1887-1948), a German artist whose first collages appeared in 1918. Discovering the work of Davison and Mellis proved to be a seminal experience for the young man. Hirst was also to become completely captivated by Mellis's way of life, even her unconventional approach to providing food for herself and her guest. As far as the swimming was concerned he often complained vociferously that Mellis forced him to swim in the sea every day of his stay. But it was their beachcombing together that appeared to have made up for what he perceived as a form of daily torture, even though he admitted that this experience served not only to refresh him but also to assist his keen appreciation of all the wonders he viewed in her studio. Brit Art hero and 1995 Turner Prize winner, Damien Hirst was later to savage critics and curators who had not been persuaded that the work of Mellis deserved their patronage. However, he might have been a little less critical if he had seen Anglia TV's screening of a profile of her in 1992. This was filmed on location in both Suffolk and Cornwall. The programme featured Margaret Mellis, then in her late seventies, swimming, dancing, bicycling as well as creating one of her constructions on camera. She entitled this *Marsh Music*, claiming that this brought together the first and last loves of her life. I have not been able to learn if she got up from her deathbed in order to dance, but she had previously expressed a wish to do just that. The *Mixed Media* works of Damien Hirst dated 1983-85 serve to illustrate the influence of Davison and Mellis on his art at that time.

As far as his painting is concerned, Hirst has not been well reviewed. In October 2009, he revealed that he had been painting with his own hand in a style influenced by Francis Bacon. *No Love Lost*, his show of paintings at the Wallace Collection in London received 'one of the most unanimously negative responses to any exhibition in living memory'. Tom Lubbock of *The Independent* described Hirst's work as 'derivative, weak and boring. Hirst, as a painter, is at about the level of a not-very-promising, first-year art student'. Rachel Campbell-Johnston of *The Times* commented 'it was "shockingly bad'.

Having dwelt briefly on his painting and explained the, albeit comparatively brief, Mellis-Hirst relationship, I feel able to venture to review at least one subject that encouraged his notoriety. I find it difficult to decide if Damien Hirst's attention-grabbing artwork of a cow preserved in formaldehyde within a glass-panelled cabinet came to be inspired by Aristotle's (384-322BC) statement in the *Poetics* that 'objects such as corpses, painful to view in themselves, can become delightful to contemplate in a work of art.' Perhaps you can be left with this thought. Having said that, I must add that at the *Young British Artists* exhibition, held at the Saatchi Gallery in North London in 1992, Hirst's work entitled *The Physical Impossibility of Death in the Mind of Someone Living* was a shark, again in formaldehyde, but this time in what was described as a vitrine. This work is said to have been sold for £50,000 so it cannot be denied that this is an artist of considerable significance. Other works have since been valued a great deal higher.

Chapter Six

Royal Connections and two contemporary artists

I AM NOT too sure that any of the hundreds of painters associated with Walberswick were actually born in the village, so the cross-section of artists featured in this book either set up home there or were visitors (occasional or regular, long or short term). My selection has not been at all random, but if there has been a story to tell I have told it and added other information and associations that I trust will prove to be of added interest. There is certainly no suggestion that the work of any featured painter ranks superior to that of any other. I was challenged by a very broad canvas and it has been a delight to effect the various introductions.

My next featured painter is the allegedly 'self-taught' Edward Seago (1910-1974) who was born in Norwich, the son of a coal merchant. I came across his name in a long-established weekly magazine which featured advertisements placed by two London galleries depicting work by Seago on the occasion of the centenary of his birth. I was attracted by the image of *Beach Huts*, which features the seashore and a beautifully painted sky taking up two thirds of the canvas. As we all know, the enormous skies of both Suffolk and Norfolk have offered enticing challenges to countless artists over the centuries. Another two watercolours by Seago, entitled *Norfolk Cottages* and *Norfolk Landscape*, led me to investigate any possible connection with Suffolk and hopefully Southwold or even Walberswick. Sure enough, I was lucky enough to come across a link; it seems he spent time in the village between 1923 and 1927 as a pupil to Bertram Priestman, RA (1868-1951). Priestman taught Edward Seago a great deal about painting skies. These facts led me to the obvious thought that Seago was not particularly 'self-taught' after all. However, bearing in mind that Seago painted other subjects. Perhaps I should not be so judgmental. Priestman had a house and studio in Walberswick where a number of pupils were tutored at that time. His home was named 'Windy Haugh' but is now known as 'Coopers Thatch', in Leveretts Lane. His studio was one of a half-dozen or so riverside buildings depicted on the *Walberswick Scroll* by Doman Turner.

As it happens, Edward Seago also received advice on painting from the already mentioned, Sir Alfred Munnings, a true East

Anglian native artist. It seems that Edward Seago became adept at cultivating friendships with people that mattered, in terms of artists that he admired and patrons who might support his career. Munnings, reflecting on the paucity of his own formal training, urged Seago to seek lessons in order to avoid becoming regarded as a young potboiler. I see little wrong in a gifted person employing his talents in the cause of making a living, but I recognise that a fellow artist of the stature of Munnings would wish to advise a youngster to pursue his art for art's sake and if this generated income so much the better. Bearing in mind that Munnings was certainly regarded as dapper in appearance, and was to my mind also something of a dandy, it was clear that he enjoyed spending the income generated from the sale of his own works of art. Born in Mendham, Munnings visited Southwold regularly in order to visit his tailor, Denny of Southwold, whose clients also included Benjamin Britten, Peter Pears and George Orwell. As far as the latter client was concerned, Mr Denny thought it was really 'cloth thrown away', Orwell being 'one of those people who put on a suit and don't look well-dressed even when they put in on new'. This firm was founded in 1851 and their shop remains in the town's Market Place. Being up-to-date with the times, they have also established their own website. Sir Alfred Munnings ended his days living in Dedham Vale and in common with the Vale's own precious son, John Constable, Munnings was also a miller's son.

To return to the successful career of Edward Seago, his subjects were not by any means confined to seaside skies and landscapes. In addition to painting portraits, he also had the distinction of being redrafted as an Official War Artist in the Second World War after it was discovered that, on enlistment, he had not disclosed a heart complaint that had dogged him since childhood. The work accomplished by Seago during, or perhaps arising from the Italian Campaign in 1944-45, was featured in more than one Edward Seago Centennial Exhibition in London in early 2010. On that campaign, he was travelling alongside his life-long friend, Lieutenant-General Sir Harold Alexander, later Field Marshall the Right Honourable, the Earl Alexander of Tunis. This was, indeed, distinguished company and that was before the patronage he enjoyed from the British Royal Family, of which more later.

Of particular interest to me, bearing in mind what I have written about Imogen Holst, was Seago's portrait of her in 1962. This was entitled *Imogen Holst listening to Peter Pears* and she is seen with her hands clasped and head slightly bowed, clearly concentrating on the tenor's performance.

As already intimated, Seago's fame also spread to the Royal Family. The late Queen Mother bought so many of his paintings that the artist was persuaded to make her gifts of two each year, on the occasion of her birthday as well as at Christmas. HRH Prince Philip, Duke of Edinburgh invited Seago on a tour of the Antarctic in 1956, and the artist's subsequent paintings, considered to be among his best, are known to hang at Balmoral. Seago was also a regular guest at another royal home, Sandringham; this was for some twenty years from the year 1950. This seems logical, bearing in mind his birthplace in Norwich.

Edward Seago was known also to indulge in a little writing and I have been able to trace two books: *Sons of Sawdust: With Paddy O'Flynn's Circus in Western Ireland* (1935) and *The Country Scene*, co-written with former Poet Laureate, John Masefield, two years later. His painting, *The Tightrope Walker (The High Wire)* emanated from his spell with a travelling circus, which started at the age of eighteen. Much has been written about this prominent and rather colourful twentieth-century artist and the two books had forewords penned from royal sources, namely HRH The Prince of Wales and HRH The Duke of Edinburgh. There seems to be little doubt that these endorsements would have had a beneficial effect on sales.

Finally, amongst his better known portraits were those of HM The Queen, her father, George VI, the Queen Mother and also Nöel Coward (1899-1973), who is quoted as having said about the artist 'What he brought to his work was a lucidity, a magic. He was showing us what was there'. I think we can safely say that Edward Seago was no mere potboiler.

Having been mentioned more than just a few times earlier, Maggi Hambling (born 1945) should need no introduction. She is an artist who, to my mind, seems to crop up everywhere nowadays, although that is perhaps a wild exaggeration. It has been said that her paintings and sculptures are robust to the extent that they catch the mood of her subjects as well as an old master. My comparatively recent 'sightings' and what I shall describe as 'hearings' include an item on Radio 4's Today programme, when the BBC played an interview with Hambling by presenter, John Humphrys. This was recorded at the Vincent van Gogh Exhibition at the Royal Academy in January 2010. John Humphrys (born 1943), whom to my knowledge has never been recognised as an art critic, stated, on the subject of van Gogh something to the order, 'Of course his insanity came out in his painting' and in response Hambling said, 'Insanity is part of being a genius'. Humphrys then observed, 'Maybe you are a bit potty yourself' and she replied, hardly drawing breath, 'Perhaps more than a bit' and I could hear her chuckling.

At the time they were discussing the merits of van Gogh's portrait entitled *L'Arlésienne: Madame Joseph-Michel Ginoux, the proprietress of the Café de la Gare, Arles*. This was said to have been painted within a period of only one hour. Maggi Hambling described this as extraordinary and said that, in her view, it was one of the greatest portraits of all time, emphasising the power of the colour. Knowing that she is a considerable portrait artist in her own right I have taken this opinion seriously. She had already described van Gogh's work as 'so real and painfully powerful' so she is an obvious admirer. The second time I came across her was my viewing BBC TV's *University Challenge* at around the same time. Maggi Hambling was the subject of one of the *'Starters for Ten'*. I am pleased to say that I answered correctly and more rapidly than the students, and was also equally successful with all three of follow-up questions on the subject of this ubiquitous painter. This is hardly surprising as, not long before, I had interviewed the artist in her Suffolk home when she was pleased to show me around her two studios. She also lives in London where she has a studio on the first floor of the home she shares with fellow artist, Tory Lawrence (born 1940) whom she met in 1983. This leads me to quote Hambling when she was asked to talk, by another interviewer, about her teenage memories. She responded by saying, 'I managed to stay at art schools for seven years. When I was at Ipswich, I went around wearing duffle coats and I learned to roll a cigarette. When I got to Camberwell, London was swinging, and I was still a virgin – and so began a great deal of experimentation to see what I liked best. And the ladies won'.

Hambling told me that she paints every day of her life. Incidentally, Tory Lawrence once worked as a secretary for the late Poet Laureate, Sir John Betjeman, and it is said that she once accidentally burnt down his writing room, leaving the charred remains of half his library. Perhaps that is why she took up painting but, according to Lawrence, she left that employment of her own accord to get married and Betjeman felt that this saved him from giving her the sack. She has now become a celebrated artist to the extent that, in a *Times* article, it is stated that 'As Hambling is to the sea so Lawrence is to the sky'

Maggi Hambling in her studio

but the latter is anxious for her work not to be compared with Hambling's on the grounds that 'I hope that I really do not paint like her. It would be awful if I was doing a second-rate Hambling'. You can now judge for yourselves from the image I show below. She has become known for paintings of the East Anglian landscape that have been described as 'humble in scale' but also demonstrating authentic responses to the various chosen subjects. David Hockney is certainly known to have advised artists to paint with the heart as well as with the hand and the eye. That sounds like good advice to me and I am inclined to the view that quite a few, if perhaps not all of the painters featured in this book, have done precisely that, and their work is all the better for it.

Tory Lawrence grew up and spent a considerable time living on the Berkshire Downs in what she has described as a very horsey world, her father being a horse-trainer. Her ex-husband, John Lawrence (the second Baron Oaksey, born 1929), had a distinguished career as TV racing commentator as well as an amateur jockey, finishing second on Carrickbeg in the 1963 Grand National at Aintree, beaten by only three-quarters of a length by the winner. So it is no real surprise that Tory Lawrence has been drawn to painting horses to the extent that she exhibited her work on that subject, including landscapes around the heaths of Newmarket, at The National Racehorse Museum in High street, Newmarket from November 2011 to February 2012. It was not until 2007 that she arrived in Suffolk where her studio is situated very close to that of Maggi Hambling.

Some years previously, in the late 1990s, Hambling had an intimate relationship with the 'Soho beauty', Henrietta Moraes (1931-1999), at a time when the latter's life was drawing to a close. Hambling described her as her muse and I have since learned that Moraes' background was that of an artists' model, *bohémienne* and memoirist. During the 1950s and 60s, she was herself the muse and inspiration for many artists of London's subculture; these included Lucian Freud and Francis Bacon.

Covehithe by Tory Lawrence (2009) Oil on board

She also became a shade notorious for her marriages, as well as her love affairs. Moraes has also been described as a *femme fatale* and a *bon vivante*. No one can say that Maggi Hambling's life has lacked colour, and I am not just talking about her painting here. A book has been published entitled *Maggi and Henrietta* (Bloomsbury 2001). I must confess that I haven't read it, or even seen the paintings and drawings. On the other hand, I felt that what Maggi Hambling wrote, probably by way of introduction, is interesting, as well as a personal comment on the relationship she had with Moraes. Hambling recalls when she painted and drew Henrietta:

> 'I re-met Henrietta on 4th February, 1998, two days after my Father's funeral, at the end of a dinner following the Francis Bacon opening at the Hayward Gallery in London. Those eyes had first blazed through mine across a large Boxing Day lunch in Wiltshire five years earlier ... However arthritic or, on occasion, hung over, she gallantly climbed onto the table to pose: raw, intense, vulnerable and commanding. I

became her subject rather than she mine. Her inspiration for me was a powerful mixture of attack, encouragement and wit.'

The publication of the book coincided with the exhibition *Henrietta Moraes by Maggi Hambling* - drawings, paintings and bronzes at Marlborough Fine Art (London), October 3-28 2001. Hambling's affair with Moraes has been described as an interruption to a much longer relationship with Tory Lawrence.

Another of Hambling's controversial public sculptures is that which commemorates the life of Oscar Wilde. This can be found in Central London, in Adelaide Street, behind the Church of St. Martin-in-the-Fields, Trafalgar Square. Hambling named this sculpture *A Conversation with Oscar Wilde* and it was unveiled on 30 November 1998, by Chris Smith, the Minister for the Arts at that time. Before this and, to my mind, quite amazingly, no such representation of this ever-popular and highly significant author and playwright had existed. Just before Christmas 1995, twelve artists were asked to submit ideas, on paper, for the Wilde sculpture. Maggi Hambling is quoted as saying, 'I became obsessed with Wilde again. Having delivered my maquette, I went on drawing him, painting him, making more sculpture of him'. This sculpture has had its critics, but no one can say that it lacks the individuality of either its creator or subject.

A Conversation with Oscar Wilde by Maggi Hambling

A more recent sculpture by Maggi Hambling, this time in the form of a large heron-shaped weathervane, was commissioned by the local council in Lambeth in a series of arts and creative lighting projects. She was shortlisted, along with other local artists, to contribute something appropriate for the project and it appears that she received her inspiration for the work by discovering a connection between the old River Effra, which would have run along a similar course to Brixton Road, and the name of the nearby Heron Road. The weathervane, now known as *The Brixton Heron*, is intended to reflect the changing nature of the area and the influences coming in from all over the world. Once again, Maggi Hambling worked with J T Pegg & Sons Limited in Aldeburgh and I discovered a video on *YouTube* of the sculpture being driven up the High Street in the seaside town on the back of a pick-up truck in some form of bizarre 'test drive'. Bearing in mind that Aldeburgh has its fair share of easterly winds this might equally have developed into a test flight. Perhaps local residents are immune to strange sights around Festival time and it seemed to attract little attention despite the weathervane's height being three times that of the vehicle carrying it. Luckily, it arrived back in the Pegg works yard quite safely, no doubt soon to be onward bound for display at its permanent home, attached to a prominent building in Brixton known as the Prince and Dex building. This is an example of one of the fruits of Aldeburgh's cultural heritage being exported to an Inner London Borough.

Maggi Hambling is well known for being accessible to the media, an attitude to publicity markedly similar to that of the distinguished sculptor, Henry Moore (1898-1986). It will be recalled that one of Moore's sculptures was once situated quite close to the concert hall at Snape, where it once overlooked the nearby marshes. Anyway, being aware that Hambling was approachable, I was nonetheless more than delighted when she agreed to see me at her country home in a village in Suffolk, not too far from the coast and, of course, Aldeburgh. Now that I have learned so much about the area, I would not have been at all surprised at this artist being an obvious choice for the Britten memorial sculpture, had there been any form of competition promoted by the powers-that-be in Aldeburgh. We now know that, in fact, the entire project was her own idea. With this in mind, I can now, more than ever, appreciate that it could only have ever been John Piper as the unchallenged choice for the design of the stained glass window in Aldeburgh church.

At Hambling's cottage home, I found a collection of outbuildings and neat gardens backing on to countryside, quite near the village hall and the bridge over a narrow river. Some would call the location idyllic but, for those who really know Suffolk, such a sight is quite commonplace. The artist guided me through her two studios, one bigger than the other. I have since come to the conclusion that one of these was probably used by Tory Lawrence but I am by no means sure. Anyway, whilst I was there in the larger studio, I was able to gaze at various items of work-in-progress, all unmistakably very much 'Maggi Hambling'. Yes, I am now a great fan and on that cold winter's day, I really wanted to stay longer than I did but I was unwilling to outstay my welcome. Hambling told me that she likes to work alone and undisturbed. As a result, she is not at all active in village life, although she does have one or two friends there.

During the course of our conversation, she mentioned her then current exhibition at the Lowry Gallery in Salford, to be followed by another, a couple of months after, at the Mellon Gallery, Fitzwilliam Museum, Cambridge. She added that her book, *The Works* (including Conversations with Andrew Lambirth), was published by Unicorn Press in 2006. Andrew Lambirth reviews art exhibitions and art books for *The Royal Academy Magazine*, *The Spectator*, *Modern Painters* and several British newspapers. He was also responsible for the book, *Margaret Mellis* (Lund Humphries 2010). Hambling told me that she had also written an illustrated book on *The Aldeburgh Scallop* and this was published at the end of October 2010. I am now quite convinced that Maggi Hambling revels in all the attention she has been getting but she could not help herself commenting that I was different from most of her interviewers in that I had turned up without a tape recorder. On the other hand, it seemed that I had redeemed myself by demonstrating that I had at least done some research. She complained that it was usually the other way around. I promised that next time I would arrive properly equipped but I did not feel at all admonished.

Before long, we found ourselves talking about subjects that are rather more mundane. Maggi Hambling surprised me by admitting that she loved to watch tennis, especially at Wimbledon as she prefers the game being played on grass, rather than clay. It came up that she never takes holidays and she shuddered when I mentioned the subject. In attending the Lowry Gallery for her exhibition she had been delighted and thrilled to visit the set of ITV's *Coronation Street* because she revealed that she is an enormous fan. Following a visit to the set, she commented on how very small the bar of the 'Rover's

Return' was in real life. She also confessed that she was thrilled when one of the characters asked her to autograph his copy of the catalogue from her exhibition. I hope I am not giving away too many secrets here. I show below a study by Maggi Hambling of actress, Amanda Barrie. She once played the character of Mike Baldwin's wife on ITV's ever-popular and long-running soap opera.

Sadly for her art and all who appreciate and admire it, Hambling now suffers from arthritis. She endeavours to lessen its impact by taking, on a daily basis, two tablespoonfuls of cider vinegar in half a mug of hot water with a dash of molasses. She maintains that this typically natural remedy has proved to be a great help in easing her discomfort.

Getting her back to talking about her art, I raised the subject of portraits because I was aware of the considerable attention she paid to the comedian Max Wall (1908-1990) at one stage in her career. I particularly liked

A study of actress, Amanda Barrie, by Maggi Hambling

Max Wall and his Image (1981) in which, to my mind, she captured his reputation for being a bit of a clown. In 1980, Hambling became the first Artist in Residence at the National Gallery, London, during which period she produced a series of portraits of this unique comedian. Wall had responded to Hambling's request to paint him with a note saying: 'Re: painting little me, I am flattered indeed - what colour?' She once told an interviewer, 'I had my first vision of this face, which seems to me to be the real face of a clown; a face with no mask, no make-up, a just live, in the flesh, clown in front of me'. It was almost inevitable that she would paint him eventually, although it was many years before she did so.

Several works of Maggi Hambling are hung in London's National Portrait Gallery. These include portraits in oils of the late jazz singer and comedian, George Melly (1926-2007) as well as the distinguished English historian A J P Taylor (1906-1990). There is also a 1993 study in charcoal of actor and writer, Stephen Fry (born 1957).

Another subject for one of her portraits was Quentin Crisp (1908-1999), an English writer, raconteur and notorious exhibitionist. However, whatever his reputation, it has been said that his one and only public appearance in drag was trolling through the reception area of London's Regent Palace Hotel wearing a black silk dress. Admittedly, he was quite young at the time. Asked about further portraits she responded by saying that Richard Ingrams, the previously mentioned friend of the Pipers, is booked in for 2010 but checking a few months later she confessed that she hadn't yet got around to that one. Hambling maintains that her subjects tend to find her, rather than the other way around but this was obviously not the case with Max Wall. This particular portraitist always insists on seven consecutive days with her subject and that is a strict condition from which she doesn't encourage any deviation. This seems a way of working vastly at odds with that of the late Lucian Freud. I have read that this descendant of one of the most influential thinkers in Western culture insisted upon putting his models under very close observation for extended periods of time and the whole process, from start to finish, could take months, in some cases even years. This finds me wondering if he was just as insistent when he, at some time in his career, painted at least six members of the Duke of Devonshire's family. The Dowager Duchess of Devonshire has reported that Freud

George Melly by Maggi Hambling

had been friends with her and her late husband for many years. She has claimed to have recognised his 'prodigious talent' at an early date, mentioning that, 'although he can be scathingly critical of those he does not like, he has always been delightful company'. Lucian Freud subsequently earned the reputation of being 'the greatest living painter' during the latter years of his long and highly successful career. He was appointed a Companion of Honour in 1983 and a member of the Order of Merit ten years later. In 2008, his ruthless portrait of a woman of his acquaintance sold at auction at Christie's in New York for no less than the dollar equivalent of £23 million.

Quite extraordinarily, I read in the published correspondence between the duchess and her very close friend of long standing, the late Patrick Leigh Fermor, that she retained Lucian Freud to paint what I took to be her bathroom at Chatsworth. She commented that, prior to his starting work, the room had been 'stuffed up all to the ceiling with Sabine Women being "tweaked". It is horrific so whatever Lu does will go nicely'. If, by any chance, Lucian Freud had ever needed a *curriculum vitae* I very much doubt that he would have mentioned this particular commission, even if it did emanate from the upper echelons of the English aristocracy. The Duke and Duchess have been keen collectors of Freud's oil paintings and drawings and fourteen of these were featured at the ancestral home in a seven-room exhibition of the late duke's life in 2006. The Dowager Duchess described this section as something of a showstopper and must have included Freud's portrait of a horse, *Skewbald Mare*, a work that depicts only the horse's hindquarters. This painting was bought by Chatsworth's Works of Art Fund. She described this acquisition as 'astonishing and very moving'. Andrew, Duke of Devonshire, died in May 2004 at the age of 84.

Although that I am conscious that I have wandered off the subject of Maggi Hambling, I remain persuaded to add something that I came across when browsing through the lively correspondence between the duchess and her dear friend, Patrick Leigh Fermor. I really did not know what to make of the following quotation but, as it bears some sort of relationship to someone so closely connected to Aldeburgh and Snape, I thought that it merits a modest mention. It has been taken from something that he had sent to 'Debo', a fragment he had extracted from one of his old notebooks:

'The operas of Benjamin Britten
Should never be actually written
In ink, or sung loud
But inscribed on a cloud
With the tail of a Siamese kitten'

Neither of these two had struck me as being particularly musical, as far as their writings are concerned, but I suppose each of them found these words amusing in their own individually eccentric ways.

Getting back to the contemporary artist from Suffolk, from what I have seen of Maggi Hambling's portraiture her style tends towards the impressionistic, in what seems to me to be an individualistic way that I find refreshing. Incidentally, we have, of course, already come across Richard Ingrams as a friend of the Pipers and his collaboration with John Piper on their book *Piper's Places*. It's a small world really when it comes to connections with coastal Suffolk, however remote they seem at the time. I feel sure that Maggi Hambling would not have been aware of this friendship with the Pipers and the link to Benjamin Britten when the question of Ingrams' portrait was first raised by him or indeed her. Or did she know the background? It may not be important but I find it fascinating, not being a great believer in coincidence.

Now I really must write about Maggi Hambling and her reputation for being able to paint the sea so magnificently, especially the North Sea, which is so dear to her heart. She has even gone as far as to say that she is to the sea as John Constable was to the sky. There will be many that would wish to debate this point and all I can say is that what I have seen of her work involving the sea has left a very favourable impression on me and I would love to own one of her sea canvasses one day. In particular, I am very impressed by *Crashing Wave* (2007), an artistic interpretation that is full of energy and includes a small area of penetrating colour within the violence of the wave. This painting was donated by Maggi Hambling to the charity auction 'Art & Soul', where it sold readily thus raising money for a children's hospice. I feel almost certain that I saw this work in the art gallery at Snape in November 2009, on sale at a price of £11,000. The gallery was exhibiting her latest collection of *North Sea Paintings* in the summer of 2009. According to Geoffrey Munn in his excellent book, *Southwold...an Earthly Paradise*, it was George Crabbe who asked the profound question 'who is brave enough to paint the sea?' and the author's answer was 'very few'. Well one painter who has faced up to the challenge and triumphed has certainly been Maggi Hambling and to say that she has a continuing love affair with, at the very least, the North Sea is not, to my mind, overstating the case. I reproduce below another of Hambling's seascape paintings.

I have also come across an image of J M W Turner's work (painted in gouache, a type of paint consisting of pigment suspended in water that has greater reflective qualities than normal watercolour) entitled *The Breaking Wave* and dated 1832. This particular painting demonstrates the artist's personal fascination with the sea, perhaps even enhanced at that time by his comparatively recent visit to the east coast. In discussing this painting, Geoffrey Munn makes the point that in those days, before the advent of photography, let alone 'freeze frame' technology, the modern concept of abstraction would not have been understood, even by an artist as experimental as Turner. I have to confess that such an interesting point would never have occurred to me and it makes this particular work even more impressive to view.

It was in the 1980s that Hambling turned her attention to landscapes in general and the sea in particular. Her latest inclination is towards the abstract, featuring the highlights of vivid colour that I had noticed in her *Crashing Wave*. When chatting to her in the larger of the two studios in Suffolk, I noticed two unfinished canvasses, each depicting a cormorant, the body shape of each bird being painted with sweeping stokes of the brush. I look forward to seeing each of these works if they ever get completely finished. I found myself speculating whether she will introduce any dramatic sea colours to the surroundings of at least one bird, of a species noted for

High Sea, August by Maggi Hambling

A corner of Maggi Hambling's Suffolk studio with the unfinished studies of cormorants

mainly black plumage. However, it has to be said that, if seen in close proximity in the wild, it is possible to identify a green gloss to the feathers. Pied cormorants have white necks, chests and undersides so we shall have to wait and see what transpires from Maggi Hambling's imaginative and creative mind. One of the birds is shown on the seashore and there is ample scope for introducing vivid colours to the waves breaking gently on the beach. The other unfinished work depicts this voracious seabird rising from the waves with a fish in its beak. On the other hand, perhaps these were intended as sketches in advance of the creation of a more dramatic work of art. Perhaps I should have asked her at the time.

In the event, I decided to attend an exhibition, entitled *Maggi Hambling: Mostly Cormorants*, that was staged at The Peter Pears Gallery, Aldeburgh in early October 2010. I tried very hard to establish whether or not either of the unfinished works I saw in Hambling's studio had made it to this event. However, from the forty or so works on show, all depicting cormorants, I was unable find them, at least on that particular day. Also being shown were paintings of seals, the odd gannet and a few herons. It became quite clear, therefore, that her fascination with the North Sea, as well as its wildlife, continues to occupy a dominant place in her art.

Hambling's focus on the sea, featuring its waves in their most extravagant and untamed form, has been recognised by several exhibitions, including the one already mentioned at the Fitzwilliam Museum, Cambridge, (*Maggi Hambling: The Wave*) and also that staged by Marlborough Fine Art, London in January 2008. This was entitled *Maggi Hambling: Waves and Waterfalls*. In reviewing this exhibition, a critic referred to the artist's determination to paint the North Sea as a subject in its own right and not in relation to the land. He refers also to the reality of the North Sea, probably from his own experience, but noticeably in the most unflattering of terms. At the same time, he set out to recognise the sea's wildness and unpredictability, suggesting that Hambling's artistic interpretation of the untamed waves involved her own confrontation with the sea's raging conditions. He added that it represented, in herself, when confronted with the sea, 'a feisty elemental force to be reckoned with'. I know exactly what he means because although she comes across as meek and mild on the surface I am certain that, when she is alone with her creative instincts and a blank canvas, her personality changes to the extent that her mood matches the subject matter of the powerful and furious sea. At the same time, she sets out to express, and certainly succeeds in catching, its grandeur and beauty.

Her series of *North Sea Paintings* began at the end of November 2002, during the period between the conception of *Scallop* and its execution. This almost biographical work continues, and she says that she draws the sea early each morning in much the same way as a pianist practices scales. She then returns to settle in one or other of her Suffolk studios and works with an economy of colour, re-creating a very personal depiction of the action of the waves as they break on the surface of the sea.

Hambling's works of art, as well as her moods, have been described as 'patchy', but isn't this the case with the vast majority of talented painters? For my part, I am deeply in love with her paintings of the North Sea and, if other examples of her work fail to impress, well, that has to be accepted, not least by the artist herself. However, I do not think, for one for moment, that she will lose much sleep over this. There is, perhaps, something to be said for the view that her most recent paintings depict much more artistic freedom than her work, say, of the 1980s. I leave others to judge this, as I am more than content with what I have seen so far. I find myself looking forward to keeping in touch with her career as it progresses further on into the twenty-first century. She is an artist of our time and I trust that her association with coastal Suffolk will remain for many years to come and that she succeeds in keeping her regrettable arthritis at bay.

In 1995 Maggi Hambling was awarded an OBE for services to painting and in the New Year Honours List 2010, described as a Painter and Sculptor, she was awarded the CBE for services to Art. Having taken such an interest in her work as well as her career, and having also had the privilege of meeting her in her own home and studio, I am inclined to look upon Maggi Hambling as very much the *grande dame* of English Art. Nevertheless, this has caused me to hesitate, feeling sure that it must be an overused expression. I was correct in that it has been used before to describe English Impressionist painter, Dame Laura Knight (1877-1970) as well as artist, Bridget Riley, CH, CBE (born 1931), a notable proponent of 'op art' (also known as optical art). However, such an epithet is by no means common in respect of our shores. In these circumstances, it would perhaps be appropriate if I make use of the indefinite article and call her a *grand dame* of English art and I am content with that. However, I am not at all certain how she would respond to the way in which I have described her.

During the course of this book, I have made mention of Cedric Morris (1889 – 1982) and Arthur Lett-Haines (1894 – 1978) and their East Anglian School of Painting and Drawing. This concern was said to run on somewhat eccentric, some have said idiosyncratic, lines based upon the *carte blanche* approach that was operating in French academies in the late 1930s. This school succeeded in having a great influence on many Suffolk artists and it has been claimed that it also made an important contribution to the teaching of art in the east of England over four decades or so, which is certainly no mean achievement. How it was run was undoubtedly as a result of the personal experience acquired by these two appealing characters in their earlier lives. They spent sixty years of their lives together from November 1918, including some time in Paris. This was after a short stay at Newlyn in Cornwall. In the French capital, they mixed freely with the expatriate artistic community, which included, amongst others, writers Ernest Hemingway (1899-1961) and Aldous Huxley (1894-1963), painter Marcel Duchamp (1887-1968) as well as poet, writer, political activist and rebellious heiress, Nancy Cunard. This rather tragic woman became muse to some of the twentieth century's most distinguished writers and artists. These probably included some, if not all, of those just mentioned and it was certainly the case with Huxley, who became one of her lovers. Nancy Cunard was said to have been the model for two separate characters in two of his novels. Being included within such a group, amongst which they were regarded as distinctive figures, certainly had an influence on Cedric Morris and Arthur Lett-Haines, both of whom were, of course, painters. No doubt, Parisian experiences such as these rubbed off on them when it came to deciding how to run their very individual school of art in Suffolk.

From the very late 1930s to the early 1940s, the school's pupils included none other than Lucian Freud. He first went there at the age of seventeen, after studying for two years at the Central School of Arts and Crafts. Also attending at Benton End were Maggi Hambling (1960s) and, as mentioned previously, Kathleen Hale of *Orlando the Marmalade Cat* fame. She was considered important enough to have her own room allocated to her in the house in the 1940s. It was then, when her marriage had become strained, she had a short affair with Lett-Haines, which might explain her somewhat preferential treatment. Arthur Lett-Haines, perhaps along with Cedric Morris, appeared to have been rather ambiguous about his sexuality. At this time, Hale had confessed that, as far as her relationship with Lett-Haines was concerned, she knew (it) 'would be no bed of roses' and she also knew that she 'wouldn't be the only bush in the rose-bed'. Incidentally, Hale had first met her future art teachers in Paris in 1923 and later quoted Welsh artist, Cedric Morris as saying to her 'Do you mean to tell me, Kathleen, that you have built your slender reputation on the broad shoulders of a eunuch cat?' To my mind, that less than flattering jibe to someone who is widely regarded as a highly successful children's author is suggestive of a man who was somewhat envious of Hale's commercial success, let alone her relationship with Lett-Haines. On the other hand, perhaps that is just my occasional cynicism coming to the fore.

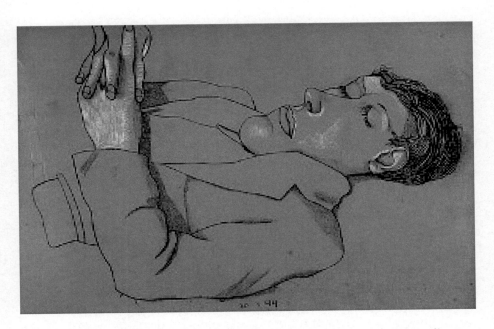

Man with folded hands by Lucian Freud, painted in 1944 when attending the East Anglian School of Painting and Drawing

As for Maggi Hambling, as an early teenager she had taken her first two oil paintings under her arm to show to Cedric Morris. Soon there were other visits to not only paint but also to help out in the kitchen, perhaps to help justify or even subsidise whatever she might have been receiving in those very early days. I have found myself speculating on just how the East Anglian School of Painting and Drawing was financed, but whatever the source of funding it cannot be denied that this educational establishment played an important part if furthering the careers of the numerous talented painters that found their way to this rather unique establishment. Morris and Lett-Haines, as mentioned previously, encouraged the school's free and easy atmosphere amidst what was clearly regarded as a family of artists striving for a common cause. To illustrate this point, there was no formal teaching at this rather unique establishment. Rather, it was an environment in which artists could explore their potential. On this basis alone, I can quite see why this proved to be a powerful attraction to the painters I have mentioned. If they had not become famous for anything else, each would certainly be awarded very high marks for individuality, thus marking themselves out by becoming someone very special.

Ultimately, it was Arthur Lett-Haines who became Maggi Hambling's mentor at that vital time in the development of her artistic core. She became imbued with the importance of hard graft in her painting. Hambling is quoted as saying that one of her lifetime best moments was when she was aged fifteen and Lett-Haines had told her to make her work her best friend. She added that it was an amazing thing to say to someone so young, because it meant that whether she was bored or happy she always able to return to her art. She emphasised that it was from that point that her life became more real. Judging by her prolific work rate nowadays, the advice she received all those years ago continues to hold good.

As I have already described, this continues to be her watchword; she can be found at her canvasses each and every day in either London or Suffolk, painting until the light fades, often missing lunch. She exists by nibbling bits of fruit throughout the day and drinking whatever she finds stored in a ready available refrigerator that occupies a prominent place in her studio. I was really delighted when she devoted some of her precious time to answering my questions about her work. After Benton End, Hambling moved on to the Ipswich School of Art and then to Camberwell before transferring to the Slade. This must have been the time that the distractions of artistic life in London started to affect her personal outlook on life generally. Mention of the Ipswich School alerts me to the fact that Maggi Hambling was asked to open a debut collection that had been assembled in a new gallery at this venue in July 2010. Charles Saatchi (born 1943), former Prime Minister, Margaret Thatcher's favourite advertising magnate and an avid collector, had recently donated his collection of modern art to the British Nation. It was the gallery at the Ipswich Art School that had been chosen to exhibit a section of his gift to the nation. At the opening, Maggi Hambling intended to say that Ipswich Art School was a leading centre of creativity from the 1930s until its closure in 1996. She was to have added 'My beginnings were at Ipswich Art School. Its restoration as a place of vision would re-focus attention on the vital richness of this place and its continuing inspiration for artists'. You might well wonder why I have appeared to allude to the fact that perhaps Maggi Hambling did not, after all, put in the planned appearance. Sadly, this is precisely what happened and only she can perhaps explain the reason for her absence. I am sure it was either forgetfulness or perhaps unforeseen circumstances but I feel sure that she would not have deliberately stayed away from this notable event.

Having written quite, some might say very, fully about a contemporary painter who delights in what coastal Suffolk has to offer, I now wish to turn my attention to another living artist, Hugo Grenville (born 1958). To say the least, he has had a varied career since leaving Eton and joining the Coldstream Guards. He went on to serve in Northern Ireland in his late teens. Even on active service he always had a painting kit on hand. Inevitably, this caused his fellow soldiers to nickname him 'Picasso'. Ian Collins has written that Grenville is possibly the only

Maggi Hambling a self portrait

professional artist to have graduated from the Guards. However, it was quite a few years afterwards that he was encouraged to take up art on a serious basis by a friend of his mother's, Nancy Farquharson. She was a staunch patron of society portraitist, Mark Gertler (1891-1939) who spent most of his life having to bear his unrequited love for Dora Carrington (1893-1932). She was an artist who lived for very many years with a member of the Bloomsbury Group, the homosexual biographer, Lytton Strachey (1880-1932), with whom she was deeply in love. She committed suicide not long after his death. How strange and tragic are both the lives and loves of others, particularly artistic people.

Incidentally, Dora Carrington's niece, Joanna Carrington (1931-2003), daughter of Noël who created Puffin books, enjoyed blissful family holidays in Walberswick and was fond of sketching and painting the beach huts. She also studied at the East Anglian School of Painting and Drawing, earning unqualified praise from Cedric Morris. She retained her connections with the area, despite living in France. During her visits to the village she stayed at Valley Farm, the home of a friend, the writer, Anthony Sampson (1926-2004). This is where Philip Wilson Steer often lodged during his working spells in the village. During her stays she was to be

The Kissing Bridge with Valley Farm, from the Walberswick Scroll

seen painting richly-coloured landscapes and seascapes that came to be shown in some London galleries. Valley Farm is depicted within the *Walberswick Scroll*, set in the background of the Kissing Bridge in 1931.

So it is very clear that Hugo Grenville's artistic credentials are certain to pass any close scrutiny because, apart from the evidence of his excellent work, he is also the nephew of Harold Peto (1854-1933), who had an Arts and Crafts approach to architecture, as did his garden designs. He was the son of Sir Samuel Peto, developer of Victorian Lowestoft and 1st Baronet, of Somerleyton Hall in Suffolk, which is widely regarded as one of the best examples of an archetypal Tudor-Jacobean mansion and one of the most beautiful stately homes in Britain. Somerleyton's rooms and magnificent gardens are open to the public.

In many respects, Hugo Grenville's artistic accomplishments are nothing short of impeccable. He once lived at Mendham, birthplace of Sir Alfred Munnings, before the family upped and moved to Crouch End in North London in 2005. His studio was then located in a former chocolate factory which had become home to a colony of artists. He also operated an art school in order to supplement his income. London continued to be the location for the family home for only a few years before the county's many natural attractions lured them back to Suffolk. They all wanted to live once more in the countryside and Hugo Grenville and his wife soon found a property not too far away from the River Waveney and only three miles from their previous home. Grenville and his family have readily admitted that the charms of the Suffolk countryside were being sadly missed and that no number of weekend visits to friends could possibly compensate for not living there permanently. He now runs his art courses from his latest country home, which is splendidly isolated. He has been able to renew and enjoy the inter-action with his students, this time in more tranquil surroundings than his London studio. Grenville has often painted in and around Southwold and Walberswick and has done so since the 1990s, on occasion accompanied by his students. He has been described as a colourist working in the Romantic tradition, being influenced by the work of Henri Matisse (1869-1954), who was very much a master of the use of colour. Grenville is a protégé of Ken Howard RA, who was crucially the Official War Artist to Northern Ireland. Elected to the Royal Academy in 1984, his work can be found in public collections including the National Army Museum, Guildhall Art Gallery, Ulster Museum and the Imperial War Museum. I mention Howard's war artist appointment because Grenville was also an Official War Artist. This was in Bosnia, his predecessor having been overcome emotionally and unable to continue with the position after being confronted with a mass

St Mark's Square. Venice – Late Winter Morning by Hugo Grenville

Woman Reclining by Hugo Grenville

grave. It was felt that Grenville would have a more detached approach to his duties as a result of his experiences in Northern Ireland.

However, there have been other influences on Hugo Grenville's work, not least as a result of his visit to a retrospective, *Fauvism at the Musée de l'art moderne de la ville de Paris* in 1999, an event that Grenville described as his personal 'road to Damascus'.

It seems impossible to be neutral in viewing Hugo Grenville's work, if only because of the almost explosive colouring. When this is coupled with his very personal interpretation of Impressionism, he seems to have created an intimate flavour as well as a spiritual intensity. When Grenville was interviewed by fellow Suffolk resident, Libby Purves, on her BBC Radio 4 *Midweek* discussion programme on the occasion of Grenville's work being exhibited at the Messum Gallery in Cork Street in London's Mayfair, another guest described Grenville's bright and colourful paintings as 'similar to flying a Spitfire on canvas'. The artist feels that the brightness expressed in his work aims to create 'a better world in paint' for the viewer. He is also a painter who sometimes thinks 'outside-the-box', in that he has worked with Philip Wells, a celebrated Performance Poet, as have other members of the artistic world such as photographers and musicians and other painters. Grenville sees a link between painting and poetry whereby he concentrates on aspects of the rhythm and metre of a poem, rather than the meaning of the words, and their relation to the colour and light expressed in his paintings. Wells has responded to Grenville's work in his poetry, finding the words to describe his paintings that the artist has confessed would never have occurred to him. Grenville has described the poetry of Wells as 'an access point to painting'.

Grenville has now parted company with Messums, regarded as the premier London gallery for East Anglian art, after a lengthy relationship. This he regards as part of a creative rebirth process. He now relies on independently curated exhibitions, as well as an American gallery, Wally Findlay Inc. who once had outlets in Palm Beach, Florida, New York, Barcelona and Los Angeles. One or two of these have now been discarded due to the deteriorated economic outlook. This change of direction affords Grenville an excellent opportunity to paint for a wider international market and he told me that this is already proving to be profitable. The painter attributes this new relationship to a freeing-up of his style, a 'creative kick', his work being now more imaginative and less representational. This has resulted in a personal decision to depict what amounts to a re-invention of the scene that is before him when painting. On the other hand, he recognises that his style is likely to continue to move forward, albeit in his favoured Romantic approach to art. So far, all has gone well and his confidence has continued to grow. The use of light has always been important in his work but his latest approach is to ignore the source of the light and to concentrate upon light radiating from within the subject. Since he described this to me, I have looked afresh at some of his more recent work and have come to appreciate the point he has made.

Having already researched the career of Hugo Grenville, I decided to arrange to call upon him in his new home in the Suffolk countryside. He was alone, apart from the comings and goings of a man who appeared to be in charge of the substantial extension that was clearly going to take place to his latest family home. The footings for an enlarged property were already in place. It was clear that Grenville, although not painting on that particular day, was a busy man, fielding telephone calls from various members of his family, dealing with me as well as matters regarding the building activities. Nevertheless, he was happy to chat about his work and soon put me at my ease.

It seems that he had no childhood ambition to become a painter. At his preparatory school, his art teacher, appropriately named Mr Black, had an abhorrence of colour. He set his class the task of copying a Spanish galleon. Grenville explained that when he and other classmates had copied the ship in pencil they were allowed to use only black, brown or yellow for colouring. If they were really lucky, they could use red followed with the special bonus of being permitted to use black ink to go round the edges. At his next school, he preferred to forego games in order to concentrate on painting on afternoons allocated for sport. It was at that school that he first made use of oils in his work.

As the family finances did not run to his attending an art school, he joined the army and, being based in London for some time, was able to attend art classes at the Chelsea School of Art in the evenings as well as part-time at the Heatherley School of Fine Art, also in

Chelsea. By the time he left the army, five years later, and having been encouraged by others, he was pretty sure he wanted to be a painter, although funding was obviously going to be a problem. He got a job with an advertising agency and became a copywriter. He was soon to realise that it was graphic design, rather than painting, that was practised at the agency. He lasted no more than eighteen months in that job, appreciating that, unlike life in the army, there was precious little freedom involved with office life. He explained that earning the Picasso nickname had nothing to do with his style but was probably due to the fact that this was the only painter that came easily to mind with his fellow soldiers. Even on active service, his paints and an easel were readily to hand and it seemed that it was not just a case of if he was to become a painter, but when. In fact, it was 1989 before he finally decided to abandon his various other activities, including that of a part-time art dealer, and became a full-time painter. Since then he has painted wherever he has happened to be, at home or abroad, landscapes as well as still lifes and figures.

As far as the spell in Bosnia as a war artist was concerned, the MOD commission was to produce one large painting which was to depict the role of the light infantry, comprising various regiments and battalions, in a humanitarian situation (actually moving into a town) in that country. It was executed back in his London studio from drawings that he had made at the time. This painting is now hanging somewhere in the Ministry of Defence in London and there are also studies in private hands after first appearing in a Messum's catalogue.

Hugo Grenville describes his latest paintings as having soft colours, not too saturated. When he first started painting, he felt that people like Walter Sickert, Philip Wilson Steer, Spencer Gore, Harold Gilman and others of that particular school were undoubtedly a big influence on his work but that is no longer the case. Grenville mentioned a particular oil on canvas painting by Wilson Steer that he described as marvellous. This is entitled *Girls Running, Walberswick Pier* dated 1888-1894 and hangs in Tate Britain where it is described as one of the most 'authentically impressionist' works produced in this country. It is reproduced opposite.

Girls running, Walberswick Pier by Philip Wilson Steer, 1888-1894, with the permission of Tate Images

Hugo Grenville went on to talk more about Philip Wells, the poet, with whom he confirmed that he collaborated very well. Wells wrote a group of poems inspired by some pictures Grenville had painted and he was thrilled when the poet went on to perform this work on the opening night of Grenville's last show at Messums' Art Gallery. Painter and poet then agreed to collaborate on another project but, unfortunately, this has not seen, in the artist's words, 'the light of day' because of other distractions. He went on to point out that what he and Wells had done together was hardly revolutionary. He then referred to Faber and Faber publishing what he described as their *Heirloom Poems* in the 1940s and 1950s when they used some of the best illustrators and artists of the day to illustrate short poems. He gave as an example T S Eliott's *The Waste Land* illustrated by painter, illustrator and graphic artist, Edward Bawden (1903-1989). Grenville then went on to say what he and Wells had in mind was eight pages long, with two illustrations and a lovely cover. We can only hope that they can get started on this project so that we can all appreciate what they manage to achieve together, particularly as, so far as he is aware, nothing like this has been done for some considerable time. I am not absolutely convinced that is precisely the case as a near neighbour of mine in south Norfolk is a very talented artist who has certainly illustrated poems written by Oliver Bernard, whose work is mentioned elsewhere. Grenville, aged 52, mentioned that his proposed project with Philip Wells had attracted the interest of a couple of publishers but, at that time, it was thought that the market was 'not quite right'. Where have I heard that before?

I found it fascinating to discover a painter working with a poet, just as other forms of the arts combine with a poet and his poetry. Benjamin Britten's collaboration with W H Auden is a notable example, as is his opera *Peter Grimes* based upon *The Borough* by Suffolk's, George Crabbe. This latter work must surely qualify as the longest poem in history. On the subject of long poems, not too long ago, whilst listening to BBC Radio 4's afternoon play I listened, deeply moved, to a narrator reading passages from Alfred, Lord Tennyson's *In Memoriam*. This contains the often-quoted words, ''Tis better to have loved and lost, Than never to have loved at all' contained within two separate verses of a poem that reached very nearly 20,000 words. This work was written in memory of his dear friend from his days at Cambridge, Arthur Henry Hallam (1811- 1833), a fellow poet who died very young. Written over a period of seventeen years, Tennyson made a start just after his friend had died, the poem being eventually completed in 1849. I feel sure that there have been, and still are, many other instances of how freshly created work can emanate from that of another artist in the world of theatre, literature, painting or indeed music.

Interestingly, Hugo Grenville happens to know Elizabeth Jane Howard quite well as she does, of course, live next door to Sargy Mann, a fellow artist whom Grenville visits extremely regularly.

He referred to the fact that most of his paintings are conceived in his mind. He added that sometimes it could take a whole day, or even more, until he has constructed and arranged, to his complete satisfaction, his latest still life subject or figure study. He then feels ready to make a start on the painting. Grenville described how he waits until the arrangement arrives at what he describes as 'the right mood' and it feels as though the layout is unlikely to be improved. This artistic work can be undertaken in London or in Suffolk. As far as the latter is concerned, he does prefer to have the feeling

The Beach from North Parade, Southwold by Hugo Grenville

of being 'comfortable' in his new, albeit then temporary, studio space, in a refurbished outbuilding. He considers it to be very important to become accustomed to how the light works and, indeed, how the space works. I found myself wondering if he has yet to achieve this now that he seems to have completed his mission with 'Suffolk revisited'. When I first met him, he did mention that in due course he would construct an entirely new studio on an area of land close to his new home. By now this may well have been achieved. One thing I can confirm; he is unlikely to be disturbed by the noise of passing traffic in the somewhat isolated location he has managed to find for his latest family residence.

The president of his American gallery describes Grenville's paintings as being of 'things remembered, paintings of reverie'. The

October Morning, Suffolk by Hugo Grenville

artist is quite happy to change the colours in accordance with the way he sees the work in his mind in order to achieve his ideal. This is on the basis that the paintings are not necessarily meant to represent reality. The same principle is also applied to his landscapes and, all in all, he feels that he paints in what he very loosely describes as a post-Impressionist idiom, drawing influence from Henri Matisse, leader of the Fauves, with a strong sense of colour and decoration. I have learned that the work undertaken by followers of Fauvism emphasise characteristic painterly qualities and strong colour over the representational or realistic values retained by Impressionism. By virtue of being aware of what his American agents have been looking for in putting together their stable of modern painters, Grenville feels that there are not too many around anymore that paint in this tradition. In this instance, he was talking about Britain and Europe. Grenville was very pleased to be asked to show in America, especially by a gallery that deals in works by Cézanne and represents the estates of Pierre Bonnard (1867-1947) and Picasso as well as Matisse.

Hugo Grenville struck me as a very contented man, loving his work, with his current ambition limited to being able to continue to paint in his chosen style and earn enough money to support his family and maintain both Suffolk and London studios. In his own words, the moment of epiphany for his family's move back to Suffolk arose from their being outside the riverside café at Walberswick, three or four years ago. It was a summer's day and his teenage boys had bought a 'shrimping and crabbing' line and were hanging it over the river's edge, their legs and feet dangling in the water. It was a special moment when they all agreed that Suffolk was their real home and they wanted to return to live there. That was more or less that, and the family is now settled into their new home, following the completion of the extension and conversion works. Perhaps he is now fully able to concentrate on his painting and teaching at what is described as his purpose-designed painter's retreat. A bolthole is still maintained in London as well as the studio, so Grenville has the best of both worlds with the artist constantly seeking inspiration derived from his regular visits to London's magnificent art galleries.

Chapter Seven

More Artists, Past and Present, and an Illustrator

IN ITSELF, BLYTHBURGH, whilst not actually situated on the coast of Suffolk is nevertheless a village with an impressive history with its original wealth being derived from the sea. It was once an active port that served to facilitate a great herring industry. This unfortunately withered away after the Reformation, when the residents, let alone the rest of the country, were absolved from an obligation to eat fish at least twice each week. As a result, the port became disused and the River Blyth silted up, leaving only the splendid church to remind its inhabitants and visitors of the much better times that had once been enjoyed.

Thankfully, not everyone stayed away as, over the years, Blythburgh has played host to some significant artists, some of whom were residents. Amongst those who lived there were Ernest Crofts (1847-1911) and Sir John Seymour Lucas (1849-1923), both Royal Academicians. There was also, as more recently, William Benner (1884-1964). Ernest Crofts was a painter of historical and military scenes whose work eventually became unfashionable, although such art has since been in more demand. He has the doubtful distinction of being possibly one of the very earliest fatalities from a motor vehicle accident; this unfortunate incident took place just outside Blythburgh in 1911, and must have caused quite a stir locally. In those days, such a happening tended to be described as a collision between two horseless carriages. Some of his work depicted the Battle of Waterloo, scenes from the English Civil War, the Duke of Wellington on a march to meet Napoleon and Oliver Cromwell at Marston Moor.

Sir John Seymour Lucas was an historical and portrait painter as well as an accomplished theatrical costume designer. Both Crofts and Lucas lived close by Blythburgh Church and Lucas had the distinction of having his own portrait painted by none other than his friend, the famous society portrait painter, John Singer Sargent (1856-1925). This work is displayed at Tate Britain. As his own reputation grew, Lucas completed a number of major works for display in various prestigious public buildings as well as those intended for royal clients. Amongst these paintings were *The Flight of the Five Members* (Houses of Parliament), *The Granting of the Charter of the City of London* (Royal Exchange), *Reception by HM King Edward VII of the Moorish Ambassador* (Royal Collection) and a portrait of *HRH the Prince of Wales in German Uniform* (Royal Collection). In almost total contrast, William Benner, to complete this trio of artists resident in Blythburgh, was inspired to paint stations situated at intervals on the narrow-gauge railway line known as the Southwold Railway. These were painted principally in the open air, in front of his subject and not at all in the style of the previously named Reg Carter. Some of Benner's paintings can be found in the Southwold Museum. He also painted elsewhere *en plein air* along the Blyth Valley. According to Richard Scott, the 'upright, schoolmasterly figure of Benner, attired in tweed jacket and tie, was a familiar figure sight around Walberswick, Southwold and Blythburgh, making his way to chosen painting locations, on a tall kit-laden black bicycle ...' All I can add is 'What a wonderful way to enjoy an artistic life'.

Not exactly of the same ilk as Carter and the Stannards in terms of illustrative and other art, was Arthur Rackham (1867-1939) and in his visits to Walberswick he too stayed at Old Farm, during a holiday in 1907. There were also subsequent visits as there is evidence of a letter written by him from another Walberswick address in 1910. Rackham established his reputation as a popular illustrator in this country during the early part of the twentieth century. However, his first commission was to come from East Anglia. This was in the latter part of the nineteenth century.

There is some history to this assignment. *Sunrise-Land* was a book that resulted in a publishing initiative in 1893 by Jarrold & Sons Limited of Norwich. This followed a reissued and refurbished book entitled *Poppy-Land*, first published in 1886 by publishers Carson and Comerford who, as two separate individuals, first published *The Stage* magazine in 1880. A formal publishing company appeared to have been in existence prior to this and was responsible for a series of carbon and other prints of stage actors towards the end of the nineteenth century. They also published *The Stage Year Book* for many years. However, I digress: *Poppy-Land*, as was the case with the intended *Sunrise-Land*, was basically an illustrated travel book featuring East Anglian counties.

Jarrolds commissioned two young artists, one of whom was Arthur Rackham. The plan was for these two gentlemen to accompany popular writer, Annie Berlyn (c1861-1943), on her travels to gather material for this new book. No doubt to the relief of the artistic couple, Berlyn was appointed to be in charge of the project. This assignment was indeed an early and very important recognition of Arthur Rackham's work. I make this point because he then went on to earn a well-deserved reputation for his book illustrations over the many years that followed.

As it happened, Rackham had previously spent a very agreeable sightseeing holiday in Norfolk with his family in 1881. During the year preceding the all-important assignment, he had been sailing with his brother, Harris, on the Norfolk Broads. Arthur was very happy to return to East Anglia during 1893-1894, this time exploring the region with his cohorts, and no doubt the fact that he was being paid for it just added to his delight. Jarrolds had given all three of them a free rein and it seems quite clear that each of these travelling companions enjoyed the company of the others. The fact that they stayed in the best hotels, enjoyed superb food and hired a wherry that was sailed on the Norfolk broads for a week provides firm evidence that a good time was had by all. The journeying during those two summers provided Rackham with an excellent apprenticeship in pen and ink drawing. He came to excel in making sketches of the local surroundings as well as water in all its forms, such as streams, lakes and rivers as well as the sea. It has been interesting to be able to study his drawings of the various female fashions of those late Victorian times.

Crag Path, Aldeburgh.
The tower on the right is one of the watch towers belonging to the old 'beach companies', which, in the days before lifeboats, used them to watch for ships in difficulty during storms, and then put to sea to try and save both the ships and their occupants.

The illustration on this page depicts *Crag Path, Aldeburgh*, then just a walkway. Rackham's portrayal of the local people taking the sea air, dressed in the fashions of the time, is a joy to see. This was a long time before Benjamin Britten moved into his Crabbe Street house that, from the rear, overlooked his back garden as well as Crag Path, the beach and the North Sea.

The scene on the previous page is taken from the book. Other such illustrations will follow. From what I have learned, the book, as was the case with its predecessor, turned out to be what is described nowadays as 'an instant bestseller'. The subject matter was expressed as a 'brilliantly evocative guide to East Anglia'. This publishing success resulted in the region becoming a Mecca for visiting holidaymakers. To take just one example, people were inspired to visit Cromer and walk along the cliffs and amongst the ubiquitous summer poppies that also came to characterise the region as a whole. Artists, both professional and amateur, were inspired to produce watercolours and oil paintings in their thousands, and no doubt some of the more professional of these were to visit Walberswick.

Below is another drawing made in this town at the same time. This was of the sixteenth century The Moot Hall, a building that once had a more central setting but coastal erosion over the years has resulted in its revised location close to the popular beach with bathing machines featured in the background. This historic, Grade I listed, timber-framed building remains standing, quite possibly in the same position today, although now accessed by an adopted road, and undoubtedly regarded as in a far less vulnerable situation.

I also discovered one of Arthur Rackham's drawings of the elderly ferryman. He was captured by the artist in the act of standing up, alone in his boat, on what appears to be the Walberswick side of the river Blyth, across the water from Southwold. The artists' colony in the village was, by then, already well-established and young Rackham, still in his mid-twenties, must have been intrigued by the presence of

How Moot Hall, Aldeburgh looks nowadays

so many painters. This led me to the conclusion that the Rackhams' family holidays from 1907-1910, and possibly beyond, were as a direct result of the artist being attracted to the village of Walberswick at the time he had been working in the area during 1893-94.

A visit was also paid to Southwold, and the drawing (page 332) of an *Old Well* with two ladies

Arthur Rackham's 'Ferryman at Walberswick' (most probably Benjamin Cross – great, great, great-uncle of the present operator of the ferry, Dani Church)

chatting, or possibly gossiping, in the foreground adds a nice touch to the scene that he had chosen to depict. It is with some pleasure that I am able to feature each of these drawings by way of illustration of Rackham's work, two being complete with the original captions.

All in all, Arthur Rackham's journeying during the two years approaching the end of the nineteenth century provided him with

Arthur Rackam's drawing of the same building made from over a century before the photograph on page 330

a comprehensive apprenticeship in the art of pen and ink drawing. It is unlikely to be disputed that the inspiration he drew over those couple of years figured prominently throughout the rest of his career. Perhaps the many admirers of his work, over what has now been more than a century, might breathe a sigh of relief that he was not drawn to joining the artists colonising Walberswick at the time of his working and holiday visits there, all those years ago. Otherwise, he might not have spent so much of his career on illustrating other very popular books, including The *Wind in the Willows* (Kenneth Grahame), *The Compleat Angler* (Izaac Walton), and *Alice's Adventures in Wonderland* (Lewis Carroll).

I feel that one aspect that I have yet to cover is work by any artist associated with Southwold

Arthur Rackham's An Old Well, Southwold

during the course of the Second World War. The painter that I have in mind practised a rather specialized art form, which featured the changes that the war had brought to the local landscape. She was Prunella Clough (1919-1999), an artist who had known and loved Suffolk dating back to the days of her affluent and rather conventional pre-war childhood. She grew to love the joy of escaping to Southwold in wartime, not only to recharge her batteries but also to improve her painting skills. She graduated from the Chelsea School of Art in 1939. One example of her work at that time is the painting entitled *Harbour Works* (1942), in watercolour, pencil and gouache. This depicts heavy structures in concrete and steel and *Shoreline and Water Defences*, completed around the same time, features not the most typical of scenes commonly associated with Walberswick and Southwold. Certain specialized structures and mines that had been placed on the beach to deter attempts at enemy landings are clearly shown in her work, *Closed Beach* (1945). These paintings by Prunella Clough are grim reminders of how war can change an idyllic scene, thankfully not irrevocably. Although she owned a house known as 'Woldside' on Constitution Hill until 1966, her creative focus was to turn to London. There were also visits to other parts the country, as well as weekend visits to France to care for an ageing aunt. Prunella Clough's aunt Eileen had pursued a Continental career in pioneering modernist architecture and design. Perhaps it was influence exerted by her aunt that inspired a fragment of Clough's penchant for industrial-looking scenes. In a 1982 interview, she said, 'Living rooms are not exactly enough. I enjoyed the drama of the exotic, which was what factories or industrial areas offered me.'

It is worth mentioning that she did have at least one connection with the Aldeburgh Festival, in that in 1953 she produced prints of masts, floats, nets and breakwaters for the Festival calendar when Mary Potter and John Piper also added contributions.

Earlier on, I mentioned a so-called 'new wave' and an ardent supporter of these more modern artists was Miss I M Birtwistle, who established the Walberswick Galleries in 1950. By doing this, she provided a valuable shop window for the artists of the day in the village and beyond. He name was Iris but she never cared for this and preferred to be known professionally by her initials. Birtwistle later moved elsewhere in Suffolk and then on to north Norfolk. Her contribution of enormous passion and energy in promoting local artists had been not only invaluable, but almost legendary. Previously, until her official gallery in Walberswick became available, Miss Birtwistle exhibited work first of all in an old battery hen hut, bought for £25, which she put in the middle of her garden. At a later date she moved to the Women's Institute hut on the village green. This became the Lantern Gallery under a future occupant.

One artist who recalled being represented in Miss Birtwistle's makeshift gallery was none other than David Hockney (born 1937). He is perhaps the most popular and versatile and, some say, the greatest living British artist of the twentieth century and beyond. However, in those days, he was very much an unknown in the world of art. I find myself speculating on who found whom at that early stage in his career? Local folklore seems to suggest that Iris Birtwistle had even sold Hockney's drawings for a fiver each before anyone had ever heard of him. However, I am hopeful that even this redoubtable gallery owner, who obviously recognised a remarkable talent when she saw it, drew the line at offering two Hockneys for the price of one. This must have been during the late fifties and possibly even the early sixties. However, assuming that the lucky purchasers of those earlier times discovered that they had a Hockney hanging on their walls, I find myself wondering if one or two decided to cash-in so that they could turn an investment of just a few pounds into a sizeable profit. Later in life, and very tragically, I M Birtwistle became blind but Richard Scott maintains that she never lost her 'feel' for good art, even after some fifteen years without the benefit of sight.

In early 2011, The Royal Academy staged a wonderful and much acclaimed sell-out show of David Hockney's newest work, all drawn in his unique style from his beloved East Yorkshire landscape, wherein lie his roots. Virtually all of this glorious art, which filled just about the entire Royal Academy, had been generated from the artist's return to painting *en plein air*, a detail that gladdened me enormously when I read it. His extensive use of incandescent colour proved to be striking enough to inspire a third leading article in an edition of that week's *Times* newspaper. His large-scale paintings took over entire walls of the gallery, thus affording a spectacular sight to his many admirers. Hockney owes a great deal to the inspiration he has drawn from the works of both Pablo Picasso and Claude Monet. I have been delighted to discover his past connections to coastal Suffolk, even though the money he received from Iris Birtwistle would not have been enough to buy him a currant bun at the Royal Academy if he had looked for one when he visited his own exhibition there. It was also fascinating to read about this artist's fascination with the latest technology for his work. He has taken to drawing on his iPad and the results were exhibited on the wall of one gallery. These were reproduced in such a way that the works were said to be indistinguishable, albeit at a distance, from oil paintings. This leaves me wondering what Miss Birtwistle would have thought of that. However, she would have been even more proud, if she had been alive, to be aware of Hockney, at last feeling able to accept an honour, this time in the prestigious and personal gift of HM The Queen, receiving the insignia of the Order of Merit. He collected this from the monarch at Buckingham Place on 22 May 2012. A vacancy, bearing in mind that this exclusive 'club' can have only twenty-four members at any one time, had been created by the death of his friend, Lucian Freud, in the previous year.

Incidentally, Stephen Spender and David Hockney became friends and the poet had a number of the artist's works hanging on the walls of his home from time to time. In 1981, Spender travelled to China with Hockney and a young man, Gregory (Greg) Evans. Hockney had taken Evans as a lover when he was in America and this young man subsequently graduated to becoming a working partner. *China Diary* (Thames & Hudson 1982) resulted from this trip, with Stephen Spender being responsible for the text with Hockney producing the pictures. Amazingly, Spender was paid the sum of £10,000 by the publisher and this was said to be the most rewarding book, in financial terms that Spender had written during the course of his entire career. The age discrepancy between the three was remarkable; Evans in his twenties, Hockney aged forty-four with Spender, at seventy-two, playing the role of the veteran. The three are said to have enjoyed a whale of a time and the trip was described as a celebration of boon companionship.

Other artists who had work exhibited at the Walberswick Galleries included Mary Potter, Jeffrey Camp (born 1923), Susan Horsfield (born 1928), Chris and Wendy Sinclair (born 1931 and 1932), Audrey Pilkington, Mary Newcomb (1922-2008) and Richard Parsons (1925-2000). Not all of these actually lived within the village but some did; others made homes nearby or, in the context of this book, should be classed as just visitors. Most have had exhibitions here and there, and all are justifiably deserving of mention because of the impressive quality of their work. These painters, as well as others, included figurative artists but all were inspired by coastal Suffolk, one producing work considered dreamlike in nature. A number of these artists are known for rich and colourful landscapes with a number executed *en plein air*. All formed part of the period of what has been called the *Winds of Change* at Walberswick. There were others, of no less consequence, but I have to draw the line somewhere. If I have to choose between these artists I would have to favour those classed as Impressionists. These works have afforded me the most satisfaction, mainly because of the added use of attractive and bold colours.

As her assistant in the gallery at Walberswick, Iris Birtwistle employed the young Jennifer Lash (1938-1993). She arrived, aged seventeen, originally to stay for a weekend and ended up remaining in the job for five years. Her employer introduced Lash to a handsome young local farmer, Mark Fiennes. They fell in love, married and had six children, including the stage and film actors Ralph (born 1962) and Joseph Fiennes (born 1970) as well as the film directors Martha (born 1964) and Sophie (born 1967). This smacks of Jennifer Lash playing a leading part in the founding of something of a show business dynasty. She dedicated her first novel to her surrogate mother. This book, one of six, was entitled *The Burial*. It was written when she was just twenty-three years old. Each of her children retained a special affection for Iris Birtwistle ever after. Acknowledged also as Jini Fiennes, Jennifer Lash became known as a painter as well as a novelist. Upon meeting Jennifer Lash in Suffolk, Dodie Smith (1896-1990), novelist and playwright who wrote *The Hundred and One Dalmatians*, remarked that Lash was, 'almost too interesting to be true'.

Incidentally, I M Birtwistle also established a reputation as a lyric poet, although she tended to belittle her talent in this genre. However, she was not without some notable admirers. These were none other than award-winning Scottish novelist, Dame Muriel Spark (1918-2006), poet, playwright and literary critic, T S Eliot (1888- 1965) as well as poet and novelist, Robert Graves (1895-1985). The latter went as far as to invite her to stay at his home in Deià, Majorca. Writing in this particular style, poets concentrate on expressing their personal and emotional feelings.

From the names of the various exhibitors at Walberswick Galleries mentioned above, but also previously, I have decided to single out Mary Newcomb. This is not merely because of her exceptional talent, but because it also gives me the opportunity to include one of her daughters, Tessa Newcomb (born 1955), who has also made a considerable name for herself as a painter. As I mentioned much earlier, this particular artist is more than just a little acquainted with Bob Jackson of Chapel Books in Westleton. Mary Newcomb once lived in Newton Flotman, just a few miles to the south of Norwich, but her residential qualifications for inclusion here are due to the fact that her later years were spent at Peasenhall, a village not all that far inland from Dunwich and also quite close to the village of Westleton where her daughter now lives. Until Tessa was aged fifteen, she lived with her parents in the small village of Needham on the Norfolk/ Suffolk border. There is no doubt that, along with other artists, Mary Newcomb's career was boosted nationally by Miss Birtwistle, as well as internationally. This led to regular exhibitions of her work at the prestigious Crane Kalman Gallery in Knightsbridge from 1970. This establishment also exhibits work by daughter, Tessa. Its owner, Andras Kalman is acknowledged appropriately in a biography of Mary Newcomb by Christopher Andreae, a writer with a long experience in art criticism. He commented that 'her drawing was mercifully free of stylisation'. Newcomb's imagery is also said to be drawn not only from observation of East Anglian life that surrounded her, but also from her memories, earlier in life as a marine biologist. Andreae's monograph includes extracts from the artist's personal diary, from which it seems clear that her talent for creativity is not restricted to her painting. She began her diary in 1986 and the first entry reads:

> 'I wanted to say these things and to record what I have seen to remind ourselves that – in our haste – in this century – we may not give time to pause and look – and may pass on our way unheeding'.

In later describing something as mundane as a man cycling rather quickly down a hill and the immediate surroundings, she observes that 'Time passes but it passes more slowly here'. This is translated into a painting entitled appropriately enough *Man Cycling Madly Down a Hill* (1988) which her biographer interprets as 'Her cyclist, charging through the overall space and colour of the painting, leaves a trail behind him like a plane across the sky'. Thus, the bicycle's momentum was everything to the artist and in her diary she notes that 'Some parts of a painting are explained in a single brush stroke and I never touch them again'. Perhaps it is in this remark that she conveys her individual style, based upon economy rather than elaboration, a technique that subsequently went on to establish her reputation. Other examples of descriptive narrative in her diary establish an individuality and unpredictable originality that are clearly demonstrated in her painting. It was said by writer, Ronald Blythe, a kindred spirit as well as being a friend of Mary, that 'she painted things that nobody else ever saw'. Incidentally, Mary Newcomb illustrated Blythe's book entitled *Borderland: Continuity and Change in the Countryside*.

Ian Collins, another friend of Mary Newcomb for some thirty years and also a writer on art, has written enthusiastically about Southwold artists. He acted as curator for a retrospective exhibition of Mary Newcomb's work at Norwich Castle Art Gallery in 2009. In his book, Collins depicts an image of Mary Newcomb's oil on canvas painting of Southwold's dramatic landmark which she completed in 1972. It is entitled The *Little Lighthouse Town*, of which she wrote 'The lighthouse stands as a guardian and a guide for us all, and lights us home'. If it is possible to get the feeling of being lost in such a small town what she says has a lot of truth, because you always know more or less where you are as long as you can see the lighthouse.

Mary Newcomb, described as a rural visionary, suffered a stroke in October 2003 and, rather sadly, that ended her painting career. After that, she confined her activities in the art world to a lively interest in other people's work. She once commented to Richard Scott that she found it difficult to understand why people valued her work so highly judging by what they were paying for her paintings. If I had been in his shoes, I might have ventured to suggest that the proprietors of the Kalman Gallery could perhaps be persuaded to offer a thoroughly professional opinion on that matter.

A painting entitled *Evening Stillness* (1999) by Tessa Newcomb was chosen by Richard Scott to adorn the front cover of his book *Artists at Walberswick*, which I regard as a personal tribute to the daughter of a fine painter whose work has captured the hearts of many of her admirers. Examples of Tessa's work, apart from subjects in the Suffolk countryside, regularly feature scenes in and about Walberswick, usually the riverside, as is the case with the book cover. More recent work depicts street scenes, both at home and abroad, as well as still life. She has given these paintings titles that, reminiscent of her mother's somewhat eccentric approach, are certainly descriptive, even though in some cases perhaps a shade unusual. I certainly took warmly to the images whilst viewing her work on the Crane Kalman website. Tessa herself says that her paintings tend to be 'set in rather unspecific places with unspecific characters so that people can make it their own story'. To me, this seems an admirable way to encourage people to become involved with her work on a personal basis rather than relying on what other people might have to say about her paintings. At the time of writing, the Kalman Gallery is staging an exhibition of her recent work to mark a book launch, T*essa Newcomb* by Philip Vann. She has truly followed in her mother's footsteps but, at the same time, she has established an enviable reputation for individuality. Tessa had paintings commissioned specially for Geoffrey Munn's book, *Southwold...an Earthly Paradise*.

It has been said that Tessa Newcomb's art arises from piercingly clear, pristine perceptions of the everyday and natural world. She maintains a prolific output, as she appears to be drawing scenes she comes across in the course of her life on what appears to be a continuous basis. Her subjects range from unkempt Suffolk allotments to curious and somewhat strange happenings in a range of Parisian squares or beside a range of canals in Venice. Her habit of wandering or cycling here and there across the spacious landscapes of East Anglia has proven to be a personally inspired, not to say readily available source, for many of her paintings. It is her unique interpretation of what she sees that marks her out as the original artist of singular vision that she has become. It is my view that she thoroughly deserves the recognition that she now commands.

It seems inevitable that there have been comparisons between her work and that of her mother, even though Tessa seems to have done her best, even from childhood, to be determined not to be subject to any form of parental influence. Her father, Godfrey, made slipware pottery and, as people were always dropping in at his showroom at home, there was no escaping the artistic world of her parents. As it happens, she might well have appeared unmoved or even embarrassed by what they did for a living. She feels that any inspiration or effect her mother's painting has had on her work, and she does admit that on occasion it has had an effect, is because it is 'in the blood'. She has summed up her mother's influence by saying 'My paintings may look a bit like my mother's but then so do I' so who can possibly lay fault to such a disarming admission? On the other hand, Tessa also recalls that in childhood she and her mother visited the home of Margaret Mellis and Francis Davison in the village of Syleham where she spotted a wonderful painting of a viaduct by Alfred Wallis; this was hanging on a wall behind a sofa. If anything was to drive Tessa Newcomb in the direction of starting out as an artist, it was that particular Wallis painting. Her admiration for this artist is also reflected in some of her further work when she took to painting scenes on the tops and sides of wooden boxes, as indeed did Alfred Wallis. She also painted on objects such music stands, cupboards and even a screen. Her decision to become an artist seems to be in conflict with a confession of hers that she didn't think she had particularly liked any paintings that she had seen until the time that she entered art school. Having read this led me to ponder just how many of us can admit to having harboured ambitions for doing something specific for a living, such as driving a train, only to eventually end up doing something completely different? From what I have read about her early days, it seems that Tessa Newcomb might have harboured a secret determination not to become an artist. Consciously or subconsciously, Tessa Newcomb found herself in a world that she has now made her own. Anyone who has a passion for the results of an imaginative approach to the landscapes as well as the inhabitants of both rural and coastal Suffolk can gain enormous pleasure from viewing and appreciating all aspects of her work. Her subjects are many and varied, but happily, as far as I am concerned anyway, these include views of the sea complete with sailing boats as well as working or resting fishermen on the shore. In closing this section on Tessa Newcomb, I am also happy to report that she, too, is an admirer of the work of Mary Potter, an artist who has been known to her since childhood.

At this point, I feel compelled to add the name of John Western (1948-1993) to the list of illustrious artists that I have chosen to feature. I met John through a dear friend of mine and I am pleased to write that John told me that he shared my love of classic sailing boats. He made many drawings in and around Walberswick in the 1980s. I am the proud owner of a painting of a medieval Suffolk moated farmhouse by John Western, a work that typifies his skill in the deft use of watercolour, thus capturing not only the building's unique characteristics but also the beautiful surroundings. He also provided the excellent design for the cover as well as other drawings for *Suffolk Houses...A Study of Domestic Architecture*, a substantial and very popular book written by Eric Sandon, FRIBA and Fellow of the Royal Society of Arts. Eric Sandon was a professional architect who worked for forty years in Suffolk and developed a deep love of the county and its many period houses. Many of those featured are listed as being of special architectural or historical interest in one of the statutory grades, if not for merely being situated within the countless conservation areas. This is what makes Suffolk such a special county, with its largely unspoiled coastline and graphically picturesque landscapes, not to forget the enormous skies that have attracted so many creative artists, writers and musicians for centuries.

Before I leave the subject of painters, I must include a contemporary artist who is very closely associated with the town of Aldeburgh. He is Derek Chambers (born 1937) who lives and works in the town whilst earning a growing reputation as a painter and printmaker. He has had solo exhibitions as well as being shown with others at the Royal Watercolour Society, the Royal Academy Summer Exhibition and the Mall Galleries, amongst other galleries. Chambers, like so many others before him, has succeeded in capturing the peculiar light and atmosphere of the seaside town. His winter 'townscapes and beachscapes' succeed in conveying, with uncanny accuracy, the feeling of the chill experienced on a cold winter's day.

The list of artists who have not only lived in but also visited the area in order to work at their craft is endless and further reading is recommended if there is a willingness to continue to explore a subject that I have found absolutely fascinating. In the meantime, I now look upon the contemporary artists, of whom I have written, along with many others, as part of the continuously active legacy of the Suffolk coast's cultural heritage.

We have come a long way and have met a great number of creative people of considerable talents in their own fields of activity. Coastal Suffolk has been threatened by the North Sea on almost a continuous basis for many centuries. For me, Geoffrey Munn's closing paragraphs in his book, *Southwold; An Earthly Paradise*, make rather depressing reading, following page upon page proclaiming the natural delights of the town and its surroundings that have served to attract any number of artists and writers over the years, let alone actors as well as other talented and creative people. Munn sees it as inevitable that the town will eventually succumb to the 'ruminating mouth of that insatiable and indefatigable beast: the sea', as have Dunwich and Easton. By way of example, he mentions that the village of Covehithe already nears the end of its existence. I find myself refusing to contemplate any prospect of the demise of Southwold. It is my view that the ever-popular and valuable real estate means far too much to many very important people who would simply exercise considerable influence to secure the necessary funding for the construction of effective sea defences if global warming threatens the area. However, I am more than willing to concede that my attitude owes more to romanticism than reality, but this does not necessarily mean that I am wrong. I cannot possibly accept that man's enthusiastic resourcefulness, allied with the country's top civil engineering skills, is incapable of prolonging the existence of 'the wold' described in the poem of summer visitor, William Morris. This work was entitled *The Earthly Paradise* (written around 1868) and provided the title for the book by Geoffrey Munn. Somehow, the necessary finance will be found from one source or another, even in the most straitened of economic conditions. A landscape that has inspired so many for over two hundred years and more simply cannot be allowed to be lost forever. After all, if Southwold succumbs it is inevitable that Walberswick will suffer the same fate. Who would be interested in painting or writing about a sea that had overwhelmed such treasures? I am unashamedly optimistic by nature and refuse to entertain such thoughts of destruction.

At this point, I thought that it would be fitting to include some notes on just a few of the other contemporary painters who are still working in and around coastal Suffolk. In doing so, I will touch upon how or why they were first drawn to the area and how much their art was involved with the move. What really struck me were the common factors, such as appreciation, interpretation and individuality, which have been so much in evidence throughout this research process, involving a spread of some two hundred years of creative art in its various forms.

Paula Nightingale first studied painting at Beckenham Art School, where Mary Potter had formerly attended, as far back as 1916, before progressing to the Slade School of Art. In the case of Paula Nightingale, she went on to the Royal College of Art before winning a scholarship to Munich where etching tended to dominate over painting. There followed various travels and, of course painting, in exotic parts of Europe in a London bus. On returning to the UK, moving house six times in nine months after having become a single mother responsible for four young children, she eventually wound up in a winter let in Aldeburgh. This was her first connection with coastal Suffolk and she hasn't travelled too far since those early days. They all lived in a house on the beach that overlooked the fish huts, one of which belonged to Billy Burrell, friend of Benjamin Britten. Before long, Nightingale had moved on to renting a small cottage, with only two bedrooms, right on the edge of the sea at Thorpeness, which she eventually purchased. This was where her youngest child, Rosie, was born. Living in such cramped conditions led to a larger property at Leiston, which earned income from being partly sub-let, and to a period of modest prosperity with her paintings finding a ready market, thanks to Thompson's Galleries in Aldeburgh and London. Since being in coastal Suffolk, she found herself constantly returning to the seashore, in her words, 'forever seeking the elusive light striking the groups of figures' she found there. Viewing the extensive gallery on her website reveals how such beach scenes figure so prominently in her work, although these are by no means the only subjects that she captures so vividly in oils. It is her versatility that has led to her work being in such demand for private collections both at home and internationally. She now lives in a boathouse on the Norfolk Broads, working as intensely as ever, having been drawn to the area's unique landscapes, ever-changing seasons, spirit and history which she describes as 'layers of time'. She is a regular exhibitor and has not neglected the sea, often driving down to the cliff at Pakefield, which serves as an excellent vantage point for viewing figures on the beach. It seems

End of Season by Paula Nightingale

certain that Paula Nightingale has found a successful niche that, just as importantly, satisfies her hunger for artistic fulfilment. The image of her work that I feature here depicts also her youngest daughter, Rosie.

Another painter who is still actively working in and around Walberswick, where she continues to live, is Eveline Hastings (born 1933). Her father had been a sculptor and he had recorded in his diary a note of an early 1930s visit to the village in which he mentioned 'the arty colours in which the houses were painted and a sighting of "clouds of nightjars" in the evenings'. It seems that nothing much has changed since then, according to *The Suffolk Tourist Guide*. There was another pre-war family connection in that her maternal grandfather decided to set up home there with his mistress. Unfortunately, and not many years after, he died there and is buried in the churchyard. As far as Eveline Hastings is concerned, she was driven over a wild-looking heath to Walberswick in the 1950s. She had been staying with an art school friend in Halesworth but this chance friendship resulted in regular visits to the village and soon she started painting there, eventually buying a cottage and living there permanently after giving up her home in London.

Eveline Hastings first studied at the Wimbledon School of Art before graduating in painting from the Slade School of Fine Art. Amongst her teachers were realist painter, Sir William Coldstream (1908-1987), Claude Rogers (1907-1979) and Lucian Freud. In an artistic career spanning over sixty years she continues to exhibit in mixed exhibitions around the area, notably, since 1998, at Chappel Galleries, Essex (she had a solo exhibition there in 2008). Her work has been shown at Royal Academy Summer Exhibitions, Young Contemporaries and Artists in Adult Education amongst other venues in London including solo and other events at the Piers Feetham Gallery in Fulham. I find her work beautifully executed, showing a thorough understanding by working directly from her subjects. In other words *en plein air*,

Thorpeness Beach by Eveline Hastings

experiencing fleeting changes of light and colour whilst benefiting from the feeling of the wind and sun as part of the visual experience. Until 1990, Eveline Hastings was employed by the Inner London Education Authority in teaching adults at a time when this form of education was at its most exciting and pleasingly widespread. She found great satisfaction in offering an art education that could lead to a qualification to people whose other commitments precluded them from full-time study. Her work is included in private collections in Europe as well as the USA.

Working from her studio in Blythburgh, Mary Gundry (born 1951) regards the local area as a constant source of inspiration, with watercolour regarded as her favourite medium although she also works in other media including oil and charcoal. She was born and brought up on the coast of North Norfolk and has always lived in East Anglia. Spicer has retained a deep-rooted love of the beach

Girls Running by Mary Gundry

and the traditions that go with it - buckets and spades, sandcastles, windbreaks, beach huts, picnics and paddling. Mary is recognised for her watercolours of children at play, although her work now has a much broader subject base with a bias towards figurative work and movement. The following image is a fine example of her work, which could be regarded as stylistically close to Philip Wilson Steer. The same could perhaps be said of Paula Nightingale's work.

Mary Gundry formerly ran a gallery in Southwold's High Street and, after a period when she concentrated more on her painting, she opened another one in Halesworth. In the past she has exhibited at the Mall Galleries in London as part of the Royal Institute of Painters in Watercolour and Society of Women Artists exhibitions. Mary Gundry, by working industriously over a period of twenty years whilst making a living from her art, is certainly part of coastal Suffolk's culture heritage. It is good that she enjoys a following from people who find pleasure in the results of her painting.

Another artist living in the Waveney Valley, bearing in mind that Hugo Grenville's home and studio can be found there, is Mary Spicer (born 1954). She has worked as a full-time artist for the last ten years and, although she may have come to painting late in life, she has a degree in Fine Art, a Post-Graduate Teaching Certificate and an M.A. (Art and Design in Education). She told me that she has grown to love the landscape that is immediately around her. She just loves and appreciates the vast open skies and sweeping stretches of farmland that she regards as a big challenge. In her chosen style, she deals with the revealed drama by recording light and shadow or by placing the horizon line close to the top or bottom of the picture. Mary Spicer concentrates on recording the grooves and furrows that are

Gorse Blaze in November by Mary Spicer

created by farm machinery as these criss-cross the picture space, fill with rain and hold pockets of light that are reflected back from the sky. More recently, she has started to tackle the huge skies and the cloudbanks that loom over the fields, casting huge shadows as they travel over brilliant yellow rape fields. She has come to regard Dunwich Heath as a source for much inspiration, particularly in the autumn, when decaying bracken, purple heather and brilliant gorse sing out against clear blue skies. Light and shadow create dramatic effects that must be quickly caught, both transparent and opaque materials are used on watercolour paper and as much as possible is done on site. A good example of her work in this respect is shown below and a fellow artist has described this as a good response to the landscape.

To take up, once more, the word 'response', Mary Spicer has written that her work is a personal response to the natural world; she is conscious of its fragility and, through her painting, she wants to remind people of the extraordinary sights and moments that might otherwise be missed daily. She feels, quite deeply, that we might be in danger of losing our connection to the land and in the process perhaps leaving behind something of ourselves. As long as she continues to paint with such profound thoughts within her, the results will certainly speak for themselves.

Mary Spicer's work is shown in a number of galleries throughout East Anglia, notably at the St. Giles' St. Gallery, Norwich and the John Russell Gallery in Ipswich, as well as at The Forum in Norwich.

Having written quite extensively about the more notable music and literary connections, as well as the many painters associated with coastal Suffolk, I shall now move on to a subject which involves the dramatic and musical performances on the county's various theatrical stages over the years. I shall include periods covering past centuries as well as more contemporary times.

PART FOUR

THEATRICAL PERFORMANCES AND OTHER MUSICAL CONNECTIONS

Everybody has his own theatre, in which he is manager, actor, prompter, playwright, sceneshifter, boxkeeper, doorkeeper, all in one, and audience into the bargain

Guesses at Truth, Series I

Julius Charles Hare (1795-1855) and Augustus William Hare (1792-1834)

The theatre is irresistible; organise the theatre!

Irish Essays. The French Play in London

Matthew Arnold (1822-1888)

Chapter One

The Theatre in all its regional as well as national aspects, some musical personalities and the 'Freud' connections in Suffolk

IN 2009-2010, ARTS Council England budgeted to spend more than £575 million of public money derived from the government and the National Lottery. This, they championed, is the bedrock of support for the arts in England. More cynically it is depicted by some as an example of modern-day lack of support for the Arts, in that the demand always seems to outstrip the supply as far as subsidies are concerned for the worlds of theatre, classical music, ballet and opera amongst other forms of the 'Arts'. However, art itself is defined by the Oxford English Dictionary as 'Human creative skill, its application or work exhibiting this'. Creative activity, imaginative designs, sounds, and ideas are also featured in the definition of the 'Arts' and a small proportion of government subsidy is reserved for what is described as 'Creativity, Culture and Education'.

By March 2011, the Coalition Government's cuts had come into effect and the overall budget was necessarily reduced to £450 million. After allocation to Strategic Funds of £202 million and £200 million to the Capital Programme, the remaining £48 million was allocated to the total Grant for the Arts. This must have resulted in many painful decisions, but with the scale of the country's dire economic situation it is difficult to see how these decisions could have been avoided. As far as coastal Suffolk is concerned, Aldeburgh Music have announced that they had been offered support of £1,308,200 for 2012-2013 which must represent recognition of the esteem in which this organisation is held, even in the demanding financial conditions that exist at the present time.

With this information in mind, it seems to be an appropriate juncture to introduce the subject of the world of theatre, particularly due to the fact that Jill Freud's Summer Theatre, totally unsubsidised by Arts East, has been such a mainstay of popular entertainment in Southwold, and later Aldeburgh, for well over a quarter of a century. Her regular seasonal productions are now regarded as something of an annual festival. In fact, when you come to think about it, most theatre-loving, middle aged people in the area have been accustomed to having the Summer Theatre available every year from July to September throughout their adult lives. This surely qualifies Jill Freud the accolade of having created something of a regional institution. Somehow, I am not sure she would look at it that way.

Nevertheless, it has to be said that there were theatrical connections with coastal Suffolk a very long time ago and certainly before Jill Freud and her thoroughly professional team arrived on the scene. Tony Falkingham, Co-Artistic Director and one of the company's theatre directors, told me that Southwold had a history of the theatre going back to the early part of the twentieth century. He has been with the company since 1991, some seven years after it secured its permanent home. He has since become something of an institution in Southwold. He is a non-driver and the sight of Tony pedalling majestically down the town's High Street is said to be regarded as a sure sign that summer had certainly arrived on this particular section of the Suffolk coast. But he is, of course, just a part of the entire team that makes up the theatre company, and the following photograph that was taken in 2006 at the time of the production of *Charley's Aunt*, directed by Tony Falkingham, will give an indication of just how many people are involved each summer season.

What better place to make a start on past theatrical connections is there other than the arrival of William Shakespeare in the area. Shakespeare's actual birth date is unknown but he is known to have been baptised in 1564; his death is recorded as being in the year 1616. The visit to coastal Suffolk took place in October 1608, and possibly again some two years later, as a member of a group of itinerant actors known as 'The King's Men', formerly 'The Lord Chamberlain's Men'. Shakespeare was said to be part owner of this theatrical company, possibly because the group company was intimately connected with London's Globe Theatre, in which Shakespeare acquired a partnership in or around 1585. I will agree that I am using some artistic license here in that all I am able to do is to confirm that it is a matter of record that this troupe performed at those dates at Dunwich. If just one such visit by the Bard ever took place, the event could not possibly be ignored. To be absolutely authentic on this subject there appears to be no genuine evidence of this genius of literature being in such close proximity to Aldeburgh and Southwold other than the fact that

A gathering of the Summer Theatre team. Jill Freud sits centre stage and Tony Falkingham is on the far left, nearest the door

a portion of Shakespeare's acting career was certainly as a member of The Kings Men. At least one historian appears convinced that Dunwich was so honoured, but bearing in mind that Shakespeare's retirement was due to take place in 1613 it would appear that any such visit was certainly late in his career. However, this is not inconceivable as he was said to have been active throughout his calling as a performer, writer and playwright.

Towards the end of the nineteenth century, if not before, the increasing popularity of Southwold as far as summer visitors were concerned resulted in the town drawing the attention of actors. Performances took place in the manner of full-blown productions under canvas as well as in sideshows on the beach. The advent of the railway line from Halesworth to Southwold via Blythburgh and Walberswick in 1879 certainly facilitated the increasing influx of visitors, especially during the summer months.

As far as Jill Freud's important, not to say highly-regarded, contribution to theatre in East Anglia is concerned it all began in 1980 when she formed Jill Freud and Company as a small group of actors and production staff touring popular classics in the eastern region. It was over mince pies and mulled wine after a Christmas show at St Edmund's Hall, Southwold in 1983 that the Hall Committee invited Jill to consider presenting their official Summer Season for the following year. This resulted in the provision of a very welcome base for her theatrical company; at a later date there was to be the addition of the 'branch office' at the Jubilee Hall in Aldeburgh. This building was, of course, formerly the home of the town's now long-established music Festival. Jill has said that her primary motivation for her theatre company was to provide work for actors. By now there must be quite a number of those who not only continue to appreciate the acting opportunities that have been afforded to them but also the highly enjoyable times they have spent in fashionable Southwold, as well as Aldeburgh, during the months of high summer.

So that is how the Summer Theatre in its present form started in Southwold and later at Aldeburgh. Strangely enough, my researches have led me to the discovery that during medieval times, East Anglia, had established a dominance over all other regional theatrical traditions in England. East Anglia was then loosely defined as the two main counties of Norfolk and Suffolk, together with parts of the two main adjoining counties. More specifically, these were Cambridgeshire, east of the river Ouse as well as Essex, north of the river Blackwater. Of the list of all towns and villages sponsoring or partaking in some kind of dramatic performances that flourished all over England, nearly forty per cent were located in the four counties just mentioned. Not only that, but more recent scholarship has doubled and even trebled the numbers and, therefore, increased the overall percentage already stated.

The original source for such information was E K Chambers (*The Mediaeval Stage*) at the beginning of the twentieth century but this venerable institution of reference has since stated how curious it has been to observe in what relatively insignificant villages it was found possible to organise plays from time to time. 'Cycle' plays as they became known, were the characteristic form of drama played in England in the Middle Ages, but in East Anglia it appears that 'non-cycle' productions were the time-honoured norm. Perhaps I should also explain that in medieval times there were three types of liturgical drama, namely Mystery, Miracle and Morality plays. Mystery plays presented an event or series of events taken from the Bible. Miracle plays tended to feature an event or legend from sources that are personified but intended to teach a religious or moral lesson. Morality Plays took the form of medieval verse drama that was designed to enlighten and discipline the audiences. These were, in part, a development of the Mystery Play but, to my mind, represented an early form of propaganda.

In these circumstances, East Anglia seemed to be out of step with the rest of the country but this may explain the greater recognition when measured in terms of packed audiences. However, perhaps this was also due to the more numerous venues that had sprung up for all these dramatic performances. Another explanation has been East Anglia's reputation as a rural area comprising any number of prosperous villages and small towns. Groups of these seemed to have clubbed together to put on performances in churchyards or purpose-built 'rounds' that were also a feature in Cornwall. 'Rounds' have been described as suggesting a circular acting area enclosed in a raised bank which is punctuated with scaffolds. Bearing in mind that London's Globe Theatre is a faithful reconstruction of the open-air playhouse, first built in 1599, it seems that the rounds became the established norms for these early theatrical productions.

It seems clear from what I have read of the theatrical tradition of East Anglia that the plays from this region, when considered as a body of dramatic texts, emerge as quite astonishing theatrical experiments suggesting a richness and diversity of theatrical practices unmatched in any other region of the country. Quite frankly, I find this astonishing but, on the other hand, why shouldn't this be the case? I invite you to consider the fact that in days gone by it was the geographical position, as well as the topography of the region, that set it apart from elsewhere in England. Perhaps this is why historians have felt that these features also influenced its theatrical fortunes. For instance, there is the proximity to northern Europe and the Netherlands, which brought not only the recurrent threat of invasion but also the possibility of trade and the collateral development of roads, ports and inland centres of commerce. It seems that the region supported a burgeoning population well before the invasion by the Normans and, difficult though it may be to accept nowadays, from the eleventh century forward it ranked as the most densely peopled area in Great Britain. During the next three hundred years or so, the region's communities continued to grow, not only in size, but also in number and prosperity as the cloth trade developed. The wool trade alone brought wealth to many East Anglian merchants and everyone will be aware of the so-called 'wool churches' that were built in the region from the profits of wool trading. One church that springs immediately to mind is that at Long Melford, Suffolk. This is widely regarded as one of the finest wool churches in England, built largely from 1467-1497 and widely out of scale for the needs of the parish it served. The same applied in villages elsewhere, such as Lavenham. But, once again, I am leaving the subject, although these albeit somewhat remote facts do serve to help illustrate the points about regional GDP rather well. It's not the Yorkshire expression 'Where there's muck there's brass' that then reigned supreme in East Anglia: it's more like 'Where there's wool there's cash, and where there's cash there's wealth, and where there's wealth there's theatre'.

It was not just the very nature of the region that set it apart from the rest of the country. East Anglia had its large urban centres, such as Norwich and to a lesser degree, Ipswich, Bury St Edmunds and Thetford. However, it was the enormous number of small communities that offered quite different kinds of theatrical opportunities from those that were readily available in those great population centres of England that played host to the tradition of the civic cycle play. In those far-off days, East Anglia possessed a uniquely dense and rural society, one with very definite literary pretensions, being home to an amazing array of writers during the late Middle Ages. These included two of the time's most celebrated female authors, namely Julian of Norwich (1343-1413) and Margery Kempe (1373-1439), both of whom were considered mystics in their day. Amongst the non-mystical, male authors were the prolific John Lydgate (c.1370-1449), John Skelton (c.1460-1529), John Bale (1495-1563) and Nicholas Udall (1505-1556). There were many others, all serving as evidence that East Anglia's cultural heritage stretches back even further than the period I am seeking to chronicle when dealing with, in the main, merely coastal Suffolk. However, I trust that I may be forgiven for regarding all this as representing solid background for the influences of literature as well as music, painting and theatre that were to emerge within my chosen area during the years that I have described previously.

As far as the entire East Anglian region is concerned, it seems that no other area in England during the 175 years between 1375 and 1550, with the possible exception of London, could boast so many prominent, identifiable, erudite and bookish figures and their literary accomplishments. Of the writers named above, both Lydgate and

Skelton were among the few of those times who were associated with playwriting, civic pageantry and mummery, although John Bale and Nicholas Udall were also associated with the English drama of their particular period. In addition, there is evidence of an astonishing number of anonymous dramatists who made their own contributions here and there throughout the region. All in all, I feel that what has been happening in Southwold and Aldeburgh as a result of Jill Freud's considerable efforts for something approaching thirty years can now be seen in a fresh context as far as the region's theatrical tradition is concerned.

Returning to the non-cycle plays of East Anglia in medieval times, an important issue that set them apart from the cycle plays staged elsewhere was the unlikely inclusion of a 'profit' element. In other parts of the country the plays were the means whereby the educated were displaying power and wealth to what were described as the unlettered ... in other words some form of pious education for the masses. In the more prosperous East Anglia, the profits from the established style of plays often served to finance important parts of capital building campaigns. The proceeds went towards the building of entire churches, replacing roofs and adding additional features to religious buildings. All of these profit-making activities helped to build communities as well as instil a feeling of financial wellbeing, no doubt serving also to account for the huge popularity of the productions throughout the region. One of the unquestionable attractions for theatregoers was the tradition that the plays tended to be accompanied by a day's eating and drinking, as well as affording an opportunity to participate in various games.

All of this went on for at least three or four generations during the late fifteenth and sixteenth centuries and almost invariably involved cooperative ventures with other communities. Sponsorship was inclined to be undertaken by perhaps just one of the nearby larger towns or villages. By no means were all of the productions on such a large scale and there developed, at this time, a second pattern of single performances, locally sponsored and more locally attended. There was also the much sharing of skills and resources between the communities in ways apparently unknown elsewhere in the country. Play books were copied for performances in other towns and it seems clear that such important matters as Performing

Rights were not of any real concern in those days. In modern times the laws of copyright reign supreme and have to receive the closest attention from producers and directors before staging any theatrical production that is not out of copyright. In the mid-fifteenth and sixteenth centuries, several permanent performance sites existed and I have seen references to such places in Great Yarmouth, Norfolk and the village of Walsham-le-Willows, near the historic town of Bury St Edmunds, Suffolk.

Having referred to early theatre in the region of East Anglia in medieval times, this may now be an appropriate point to refer to history of regional theatre in the whole of Britain during the twentieth century to the present day. This may also assist us in, once again, placing the theatrical activity seen in coastal Suffolk in a more clearly defined context. Dominating all have been two main trends; the decline of the commercial touring circuit from its peak in the Edwardian period and the subsequent growth of the repertory movement from campaigns and experiments at the turn of the nineteenth and twentieth centuries to its current status as a provider of theatre in the regions. The repertory movement itself was inaugurated in Manchester by Miss Annie Horniman (1860-1937), first at the Midland Theatre in 1907 and a year later at the Manchester Gaiety, the first full-scale modern repertory theatre. Unfortunately, this enterprise collapsed after the First World War and in 1921 the latter theatre was sold to a cinema company. Previous to her activities in Manchester, Annie Horniman had, as a result of her friendship with Irish poet and dramatist, W B Yeats (1865-1939), agreed to fund the opening of the Abbey Theatre in Dublin in 1904 as a home for the Irish National Theatre. Horniman had worked as an unpaid secretary, being able to do so as she was an independently wealthy woman. The good news is that as a result of Horniman's initiative, England now has an impressive scattering of such theatres, especially in cities and large towns. One or two that come immediately to mind are the Bristol Old Vic and the Belgrade Theatre in Coventry (purpose-built in 1958) but there were certainly others, particularly in the cities of Birmingham and Liverpool, which represented twin beacons of the repertory movement. Other locations more than worthy of mention are Sheffield and Nottingham. Recent years have seen interesting and lively variations of the pattern, such as the partial revival of the touring circuit with the help of public subsidy from the Arts Council.

There has also been the emergence of small-scale community theatre touring to non-theatre venues.

The famous names of stage and screen that first started out in repertory are literally countless but of some interest, particularly to those born between the wars, will be the future stars that made it big from Miss Horniman's Company in Manchester. These were Robert Donat (1905-1958), Rex Harrison (1908-1990), Michael Redgrave (1908-1985) and Cecil Parker (1897-1971). None of these stalwarts of cinema and theatre, or indeed their work, require further introduction from me.

The touring theatre in itself can be regarded as covering a broad spectrum, with the larger and more strategically placed houses being in a position to attract the finest companies with the less important venues catering for the various second-, third- and even fourth-ranked companies. Nowadays, many productions that subsequently end up in a West End theatre have been tried out in the provinces and as far as East Anglia is concerned these ' previews' can be seen from time to time in both Cambridge and Norwich. On the other hand, West End productions continue to tour the country on a regular basis, after their usually successful London runs have come to an end. One can only marvel at how it is possible to transport complete productions with elaborate sets with such relative ease. Such a practice has provided severe competition to far less well-endowed theatrical companies throughout the nation. I feel that this is to be regretted, although it must be borne in mind that this does provide provincial audience with an opportunity to see the stars in action at their local venues.

The viability of, not to mention the element of trust shown in, the touring system is best demonstrated by the boom in building new theatres or renovating old theatres from the mid-1890s to the outbreak of the First World War. This construction activity took place in Britain's larger cities as well as seaside locations such as Blackpool and Brighton. However, the arrival of talking pictures in the nation's picture-houses provided strong competition, so it was this revolutionary element in popular entertainment that was to signal the end to a rich era in theatre construction. The result was a huge depletion in the number of touring companies but, thankfully, not their total elimination. So it seems that, over the years, it has been inevitable that there should be odd pockets of activity in theatre production of one sort or another. There have certainly been new theatres and this brings to mind the Yvonne Arnaud Theatre in Guildford that opened its doors in 1965. It must not be overlooked that the advent of post-war television in the 1950s, followed by its rapid growth when the commercial TV companies were formed, also provided stiff competition to 'live' theatre. The twentieth century brought massive changes in popular entertainment, but throughout all attendant vicissitudes, including local single-screen cinemas converted to bingo halls, the form of enjoyment provided by the theatre industry has remained popular in its own right. This is probably due to the fact that there is a significant body of people in this country who prefer 'live' entertainment compared with that usually on offer via the vast array of screens of varying sizes in the nation's homes and ubiquitous multiplex cinemas.

In reciting this brief background to the theatre business, I have ignored the people involved. Theatres require owners, managers, stage managers, production staff, artistic and technical direction, set and costume designers, set builders, box office and front-of-house staff ... the list goes on and on but it is the actors that have that essential, direct contact with the public. The actors have a variety of outlets for their talent nowadays but, from the little I know about the profession, there always seem to be very large numbers 'resting', indicating that there is just not enough work available for everyone to be employed on a viably regular basis. There have always been the big names in cinema, television and theatre but for every major star there must be literally thousands of others in the profession, most of them waiting for the big break. That is why regional theatre in its various forms is important and it needs to be cherished if it is to survive during the twenty-first century. Jill Freud certainly recognised this when establishing her popular Summer Theatre company in Southwold.

I have dealt with the theatre in its various aspects and I will now refer to some musical connections with both Southwold and Aldeburgh, albeit of a different form to what we have come to expect from the Britten-Pears dominance of this subject in their particular bailiwick.

It must surely be agreed that the seaside town of Aldeburgh has placed host to some remarkably creative artistic talent in one form or another over the years. History may well record that it was during the twentieth century that its reputation as a cultural centre reached its zenith, thanks mainly to Benjamin Britten and his multifarious friends, not all of whom were exclusively associated with the world of music. There is, however, a current resident of Aldeburgh whose fame has been achieved in a genre that most will consider to be a million miles away from the work of the town's most well-known musical character, indeed the very person whose name is synonymous with Aldeburgh. Just because the poet-lyricist I have in mind was born in 1943 and is known for his contribution to progressive rock music does not automatically exclude him from some of the distinguished company that has been included in this chapter. Having said this, I am prepared to accept that by naming him as none other than Peter Sinfield I am by no means certain that everyone is going to claim that they have heard of him. On the other hand, many others would make claim to recognising at least some of the people with whom he has been associated over the years. But before I go too far down that route, it is necessary for me to name the legendary band, 'King Crimson' which, even to this day, enjoys a large cult following. King Crimson was formed by Robert Fripp, guitarist and keyboard player, the husband of singer, songwriter and actress, Toyah Wilcox. His co-founders were drummer, Michael Giles (born 1942), Peter Sinfield, multi-instrumentalist, who came up with the band's name, Ian McDonald (born 1946) and Gregg Lake (born 1947). Lake was later to achieve further fame with Emerson, Lake and Palmer, an extremely popular band in the seventies that sold over 40 million albums. Being regarded as an indifferent vocalist and with a guitar skill significantly inferior to that of Robert Fripp, Sinfield's principal role in the band was that of lyric writer. However, he was also in charge of the light show at their concerts, as well as offering advice on artwork, album design and other details relating to the band's releases.

Describing him as merely a lyricist does not really do justice to the fact that Peter Sinfield wrote all of the words for the legendary debut album, *In the Court of the Crimson King* (1969) which included *21st Century Schizoid Man*, said to be ex-Prime Minister, Tony Blair's favourite song. The album, which has an extraordinary cover, as shown below, has been described as absolutely fantastic, being still in the top 100 of the most extraordinary albums ever made and notable for an incredible standard of musicianship as well as marvellous harmonic quality. Over the years, King Crimson has disbanded, only to re-form on several occasions, often with changes in personnel. The band continues to remain active with a reputation for continued progressive development. Sinfield made his exit as long ago as 1971, following a break-up of the partnership with Robert Fripp.

Album cover of The Court of the Crimson King © Barry Godber (1946-1970)

Musically, Peter Sinfield has been largely influenced by Bob Dylan (born 1941) and Donovan (born 1946). Hearing Donovan's opening line of *Colours*: 'Yellow is the colour of my true love's hair' was, as Sinfield has stated, the defining moment when he decided he had the desire and ability to start writing songs. At the time of his association with the King Crimson band, his lyrics were described as psychedelic. In this context, Sinfield is best known for a distinctive approach to the sounds of words, filled with surreal (and sometimes fiercely sexual) imagery, and a special facility with water-images and ideas involving inspiration drawn from the sea. This is one single factor that can be viewed as being in common with certain parts of Benjamin Britten's repertoire.

Later in his career Peter Sinfield adapted his writing for pop music, and co-wrote a succession of hits that were to be sung by artists such as Celine Dion (born 1968), winner of the 1988 Eurovision Song Contest, Cher (born 1946) and Cliff Richard (born 1940), who missed being the Eurovision winner in 1968 with *Congratulations* by the margin of just one vote. He is also associated with Leo Sayer (born 1948) and the singing group Bucks Fizz, another Eurovision Song

Contest Winner in 1981. I am not really sure what conclusion I should be drawing from these Euro-facts but it seems that Peter Sinfield was not involved in either of the named successes. I am inclined to think that this particular factor is in his favour.

The other notable musical character I want to mention, this time in connection with Southwold, is the legendary bandleader, Jack Parnell who died in August 2010 at the age of eighty-seven. I first came across this remarkable musician when he was drummer with the Ted Heath Orchestra in the early 1950s when this stalwart of the 'big band' genre performed at Bristol's Colston Hall. In 1955, Parnell formed his own sixteen-piece band and was voted the country's best drummer in the *Melody Maker* poll for seven years in succession. The fact that there was a lot of good competition around in those days, including Ronnie Verrell (1926-2002), another of my early heroes, who succeeded Parnell with Ted Heath (1902-1969), and Eric Delaney (born 1924), also a well-known band leader, serves as a testament to his wonderful talent in the field of popular twentieth – century percussion. Parnell went on to feature with his band on various light entertainment shows on television such as *Sunday Night at the London Palladium*, produced by his uncle, the famous musical impresario, Val Parnell (1892-1972), as well as *The Muppet Show*. Jack was also appointed Musical Director for ATV from 1956-1981. It was because of his friendship with the late Derek Scott, who was a musical associate with that company, that he chose to spend his later years, from 1982, in Southwold. Scott had a holiday home in the town and this later became his home in retirement with his wife, Sidi, who will be mentioned later because of her choreographic and dancing connections with Jill Freud's Summer Theatre. Jack Parnell had always said that the 'heart of the band' was the drummer and it is sad to think that this particular heart will no longer be beating out the rhythm. In my own case, he leaves behind many happy memories of Sunday evenings at the Colston Hall, Bristol when I was a teenager who adored the music performed by the 'big bands'.

Whist on this particular subject, the 'Big Band Sound' could once be heard on a regular basis in coastal Suffolk. The location was none other than Pontin's Holiday Centre at Pakefield. When the man in charge at that centre was David Gwyn, he became something of a musical impresario who also revelled in the honorary title of 'Mr Big

Band of Europe'. I must confess as to not being altogether familiar with his credentials in that respect but he certainly attracted the crowds to his musical promotions, such as various forms of jazz, 'Sounds of the Sixties' as well as big band concerts at the holiday centre he managed for quite a few years. Enthusiasts of the latter genre would travel from all over the country and spend weekends listening to performances by orchestras led by Ray McVay, Eric Delaney, Syd Lawrence and Herb Miller who followed in the tradition of his brother, the late lamented and revered throughout the globe, Glenn Miller (1904-1944).

Having dwelt on some of the popular music of the twentieth century it is difficult to leave Southwold without referring also to just two more people who have a home there, namely actor, director and writer, Leigh Lawson (born 1945) and his wife, born Lesley Hornby in 1949, but far better known as 'Twiggy', the famous model, actress and singer. One of her most famous roles was as Polly Browne in Ken Russell's 1971 film of *The Boy Friend*', Sandy Wilson's, romantic musical comedy which first appeared on the West End Stage in 1954 and ran for over two thousand performances. Twiggy did, of course, have an extensive career on stage and screen and her performance in *The Boy Friend* won her two Golden Globe Awards as 'New Star of the Year' and 'Best Actress'. She made her Broadway debut in the musical, *My One and Only*, starring and co-staged by American all-round actor, singer, choreographer, director, Tommy Tune (born 1939), for which she earned a Tony nomination. She appears far more on our television screens nowadays in the Marks and Spencer fashion advertisements, a campaign that has run since 2004. Twiggy claims that she was 'discovered' for this assuredly lucrative assignment whilst eating lunch in a Southwold pub after she and her husband had been walking on the town's gusty beach.

Incidentally, Leigh Lawson trained at RADA and has enjoyed a long career, including appearances on the West End stage and more widely on TV and in films. In 1999, he co-wrote and directed the musical *If Love Were All*, which tells of the friendship between West End actress and musical comedy performer, Gertrude Lawrence (1898-1952) and Noël Coward. He has also directed in the West End and on Broadway.

Another modern musician who lives in a village within the coastal strip of Suffolk, around the Middleton-Westleton area, is none other than Neil Innes (born 1944), once a member of the 1960s Bonzo Dog Doo-Dah Band, a musical combination that combined elements of music hall, traditional jazz, psychedelic rock and avant-garde art. Innes was also better known for his collaborative work with the Monty Python team which did, of course, include Michael Palin (born 1943), another resident of coastal Suffolk. Innes had previously studied at the Norwich School of Art before moving on to Goldsmiths' College where he met his future wife, Yvonne Catherine Hilton who was studying drama. At Goldsmiths', Neil Innes was awarded a degree in Fine Art and rather surprisingly went on to what can certainly be described as a very successful music career, writing most of the band's songs, including *I'm the Urban Spaceman*, their sole hit (produced by Paul McCartney and Gus Dudgeon under a pseudonym, Apollo C Vermouth). This work won the prestigious Ivor Novello Award for Best Novelty Song in 1968. Another of his musical successes was the song, *Death Cab for Cutie*, which featured in The Beatles' film, *Magical Mystery Tour*.

It was in the mid-1970s that Neil Innes became so closely associated with the TV series *Monty Python's Flying Circus* where he could be found performing as well as writing songs and sketches. Other musical and writing successes followed, including the composition of songs for the film, *Monty Python and the Holy Grail*, in which he appeared as a head-bashing monk. Later he had a small role in Terry Gilliam's 1977 fantasy and black comedy film, *Jabberwocky*, which starred Michael Palin. The name was taken from a nonsense poem of the same name by Lewis Carroll (1932-1898). As a result of what happened throughout this stage of his career, Innes was often referred to as 'the Seventh Python'. He likes to describe himself as a musical comedy satirist, perhaps one of Britain's greatest over the past half-century, and who could argue with that? He even went on to become closely involved with, and star in, the 2008 musical documentary film, *The Seventh Python*, which featured Michael Palin and other *Python* team members, John Cleese, Eric Idle and Terry Jones. No doubt this movie seemed like a good idea at that time and although it could not be described as a particularly outstanding success in this country it did receive an award at the 2009 Las Vegas Film Festival and was the opening selection for the Pacific Palisades Film Festival in the same year. I am wondering if this production was helped by the tag line, which purported to promote the accidental career of 'the most famous rock star you have never heard of'. I watched the trailer on *YouTube* ... very 'pythonesque'.

I think most would agree that an extremely varied group of very special individuals are associated with coastal Suffolk and Neil Innes is a perhaps a prime example

I find it impossible to conclude this chapter without referring to the various generations of the Freud family and their connections with the Southwold-Walberswick area. Perhaps now would be a good time to tell you a little of the family history, although you will have read elsewhere of the literary accomplishments of Esther Freud.

It all started in 1934 when Lucie and Ernst Freud, an architect and the youngest son of Sigmund Freud, founder of psychoanalysis, bought a holiday home in Walberswick. They were parents to three children that included Lucian and Clement. The family had arrived in England in 1933 as refugees from the Nazis and, as Sir Clement so typically described it in his autobiography, *Freud Ego*, 'before this habit had caught on'. They took lodgings in Clarges Street in London's Mayfair, not far from the Ritz Hotel, before moving to St John's Wood. It is evident that they soon became aware of the highly fashionable addresses to be found in London. Perhaps it was the architecture that attracted the head of that part of the Freud family that arrived in England when the political situation in Germany cannot have generated a comfortable environment for this particular Jewish family of five.

Even in this, the second decade of the twenty-first century, the Freud family have retained their close association with the area, with several generations continuing to enjoy all that coastal Suffolk continues to offer. Their influence on the culture of not only the locality but also nationally, as well as internationally, continues to thrive. I am thinking here of not just the theatre and literature but, by virtue of marriage, film production and direction, screenwriting, TV production and broadcasting.

Although the artist, Lucian Freud grew up knowing Walberswick and Southwold it cannot be said that the focus of his artistic creativity and inspiration had been, in any way, influenced by these very early East Coast experiences. According to his daughter, Esther, 'My father is just about the only member of my family who doesn't love Walberswick. He said he would never paint there because he would be put off by all the amateur lady artists wearing amber necklaces'. To say the least, this is nothing less than an enormous insult if it is to be taken seriously, but I am inclined to feel that his tongue must have been firmly in his cheek at the time this comment was made. I feel certain that such a throwaway remark was not intended to be directed at the rich cultural heritage of this remarkable village. However, it was probably at the family home in Walberswick that Lucian Freud started to develop his genius for portraiture and this is probably where he made a drawing of his mother, one of the earliest of his series of her portrait over the years. We have already learned that he went on to attend the East Anglian School of Painting. This was in 1939 and he was aged just sixteen. I would have thought that Lucian Freud's parents had certainly supported their son with this move, once that he had made his wishes known. So, if nothing else, Ernst Freud's choice of Walberswick as the family home did lead to some early tuition at a place where other notable artists had also studied and were continuing to study alongside him.

This school of art was first established in 1937 at Dedham, then later relocated to Benton End, near Hadleigh, by the previously mentioned Cedric Morris and Arthur Lett-Haines, who favoured the 'free rein' approach that was then current in French academies. The latter was fond of describing himself as an English surrealist. Both men were distinguished painters who had spent the 1920s in Paris where they were to rub shoulders with the likes of Juan Gris (1887-1927), Spanish painter and sculptor noted for his association with the emergence of Cubism, as well as Marcel Duchamp (1887-1968), a French American artist whose work was connected with the Surrealist movement. As far as the history of their school of art is concerned, their original building in Dedham was destroyed by fire in July 1939 and it is said that local artist, Alfred Munnings had himself driven around the smoking ruins gloating at the destruction of what he saw as a dangerously radical tendency. Lucian Freud, rumoured to be the pupil who caused the fire, did not study there for too many years, as by 1941 he had become a merchant seaman, being invalided out of that service in 1942. It strikes me that this must have been somewhat of a hazardous occupation during the war, having regard to the constant attacks on shipping convoys by the German U-boats. After a brief return to the tutelage of Cedric Morris in Suffolk, by which time the school had moved to Hadleigh, Lucian Freud returned to London. From then on, his cultural connections with Suffolk sadly came to an end. I am a great admirer of a portrait of his daughter, Esther, oil on canvas 1982-1983, that was almost certainly executed in his studio and not at her current holiday home in Walberswick.

In commenting in her autobiography on Lucian Freud, none other than Kathleen Hale, another student of Morris and Lett-Haines, wrote:

> 'He was a strange lad, as sharp as a needle, and sophisticated beyond his years. Even at that age (16) his work was extraordinary – uncompromisingly weird, beautifully drawn, with an ascetic economy of free line, and showing perversely the opposite of reality. He has since become an almost microscopic Realist – a complete reversal of the usual development from studentship to maturity. At Benton End he was like a being from another world and his presence at the school had a galvanizing effect on other students.'

Bearing in mind that Esther Freud, her equally-gifted husband and their family retain their close connections with Walberswick, not to mention the artistic activities in the area, you can see that the Freud clan are more or less certain to continue the association through future generations now that they have established such a powerful base in coastal Suffolk.

Chapter Two

Historical associations and how seasonal theatre has developed in contemporary Southwold and Aldeburgh

GIVEN WHAT HAS now been learned from my necessarily brief account of the region's theatrical history, Jill Freud's Summer Theatre is perhaps best classed as 'seasonal repertory'. The theatre-going citizens of Southwold and Aldeburgh, not to mention residents of nearby towns, villages and settlements as well as, from what I have heard, even further afield, must feel rather thrilled that they have such ready access to enormously pleasing entertainment without the need to travel to the West End or elsewhere. Given its earlier status as a touring company, albeit on a limited scale and for only a couple of years or so, it is easy to understand why Jill Freud leapt at the chance to enjoy the comforts of a permanent home for her company's popular productions. There may well be similar ventures of this nature elsewhere in the United Kingdom, quite apart from East Anglia, but what is offered on this section of the Suffolk coast does strike me as being rather unique, given its genesis. This said, the Summer Theatre at the rather sedate seaside town of Frinton-on-Sea in Essex has an impressive history. It has been established for some seventy years and runs for more or less the same number of weeks as Jill's company, but in only one location, the McGrigor Hall, Frinton. This company also appears to be run on a repertory basis and in 1974 faced closure for economic reasons and would have been lost but for the timely intervention of the popular theatre and cinema actor, Jack Watling (1923-2001). He described this as his proudest achievement in that, with his own money, he mounted a whole season, which saved the enterprise from virtually certain collapse until new funding was forthcoming. On the other hand, it must not be forgotten that Southwold has supported seasonal theatre in the town, in one form or another, for over fifty years. This has afforded today's Summer Theatre the strong foundation that Jill Freud and her team have done so much to preserve, as well as build upon when giving effect to thoroughly professional improvements, both on and off the stage.

Having said this, the town of Southwold can lay claim to some history of early theatre, although not so far back as has been mentioned for elsewhere in the region. Paul Scriven, MBE, a vice-president of Southwold Museum and Historical Society, has done some valuable research on the subject and in an article for the society's newsletter he referred to the diaries of someone he describes as an avid chronicler of Southwold in the nineteenth century. It was Mr James Maggs, who recorded that on 27 September 1837, the Atkins Theatrical Co. arrived in the town, leaving on 6 October in the same year, presumably after a number of performances. Similarly, the Abbotts Theatre company left the town on 22 June 1849 but there is no record of their arrival or what had been played. Maggs also recorded a concert at the Town Hall on 13 October 1851 and there are further references to various forms of entertainment, including music and songs. I can't say that this provides massively firm evidence of a huge demand for organised entertainment in Southwold and my view appears to be supported by what Mr Scriven writes about the 'great Fisher family' who were responsible for building theatres elsewhere in Suffolk, namely in the towns of Lowestoft, and Beccles. There was also one at Bungay that was capable of holding an audience of not less than 300-400. However, there is no record of anything similar in Southwold, a town that was considered as not being capable of attracting the best patronage for the 'Fisher' type of theatrical ventures.

Nevertheless, there is some evidence, derived from theatrical programmes dating as far as back as 1808, which involved a tragedy, a farce and comic songs, all performed on the same evening in the seaside town. Other theatrical productions followed during the next two years at various venues. It was not until 1832 that records began to give details of similar programmes of entertainment. However, it was much nearer the end of the nineteenth century before members of the town's population were able to witness a reasonable offering of theatrical performances by amateur players. The town's New Pavilion offered an excellent venue for concert parties just before World War II and it is known that a famous female comedy act, Elsie (1893-1990) and Doris Waters (1904-1978) appeared there around that time. This pair was more popularly known by their stage names, 'Gert' and 'Daisy'. Their brother was the well-known actor, Jack Warner OBE (1895-1981), famous as TV's PC *Dixon of Dock Green*. During the post-war years, there were many local entertainments in Southwold and from the 1950s to the 1960s and beyond a number of repertory groups were regularly performing seasons of plays in the town. Paul Scriven has made the point that the Southwold's records are by no means complete as far as the cultural life of the town is concerned. However, any reservations that may have been held have surely been laid to rest by the huge success of Jill Freud's now well-established Summer Theatre. Nevertheless, it does seem to me that neither Southwold nor Aldeburgh would be capable of supporting a viable theatre company for a significantly extended season, let alone on an all-the-year-round basis. What the company is doing now is probably just about right, given their available resources, supplemented by local sponsorship and voluntary support.

When the opportunity presented itself back in 1983, Jill wanted to be certain that two members of her original team, Mark Sterling, Production Manager and Michael Richmond, Director, would be happy to join this new venture. Once given that assurance, the company, now incorporated under a charitable trust, has since gone from strength to strength with the small team being enhanced by the arrival of Anthony Falkingham as a further director. The permanent team was complete and remained that way until the death of Michael Richmond. He was replaced by Peter Adshead who is perhaps best known for having established, in association with others, a small, traditional repertory company, Hollow Crown Productions, in the year 2005. Since then, he has gone on to earn a fine reputation in the world of theatrical production, as well as in training and encouraging new talent.

It is now taken as read that the director of a theatrical production is a vitally essential member of the team but, as with the theatre generally, there is a history to the art of direction, part of the multifaceted knack required for the process of creating what is universally accepted as pure 'theatre'. In much earlier times, the need to shape the theatrical event was thought best to come from within those involved with the activity but matters developed to the extent that a need was discerned for unification, direction and encouragement from without; in other words, there was a need for leadership. The authority to intervene was once the prerogative of the playwright or a lead actor (sometimes the same person) and this remained the norm until the late nineteenth century. Earlier, William Shakespeare's career as dramatist and poet included also the art of acting, more often than not with a company of fellow actors who were also responsible for the establishment of the original Globe Theatre in London. The Bard was not known in the role of director, as we now know that such a concept was not emerge for something approaching three hundred years or so. The modern version of directing a theatrical production grew from the work of the Duke of Saxe-Meiningen of Prussia (1826-1914) and his stage manager, a former actor, Ludwig Chronegk (1837-1890). Further work was nurtured by pioneers such as André Antoine (1858-1943), Constantin Stanislavsky (1863-1938) and Max Reinhardt, whose name featured in an earlier chapter. The latter gave up acting completely in 1903 to devote the whole of his energies to directing.

Let us take some of these individuals one at a time: Saxe-Meiningen, by making use of his knowledge of the history of art, allied with his personal drawing skills, designed highly detailed, historically accurate scenery, costumes, and properties for the theatre. In addition, he choreographed the large crowd scenes that were to stun audiences, not only in London but also across Europe. He and his Meiningen Ensemble toured Europe extensively, and had a profound effect on theatre production across the continent. For this work in early-twentieth-century theatre, he has become known as the first modern director and his credentials certainly appear to merit this accolade. Chronegk acted with the Meiningen company from 1866-1870 but from the time he was appointed stage-director he revolutionised German stage methods, not without criticism from within the business. In addition, Russian actor and theatre director Stanislavsky's innovative contribution to modern European and American realistic acting remained at the core of mainstream western performance training for much of the nineteenth century. André Antoine, French actor, theatre manager, film director, author, and critic is considered to be the inventor of modern *mise en scène*, an expression used to describe the design aspects of a production, in his native country. Max Reinhardt, by employing powerful staging techniques, and harmonising stage design, language, music and choreography, introduced new dimensions into German theatre.

It is clear that all of these talented and creative people must surely be regarded as trailblazers for the state-of-the-art theatrical practices that are so commonplace nowadays, all over the world, but principally in London's West End as well as on Broadway. It is not difficult to imagine just how impressed these early pioneers would be at what is being achieved by their modern counterparts, who sometimes have millions of pounds to spend on extravagant musical and other dramatic productions in London. But it must not be forgotten that the vital skill of interpretation lies at the heart of theatrical practice, not least in some of the classical dramas. Consequently, the presence of no less than four directors in Jill Freud's team of five ensures that the vital combination of skill and experience comes into play when the time arrives for the selection of the five productions that will be staged for the following season. The choices tend to be on the lines of, but not invariably, a thriller or two, something dramatic with perhaps an element of comedy, a traditional farce, not forgetting an outright comedy or possibly a musical. As usual, the focus will always be on ingredients designed to secure a series of box-office successes, with the minimum requirement of at least covering their overall costs. This is an essential prerequisite if the company is to survive without official subsidy, even throughout the course of the most adverse financial climate.

Let us now reflect on some other aspects of the Jill Freud's Summer Theatre's history. We are now aware of its origins, but it is not generally known just how basic the facilities have been over the years. Although there are now buildings in both Southwold (St Edmund's Hall) and Aldeburgh (Jubilee Hall) which become converted to theatres for a period of ten weeks in each summer season, it was only the introduction of raked seating that has ensured that vital ingredient for a happy audience; a good view of what is happening on stage. Even then it was a matter of luck that Jill's husband, the late Sir Clement Freud (1924-2009) happened to spot a diary item in London's *Evening Standard* that the Ford Motor Company wished to dispose of a mobile theatre that contained raked seating. It was snapped up without delay, Sir Clement always having an eye for a good deal. The spirits of the team were transformed to optimistic radiance. Supporters of seasonal theatre in Southwold would soon be aware of the distinct visual improvement and it was then up to the team to think in terms of a quantum leap, not only in facilities but also of hiring staff and actors to ensure that the company could plan an ambitious series of productions for the following season. Although Sir Clement (known as 'Clay' to his family and friends) held no official position with the Summer Theatre Company, he was always very active behind the scenes and his generosity in so many ways over the years was an important contributory factor to the company's success. His traditional speech on each season's opening night was always an outstanding success, not least because of his outrageous jokes. He remains sadly missed.

Comparisons are said to be odious, or even odorous if we are to be guided by the comic character, Dogberry, in Shakespeare's *Much Ado About Nothing*. It appears that the Bard intended this phrase to be ironical in that the original expression featuring the word 'odious' dates back to circa 1440 but I am again guilty of digression. All that I really set out to do is

A scene from a 1994 production of 'How the Other Half Loves' featuring Elizabeth Downes and Cheryl Kennedy and directed by Kit Thacker

to contrast the now well established, Jill Freud's Summer Theatre with the Aldeburgh Festival. The administration of the former has the outward appearance of running like a well-oiled machine but is that really the case? I doubt it, as I feel sure that there are the odd hiccups just as they happen in other organisations. However, the fact remains that the theatre company operates without any public subsidy and the professional actors, directors, designers and everyone else concerned with staging the shows do so without any expectations of earning large sums of money. Indeed, and for some years, the height of the company's ambitions has been to at least break even, a happy state that relies heavily on having to achieve, on average, something approaching a sell-out for each performance. Fortunately, they seem to often succeed in that particular aspiration and long may their extensive string of successes continue.

My original plan was to write a book about Jill Freud, until she succeeded in persuading me otherwise. Nevertheless, I have been unable to resist the urge to enlighten you on at least a few interesting fragments of information that have, to my mind, shaped the course of the way she has chosen to live her very eventful, not to say, highly active life. Over the years, the enthusiastic energy she has displayed in everything she set out to do must have acted as an inspiration, not only to her family but also to all of her friends and colleagues.

Jill was born in 1927 and in 1942, as June Flewett, the name with which she was baptised, she was evacuated to the Oxford home of writer, academic, essayist and literary critic C S Lewis (1898-1963). It has to be said that this was a wartime event that clearly changed her life. The young June, she changed her name for professional reasons at a later date, made a huge impression on the novelist and he wrote that when June goes 'the only bright spot in our prospect' goes with her. Jill Freud, as I shall now refer to her, won a place to the Royal Academy of Dramatic Art in 1945 and it was only with the financial support of Lewis that she was able to do so. Soon after she graduated, Jill embarked upon a successful career in the West End under the stage name, Jill Raymond, co-starring with, among others, Michael Redgrave (1908-1985) as well as appearing in films and on television both before and just after she met and married Clement Freud in 1950. Jill recalls that a newspaper headline at that time read 'West End star marries cook'. This reminds me of what the late Paul Eddington wrote in his biography, tragically entitled *So Far, So Good*. This book was published just two weeks before he died of skin cancer in 1995. Along with many other, celebrities Eddington attended Princess Diana's first public engagement, switching on the West End's Christmas lights. Paul found himself standing next to Clement Freud and remarked, 'Aren't we lucky; we could have been saddled with some night club floozie.' Eddington then added, 'Sorry! Of course, you're a night club floozie yourself, aren't you!' He was not too surprised when he got what he deserved, a typical frosty look. Paul had to confess that his sense of decorum did sometimes desert him. It seems that he had suddenly recalled Sir Clement's spell as the owner of a popular club, situated over the Royal Court Theatre in Sloane Square in the early 1950s. However, more probably, it might have been Clement Freud's seat on the board of the Playboy Club in Park Lane. During the last war, he was a trainee chef at London's Dorchester Hotel. The kitchen there, at that time, Freud described as 'a hell-hole of a huge dank building regardless of inconvenience to staff'. Describing various characters and goings-on during those days, Freud earned praise for painting in his own words, 'a rich, vivid uproarious picture'. It seems that I have strayed from the subject once again, but I cannot resist the odd anecdote.

It was not until the 1970s that 'Jill Raymond' resumed her acting career, mainly on television, before getting involved with her touring theatre company under her married name. This led eventually to her Summer Theatre at Southwold and later at Aldeburgh. Nowadays, when she appears in their productions, and she continues to do so on a regular basis, she appears under the name Jill Freud. I would venture the opinion that Jill is not without a lot of commonsense ability in the art of marketing, bearing in mind her husband's spell as a popular Liberal Member of Parliament for the constituency of Ely.

I have skated far too quickly over the years that she spent with C S Lewis. Due to the importance of these in her life, I feel that I should write just a little more on the subject due to the nature of the people she met when living in that household. It was also the fact that she tended to be treated as a young adult, rather than just a child, that must have accelerated her maturity, not to mention her knowledge of literary matters. In this respect, Jill recalls being taken to tea at the home of professor J R R Tolkien (1892-1973), writer, poet and philologist. C S Lewis was like an adoptive parent to Jill and he had a significant influence on her development, as did, no doubt, his other literary friends together with the dons who formed an informal group called 'The Inklings'. Lewis encouraged her to read and made available any book she wanted, even suggesting that she could purchase books at Blackwell's and have them charged to his account. In the event, she remained far too shy and inhibited to take advantage of such generosity. She has described having the benefit of the company of two erudite men at supper each evening, listening attentively to the discussions between them. The other man was 'Warnie', Lewis's alcoholic brother. Another member of the household was Janie Moore, Lewis's adoptive mother, the brothers' real mother having died of cancer when they were just boys. There was more to the relationship between C S Lewis and 'Mrs Moore' than appeared on the surface. Janie Moore was twenty-six years the author's senior, but Jill was not aware of that at the time. When Mrs Moore was unable to look

A scene from the 2006 production of 'Death in Act Two' with Jill Freud and Jeffrey Perry directed by Richard Frost

after the household affairs properly, due to an indisposition, Jill returned to Oxford after her school examinations and remained there on and off for two years as a paid help, thus delaying her entrance to RADA.

Ever since her theatre company became such a central part of her life in the early 1980s, Jill has continued to act in various productions and many of her many supporters will be very happy for this activity not to become a part of the history and no longer of the present as each season comes along.

Chapter Three

More on the history of Southwold and Aldeburgh's Summer Theatre and the birth of The Jill Freud Company

SO JILL FREUD'S permanent team, although never likely to be endowed with limitless funds, has succeeded in mounting highly-entertaining theatrical productions for the benefit of coastal Suffolk's residents and visitors alike. The Summer Theatre's audience support and sustained popularity stand as testament to the entire company's hard work that commences within weeks after the closing curtain falls on the year's final performance. Without such tremendous dedication, there would be no prospect of such uninterrupted success and, somehow, one feels that a tradition has been established to such great effect that it certainly seems highly unlikely if it will ever falter. Even today's stalwarts cannot go on forever but the excellent quality of the latest recruit represented an encouraging indication that, as with the Aldeburgh Festival, the show will go on ... and on ... and on. We all very much hope and trust that this will prove to be the case. Such a solid foundation is unlikely to be lacking in future support, but it was inevitable that the time would come when the 'guiding light' would need to be replaced.

A November 2011 announcement revealed brief details of the future management structure of the production company. After twenty-eight years of sole responsibility, Jill Freud decided that the time had become appropriate for a new partnership to take on the task of ensuring the company's continued existence and also its future success. It must have reassured the loyal patrons that the existing management team, Anthony Falkingham, Mark Sterling and, more latterly, Peter Adshead, which had worked so closely with Jill Freud over a number of years, had incorporated itself as ASF Productions, trading as The Jill Freud Company. This new company has made it their business to undertake all future management and seasonal planning, thus ensuring not only the all-important continuity of purpose but also the maintenance of standards. Thus, the foreseeable future has been secured.

Unlike painting and literature, the arts of the individual, both the theatre and music require professional organisation to enable creative and performing talent to be made available to the supporting public. The Aldeburgh Festival is a fine example of how an original concept has become a permanent fixture, something that is likely to continue almost indefinitely as long as there is a market for what is on offer. It is now hoped that the same will apply to The Jill Freud Company. Jill continues as an active patron and remains on the board of the trust.

Jill Freud has always been deeply conscious of the fact that the season of summer theatre will probably need regular outside financial support, in one form or another, sooner or later, and, in this respect, she is very proud of the fact that two of their productions have already had a direct 'after-life'. In 2008, they took *The Lady Vanishes* to the Yvonne Arnaud Theatre in Guildford, and Mark Sterling's company took it out again in early 2010. In 2009, he transferred their production of *Crooked Wood* once again to the Yvonne Arnaud. Jill played a leading role in that one. The touring of productions that stem from the Suffolk coast is something that Jill, Peter Adshead and Mark Sterling remain particularly keen on promoting and then undertaking. Such ambitious plans will, hopefully, aid the financial position of the company, thus helping to preserve its future.

Another director who is closely associated with Jill Freud's theatre company is Richard Frost, who trained as an actor at the Central School for Speech and Drama, where he met Anthony Falkingham who was on the staff there, and also at the Webber Douglas Academy of Dramatic Art in London which is now closed. Richard had been invited to direct a production of *Corpse!* in Southwold in 1996 and although, at that time, he had never previously visited the town he has since enjoyed directing more than the odd few plays since then. These included *Hindle Wakes* in 1999, *Death in Act Two* in 2006, *Holiday Snap* in 2010, a play by Michael Pertwee (1916-1991) that also featured Jill Freud and *Abigail's Party* also in 2010, a play by Mike Leigh (born 1943). This work once starred Alison Steadman (born 1946) as the monstrous Beverly and was featured highly successfully on national television.

Frost told me that a fine example of the status earned and enjoyed by Jill Freud's Summer Theatre is how the word has spread within the theatre world regarding the high standard of the productions and acting. He mentioned Phil Clark, a freelance theatre director who has thirty-five years of creating innovative and exciting theatrical productions, some of which were notably at the Sherman Theatre in Cardiff. He had heard about Southwold Summer Theatre from some of the company's actors and asked Jill Freud if he could perhaps direct a play for her. His request was granted and in 2010 he directed *Dangerous Obsession* by N J Crisp (1923-2005), a prolific television writer, dramatist and novelist. In the sixties, after writing some single dramas, Crisp moved to writing serials and turned out many scripts for several BBC series including *Compact, R3, Dixon of Dock Green, Dr Finlay's Casebook, Colditz* and *Secret Army*. Phil Clark went on to direct for the theatre in New York. This was *Skellig*, a play that was originally presented at the Young Vic in 2003 as a stage revival of David Almond's Carnegie Award-winning novel of the same name, adapted by the author himself. This play opened in March 2011 at the New Victory Theatre, off-Broadway at West 42nd Street. From Southwold to Broadway strikes me as New York's gain and coastal Suffolk's loss, but I feel sure that he will be back.

I was interested in some background information on how the company worked and Richard Frost told me that rehearsals can take place at various venues in and around Southwold, over a period of three weeks. For instance, rehearsals could be held in the barn at a Walberswick property owned by members of the Freud family, within the Girl Guide's Hut in Cumberland Road or perhaps in rooms at St Felix School, Southwold. Members of the company really feel part of the local community during the summer months of theatrical activity. It's not always the same actors, but many do return time and time again alongside a handful of new faces each season. The same applies to directors, so the company retains a certain freshness, a factor which is thought to be very important. For his work in 2010, Frost was living in the town for a total of seven weeks. The fourth play for the season will already be in rehearsal during the first week's run of the first production. The last play of the season will start being rehearsed on the morning after the opening night of the fourth play. Theatrical activity in and around the town of Southwold is certainly quite hectic but it must be borne in mind that this is only after month upon month of planning, auditioning, designing and building sets, assembling the costumes and all of the complicated paraphernalia of mounting five productions over a nine week season. There will be only a few months inactivity until such time as the stalwarts start all over again. One can only marvel at their enormous energy as well as dedication to the cause of Summer Repertory Theatre in Southwold and Aldeburgh.

Being aware that, from time to time, even the best organised productions can suffer a lapse, especially with mislaid props or even their non-existence on stage for a crucial part of the play, I am assured that Jill Freud's company, after over almost thirty successive seasons are very methodical and orderly in their planning. Richard Frost felt that the technical team maintained an extraordinary level of efficiency. However, I am sure that at some time in the future there will be a staging of say *Dial M for Murder* when it is suddenly discovered that the telephone, absolutely crucial to the plot, is found to be missing from the set. Richard Frost recounted a story of when this once happened, during a performance by another repertory company: the situation was resolved by an actress who was running the company. She borrowed a cloth cap from a stagehand and a coat from someone else. She knocked upon the set's door and entered stage left announcing 'I'm from the GPO and have come to install your 'phone'. This quick thinking served to save the day on that particular occasion but these things do happen, although not, apparently, in Southwold. I am quite sure that, having written that piece, it will now be the kiss-of-death for such a fine reputation.

As far as each season's productions are concerned, the plays are chosen in January in each year, an exercise that is followed by Anthony Falkingham applying for and then obtaining the necessary rights for performance followed by the directors getting together for an initial meeting in February. Eventually the auditions for the actors take place in London, occasionally in the past at Jill Freud's spacious flat and others at the well-known audition venue, The Drill Hall, Chenies Street. After these have been completed, the various casts are chosen. Maurice Rubens, the set designer, of whom Jill Freud, in particular, has the highest opinion, starts building the models for the sets in March, after first researching the plays. He then starts building the sets in the Southwold workshop at the end of April or the beginning of May each year. Designing and building workable sets for such confined spaces for the performances at St Edmund's Hall, Southwold as well as the Jubilee Hall, Aldeburgh provides Maurice with considerable challenges. Southwold, in particular, is famous for its 'graveyard run'. For example, if it is necessary for an actor to exit the small 'stage left' to be followed by the next entrance at 'stage right' the only way this can be accomplished is for the actor to leave the building and run through the cemetery grounds to arrive at the door adjacent to the other side of the stage and to wait for the cue to make the necessary entrance. It is the fact that Maurice Rubens invariably succeeds in his task that justifies Jill Freud's description of this very talented stage designer as a 'real genius'. Perhaps Rubens' success comes from always having it in mind that he wants to assist those actors obsessed with the advice of Noël Coward on acting: 'learn the lines and don't bump into the furniture'. He has designed all of the Summer Theatre's productions since 1991, invariably on a tight budget and habitually accompanied by the ever-present spatial problems. In his writings on the occasion of the twentieth year of the production company's summer shows, he described how he had felt both elated and anxious when getting his annual telephone call from Jill Freud saying, 'Can we do it again?' We must all be grateful that he continues to respond, 'Yes, darling, I've got a pencil ready.' Perhaps, now that such important changes have taken place, he will have to rehearse the equivalent response that will need to be addressed to a member of the new team.

Costume design and wardrobe responsibilities are the under the control of Miri Birch, who also works in a similar capacity for the White Horse Theatre which is based in Germany. The lighting for each set is designed by James Laws, who has an impressive track record in doing the same for the London Mozart Players across the country. Sidi Scott choreographs appropriate productions, having enjoyed a career in the West End in such shows as *Carousel* and *Kiss me Kate*. Her late husband, Derek Scott (1921-2006) was musical director for the company, having, in his working career, seen service as musical associate on the internationally famous *Muppet Show*. In this capacity, he contributed musical ideas, commissioned musical arrangements and accompanied guest stars as well as writing the theme music heard in many *Muppet Show* sketches. He also provided all of the piano solos for *Rowlf* (a character in the *Muppets*). Other aspects of Derek's musical career as a professional were equally impressive in that he also wrote theme music for various ITV productions such as *General Hospital* and ATV's *Hancock*. It was after this very talented couple had retired to Southwold that a chance meeting with Jill Freud in the town's High Street resulted in their getting so heavily involved with her theatre company. Being prominent members of the team has brought sheer professionalism to so many performances over the years. Not least amongst their successes together was the production of *Cinders*, a 1920s theatrical masterpiece staged in 2000, a show that thoroughly deserved its rave reviews. Leading lights in West End musical comedy, Bobby Howes (1895-1972) and Binnie Hale (1899-1984) starred in the original production at London's Adelphi Theatre in 1929 but the Southwold staging by Anthony Falkingham was heaped with praise. The musical director who subsequently succeeded Derek Scott in that capacity is Jonathan Rutherford, who studied at the Yehudi Menuhin School and whose work in the theatre included the West End productions of *Annie* and *The Sound of Music* with Petula Clark. Having been in the audience at the company's 2010 production of the sophisticated musical, *Cowardy Custard*, directed by Anthony Falkingham, I can only marvel at Jonathan's rare talent for playing the musical accompaniment on the piano for something approaching three hours with just one interval. He gave everyone there at Southwold, including the players, enormous musical enjoyment during the course of a memorable evening's entertainment that featured popular elements of Noël Coward's repertoire, including songs as well as readings from his biographical writings. I was also impressed by Maurice Ruben's set. He must have performed miracles with the design and Sidi Scott's brilliant choreography prevented the performers from bumping into each other in such a very confined space for a music and dance performance.

The towns of Southwold and Aldeburgh, not to mention a considerable following from surrounding counties in East Anglia, continue to cherish the summer theatre and long may it continue. At the time of going to press, the 2012 Summer Season has started, so it remains very comfortably business as normal. Bearing in mind that it was Jill Freud who first suggested that I might consider writing a book based upon the cultural heritage of coastal Suffolk, this is perhaps a good note on which to end the main narrative.

EPILOGUE

IN FUTURE YEARS, it will be almost impossible for me to visit parts of coastal Suffolk without being aware of what I have written here. However, the story is of a continuous nature, bearing in mind that there remains the living legacy for all to see as well as enjoy. The Aldeburgh Festival has become a celebrated institution and Aldeburgh Music, coupled with the educational work that is done at Snape, has developed into something of an industry. The Arts Council of England has now nominated this establishment as a National Centre of Excellence. Their most recent and heavily-subsidised £16 million development of what is collectively known as the Hoffman Building, incorporating the 340-seat Britten Studio, orchestral rehearsal space and other facilities, has moved the organisation into a new era for what has been described as the 'creative campus'.

The year 2012 saw the formation of a new and unique international project, the Aldeburgh World Orchestra. No less than 124 of the most talented young musicians from across the globe will be led by acclaimed British conductor, Sir Mark Elder (born 1947), musical director of Manchester's Hallé orchestra, in performances of Britten, Mahler, Shostakovich and Stravinsky, as well as the world première of a new commission. This exciting new orchestra was in Suffolk in July 2012, as part of the London 2012 Festival, which was a culmination of the 2012 Cultural Olympiad. There were high profile performances at Snape Maltings, as well as major London and European venues, including the Amsterdam Concertgebouw. In the lead up to this exciting new orchestral venture, the Britten–Pears Orchestra extended its intake to draw top-calibre international young artists from every continent. As well as providing an exceptional artistic opportunity for the participants in 2012, the project also created a matchless legacy of international connections for the Britten-Pears Programme.

The Britten-Pears Foundation Library continues to act as the portal for their comprehensive range of research resources. I know from my own experience that their levels of service and cooperation are impeccable.

No doubt, as long as the creative mind of P D James continues to function on what seems to be an everlasting basis, Commander Adam

Dalgleish will carry on making his investigative forays into coastal Suffolk and beyond. The Summer Theatre at Southwold and Aldeburgh will also continue to delight. Just as I did, visitors and residents will stumble across artists working *en plein air*, as some things just do not change, especially the coastal landscape with its splendidly serene marshes on a quiet day. There is undoubtedly an almost mystical atmosphere around the areas I have described and I fail to see how that can lose its influence as long as the culture continues to live on and there remain enough people willing to carry forward the rich inheritance for the benefit of successive generations.

Now, more than ever, I am absolutely convinced that writers poets, painters and musicians as well as people involved with the theatre in all its aspects, stand apart from other individuals because all have lived for their art and a great number continue to do so. These are the people, both collectively as well as individually, that represent the cultural legacy of coastal Suffolk. Single-mindedness in the pursuit of one's art cannot possibly be considered as a vice, but there will always be personalities in a close relationship to the artist who might entertain an alternative opinion. For painters, writers and composers the creative process is likely to involve long periods of seclusion and this can be very hard on those close to them. Those of us who enjoy and are entertained by the fruits of the sacrifices that have been made can be only grateful for such a prolific supply of books, music, paintings, sculptures and entertainment. As long as our insatiable appetite for such pleasures remains, the output will surely continue. On the other hand, there will always be individual artists, writers and musicians who would be happy to produce the work in any event, leaving the commercial side to those who consider it to be an all-important and economically inevitable fact of life in the competitive world in which we all live nowadays.

For my part, I shall continue to browse the area's bookshops, visit art galleries and listen to music and be grateful that I now know so much more about what drives people to produce works of art. For that, I shall always be grateful.

The contents of this book have been written from the viewpoint of an average person having nothing more than an enthusiastic interest in the arts, but with no claims to be able to criticise from an informed, let alone a learned standpoint. I feel sure that this has been all too evident. On the other hand, since completion of the project I have become aware that my attitude to the arts has changed irrevocably and, hopefully, for the better. My appreciation has also been transformed and, in future, I will be doing more much thinking about what I am reading, watching, viewing as well as hearing. If the same applies to others, so much the better, but I will certainly settle for what has happened to me.

Inevitably, in researching much of what has been written in this volume I have come up with more questions than answers when considering the lives of various individuals. For instance, why were John and Myfanwy Piper so attracted to the music of Benjamin Britten? What drove John to immerse himself in so much intricate design work on the sets and costumes of various operas and why did Myfanwy feel irresistibly drawn to becoming a librettist? I cannot believe that it was purely for commercial reasons, however deep were the financial worries associated with the education of the couple's children. In more modern times, just how does Esther Freud manage to find time to write her well-received novels as well as deal with the day-to-day requirements of family matters? She runs two homes and, at the same time, she appears able to carry out a normal married life with a husband who always seems to be in demand with his prolific acting and directing activities.

Jill Freud is well into her eighties and will always be remembered for being so very closely associated with her highly successful Southwold Summer Theatre. The 2012 programme is as intriguing as ever and is certain to entertain the loyally enthusiastic audiences that turn up each year.

Coming across an artist from the industrial north of England working *en plein air* near Walberswick was a real bonus and served to provide me with convincing evidence that the attraction of the area remains as powerful as ever. Here was a man prepared to make the effort to follow in the footsteps of Charles Rennie Mackintosh and many others. I found it unnecessary to ask him what drew him there. His contentment at his work, oblivious to moving traffic and the odd inquisitive motorist, was an added inspiration to me; his subsequent ready cooperation encouraged me to persevere with the sometimes overwhelming task of telling this remarkable story. Additionally, I found considerable joy in featuring contemporary painters from the area, and found their enthusiasm equally infectious when having to deal with the more administratively boring aspects of bringing a project such as this to a close.

In the course of my research, as well as in the actual writing, I found myself speculating, indeed fantasizing, on how wonderful it would be to hire, say, the Jubilee Hall in Aldeburgh or the St Edmund's Hall in Southwold. I could then set about throwing a series of parties for all of the people who have made their individual contributions to the cultural heritage of this particular section of coastal Suffolk over the last two hundred years or so. Whether the invited guests would be able to hear anyone else speak at such fanciful gatherings would probably prove exceedingly difficult. I can only imagine what contemporary television and radio's arts programmes would make of it with their state-of-the-art cameras and sound equipment. As for the eager presenters, they would be in their element with such rich pickings being so freely available.

It seems that I was not the only one speculating on these lines as it came to my notice that, on a much smaller scale, Alan Bennett (born 1934) has written a play on an imagined meeting between W H Auden and Benjamin Britten that might have taken place in the year before Auden's death in 1973. In reality, the pair had not met since 1953 when Auden gave a lecture at the Aldeburgh Festival. Britten did, of course die in 1976 at the age of only sixty-three. You have now read about the background to this parting of the ways. The imagined discussion that formed the dialogue in Bennett's play was inevitably about creativity, passion and inspiration. I would have hoped that this would also have been the case for my own, make-believe social events. On the other hand, perhaps most of the passion would be of a dissimilar nature.

The first half of Bennett's dramatic piece is devoted to the poet being interviewed by his future biographer but it is the second half that really interested me. Britten, as we have already seen, was thought to have been a model of sexual restraint even though he was a self-confessed admirer of young boys, whereas Auden was something of an intellectual bully and a devoted apostle to sexual freedom.

In Bennett's play, it is Britten's personal anxiety about his opera, *Death in Venice* (first performed in 1973 so the setting of the play is contemporary as far as the opera is concerned) that forms the main subject for debate between the two men. The composer confessed being troubled by any thought of the work being regarded as a self-revelation. As one critic once wrote, the opera 'sums up the conflict of innocence and experience that obsessed Britten all his life'. On the other hand, Auden was desperate to write the libretto or at least be heavily involved with it. We now know that it was to Myfanwy Piper, and not to Auden, that Britten entrusted a work in which he had perhaps sailed rather too close to the wind on a personal basis. We have also learned of the rather delicate nature of the discussions that took place between the real-life composer and his librettist regarding her own private, but similar experiences. It would perhaps also be best not overlook the added poignancy of Auden's sham marriage to Thomas Mann's daughter that had taken place in 1935. Bennett certainly chose a rich subject on which to exercise his imagination. His play, *The Habit of Art,* was first performed at the Lyttelton in London in November 2009 by the National Theatre Company and has been on tour to the provinces. I saw it in Birmingham with members of my family and we all agreed that it was a very entertaining, as well as a thought-engaging, evening.

Almost finally, I cannot bring myself to the point of writing even a muted apology for what some would say is the disproportionate space I have given to the life and works of Benjamin Britten during the course of this story of the massive cultural history of Suffolk's coastal strip. Britten introduced prolific quantities of music to the area surrounding the town of Aldeburgh, its beach and later to the river and marshes at Snape. It was in 1959 that Britten sought the financially-related assistance of Henry Moore and other artistic friends in seeking to fund the improvements to the town's Jubilee Hall; their relationship had gone back to the 1930s. Now the Britten-Moore legacy lives on with the introduction in 2011 of a further bronze by Moore alongside the concert hall at the former maltings. Furthermore, I have been incredibly impressed by the continuing enthusiasm and scholarship of all those associated with the Britten-Pears Foundation, together with those at the library and Aldeburgh Music, an elite organisation that continues to expand to the benefit of so many young and gifted musicians.

On quite another note and, as a lover of most forms of sport, it has been particularly pleasing for me to discover that both Benjamin Britten and Peter Pears enjoyed their sporting interludes, away from composing, performing and debating serious matters. They regularly indulged themselves in games of tennis, swimming, playing cricket and, it seems, a little sailing. Is it conceivable that it was their extra-curricular sporting activities that served to temporarily, but also beneficially, separate them from their creative as well as inspirational association with their many artistic friends? In other words, a form of escapism.

A fellow schoolboy at South Lodge preparatory school in Lowestoft recalled not only his friend, Ben's, love of the game of cricket but also his already recognised talent as a musician. It seems that the young Britten was invariably required to field in the deep as, even in those early days, it was expected that he would ultimately become a concert pianist. The headmaster, fearful that his prize pupil's fingers might become damaged, was once heard to call out when a high ball was hit in the future composer's direction, 'You're not to catch it Britten! You're not to catch it!' What young Ben thought about this over-protective instruction is not recorded but I am willing to wager that he would have ignored such a command in order to do his very best to play his part in dismissing the big-hitting batsman. Otherwise, and to coin a phrase, it just wouldn't have been cricket. A choice between sportsman or musician? Of course not, but he could have been relied upon to get his priorities right in such circumstances. I feel quite certain about that.

ACKNOWLEDGEMENTS

I am deeply indebted to a large number of people for the help, various permissions, interviews and the overwhelming support I have been given during my research and the writing of this book. Although I will do my best not to exclude anyone I trust that I can be forgiven if I do so, purely as a result of my inefficiency in keeping proper records. However, those I have remembered include Jill Freud, Richard Scott, Glenn Barnes, Jude Brimmer, Maggi Hambling, Elizabeth Jane Howard, Hugo Grenville, Richard Frost, Anthony Falkingham, Barry Tolfree, Tony Cardy, Richard Webster, Mel Gooding, Amelia Morgan, Mark Paterson, Barry Hughes, Dr Nicholas Clark, Dr Diana Dixon, Alison Barnes, D J Taylor, Simon Fletcher, Bob Jackson, Tiggy Gabrielle Jackson Newcomb, Robert Soden, Alison Rawson, Mary Spicer, Eveline Hastings, Paula Nightingale, Tory Lawrence, Mary Gundry, Geoffrey Munn, Basil Scott and Jane Alexander. Jonathan Merrett's as well as Kate Gibney's generous contributions are also greatly appreciated.

I must also gratefully acknowledge the ever-present support, advice and encouragement from my wife, Beverley, Elizabeth Graham and Kate Auty.

Amongst the various bodies and institutions that made services available to me were the Tate Gallery, Britten-Pears Foundation, Walberswick Parish Council, Aldeburgh Music, Norfolk County Council Library, Diss Museum and the Southwold Museum and Historical Society. Again, I must say that there were probably more and I readily apologise for my omissions although I must also give credit to *The Oxford Dictionary of Quotations (Second Edition, 1975)*.

BIBLIOGRAPHY AND SOURCE MATERIAL

Amis, K, Memoirs (Penguin Books, 1992)

Andreae, C, Mary Newcomb (Lund Humphries, 2006)

Bankes, A and Reekie, J (Compilers), New Aldeburgh Anthology (The Boydell Press, 2009)

Banham, M (Ed), The Cambridge Guide to the Theatre (Cambridge University Press, 2000)

Barnes, A, Arthur Rackham in East Anglia (Poppyland Publishing, 2005)

Beadle, R (Ed), Medieval English Theatre (Cambridge University Press, 1994)

Bernard, O, Getting Over It: An Autobiography (Peter Owen, 1992)

Bernard, O, Moons and Tides (Mirror Press, 1978 but republished in 1989 as Moons and Tides, Walberswick by The Southwold Press)

Bernard, O, Verse &c. (Anvil Press Poetry, 2001)

Birkenhead, The Earl of, John Betjeman's Collected Poems (John Murray (Publishers) Limited, 1958)

Blythe, R, Aldeburgh Anthology (Snape Maltings Foundation in association with Faber Music, 1972)

Blythe, R, Outsiders...a Book of Garden Friends (Black Dog Books, 2008)

Blythe, R, The Bookman's Tale (Canterbury Press, 2009)

Blythe, R, The Stories of Ronald Blythe (Lucas Books, 2002)

Boyden, M and Buckley, J (Eds), Opera: The Rough Guide (Rough Guides Limited, 1997)

Brook, D, The Romance of the English Theatre (Rockliff, 1952 (Revised edition))

Bucknell, K (Ed), Christopher Isherwood Diaries, Volume One (1939-1960) (Methuen, 1996)

Cavaliero, G, John Cowper: Novelist (Clarendon Press, Oxford, 1973)

Church, D and Gander, A, The Story of the Southwold – Walberswick Ferry (Dani Church with Design by Holm Oak Publishing, 2009)

Collins, I, Making Waves...Artists in Southwold (Black Dog Books, 2005)

Eddington, P, So Far, So Good (Hodder & Stoughton, 1995)

Eric J, Kingsley Amis: A Biography (Hodder & Stoughton, 1995)

Evans, J (Ed), The Diaries of the Young Benjamin Britten 1928-1938 (Faber and Faber, 2009)

Forster, E M, Aspects of the Novel (Edward Arnold, 1927)

Freud, C, Freud Ego (BBC Worldwide Limited, 2001)

Freud, E, The Sea House (Hamish Hamilton, 2003)

Gooding, M, Whalley, E, Winner, C, Margaret Mellis ... A life in Colour (Sainsbury Centre for Visual Arts (SCVA), 2008)

Grenfell, J, In Pleasant Places (Macmillan, 1979)

Grenfell, J, Joyce Grenfell Requests the Pleasure (Macmillan, 1976)

Grogan, C (Ed), Imogen Holst...A Life in Music (The Boydell Press, 2007)

Hale, K, A Slender Reputation (Frederick Warne, 1994)

Hambling, M, The Aldeburgh Scallop (Full Circle Editions, 2010)

Hamilton, J, Arthur Rackham ... a Life with Illustration (Pavilion Books, 1990)

Harewood, The Earl of, The Tongs and the Bones (Weidenfeld and Nicolson, 1981)

Headington, C, Peter Pears: A Biography (Faber and Faber, 1992)

Heiney, N, The Silence at Song's End (Songsend Books, 2007)

Hemmings, D, Blow-Up and Other Exaggerations (Robson Books 2004)

Howard, E J, Slipstream: A Memoir (Macmillan, 2002)

Isherwood, C, Christopher & His Kind (1929-1939)
(Eyre Methuen, 1977)

Isherwood, C, The Berlin of Sally Bowles (The Hogarth Press, 1975)

James, P D, Time to be Earnest ... A Fragment of Autobiography (Faber and Faber, 1999)

James, P D, Unnatural Causes (Faber and Faber, 1967)

Jobson, A, Suffolk Remembered (Robert Hale and Company, 1969)

Lahr, J (Ed), The Diaries of Kenneth Tynan (Bloomsbury, 2001)

Lehmann, J and Parker, D (Eds), Edith Sitwell: Selected Letters (Macmillan, 1970)

Lewis, J, Cyril Connolly...a Life (Jonathan Cape, 1997)

McGovern, U (Ed), Chambers Biographical Dictionary (Chambers Harrap Publishers, 2002 (7th Edition))

Miller, J (Ed), The Best of Southwold (Sutton Publishing, 1998)

Mitchell, D, Britten & Auden in the Thirties: The Year 1936 (Faber & Faber, 1981)

Mitchell, D and Evans, J (Compilers), Benjamin Britten: Pictures from a Life 1913-1976 (Faber and Faber, 1978)

Mitchell, D and Reed, P (Eds), Letters from a Life: Selected Letters and Diaries of Benjamin Britten,
Volume One 1923-39 (Faber and Faber, 1991)
Volume Two 1939-45 (Faber and Faber, 1991)
Volume Three 1946-51 (Faber and Faber, 2004)

Mosley, C (Ed), In Tearing Haste: Letters Between Deborah Devonshire and Patrick Leigh Fermor (John Murray, 2008)

Munn, Geoffrey C, Southwold...an Earthly Paradise (Antique Collectors' Club, 2006)

Potter, J, Mary Potter...a Life of Painting (Solar Press, 1998)

Reid, P (Ed), Letters from a Life: The Selected Letters of Benjamin Britten 1913-1976, Volume Four 1952-1957 (The Boydell Press 2008 in association with The Britten-Pears Foundation, 2008)

Rendell, R, Ruth Rendell's Suffolk (Hutchinson, 1992)

Scarfe, N (Ed), John Constable's Correspondence II (Suffolk Records Society, 1964)

Scott, R, Artists at Walberswick...East Anglian Interludes 1880-2000 (Art Dictionaries Ltd., 2002)

Sherry, N, The Life of Graham Greene (Volume 2: 1939-1955) (Jonathan Cape, 1994)

Spalding, F, John Piper: Myfanwy Piper...Lives in Art (Oxford University Press, 2009)

Sutherland, J, Stephen Spender: The Authorised Biography (Viking, 2004)

Tolhurst, P (Anth), A Distant Cry...Stories from East Anglia (Black Dog Books, 2002)

Taylor, D J, Orwell ... the Life (Chatto & Windus, 2003)
Tynan, K and Eban, E (Eds), Kenneth Tynan Profiles (Nick Hern Books, 1989)

Willsher, J, The Dedalus Book of English Decadence (Dedalus, 2004)

Willsher, P, Fred Pontin: The Man and his Business (St David's Press, 2003)

Vann, P, Tessa Newcomb (Sansom, 2010)

Wallace, D, The Face of Britain Series: East Anglia (B T Batsford Ltd, 1947-8)

Wilson, M, Mary Wilson: New Poems (Hutchinson, 1979)

I also read:

Barker, P, The Ghost Road (Penguin Books, 1996)

Betjeman, J (illus by J Piper), Church Poems (John Murray (Publishers) Limited, 1981)

Hale, K, Orlando (The Marmalade Cat): The Seaside Holiday (Frederick Warne, 1991 (revised edition) First published by Country Life, 1952)

Howard, E J, Falling (Macmillan, 1999)

James, P D, Cover Her Face (Faber and Faber, 1962)

James, P D, Unnatural Causes (Faber and Faber, 2006)

Forster, E M, Maurice (Penguin Books, 1972)

Freud, E, Summer at Gaglow (First published as Gaglow by Hamish Hamilton, 1997)

Freud, E, The Sea House (Ecco, an Imprint of Harper Collins, 2004)

Myerson, J, Something Might Happen (Jonathan Cape, 2003)
Sweet, M, The West End Front...The Wartime Secrets of London's Grand Hotels (Faber and Faber, 2011)

Source material included:

BBC R4, Tales from the Stave (15 December 2009)

Bird-watching in Suffolk (Suffolk Tourist Guide, website: www. suffolktouristguide.com)

Friends of East Suffolk Performing Arts – various newsletters

Jill Freud & Company...25 Years of Theatre, Southwold and Aldeburgh (Leiston Press, 2008)

Mary Newcomb's Odd Universe (Norfolk Museums & Archaeology Service and East Anglia Art Fund, 2009)

The Oxford Dictionary of Art (Oxford University Press, 2004)

Turner and the Masters (Tate Publishing, 2009)

LIST OF ILLUSTRATIONS

INDEX